Small Firm Dynamism in East Asia

Edited by

FARRUKH IQBAL
World Bank, Washington, U.S.A.

and

SHUJIRO URATA
Waseda University, Tokyo, Japan

Reprinted from *Small Business Economics*,
Volume 18(1–3), 2002

Kluwer Academic Publishers
Dordrecht / Boston / London

A C.I.P. Catalogue record for this book is available from the Library of Congress.

ISBN 1-4020-7047-0

Published by Kluwer Academic Publishers,
P.O. Box 17, 3300 AZ Dordrecht, The Netherlands.

Sold and distributed in North, Central and South America
by Kluwer Academic Publishers,
101 Philip Drive, Norwell, MA 02061, U.S.A.

In all other countries, sold and distributed
by Kluwer Academic Publishers,
P.O. Box 322, 3300 AH Dordrecht, The Netherlands.

Printed on acid-free papers

Printed in the Netherlands

TABLE OF CONTENTS

Small Firm Dynamism in East Asia: An Introductory Overview

Farrukh Iqbal
Shujiro Urata

1. Introduction

This Special Issue presents a collection of papers which examine the evolution of small and medium enterprises (hereafter SMEs) in East Asia over the past quarter century or so. East Asia is of interest because this region has experienced, on average, the highest economic growth rates in the world during this period. This has been accompanied by dramatic transformations in sectoral output and employment, in demographic patterns and in the flow and composition of domestic and international trade. It is of interest to see to what extent these transformations have affected, or have been influenced by, industrial structure as reflected in the evolution of small firms. At the same time, not all countries in East Asia have grown at similar rates nor has there been uniformity in public policies across the region. How smaller firms have coped with the different policy environments and patterns of economic transformation that have characterized the region in the recent past could be of potential importance to the formulation of public policy in other developing countries.

The papers illustrate selected aspects of the performance of SMEs in East Asia such as their contribution to employment growth, productivity change and resilience in the face of shocks. They also analyze some factors that have been responsible for the observed patterns of SME performance.[1] These factors include aspects of public policy and the overall business environment such as subcontracting (in Japan), clustering (in Japan and Indonesia), government-business coordination (in Malaysia), low cost entry and exit into business (in Taiwan), liberalization of domestic production and trade (in China), financial and technical support from public sources (in Korea and Japan) and so on. Each of the papers does not cover each factor in equal detail. Instead, the few determinants that are considered most relevant in a particular case are given most attention. What is thereby lost in terms of uniformity is compensated in part by the depth of analysis that is made possible in some of the case studies.

Two non-Asian studies have also been included in the set of papers presented here. This was done in order to accommodate some aspects of small firm behavior and experience that are not well captured in the data available in East Asia. One discusses the role of small firms in generating innovations and the role of public policy in facilitating this in the case of the U.S. (see paper by Audretsch). Another reports on entrepreneurial and locational factors that determine the survival and expansion of very small firms in Africa (see paper by Liedholm).

The rest of this overview is organized as follows. The next section provides a review of small firm experience in different countries in East Asia during the last quarter century or so with respect to growth and employment, response to economic shocks, productivity change and innovation. This is followed by a section which discusses the main factors that are thought to have determined small firm dynamism in East Asia. *Inter alia*, these two sections provide overviews of each of the papers included in this issue. The final section draws some lessons for public policy.

Farrukh Iqbal
World Bank
1818 H St. NW
Washington, DC 20433
U.S.A.

Shujiro Urata
Waseda University
Tokyo
Japan

Small Business Economics **18**: 1–12, 2002.

2. Aspects of SME dynamism in East Asia

SME experience with growth and employment: 1975–1995

Two trends are common to the experience of most East Asian economies with respect to SMEs in the last quarter century. First, SMEs appear to have either held their own or become more important when their role is measured by their share of employment and value added. Secondly, there is some evidence that, within the class of SMEs, the role of very small firms (those with less than 10 workers) has tended to decline.

Japan's pattern of economic growth since 1975 has featured a slowing phase during the late 1970s and early 1980s due to an increase in the price of oil, a major import for Japan; an expanding phase in the late 1980s, the so-called bubble economy period when oil prices declined and overconfidence set in; and a period of stagnation in the 1990s as the bubble economy collapsed and deep-seated problems in the financial sector became prominent. How did Japanese SMEs fare through all this? It would appear that, as a group, Japanese SMEs fared no better or worse than all firms taken together. For example, their share of overall employment remained fairly stable, fluctuating between 70% and 74% in the manufacturing sector. SME shares in value added and output show similar stability. However, within the SME group, there was a clear shift away from very small enterprises (1–4 employees) to larger enterprises. Between 1969 and 1996, the share of very small enterprises fell from 72% of the total to 62% with the bulk of the decline occurring in the last ten years when the overall economy has stagnated. This suggests a link between the recent liberalization of the retail sector (under pressure from the United States) and the survival rate of such enterprises (see paper by Kawai and Urata).

Unlike the case in Japan, the role of SMEs in *Korea* has undergone a dramatic transformation in the last twenty five years. The share of employment originating in SMEs (in manufacturing) rose from 46% (in 1975) to 69% (in 1997) while that of value added rose from 32% to 47%. This is all the more striking if one considers that SME shares in employment and value added had declined throughout the 1960s. Given that Korea's economy has expanded tremendously in the past quarter century (with occasional downturns as in 1997–1998), these data suggest that SMEs have been important generators of income and employment in Korea despite the general perception that Korea's economy is heavily dominated by large conglomerates. Indeed, Korean SMEs have also become well established, like Japanese SMEs before them, in two activities often associated with dynamism: exporting and overseas investment. Korean SMEs have accounted for about 35% or so on average of total exports from Korea during the last twenty years and have moved more rapidly into overseas investing than even larger Korean firms (see paper by Nugent and Yhee).

Like Korea, *Taiwan* has grown rapidly in the last quarter century but unlike Korea, it has always been thought of as a SME-based economy. An overview of the evolution of its industrial structure since the early 1980s (see paper by Aw) shows that the overall size distribution in manufacturing has stayed more or less the same with a heavy preponderance of SMEs. Within this relatively stable structure, some subsectors such as textiles and clothing show growth in the employment and output shares of SMEs while others, such as basic metals and chemicals, show some decline. Among SMEs, the number of firms in the micro category (less than 5 workers) declined while those in the small category (5–99 workers) increased. The overall impression one gains is that, with a few exceptions, SMEs in Taiwan shared substantially in the country's rapid economic growth of the past quarter century.

China presents an interesting case of market reforms and their impact. Since the late 1970s, China has gradually liberalized its economy and has allowed individuals to set up rural and urban enterprises in a wide range of economic activities. What has been the impact on small enterprises? The evidence to date shows that SMEs in China have gained substantially from liberalization.[2] While employment data show a relatively constant share for SMEs, value added data suggest an increase in share of total output from 57% in 1980 to around 66% in 1996 (see paper by Wang and Yao). Given that overall national output was itself growing at around 11% per annum over this period, this suggests a very dynamic SME sector.

Indonesia experienced strong economic growth in the 1970s with the help of high oil prices, a period of stagnation in the 1980s when oil prices declined and another period of strong economic growth after 1986 when substantial trade and investment liberalization enabled a dramatic surge in labor-intensive manufacturing export production. Recently, the regional financial crisis of 1997–1998 dealt Indonesia a severe shock from which it has not yet fully recovered. How have its SMEs done through the twists and turns of the economy in the past quarter century? Unfortunately, the data needed to track the performance of the SME sector are not as good for Indonesia as for many of the other countries in East Asia. Nevertheless, it is generally believed that SMEs in Indonesia benefited significantly from the turn to labor-intensive exports in the late 1980s and were not any worse affected by the 1997–1998 downturn than larger firms. The paper by Berry, Rodriguez and Sandee notes that even very small enterprises (establishments of 5–19 workers) shared in Indonesia's export success in the last two decades. Total exports from this group rose from a level of $137 million in 1983 eighteen-fold to a level of $2.1 billion in 1992, or an almost three-fold increase as a proportion of total manufactured exports (from 4% to 11%). A significant amount of exportable output was also undoubtedly provided by the SME sector to larger firms under sub-contracting arrangements.

Thailand is one of the few countries in East Asia which shares only one of the two trends noted at the beginning of this section. Unlike the other cases, in Thailand, the overall share of small and medium firms in total employment fell from 60% to 52%. At the same time, as in other East Asian countries, one observes a decline in the share of the smallest firms (with less than 10 workers) from 12% to 6% (see paper by Wiboonchutikula).

SMEs and the absorption of shocks

There are several reasons why it is of interest to investigate how smaller firms cope with economic shocks. First, if it is the case that small firms are better able to adjust to business cycle swings or large exogenous shocks, this would clearly be of help to development strategy. Second, if it can be determined which types of shocks put small firms at greatest risk, that too would be useful for strategy formulation purposes, especially in cases where employment protection is an important objective. Finally, to the extent that policies can alter the probability of success or failure in coping with shocks, it would be useful to know which set of policies is most effective and under what conditions.

The recent crisis in East Asia provides an opportunity to examine the link between industrial structure and economic resilience. The relative impact of the crisis by size of firm can be judged in part by the effects on capacity utilization and employment. The table below summarizes some results from a survey sponsored by the World Bank in five crisis-afflicted East Asian countries towards the end of 1998. It shows that in all the five cases considered large firms tended to have higher rates of capacity utilization after the crisis than smaller firms. If we assume that firms of both size groups had the same rate of capacity utilization before the crisis, this result might suggest either that large firms were not as badly affected by the crisis in 1997–1998 or were recovering faster. However, we do not have data on capacity utilization rates by firm size before the crisis and so cannot be definite in our inference. The table also shows that, for two of the five cases (Korea and Malaysia), a smaller share of small firms reported fewer workers after the crisis thus suggesting that they had engaged in less retrenchment of their workforces, an outcome consistent with the shock absorption view. However, the results are not uniform. Two other cases (Thailand and Indonesia) show the opposite result, that is, a relatively higher share of small firms report fewer workers after the crisis. The fifth case (the Philippines) is evenly split. The inability to clearly discern the role of size in coping with exogenous economic shocks from such aggregate data as shown in the table suggests that more detailed investigation is needed.

Berry, Rodriguez and Sandee investigate the impact of the crisis on small firms in Indonesia at a more disaggregated level. In Indonesia's case, the crisis resulted in a major economic contraction with GDP declining by about 14% in 1998 alone and the Rupiah depreciating by around 60% in real terms during 1997–1999. In the face of such a crisis, it is inevitable that most economic groups

TABLE I
Impact of 1997 crisis on East Asian firms

		Capacity utilization level after crisis	Share of firms with fewer workers after crisis
Korea	Small	71	61
	Large	77	80
Indonesia	Small	51	54
	Large	63	45
Philippines	Small	76	50
	Large	79	50
Malaysia	Small	64	29
	Large	73	40
Thailand	Small	57	56
	Large	67	45

Note: For the purposes of this survey, SMEs were defined as firms with less than 150 workers.
Source: Dwor-Frecaut et al., *Asian Corporate Recovery*, World Bank, 2000.

will suffer setbacks. Indonesian SMEs were no exception. A survey of 800 small scale enterprises conducted during 1998 revealed that as much as 72% had experienced some economic loss from the crisis. Other sources report that small scale garment producers have been badly affected by the decline in the flow of imported cloth and other raw materials on which their output depends. Other small scale industries dependent on imported inputs or strong domestic demand, such as small clove cigarette producers, have also been hurt by the crisis. Nevertheless, the bulk of the evidence, admittedly impressionistic and qualitative in nature, suggests that smaller firms have been weathering the crisis better than might have been expected and perhaps better than larger companies. In particular, SMEs with a link to export markets have done quite well and have been experiencing a strong surge in demand for their products which have become competitive due to the substantial depreciation of the Indonesian Rupiah. Examples include the SME furniture industry of Jepara and the traditional batik cloth weaving industry of Central Java. Overall, small and medium exporters have laid off fewer workers than non-exporters as a group.

Similar issues can also be explored for the case of business cycles rather than large exogenous shocks. Business cycle swings in fast growing economies could be moderated if the requisite structural adjustments are made swiftly. Given that SMEs typically have higher labor turnover and corporate failure rates than large enterprises, face lower entry and exit costs, and are less prone to engaging in collective action to forestall labor retrenchment or bankruptcy, an economy that has a higher proportion of SMEs is more likely to be able to adjust smoothly. Taiwan is said to exemplify such a model and is generally thought to adjust quite swiftly to business cycle swings and large external shocks. Evidence of high turnover among Taiwanese firms is provided in the paper by Aw and it might be noted that Taiwan was among the local economies that were not significantly affected by the East Asian crisis.

Wiboonchutikula investigates the shock absorption nature of SMEs by looking at the relative performance of small and large firms over the business cycle in Thailand. He divides the period 1987–1996 into sub-periods of varying industrial growth and finds that employment growth among smaller firms rises at a faster rate when overall industrial growth is slower. In other words, employment in SMEs tends to move countercyclically. At the same time, employment growth among large firms is seen to move pro-cyclically, rising more during periods of rapid economic growth. This is consistent with the view that economic conditions are slack larger firms lay off workers who are then absorbed in smaller firms, especially in the service sectors and most likely in the form of self-employment.

Korea presents an interesting case. On the one hand, it is clearly less of a SME-oriented economy than Taiwan. The relatively bigger impact of the East Asian crisis on Korea is consistent with this observation. On the other hand, as Nugent and Yhee show, SMEs have become more prominent in Korea's industrial structure in the last quarter century or so, accounting for progressively higher shares of employment and value added. Accordingly, the Korean economy should have become more resilient over time to business cycle swings and large shocks. While it is hard to compare resilience over time in a statistically rigorous fashion, casual empiricism shows that the Korean economy did recover rather quickly from the financial crisis of 1997–1998, an observation that is consistent with the high proportion of SMEs in its industrial structure.

Total factor productivity performance

Several papers in this Special Issue provide assessments of the technical progress achieved by SMEs as measured by total factor productivity growth.[3] Urata and Kawai analyze TFP level and growth by firm size for the manufacturing sector in Japan during 1966–1996. Their results suggest that smaller firms (with less than 100 employees) in Japanese manufacturing do show positive levels of TFP growth throughout the three decade long period considered. Indeed, they managed to make progress even in the stagnant first half of the 1990s. So there is clearly evidence of dynamism in this regard. However, in relative terms, smaller firms do not seem to have done quite as well as larger firms. For most of the period considered, larger firms had higher rates of TFP growth than smaller firms; the only sub-period in which smaller firms had the edge was 1966–1972. Also, in 1996, larger firms clearly had higher levels of TFP than smaller firms on average. However, there is considerable variation in performance across subsectors within manufacturing. Small establishments show higher levels of TFP in the machinery subsectors which do not require large scale facilities and in which many innovative parts and component manufacturers are to be found. By contrast, larger firms have higher TFPs in the metal production industries, such as iron and steel, which are distinguished by high minimum efficient scales of production. So the computed TFP levels appear to be affected by both technological and scale factors.

The generally inverse relation between measured TFP levels and firm size noted above for Japan is also found for Taiwan. In regressing firm level TFP with firm size and age, Aw finds that the larger the firm size the greater the average productivity. However, the relationship is nonlinear in that the gain in productivity is much higher in going from micro-size firms (with less than 5 workers) to small size firms (with between 5 and 99) workers than in going beyond to medium (100–299 workers) and large (300 plus workers) firms. On the basis of the estimated coefficients, Aw concludes that the productivity advantage of increasing firm size is significant only among the size group featuring less than 100 workers, that small firms are only marginally less productive than medium-sized firms and, finally, that the productivity levels of large firms are not significantly different from those of medium-size firms.

Nugent and Yhee report on evidence from Korea. They note that wide variations exist in the estimates of TFP growth reported by different researchers using different assumptions and time periods. With this qualification, they make two points. First, that TFP growth in Korea has tended to be highest in the metal products and machinery subsector which has very few SMEs. Second, in general, sectors in which SMEs are over-represented tend to have lower TFP growth rates than sectors in which SMEs are under-represented. Finally, on the basis of their own analysis, they conclude that TFP tends to rise with firm size through the 101–200 class but then declines.

Wang and Yao analyze TFP growth in the case of China. They find that small firms in China have had a higher growth rate of TFP during the period 1981–1995 than larger firms but that, despite this dynamism, the average TFP level of small firms remains lower. They also report that, in general, both TFP levels and growth among collective and private firms are higher than those of state-owned firms, a finding which suggests that type of ownership is also an important consideration.

The above review of TFP performance in selected countries of East Asia shows that SMEs have been dynamic in that their TFP indices have risen over time; they clearly appear to have contributed to the region-wide experience of rising productivity in the last quarter century. However, they have not demonstrated a clear advantage over large firms in this regard. The evidence is mixed. Whereas in China, smaller firms have tended to do better than larger firms, the cases of Japan and Korea show the opposite relationship to hold and the Taiwan analysis supports a non-linear relationship between size and TFP growth.

SMEs and innovation

The rate of innovation is another measure of the dynamism of firms. Until very recently the conventional wisdom was that large corporations were better placed to engage in innovation because their scale made it possible for them to invest in R&D.[4] Indeed, if R&D expenditures are used as a proxy for innovation, it would appear that larger firms undertake more innovative activity. However, R&D expenditures are only a measure of inputs into the process of technological advance and not a measure of the outputs. A better measure of innovation output is the rate of patenting. Measures of patenting rates by firm size are now available for some developed economies. In the case of the U.S., Audretsch shows that the rate of innovation across firm size varies considerably from industry to industry. While large firms generate most of the innovations in such industries as pharmaceutical products and aircraft, small firms have a higher rate of innovation in such industries as computers, process control instruments, and plastics products. Indeed, the relative innovation performance of small firms in the U.S. is even more impressive when we consider that their R&D expenditures are far lower than those of large firms. Similarly, when adjustments are made for size, small firms appear to be more dynamic than large firms on average. For example, Audretsch reports that when adjusted for employment the small firm innovation rate in the U.S. is around 0.31 on average while that for large firms is around 0.20.

Urata and Kawai also provide some data on innovation inputs and outputs by firm size in the case of Japan. First, looking at innovation inputs, they show that larger firms are more likely to engage in R&D activities. Thus, while 44% of firms having more than 300 workers report in-house R&D with full-time research staff, less than 10% of smaller firms (say with less than 50 workers) report doing in-house R&D. However, smaller firms appear to be as active as larger ones in obtaining R&D from other sources such as universities and research institutes, both public and private. Second, looking at gross innovation outputs, they show that large firms have a higher rate of patenting than smaller firms. For example, while firms with more than 300 workers were patenting at the rate of 174 patents per establishment in 1987, the rate for smaller firms ranged from as low as 3.9 to only as high as 13.7 per establishment. This pattern persists across all manufacturing sectors and for both 1971 and 1987, the two years for which such data are reported by Urata and Kawai. However, unlike Audretsch, they do not report data for patenting rates adjusted by employment, and so it is not possible to compare the per person patenting productivity of smaller and larger firms.

3. The determinants of SME dynamism

Clusters and agglomeration

Clustering refers to the geographic concentration or agglomeration of inter-connected companies in particular business fields. In recent years, there have been several conceptual analyses and empirical reviews of the role of clusters in the competitiveness of industries, regions and countries. It is generally thought that clustering is especially important for smaller firms because they stand to benefit relatively more from the economies of scale, reduction of transport costs, pooling of labor, and technology spillovers that are enabled or promoted by clusters.

Yamawaki reviews the evolution and structure of clusters in the case of Japan. He focuses on two aspects, namely, what gives rise to clusters and what benefits are acquired by small firms from being in clusters. He confirms that clusters are indeed a small firm phenomenon in Japan in that the average size by employment of firms that exist within clusters is around 10, ranging from as low as 6 (for textile firms) to 24 (for garment firms). In order to determine what gives rise to clusters he reviews the history of 14 industrial clusters covering a wide range of industries and locations within Japan. He notes that it is difficult to generalize about the main determinants of the tendency to cluster since there appears to be a lot of variation in this across different clusters. Thus, in some cases, the existence of a leading large firm was the dominant determinant. Examples are the general machinery cluster that came up around the construction machinery giant, Komatsu Corporation in Komatsu and the automotive parts cluster that grew up around Fuji Heavy Industries in Ota. In other cases, a pooled labor market was an important consideration. A relevant example is the apparel cluster in Gifu which developed around the availability of part-time female labor in the local area The presence of public research and standards-testing facilities was another important determinant for some clusters. Examples include the textile cluster in Hyogo where a public technology center was first established over a hundred years ago in 1894.

What benefits do small firms derive from being part of clusters? Yamawaki presents results from a survey of such firms carried out in 1996. According to the responses received, it would appear that the four most important benefits of clustering perceived by small firms are specialization, ease of procurement, diffusion of technology and public policy support. Clustering supports suppliers with specialized skills and this allows for a division of labor that results in lower costs. The fact that many firms cited technological diffusion and cooperation as an important factor suggests that there is considerable knowledge spillover within clusters. Finally, policy support provided by regional local government authorities, typically in the form of public testing, research and technology development centers, appears to make a difference. Indeed, the last two factors are connected in that public technology development centers facilitate the transfer of knowledge across firms within the same region. It is also interesting to note that access to labor markets and skilled workers is not cited by the surveyed firms as being very important. There might appear to be a contradiction in the finding that the existence of specialized firms is important to cluster-based firms but the availability of specialized skills is not. This could be explained by the fact that the dominant source of skills acquisition in Japan is on-the-job training and the skills thereby acquired may be too firm-specific to be useful to others. Seniority-based patterns of compensation may also discourage labor spillovers across firms. Finally, labor raiding or recruiting skilled workers from other firms within the cluster may not be considered an ethical business practice in Japan and may, therefore, be avoided.

Berry, Rodriguez and Sandee provide some evidence of the importance of clusters to small firms in Indonesia. They note that a number of SMEs have become successful exporters of rattan furniture, wood furniture, and garments. In each of these cases, subcontracting with foreign firms and clustering have played an important role. Indeed, differences can be noted between the performance of clustered and dispersed enterprises. Clustered enterprises are more likely to be in the exports business and to adopt process and product innovations. Examples include the Jepara furniture cluster of about 2000 small enterprises (and 100 large and medium ones) which has become active in exports. Close contact with foreign buyers has resulted in rapid upgrading and diversification of furniture product lines. This is in contrast to other sources of furniture supply in Indonesia which are characterized by more dispersed production and which have tended to grow less rapidly, be focused more on the domestic market, and stay with a narrower product line.

Clusters may also be relevant to the extent that they stimulate innovation through knowledge spillovers. Small firm innovation depends on knowledge inputs. Given that small firms tend not to spend large amounts on R&D expenditures, it is fair to assume that such inputs are not generated primarily by the own efforts and resources of the firms. It is more likely that such inputs are obtained from knowledge spillovers generated in part by proximity to universities, research and training institutes and in part by proximity to other firms.[5] Of course, such spillovers are available to all firms, small or large, but they are likely to be relatively more important for smaller firms than for larger ones. Evidence of the importance of knowledge spillovers is provided by Audretsch who shows that innovation is clearly a large city phenomenon in the U.S. in that the rate of innovation per capita is highest in densely-populated metropolitan areas and considerably lower in non-urban areas. Clearly, the concentration of universities, research institutes, skilled workers, and other firms that is to be found in large cities makes a difference. Reviewing the growing literature on the subject, Audretsch makes the following general observations about the processes and patterns involved. First, knowledge spillovers tend to be geographically bounded in the sense that they tend to have a larger impact on firms which are geographically proximate to the areas where the knowledge is created than on firms which are more distant. Second, this boundedness is more pronounced for "tacit knowledge" spillovers than for other types of knowledge where by tacit knowledge is meant the type that is spread by informal, direct and repeated contacts and social networking. A popular example of this is the networking to be found in California's Silicon Valley. Third, the impact of tacit knowledge spillover varies by industry life cycle, being greatest during early stages prior to the establishment of dominant designs and product standards. Fourth, sharing a common base of generalized knowledge (as is made possible by links to a common dominant university, for example) is more conducive to innovation than is specialization.[6]

Subcontracting

Subcontracting has often been pointed to as a distinctive aspect of industrial structure in Japan and, to a lesser extent, in Korea and Taiwan. The relative economic success of these countries suggests that it would be useful to ask whether subcontracting leads to higher static and dynamic efficiency. Are the profits or productivity, for example, of the firms that engage in subcontracting as purchasers higher than of those who do not? Does subcontracting free-up such firms to engage in more managerially and technologically sophisticated activities? One can ask similar questions regarding the impact on firms that engage in subcontracting as suppliers. Does this increase their profits? Does it enable them to get linked to technologically more sophisticated supply chains with attendant long-run benefits? The latter set of questions is more relevant for our present purposes since those who engage in subcontracting as suppliers are usually small or medium in size.

Some of these questions are tackled empirically in the paper by Kimura. He uses firm level data from a 1994 survey of Japanese corporations in the machinery sector, a sector in which subcontracting arrangements are particularly prominent. He is able to distinguish four types of firms in his sample: (1) those who do not engage in subcontracting either as purchasers or as suppliers; (2) those who engage in subcontracting as suppliers but not as purchasers; (3) those who are involved as both suppliers and purchasers; and (4) those who are involved as purchasers but not as suppliers. Two interesting results emerge from the statistical analysis of the links between firm status vis-à-vis subcontracting and other firm characteristics. First, there is little evidence that subcontracting leads to higher profits. The probability of using a subcontractor is not significantly related to the proxy for profits (ratio of operating surplus to total sales). Nor is the probability of being a subcontractor significantly related to this proxy. Indeed, summary sample statistics suggest that completely independent firms, that is, those who do not work with, or as, subcontractors, have a higher profit level on average than the other three categories noted above. Of course, these findings need to be qualified since they pertain to only one sector and one year and the data sample itself is limited to firms above a certain size (with more than 50 workers and capital of more than 30 million yen). Nevertheless, the argument that subcontracting might be a source of efficiency or profit advantage for either purchasers or suppliers is not supported by Kimura's empirical analysis. The popularity of this arrangement in Japan must, therefore, rest on its other perceived advantages.

Second, the link between subcontracting and technological sophistication is complex. Kimura finds that the probability of using a subcontractor is higher for firms with higher R&D expenditures. What is cause and what effect is not clear from this link. It may arise because technologically more sophisticated firms find it convenient and cheaper to subcontract aspects of their work that are simpler. It may also reflect the fact that those who subcontract find it easier to turn their management energies to technologically more advanced pursuits.

While Kimura provides data on the link between subcontracting and profits, Urata and

Kawai and Aw analyze the link between subcontracting and productivity for the cases of Japan and Taiwan respectively. Urata and Kawai find a statistically significant and positive relationship between TFP (measured as both growth and level) and subcontractor status (as a supplier). However, Aw does not find a similar result for Taiwan. Using the proportion of firm revenues derived from subcontracting activities as a measure of subcontracting and holding constant firm size and age, she finds no statistically significant relationship between subcontracting and TFP growth in any but one (textiles) of the nine sectors she analyzes. On the whole, therefore, the papers in this Special Issue do not make a convincing empirical case that subcontracting is an important determinant of firm profits and dynamism.

Market friendly policies

Something that all developed countries and many developing countries take for granted is the prevalence of market friendly policies allowing for substantial freedom to private entrepreneurs to choose occupations and businesses and, in their businesses, what to produce and how to produce it. In China, however, this has only been possible since the late 1970s (in agriculture) and the 1980s (in various manufacturing industries). Nevertheless, within the last two decades, as gradual liberalization occurred, the SME sector in China has displayed great dynamism. As already noted, by 1995, it had come to account for roughly 63% of industrial output and 74% of industrial employment. Just fifteen years earlier, its share of industrial output stood at 57%. The enormity of this achievement can be gauged in part by the fact that the overall economy grew at a rate of roughly 11% per annum over this period and in part by the fact that SMEs grew despite continuing biases in the allocation of official credit towards larger and state-owned firms.

According to Wang and Yao, China's SME sector grew dramatically because it benefited from the withdrawal of state control in several ways. First, decontrol of agriculture allowed for the proliferation of small family farms. Second, the government's earlier policies of favoring heavy industry development had left a huge vacuum in the consumer goods market which small firms began to fill in the 1980s. Third, opening up to foreign trade allowed small scale producers to move into labor-intensive exports. Indeed, so attractive were the opportunities offered by the move to market economics that even many local governments and community groups set up new enterprises, adding to the growth of collectively-owned TVE's or town and village enterprises. The lesson to be drawn from this is that SMEs in developing countries stand to benefit tremendously from market-friendly policies which encourage the growth of domestic and international trade in labor-intensive products.

Government-business coordination

Local government-business coordination is identified as a key factor in the performance of small and medium industries in Malaysia in the paper by Rasiah. He shows this by contrasting the performance of small and medium size subcontractors producing machine tools for microelectronic multinationals at two different locations in Malaysia. While demand for machine tools grew strongly in Malaysia during the 1980s and 1990s as a result of the expansion of the foreign-investment led production of microelectronics, the development of the local machine tool industry differed widely among regions. Comparing the cases of Penang and Kelang Valley, which had similar starting conditions, Rasiah finds that the local machine tool industry developed far more successfully in the former location. On the basis of data collected through firm level interviews, Rasiah concludes that this was due to differences in the nature of government-business links in the two locations. The local government in Penang provided various types of support to local SMEs as well as to multinationals. In particular, it got involved in ensuring that multinationals seeking subcontractors and subcontractors looking for work could be matched and were given maximum information about each other. The relatively autonomous state government of Penang was also able to bypass the national government's indigenous entrepreneur preference policies and divert business to capable local Chinese-owned SMEs. By contrast, links between microelectronics multinationals and local machine tool firms did not develop to the same extent in Kelang Valley, mainly because of a lack of effective government-business coordination.

Public technical and financial support

Many East Asian countries have provided technical and financial support to SMEs over the past quarter century or so. Technical support has been provided in the form of research institutes, testing and standards laboratories, science parks, productivity advisory services, and trade promotion centers. These have not necessarily been for the exclusive use of SMEs but they have tended to be more heavily used by SMEs than by larger firms. Financial support has been provided in the form of directed and sometimes subsidized credit through public and private banks, credit guarantees, and selected tax benefits. While noting that the lack of rigorous data on program benefit and costs makes it difficult to evaluate many of these programs, Nugent and Yhee provide a useful account of the effectiveness of public technical and financial support programs for SMEs in the case of Korea. They note that financial support in particular tends to be widely used and highly rated by Korean SMEs. Broadly speaking, the technical assistance on offer is also generally viewed as useful but not as highly rated as financial support. A similar pattern is reported for Thailand by Wiboonchutikula on the basis of a survey of SME needs. Most firms gave higher priority to reduced interest rates and better access to loans than to marketing and training programs. On the other hand, Kawai and Urata find that small firm start-up in Japan is deterred by the availability of special credit programs. They interpret this finding to mean that subsidized loans protect incumbent SMEs and so constitute a barrier to the entry of new smaller companies. They also note that the Japanese SMEs make heavy use of public technical and research centers and that the acquisition of patents and technical knowledge from outside the firm is a significant determinant of SME total factor productivity levels and growth. Finally, Audretsch notes the success of a program in the U.S. that combines financial and technical support by providing funds for innovation by small businesses. This program, known as the Small Business Innovation Research Program (SBIR), requires each participating government agency to reserve a portion of its research budget for small firms and provides for support not only at the research stage but also at the commercialization stage. Audretsch reports that SMEs receiving SBIR support show faster rates of growth than those that do not and that a significant number of beneficiary firms would not have been started in the absence of such support.

Owner/firm characteristics and SME dynamism

The set of characteristics discussed so far are in one sense external to the firm. They pertain to the environment within which firms operate. However, other characteristics which relate more directly to firms might also be considered. Such characteristics would include the human capital of the owner, with better educated and more experienced entrepreneurs likely to do better than those with less education and experience. Gender might be an important factor also to the extent that women, for example, might be less risk averse and, therefore, female-owned firms might be more likely to survive but less likely to grow. The location of the firm in an urban or rural area, more or less distant from markets, might also be an important consideration. Unfortunately, direct information on the role of such factors is not available in the papers pertaining to East Asia that are included here. This gap is filled instead by the paper by Liedholm based on data from a Latin American and 5 African countries.

Liedholm discusses the determinants of both firm survival and firm growth. Citing other studies using African data, he notes that the probability that a firm will close or "die" during a given year is clearly related to locational factors. Urban firms, regardless of size, are more likely to survive than rural-based firms and firms located in commercial districts more likely to survive than those operated out of the home, for example. Thus, proximity to markets appears to be an important determinant of firm survival in Africa. Gender does not seem to matter in that firms that close on account of business setbacks and failures are just as likely to be headed by females as by males. Turning next to the determinants of firm growth (measured by number of employees) Liedholm reports results from his own statistical analysis. Locational variables are once again found to be important.

Enterprises operating in the urban areas and in commercial districts grow faster than rural and home based enterprises. The gender of the owner is also a statistically significant determinant of enterprise growth with male owners doing better than female ones. Finally, while relevant measures are not available in Liedholm's data, he reports from other studies that human capital does matter. Prior vocational training of owners is found to lead to faster firm growth. So also is previous experience in other businesses. However, the results are somewhat mixed for measures of formal schooling with some studies reporting a statistically significant positive relationship and others not.

Firm size and growth

Initial firm size is also commonly thought to affect dynamic performance. The assumption is that firms which are below a certain size are unlikely to survive and grow because they face a tough business and policy environment. Certainly, the higher rate of enterprise closures that is typically found for smaller firms in comparison to large ones suggests that this might be a plausible assumption. However, two of the papers in this Special Issue suggest that this may not be the case. First, Liedholm reports results from Africa showing that initial size is inversely related to enterprise expansion. Firms which are smaller at start-up appear to add more jobs per firm than larger enterprises within the sample. Second, Aw shows in the Taiwan case that the causality may run from performance to size rather than from size to performance. In other words, more productive firms grow larger while less productive firms grow smaller or exit. Thus, Aw shows that employment growth among Taiwanese firms is positively related to initial levels of productivity (measured by TFP) in all but two of the nine sectors in her sample. At the same time, employment growth is negatively related to initial firm size. In other words, controlling for initial productivity, the larger the firm the slower it expands. This suggests quite strongly that firm size, by itself, is not a source of advantage but productivity is. There may still be other reasons why smaller firms may face higher risks of closure and bankruptcy but size by itself need not be the deciding determinant of success or failure.

4. Concluding observations

The papers included here do not all explicitly set out to analyze implications for public policy. Nevertheless, it may be useful to see what conclusions might be implied in the data and results that are presented. First, we should note that the results do not make a strong case for the proposition that firm size should be an important focus of public policy. For example, the results do not show unambiguously that small firms are inherently more productive or dynamic than large firms. In some cases they are, but in others, not. There appears to be a lot of variation within the SME category itself, with productivity differences being larger in some cases among SMEs than between SMEs and large firms. Moreover, productivity seems to be influenced by several factors other than size, such as sector of operations. Finally, it would appear that the causal relation may run from productivity to size rather than the other way around.

Second, while some papers show that certain factors are likely to have contributed to small firm dynamism, clear implications for public policy do not necessarily flow from these observations. For example, it might well be the case that clustering promotes small firm development. However, clustering seems to happen on a largely voluntary basis, driven by historical and geographical considerations, and does not seem to be linked to any specific government intervention (other than the provision of general infrastructure such as roads and ports). Similarly with subcontracting. The presence of subcontracting appears to be largely related to endogenous decisions made by firms and not to any particular aspect of the public policy environment. And the decisions thus made apparently involve complexities which are not reducible to simple outcomes for profitability or productivity.

There is one area, however, where public policy intervention seems to make a noticeable difference. This is the technical assistance provided in the form of public testing, research and technology dissemination centers (as in Japan, Korea and Taiwan), skill development centers (as in Malaysia), and universities (as in Japan and the U.S.). These forms of assistance are functional and not necessarily size-specific. They consist of the production and dissemination of knowledge and skills which, while available to all firms, could have a proportionately bigger role in the economics of smaller firms that do not have the capital or economies of scale to invest in in-house R&D activities.[7]

This suggests that the focus of public policy should shift away from size to the enabling environment within which all firms can contribute to innovation and job growth. When viewed through the lens of size alone, small firms are likely to appear to need protection largely on income distribution grounds since a strong case cannot be made for them on efficiency and static productivity grounds. On the other hand, if the dynamic evolution of firms is given more weight, innovation-oriented public policies can be followed which, while size-neutral in design, could have disproportionately larger positive externalities for small firms.

Acknowledgements

The papers published in this Special Issue were originally commissioned for a project on The Role of Small and Medium Enterprises in Development, organized by the World Bank Institute with funding support from the Policy and Human Resources Development Trust Fund of the Government of Japan.

Notes

[1] Unless otherwise noted, the policy and empirical focus of the papers included here is on small and medium enterprises in the manufacturing sector only.

[2] Note that China's definition of SME's differs from that generally encountered in the literature. Production capacity is used to define firms by size for industries with a limited number of products (such as iron and steel) while the original value of fixed capital is used for firms with a diverse range of products.

[3] The reader should keep in mind the pitfalls and controversies surrounding the measurement and interpretation of total factor productivity. These are briefly noted in the paper by Urata and Kawai.

[4] The study of the link between size and innovation was transformed by the publication of *Innovation and Small Firms* by Zoltan Acs and David Audretsch in 1990. They found that small firms in the U.S. enjoyed an innovative advantage on a per employee basis. Similar findings are reported for other countries as well including the Netherlands, the United Kingdom and Italy (see references in Thurik, 1996).

[5] One might conceive of other forms of knowledge spillover as well, some that may be more relevant in a developing country context. For example, it is often claimed that significant knowledge spillovers occur via international trade through interaction with foreign buyers and equipment suppliers. It is also possible that direct foreign investment projects could lead to knowledge spillovers for host countries.

[6] While much has been written about technology, geography and regional economic development in developed country contexts (see, for example, the Special Issue of *Small Business Economics*, 1996, Vol. 8, No. 2) little is available on the developing country experience in this regard.

[7] Evidence of a disproportionately larger effect on small-firm innovation arising from the spillovers from university research is reported for the case of Italy in Audretsch and Vivarelli, 1996.

References

Acs, Zoltan J. and David B. Audretsch, 1990, *Innovation and Small Firms*, Cambridge: MIT Press.

Audretsch, David B. and Marco Vivarelli, 1996, 'Firm Size and R&D Spillovers: Evidence from Italy', *Small Business Economics* **8**, 249–258.

Dwor-Frecaut, Dominique, Francis Colaco and Mary Hallward-Driemeir (eds.), 2000, *Asian Corporate Recovery: Findings from Firm-Level Surveys in Five Countries*, Washington D.C.: The World Bank.

Thurik, A. Roy, 1996, 'Introduction: Innovation and Small Business', *Small Business Economics* **8**, 175–176.

The Dynamic Role of Small Firms: Evidence from the U.S.

David B. Audretsch

ABSTRACT. This paper provides a conceptual and empirical account of the dynamic role of SMEs in the U.S. economy. Evidence is provided to show that SMEs are important sources of employment growth and innovation. For example, the net employment gain during 1990–95 is shown to be greater among smaller firms than among larger firms. Furthermore, while large firms often produce a larger number of patents per firm, the patenting rate for small firms is typically higher than that for large firms when measured on a per-employee basis. It is noted that public policy is shifting away from traditional measures which were based on a static conception of industrial organization and thus emphasized anti-trust, regulation and public ownership solutions, towards measures which are geared towards supporting the dynamic role of SMEs. These measures focus on providing an enabling environment for enterprise start-ups, job creation, knowledge spillovers and technological change.

1. Introduction

As recently as the 1980s, there were serious concerns about the ability of the United States to withstand competition in the global economy, to create jobs, and to continue to develop economically. Lester Thurow bemoaned that the United States was "losing the economic race,"[1] because, "Today it's very hard to find an industrial corporation in America that isn't in really serious trouble basically because of trade problems. . . . The systematic erosion of our competitiveness comes from having lower rates of growth of manufacturing productivity year after year, as compared with the rest of the world" (Thurow, 1985, p. 23). W. W. Restow predicted a revolution in economic policy, concluding that, "The United States is entering a new political era, one in which it will be preoccupied by increased economic competition from abroad and will need better cooperation at home to deal with this challenge."[2] The influential study, *Made in America*, directed by the leaders of the MIT Commission on Industrial Productivity (Dertouzos and others, 1989), even reached the conclusion that for the United States to restore its international competitiveness it had to adapt the types of economic policies targeting the leading corporations in Japan and Germany.

The 1990s proved those economists and scholars mistaken, or at least too zealous in their inclinations. The last decade has seen a remarkable reemergence of competitiveness, innovative activity, and job generation in the United States not seen in many years. Not only was this economic turnaround largely unanticipated by many scholars and members of the policy community, but what was even more surprising than the resurgence itself was the primary source of the resurgence; that is, small firms.

As scholars began the arduous task of documenting the crucial role played by small and medium enterprises (SMEs) in the United States as a driving engine of growth, job creation, and competitiveness in global markets (Audretsch, 1995), policy makers responded with a bipartisan emphasis on policies to promote SMEs.[3] For example, in his 1993 State of the Union Address to the country, President Bill Clinton proposed, "Because small business has created such a high percentage of all the new jobs in our nation over the last 10 or 15 years, our plan includes the boldest targeted incentives for small business in history. We propose a permanent investment tax creditor the small firms in this country."[4] The Republican response to Clinton was, "We agree with the president that we have to put more people to work, but remember this: 80 to 85 percent of

Ameritech Chair of Economic Development
Institute of Development Strategies
Indiana University
SPEA, Suite 201
Bloomington
IN 47405-2100
U.S.A.

Small Business Economics **18**: 13–40, 2002.

the new jobs in this country are created by small business. So the climate for starting and expanding businesses must be enhanced with tax incentives and deregulation, rather than imposing higher taxes and more governmental mandates."[5]

One of the puzzles posed by the important contribution of small firms to the resurgence of the U.S. economy is that the share of economic activity, measured in terms of share of total establishments, employment, or output, has not dramatically increased over the last 20 years (Acs and Audretsch, 1993). In fact, a meticulous comparison documenting the role of SMEs across a broad spectrum of countries revealed that the share of economic activity accounted for by SMEs is considerably less than in, for example, Japan, Germany, the United Kingdom, Italy, and The Netherlands.

If SMEs are so important to the U.S. economy, then how come SMEs account for such a small share of economic activity, at least relative to other economies? The answer to this question lies in a crucial distinction between the static role and the dynamic role of SMEs.

In the second section of this paper we contrast the static role and dynamic role of SMEs. In the third section we examine the policies that have contributed to promoting the dynamic contributions of SMEs. Finally, in the fourth section, a summary and conclusions are provided.

2. Evolution of SMEs

Static and dynamic context

Two disparate views about the impact of small firms on economic efficiency have emerged in the economics literature. On the one hand is the traditional, static, view in the field of industrial organization that views small firms as imposing excess costs on the economy as a result of a scale of production that is too small to be efficient. According to this traditional view, the inefficient scale of operations results in lower levels of productivity for small firms and lower wages for their workers. The shift in economic activity that has taken place over the previous two decades away from large corporations and toward new and small firms may be interpreted as causing a decrease in the standard of living of Americans. Shifting employment out of high-productivity and high-wage firms and into lower productivity and lower-wage (small) firms, according to this traditional view, reduces the well-being of the American population, and any policies that shift economic activity out of small firms and back into large corporations should be encouraged, since they will increase the American standard of living.

On the other hand is the nontraditional, dynamic, view. With the hindsight of some 15 years, it is clear that the dynamic view of small-firm efficiency is more consistent with not just the recent wave of theories about the evolutionary role of small and new firms, but also with the compelling empirical evidence that analyzes firms and industries through a dynamic lens (Caves, 1998).

The purpose of this paper is to explain this dynamic role played by small firms in the U.S. economy. A particular emphasis is placed on the contribution of small firms to innovation, job generation, and international competitiveness.

Static role

The static role of SMEs in the United States is documented in Table I. The source of the data is the Longitudinal Establishment and Enterprise (LEEM) file, which is produced jointly by the U.S. Small Business Administration (SBA) and the U.S. Bureau of the Census. A more thorough and detailed explanation and documentation of the LEEM database can be found in Audretsch (1995).

According to the SBA, the definition of a small firm is one with fewer than 500 employees. In every major economic sector, most of the businesses are SMEs. For example, in manufacturing, only around 49,000 of the 388,000 businesses (establishments) are owned by large firms.

In Table II the distribution of employment by firm size is shown. Because a larger firm employs more people than a SME, the firm-size distribution measured by employment is not as skewed as in Table I, where it is measured by the number of establishments. Still, most Americans work in SMEs. However, the share of employment accounted for by SMEs varies considerably across major economic sectors. For example, in construction only a small share of employment is in large firms. By contrast, in manufacturing around two-thirds of employment is in large corporations.

In Tables I and II establishments are classified according to the size of the enterprise to which they belong. Table III shows that if the establishments are classified according to establishment size, then an even greater share of establishments are accounted for by SMEs. Similarly, Table IV shows that the employment share of SMEs is even greater if the employment were classified according to the size of the establishment and not the size of the enterprise.

One of the most striking findings emerging in this static view of industrial organization is that small firms generally operate at a level of output that is too small to sufficiently exhaust scale

TABLE I
LEEM establishment distribution by firm size and establishment industry: 1995

Firm size	Establishment industry									
	Agra-services	Mining	Construction	Manufacturing	TCPU	Wholesale	Retail	FIRE	Services	Uncoded
0	22,539	2,238	96,543	27,212	28,875	40,618	126,378	52,374	236,236	25,352
1–4	49,759	10,029	306,478	100,551	96,342	172,102	468,307	261,041	1,078,044	21,973
5–9	19,262	3,417	111,382	60,442	34,663	79,305	229,549	60,036	395,712	3,188
10–19	9,967	2,576	62,891	52,575	23,759	59,668	153,936	33,534	217,715	1,097
20–49	3,707	2,084	35,052	48,424	18,514	48,351	116,609	28,471	142,859	404
50–99	785	951	9,111	22,033	8,446	21,676	50,563	17,995	62,258	30
100–249	399	809	4,275	18,612	7,901	18,983	47,050	18,332	62,210	18
250–499	168	603	1,360	9,923	5,055	10,275	31,708	11,729		
500–999	214	625	931	8,376	4,683	9,302	29,065	12,139		
1000+	946	3,991	3,810	40,229	56,194	56,624	305,629	132,215		
Total	107,746	27,323	631,833	388,377	284,432	516,904	1,558,794	627,866	2,378,412	52,067

Source: Tabulations of the prototype Longitudinal Establishment and Enterprise (LEEM) file, a joint project of the Office of Economic Research, Office of Advocacy, Small Business Administration, and the Center for Economic Studies of the Bureau of the Census, U.S. Department of Commerce (Acs and Armington, 1998, Table 6.3c).

TABLE II
LEEM employment distribution by firm size and establishment industry: 1995

Firm size	Establishment industry									
	Agra-services	Mining	Construction	Manufacturing	TCPU	Wholesale	Retail	FIRE	Services	Uncoded
0	0	0	0	0	0	0	0	0	0	0
1–4	103,692	20,160	642,722	227,470	199,212	369,679	1,040,824	501,333	2,244,789	36,717
5–9	126,586	22,410	728,147	404,733	223,611	513,430	1,478,920	373,335	2,540,323	20,399
10–19	130,322	33,794	837,695	714,023	302,064	732,703	1,878,676	377,532	2,705,654	14,330
20–49	101,525	53,395	1,108,886	1,433,918	457,795	1,053,428	2,653,287	521,661	3,448,373	11,360
50–99	45,497	37,959	574,168	1,308,089	339,675	684,409	1,693,721	412,520	2,561,140	1,851
100–249	36,888	44,129	485,825	1,796,540	393,102	700,693	1,440,357	492,592	3,564,147	2,490
250–499	15,172	31,067	210,453	1,276,358	235,453	373,365	768,499	322,560	2,468,592	253
500–999	10,856	38,658	141,812	1,274,762	234,024	262,512	640,040	311,394	2,311,945	2,243
1000+	59,104	345,734	397,192	10,172,347	3,538,287	1,914,731	9,481,931	3,670,767	12,851,941	2,156
Total	629,642	627,306	5,036,900	18,608,240	5,923,233	6,604,950	21,076,255	6,983,694	34,696,904	91,799

Source: Tabulations of the prototype Longitudinal Establishment and Enterprise (LEEM) file, a joint project of the Office of Economic Research, Office of Advocacy, Small Business Administration, and the Center for Economic Studies of the Bureau of the Census, U.S. Department of Commerce (Acs and Armington, 1998, Table 6.4c).

TABLE III
LEEM establishments classified by firm size and by establishment size

Employment size class	1990		1994		1995	
	Number of establishments by firm size	Number of establishments by establishment size	Number of establishments by firm size	Number of establishments by establishment size	Number of establishments by firm size	Number of establishments by establishment size
0	592,101	619,153	655,566	694,967	658,365	695,344
1–4	2,393,133	2,679,308	2,520,339	2,838,407	2,564,626	2,882,658
5–9	969,135	1,237,084	981,598	1,285,158	996,956	1,298,392
10–19	598,851	769,619	608,316	799,077	617,718	817,335
20–49	415,667	508,292	438,295	526,365	444,475	543,906
50–99	174,448	175,357	192,803	177,913	193,848	185,259
100–249	160,002	97,709	178,683	101,940	178,589	107,308
250–499	94,725	24,323	105,074	25,657	105,392	27,194
500–999	82,052	9,590	87,258	9,765	91,039	10,333
1000+	645,902	5,581	697,125	5,808	722,746	6,025
Total	6,126,016	6,126,016	6,465,057	6,465,057	6,573,754	6,573,754

Source: Tabulations of the prototype Longitudinal Establishment and Enterprise (LEEM) file, a joint project of the Office of Economic Research, Office of Advocacy, Small Business Administration, and the Center for Economic Studies of the Bureau of the Census, U.S. Department of Commerce (Acs and Armington, 1998, Table 6.1).

TABLE IV
LEEM employment by firm size and by establishment size

Employment size class	1990		1994		1995	
	Number of establishments by firm size	Number of establishments by establishment size	Number of establishments by firm size	Number of establishments by establishment size	Number of establishments by firm size	Number of establishments by establishment size
1–4	5,108,303	5,843,895	5,311,360	6,127,769	5,386,598	6,192,612
5–9	6,242,213	8,158,925	6,325,466	8,485,239	6,431,894	8,574,605
10–19	7,534,444	10,343,097	7,537,382	10,738,355	7,726,793	10,992,228
20–49	10,401,095	15,375,515	10,364,280	15,905,109	10,753,628	16,435,592
50–99	7,295,147	12,027,638	7,321,621	12,224,648	7,659,029	12,755,332
100–249	8,268,752	14,610,283	8,590,755	15,276,124	8,956,763	16,070,791
250–499	5,272,697	8,306,581	5,523,148	8,757,727	5,701,772	9,280,853
500–999	4,807,014	6,550,174	5,128,503	6,661,977	5,228,246	7,019,910
1000+	38,495,464	12,209,021	40,584,831	12,510,398	42,434,190	12,956,990
Total	93,425,129	93,425,129	96,687,346	96,687,346	100,278,913	100,278,913

Source: Tabulations of the prototype Longitudinal Establishment and Enterprise (LEEM) file, a joint project of the Office of Economic Research, Office of Advocacy, Small Business Administration, and the Center for Economic Studies of the Bureau of the Census, U.S. Department of Commerce (Acs and Armington, 1998, Table 5.7).

economies, even when the standard definition of a small firm employing fewer than 500 employees is applied. A large number of studies found that because the minimum efficient scale (MES) of output, or the lowest level of output where the minimum average cost is attained, large-scale production is typically required to exhaust scale economies in manufacturing. Any enterprise or establishment that was smaller than required by the MES was branded as being *suboptimal* or inefficient, in that it produced at average costs in excess of more efficient larger firms. Weiss (Audretsch and Yamawaki, 1991, p. 403) assumed that "The term 'suboptimal' capacity describes a condition in which some plants are too small to be efficient."

The importance of scale economies in the typical manufacturing industry relegated most small firms to being classified as suboptimal.[6] For example, Weiss (1964) found that suboptimal plants accounted for about 52.8 percent of industry value-of-shipments, Scherer (1973) found that 58.2 percent of value-of-shipments emanated from the suboptimal plants in 12 industries, and Pratten (1971) identified the suboptimal scale establishments accounting for 47.9 percent of industry shipments. After reviewing the literature on the extent of suboptimal firms, Weiss concluded that, "In most industries the great majority of firms is suboptimal. In a typical industry there are, let's say, one hundred firms. Typically only about five to ten of them will be operating at the MES level of output, or anything like it."[7]

What are the economic welfare implications? Weiss (1979, p. 1137) argued that the existence of small firms that are suboptimal represented a loss in economic efficiency and therefore advocated any public policy that ". . . creates social gains in the form of less suboptimal capacity." This actually translated into an ingenious argument against market power, since empirical evidence suggested that the price umbrella provided by monopoly power encouraged the existence of suboptimal capacity firms. Weiss (1979) went so far as to argue that the largest inefficiency associated with market power was not the higher prices charged to consumers but rather that it facilitated the existence of suboptimal scale small firms.

Wages and productivity would be expected to reflect the degree to which small firms are less efficient than larger firms. There is a large body of empirical evidence spanning a broad range of samples, time periods, and even countries that has consistently found wages (and nonwage compensation as well) to be positively related to firm size. Probably the most cited study is that of Brown et al. (1990, pp. 88–89). They conclude that, "Workers in large firms earn higher wages, and this fact cannot be explained completely by differences in labor quality industry, working conditions, or union status. Workers in large firms enjoy better benefits and greater security than their counterparts in small firms. When these factors are added together, it appears that workers in large firms do have a superior employment package." Indeed, Audretsch (1995) shows that the mean manufacturing wage in small firms that can be classified as being suboptimal is only 80.5 percent as high as their larger, optimal counterparts.

Seen through the static lens provided through traditional industrial organization and labor economics, the economic welfare implications of the recent shift in economic activity away from large firms and towards small enterprises is unequivocal. Overall economic welfare is decreased since productivity and wages will be lower in smaller than in larger firms. As Weiss (1979) argued in terms of efficiency and Brown et al. (1990) in terms of employee compensation, the implication for public policy is to implement policies to shift economic activity away from small firms and toward larger enterprises.

Dynamic view

Coase (1937) was awarded a Nobel Prize for explaining why a firm should exist. But why should more than one firm exist in an industry?[8] One answer is provided by the traditional economics literature focusing on industrial organization. An excess level of profitability induces entry into the industry. And this is why the entry of new firms is interesting and important, because the new firms provide an equilibrating function in the market in that the levels of price and profit are restored to the competitive levels. The new firms are about business as usual. They simply equilibrate the market by providing more of it.

An alternative explanation for the entry of new firms was provided for by Audretsch (1995). Audretsch shows how new firms entered the industry not simply to increase output by being a smaller replica of the large incumbent enterprises but by serving as *agents of change*. This suggested that small firms, at least in some situations, were not about being smaller clones of the larger incumbents but rather about serving as *agents of change* through innovative activity.

The starting point for most of these theories of innovation is the firm.[9] In such theories the firms are exogenous and their performance in generating technological change is endogenous.[10] For example, in the most prevalent model found in the literature of technological change, the model of the *knowledge production function*, formalized by Griliches (1979), firms exist exogenously and then engage in the pursuit of new economic knowledge as an input into the process of generating innovative activity.

The most decisive input in the knowledge production function is new economic knowledge. As Cohen and Klepper conclude, the greatest source generating new economic knowledge is generally considered to be R&D.[11] Certainly a large body of empirical work has found a strong and positive relationship between knowledge inputs, such as R&D, on the one hand and innovative outputs on the other.

The knowledge production function has been found to hold most strongly at broader levels of aggregation. The most innovative countries are those with the greatest investments to R&D. Little innovative output is associated with lesser developed countries, which are characterized by a paucity of production of new economic knowledge. Similarly, the most innovative industries also tend to be characterized by considerable investments in R&D and new economic knowledge. Industries such as computers, pharmaceuticals, and instruments are not only high in R&D inputs that generate new economic knowledge but also in innovative outputs (Audretsch, 1995). By contrast, industries with little R&D, such as wood products, textiles, and paper, also tend to produce only a negligible amount of innovative output. Thus, the knowledge production model linking knowledge generating inputs to outputs certainly holds at the more aggregated levels of economic activity.

Where the relationship becomes less compelling is at the disaggregated microeconomic level of the enterprise, establishment, or even line of business. For example, While Acs and Audretsch (1990) found that the simple correlation between R&D inputs and innovative output was 0.84 for four-digit standard industrial classification (SIC) manufacturing industries in the United States, it was only about half, 0.40, among the largest U.S. corporations.

The model of the knowledge production function becomes even less compelling in view of the recent wave of studies revealing that small enterprises serve as the engine of innovative activity in certain industries. These results are startling, because as Scherer (1991) observes, the bulk of industrial R&D is undertaken in the largest corporations. Small enterprises account only for a minor share of R&D inputs. Thus the knowledge production function seemingly implies that, as the *Schumpeterian Hypothesis* predicts, innovative activity favors those organizations with access to knowledge-producing inputs; that is, the large incumbent organization. The more recent evidence identifying the strong innovative activity raises the question, *Where do new and small firms get the innovation producing inputs; that is, the knowledge?*

One answer, proposed by Audretsch (1995), is that, although the model of the knowledge production function may still be valid, the implicitly assumed unit of observation – at the level of the firm – may be less valid. The reason why the knowledge production function holds more closely for more aggregated degrees of observation may be that investment in R&D and other sources of new knowledge spills over for economic exploitation by third-party firms.

A large literature has emerged focusing on what has become known as the *appropriability problem.*[12] The underlying issue revolves around how firms that invest in the creation of new economic knowledge can best appropriate the economic returns from that knowledge (Arrow, 1962). Audretsch (1995) proposes shifting the unit of observation away from exogenously assumed firms to individuals; that is, agents with endowments of new economic knowledge. But when the lens is shifted away from focusing on the firm as the relevant unit of observation to individuals, the relevant question becomes, *How can economic agents with a given endowment of new knowledge best appropriate the returns from that knowledge?*

The appropriability problem confronting the individual may converge with that confronting the firm. Economic agents can and do work for firms, and even if those economic agents do not, the economic agents can potentially be employed by an incumbent firm. In fact, in a model of perfect information with no agency costs, any positive economies of scale or scope will ensure that the appropriability problems of the firm and individual converge. If an agent has an idea for doing something differently than is currently being practiced by the incumbent enterprises – both in terms of a new product or process and in terms of organization – then the idea, which can be termed as an innovation, will be presented to the incumbent enterprise. Because of the assumption of perfect knowledge, both the firm and the agent would agree on the expected value of the innovation. But to the degree that any economies of scale or scope exist, the expected value of implementing the innovation within the incumbent enterprise will exceed that of taking the innovation outside of the incumbent firm to start a new enterprise. Thus, the incumbent firm and the inventor of the idea would be expected to reach a bargain by splitting the value added to the firm contributed by the innovation. The payment to the inventor – either in terms of a higher wage or some other means of remuneration – would be bounded between the expected value of the innovation if it is implemented by the incumbent enterprise on the upper end and by the return that the agent could expect to earn if the agent used it to launch a new enterprise on the lower end. Thus, each economic agent would choose how to best appropriate the value of this endowment of economic knowledge by comparing the wage the agent would earn if the agent remains employed by an incumbent enterprise, w, to the expected net present discounted value of the profits accruing from starting a new firm, π. If these two values are relatively close, then the probability that the agent would choose to appropriate the value of this knowledge through an external mechanism such as starting a new firm, $Pr(e)$, would be relatively low. On the other hand, as the gap between w and π becomes larger, the likelihood of an agent choosing to appropriate the value of this knowledge externally through starting a new enterprise becomes greater, or

$$Pr(e) = f(\pi - w).$$

The model proposed by Audretsch (1995) refocuses the unit of observation away from firms deciding whether to increase their output from a level of zero to some positive amount in a new industry to individual agents in possession of new knowledge that, owing to uncertainty, may or may not have some positive economic value. It is the uncertainty inherent in new economic knowledge, combined with asymmetries between the agent possessing that knowledge and the decision making vertical hierarchy of the incumbent organization with respect to its expected value, that potentially leads to a gap between the valuation of that knowledge.

How the economic agent chooses to appropriate the value of this knowledge, that is either within an incumbent firm or by starting or joining a new enterprise, will be shaped by the knowledge conditions underlying the industry. Under the routinized technological regime the agent will tend to appropriate the value of new ideas within the boundaries of incumbent firms. Thus, the propensity for new firms to be started should be relatively low in industries characterized by the routinized technological regime.

By contrast, under the entrepreneurial regime the agent will tend to appropriate the value of new ideas outside of the boundaries of incumbent firms by starting a new enterprise. Thus, the propensity for new firms to enter should be relatively high in industries characterized by the entrepreneurial regime.

Audretsch (1995) suggests that divergences in the expected value regarding new knowledge will, under certain conditions, lead an agent to exercise what Hirschman (1970) has termed as *exit* rather than *voice*, and depart from an incumbent enterprise to launch a new firm. But who is right, the departing agents or those agents remaining in the organizational decision making hierarchy who, by assigning the new idea a relatively low value, have effectively driven the agent with the potential innovation away? *Ex post* the answer may not be too difficult. But given the uncertainty inherent in new knowledge, the answer is anything but trivial *a priori*.

Thus, when a new firm is launched, its prospects are shrouded in uncertainty. If the new firm were to be built around a new idea (i.e., potential innovation), then it is uncertain whether there is sufficient demand for the new idea or if some competitor will have the same or even a superior idea. Even if the new firm were to be formed to be an exact replica of a successful incumbent enterprise, it is uncertain whether sufficient demand for a new clone, or even for the existing incumbent, will prevail in the future. Tastes can change, and new ideas emerging from other firms will certainty influence those tastes.

Finally, an additional layer of uncertainty pervades a new enterprise. It is not known how competent the new firm really is, in terms of management, organization, and workforce. At least incumbent enterprises know something about their underlying competencies from experience. A new enterprise is burdened with uncertainty as to whether it can produce and market the intended product as well as sell it. In both cases the degree of uncertainty will typically exceed that confronting incumbent enterprises.

This initial condition of not just uncertainty, but greater degree of uncertainty vis-à-vis incumbent enterprises in the industry is captured in the theory of firm selection and industry evolution proposed by Jovanovic (1982). Jovanovic presents a model in which the new firms, which he terms *entrepreneurs*, face costs that are not only random but also differ across firms. A central feature of the model is that a new firm does not know what its cost function is (i.e., its relative efficiency) but rather discovers this cost function through the process of learning from its actual post-entry performance. In particular, Jovanovic (1982) assumes that entrepreneurs are unsure about their ability to manage a new-firm startup and therefore their prospects for success. Although entrepreneurs may launch a new firm based on a vague sense of expected post-entry performance, they only discover their true ability – in terms of managerial competence and of having based the firm on an idea that is viable on the market – once their business is established. Those entrepreneurs who discover that their ability exceeds their expectations expand the scale of their business, whereas those discovering that their post-entry performance is less than commensurate with their expectations will contact the scale of output and possibly exit from the industry. Thus, Jovanovic's model is a theory of *noisy selection*, where efficient firms grow and survive and inefficient firms decline and fail.

The role of learning in the selection process has been the subject of considerable debate. It has been referred to as the *Larackian* assumption that learning refers to adaptations made by the new enterprise. In this sense, those new firms most flexible and adaptable will be the most successful in adjusting to whatever the demands of the market are. As Nelson and Winter (1982, p. 11) point out, "Many kinds of organizations commit resources to learning; organizations seek to copy the forms of their most successful competitors."

Conversely, the interpretation that the role of learning is restricted to discovering if the firm has the *right stuff* in terms of the goods it is producing as well as the way the goods are being produced. Under this interpretation the new enterprise is not necessarily able to adapt or adjust to market conditions, but receives information based on its market performance with respect to its *fitness* in terms of meeting demand most efficiently vis-à-vis rivals. The theory of organizational ecology proposed by. Hannan and Freeman (1989) most pointedly adheres to the notion that, "We assume that individual organizations are characterized by relative inertia in structure." That is, firms learn not in the sense that they adjust their actions as reflected by their fundamental identity and purpose, but in the sense of their perception. What is then learned is whether or not the firm has the right stuff, but not how to change that stuff.

The theory of firm selection is particularly appealing in view of the rather startling size of most new firms. For example, the mean size of more than 11,000 new-firm startups in the manufacturing sector in the United States was found to be fewer than eight workers per firm (Audretsch, 1995).[13] While the MES varies substantially across industries, and even to some degree across various product classes within any given industry, the observed size of most new firms is sufficiently small to ensure that the bulk of new firms will be operating at a suboptimal scale of output. Why would an entrepreneur start a new firm that would immediately be confronted by scale disadvantages?

An implication of the theory of firm selection is that new firms may begin at a small, even suboptimal, scale of output, and then if merited by subsequent performance expand. Those new firms that are successful will grow, whereas those that are not successful will remain small and may ultimately be forced to exit from the industry if operating at a suboptimal scale of output.

Subsequent to entering an industry, an entrepreneur must decide whether to maintain its output by expanding, contracting, or simply exiting. Two different strands of literature have identified several major influences shaping the decision to exit an industry. The first and most obvious strand of literature suggests that the probability of a business exiting will tend to increase as the gap between its level of output and the MES level of output increases.[14] The second strand of literature points to the role that the technological environment plays in shaping the decision to exit. As Dosi (1982) and Arrow (1962) argue, an environment characterized by more frequent innovation may also be associated with a greater amount of uncertainty regarding not only the technical nature of the product but also the demand for that product. As technological uncertainty increases, particularly under the entrepreneurial regime, the likelihood that the business will be able to produce a viable product and ultimately be able to survive decreases.

An important implication of the dynamic process of firm selection and industry evolution is that new firms are more likely to be operating at a suboptimal scale of output if the underlying technological conditions are such that there is a greater chance of making an innovation (i.e., under the entrepreneurial regime). If new firms were to successfully learn and adapt, or are just plain lucky, then those firms will grow into viably sized enterprises. If not, then those firms will stagnate and may ultimately exit from the industry. This suggests that entry and the startup of new firms may not be greatly deterred in the presence of scale economies. As long as entrepreneurs perceive that there is some prospect for growth and ultimate survival, such entry will occur. Thus, in industries where the MES is high, it follows from the observed general small size of new-firm startups that the growth rate of the surviving firms would presumably be relatively high.

At the same time, those new firms not able to grow and attain the MES level of output would presumably be forced to exit from the industry, resulting in a relatively low likelihood of survival. In industries characterized by a low MES, neither the need for growth nor the consequences of its absence are as severe, so that relatively lower growth rates but higher survival rates would be expected. Similarly, in industries where the probability of innovating is greater, more entrepreneurs may actually take a chance that they will succeed by growing into a viably sized enterprise. In such industries one would expect that the growth of successful enterprises would be greater, but that the likelihood of survival would be correspondingly lower.

That the role of SMEs seen through a dynamic lens is considerably different than through a static one is made clear in Table V, which shows the percentage change between 1990 and 1995 in employment owing to new firms (births), exits (deaths), additional employment in existing firms (expansions), and decreases in employment in existing firms (contractions). For example, there was a 12.76 percent increase in employment owing to the birth of new firms in manufacturing between 1990 and 1995. However, employment change owing to births was considerably greater by SMEs than by large corporations. There were nearly one-third new jobs created by new firms with fewer than 20 employees. Similarly, there was an increase in employment of SMEs of 144.69 percent resulting from the startup of new firms.

However, there was also a considerable number of jobs lost as a result of firms going out of business, classified as deaths in Table V. The overall employment birth rate of 12.76 percent in manufacturing was more than offset by a loss in employment owing to a death rate of 15.92 percent. Just as the birth rate is greater for smaller enterprises, so is the death rate. The share of 1990 employment lost owing to firms exiting was 12.79 percent for large corporations, 19.37 percent for enterprises having between 20 and 499 employees, and 28.69 percent for enterprises with fewer than 20 employees.

The expansion rate is also inversely related to firm size, with the smallest enterprises exhibiting an expansion rate of nearly one-third, while the large corporations exhibited an expansion rate of just over 10 percent. However, the contraction rate follows a different pattern than do the birth, death, and expansion rates. This is because the contraction rate is actually the greatest for large corporations and the lowest in enterprises with fewer than 20 employees. The high contraction rate for corporations, 16.62, percent reflects the high degree of corporate downsizing that has occurred in the 1990s.

The high degree of corporate downsizing combined with relatively low employment birth and expansion rates resulted in a net decrease in employment in large corporation of 8.47 percent

TABLE V
1990–1995 employment changes by establishment change type, industry, and firm size (base year method)

Industry	Firm employment	1990 establishment employment	Births	Deaths	Expansions	Contractions	Net
			(as a percentage of 1990 employment in same employment size category)				
Manufacturing	<20	1,354,055	30.38	–28.69	31.27	–11.72	21.25
	20–499	5,863,336	14.31	–19.37	18.67	–13.05	0.57
	500+	11,956,053	10.01	–12.79	10.93	–16.62	–8.47
	All	19,173,444	12.76	–15.92	14.73	–15.18	–3.61
Other productive	<20	2,559,336	38.51	–34.52	26.15	–14.39	15.75
	20–499	2,831,202	17.61	–25.47	14.54	–22.08	–15.41
	500+	1,127,345	20.49	–24.12	13.89	–24.22	–13.97
	All	6,517,883	26.32	–28.79	18.98	–19.43	–2.93
Distributive	<20	6,059,802	34.29	–33.39	20.65	–11.90	9.66
	20–499	9,075,659	27.57	–25.14	13.04	–14.82	0.65
	500+	11,054,412	31.74	–21.16	12.61	–14.41	8.79
	All	26,189,873	30.89	–25.37	14.62	–13.97	6.17
Services	<20	8,911,767	35.54	–27.36	27.20	–12.23	23.14
	20–499	13,467,494	30.79	–21.61	19.89	–15.82	13.24
	500+	19,164,668	28.88	–17.77	15.67	–14.91	11.87
	All	41,543,929	30.93	–21.07	19.51	–14.63	14.73
All	<20	18,884,960	35.17	–30.36	25.25	–12.38	17.68
	20–499	31,237,691	25.57	–22.56	17.18	–15.58	4.61
	500+	43,302,478	24.18	–17.42	13.53	–15.50	4.79
	All	93,425,129	26.87	–21.76	17.12	–14.89	7.34

Source: Tabulations of the prototype Longitudinal Establishment and Enterprise (LEEM) file, a joint project of the Office of Economic Research, Office of Advocacy, Small Business Administration, and the Center for Economic Studies of the Bureau of the Census, U.S. Department of Commerce (Acs and Armington, 1998, Table 8.1a).

between 1990 and 1995. At the same time, the high employment birth and expansion rates combined with lower death and contraction rates resulted in a net increase in employment, 21.25 percent for firms with fewer than 20 employees.

The dynamic pattern of employment creation in manufacturing is typical for the entire U.S. economy. In every major sector (1) the birth rate of SMEs exceeds that in large corporations, (2) the death rate of SMEs exceeds that of large corporations, (3) the expansion rate of SMEs exceeds that of large corporations, (4) the contraction rate of large corporations exceeds that of SMEs, and (5) the net employment gain is the greatest in SMEs.

Table VI shows that while the numbers of enterprises and new enterprises have been growing over time, the rate of growth has been fairly constant. The dynamic contribution of SMEs documented in Table IV does not seem to be restricted to just several years but is now characteristic of the U.S. economy.

Table VII shows that SMEs contribute not only the greatest amount of net employment creation but also the greatest amount of turbulence. The sum of employment creation plus destruction is identified as reallocation in Table VII.

Analysis of SMEs through a dynamic framework reveals that their impact is considerably more significant than when analyzed through a static framework.

Innovation

Not only was the large corporation thought to have superior productive efficiency, but conventional wisdom also held the large corporation to serve as the engine of technological change and innovative activity. After all, Schumpeter (1942, p. 106), "What we have got to accept is that the large-scale

TABLE VI
Change in the number of U.S. businesses with employees, fiscal years 1982–1995 (thousands)

Year	Firms at end of each year	Successor firms	New firms	Sum: new and successor	Terminations	Net rate of growth (percent)
1995	6,057	164	819	983	871	1.09
1994	5,992	137	807	944	803	2.40
1993	5,851	136	776	911	801	1.93
1992	5,741	138	737	875	819	0.95
1991	5,687	140	724	864	818	0.84
1990	5,639	146	769	915	846	1.27
1989	5,568	153	743	896	826	1.10
1988	5,513	153	755	907	752	1.71
1987	5,420	163	775	939	717	3.64
1986	5,230	175	741	916	801	1.70
1985	5,142	166	722	888	746	2.67
1984	5,009	164	691	855	687	3.54
1983	4,837	171	633	804	720	1.26
1982	4,777	185	595	781	707	1.55

Source: Adapted by U.S. Small Business Administration, Office of Advocacy, from data provided by the U.S. Department of Labor, Employment and Training Administration, based upon state employment security agencies' quarterly reports, 1995.

TABLE VII
Establishment employment flows by initial year establishment size classification: 1994–1995
[percent change in establishment jobs (based on mean employment in size class)]

Initial establishment employment	1994 employment	Net	Creation	Destruction	Reallocation
1–4	6,127,769	18.2	36.2	–17.9	54.1
5–19	19,223,594	5.0	20.8	–15.8	36.6
20–49	15,905,109	3.5	17.5	–14.0	31.5
50–99	12,224,648	3.2	15.9	–12.7	28.6
100–499	24,033,851	2.1	13.5	–11.5	25.0
500–999	6,661,977	–0.6	10.2	–10.8	21.0
1,000–4,999	9,934,405	–0.9	8.0	–8.9	16.9
5,000+	2,575,993	1.5	10.1	–8.5	18.6
Total	96,687,346	3.6	16.6	–13.0	29.6
Mean establishment employment	**1994 employment**	**Net**	**Creation**	**Destruction**	**Reallocation**
1–4	7,125,242	4.4	33.4	–29.0	62.4
5–19	19,087,849	3.4	20.1	–16.7	36.7
20–49	15,683,617	4.1	17.6	–13.6	31.2
50–99	12,073,947	4.7	16.4	–11.7	28.1
100–499	23,798,729	4.0	13.8	–9.8	23.6
500–999	6,571,009	2.6	11.1	–8.6	19.7
1,000–4,999	9,818,110	2.2	9.0	–6.8	15.9
5,000+	2,528,843	1.1	7.3	–6.1	13.4
Total	96,687,346	3.6	16.6	–13.0	29.6

Source: Tabulations of the prototype Longitudinal Establishment and Enterprise (LEEM) file, a joint project of the Office of Economic Research, Office of Advocacy, Small Business Administration, and the Center for Economic Studies of the Bureau of the Census, U.S. Department of Commerce (Acs et al., 1999, Table 2).

establishment has come to be the most powerful engine of progress." A few years later, Galbraith (1956, p. 86) echoed Schumpeter's sentiment when he lamented, "There is no more pleasant fiction than that technological change is the product of the matchless ingenuity of the small man forced by competition to employ his wits to better his neighbor. Unhappily, it is a fiction."

Knowledge regarding both the determinants and the impact of technological change has been largely shaped by measurement. Measures of technological change have typically involved one of the three major aspects of the innovative process: (1) a measure of inputs into the process, such as R&D expenditures, or the share of the labor force accounted for by employees involved in R&D activities; (2) an intermediate output, such as the number of inventions that have been patented; or (3) a direct measure of innovative output.

The earliest sources of data, R&D measured, indicated that virtually all of the innovative activity was undertaken by large corporations. As patent measures became available, the general qualitative conclusions did not change, although it became clear that small firms were more involved with patent activity than with R&D. The development of direct measures of innovative activity, such as databases measuring new product and process introductions in the market, indicated something quite different. In a series of studies, Acs and Audretsch (1987, 1988, 1990) found that while large firms in manufacturing introduced a slightly greater number of significant new innovations than small firms, small-firm employment was only about half as great as large-firm employment, yielding an average small-firm innovation rate in manufacturing of 0.309, compared to a large-firm innovation rate of 0.202.

As Table VIII shows, the relative innovative advantage of small and large firms varies considerably across industries. In some industries, such as computers and process control instruments, small firms provide the engine of innovative activity. In other industries, such as pharmaceutical products and aircraft, large firms generate most of the innovative activity. Knowledge regarding both the determinants and the impact of technological change has been largely shaped by measurement.

Audretsch (1995) concluded that some industries are more conducive to small-firm innovation while others foster the innovative activity of large corporations corresponds to the notion of distinct technological regimes; that is, the routinized and entrepreneurial technological regimes. According to Winter (1984, p. 297), "An entrepreneurial regime is one that is favorable to innovative entry and unfavorable to innovative activity by established firms; a routinized regime is one in which the conditions are the other way around."

New firm startups

Empirical evidence in support of the traditional model of entry, which focuses on the role of excess profits as the major incentive to enter, has been ambiguous at best, leading Geroski (1991, p. 282) to conclude, "Right from the start, scholars have had some trouble in reconciling the stories told about entry in standard textbooks with the substance of what they have found in their data. Very few have emerged from their work feeling that they have answered half as many questions as they have raised, much less that they have answered most of the interesting ones."

Perhaps one reason for this trouble is the inherently static model used to capture an inherently dynamic process. Neumann (1993, pp. 593–594) has criticized this traditional model of entry, as found in the individual country studies contained in Geroski and Schwalbach (1991), because they "are predicated on the adoption of a basically static framework. It is assumed that startups enter a given market where they are facing incumbents which naturally try to fend off entry. Since the impact of entry on the performance of incumbents seems to be only slight, the question arises whether the costs of entry are worthwhile, given the high rate of exit associated with entry. Geroski appears to be rather skeptical about that. I submit that adopting a static framework is misleading. . . . In fact, generally, an entrant can only hope to succeed if he employs either a new technology or offers a new product, or both. Just imitating incumbents is almost certainly doomed to failure. If the process of entry is looked upon from this perspective the high correlation between gross entry and exit reflects the inherent risks of innovating activities. . . . Obviously it is rather difficult to break loose from the inherited mode of

TABLE VIII
Number of innovations for large and small firms in the most innovative industries

Industry	Total innovations	Large-firm innovations	Small-firm innovations
Electronics computing equipment	395	158	227
Process control instruments	165	68	93
Radio and TV communication equipment	157	83	72
Pharmaceutical preparations	133	120	72
Electronic components	128	54	73
Engineering and scientific instruments	126	43	83
Semiconductors	122	91	29
Plastics products	107	22	82
Photographic equipment	88	79	9
Office machine	77	67	10
Instruments to measure electricity	77	28	47
Surgical appliances and supplies	67	54	13
Surgical and medical instrument	66	30	36
Special industry machinery	64	43	21
Industrial controls	61	15	46
Toilet preparations	59	41	18
Valves and pipe fittings	54	20	33
Electric housewares and fans	53	47	6
Measuring and controlling devices	52	3	45
Food products machinery	50	37	12
Motors and generators	49	39	10
Plastic materials and resins	45	30	15
Industrial inorganic chemicals	40	32	8
Radio and TV receiving sets	40	35	4
Hand and edge tools	39	27	11
Fabricated platework	38	29	9
Fabricated metal products	35	12	17
Pumps and pumping equipment	34	18	16
Optical instruments and lenses	34	12	21
Polishes and sanitation goods	33	13	19
Industrial trucks and tractors	33	13	20
Medicinal and botanicals	32	27	5
Aircraft	32	31	1
Environmental controls	32	22	10

Note: Large and small-firm innovations do not always sum to total innovations because several innovations could not be classified according to firm size.
Source: Audretsch (1995).

reasoning within the static framework. It is not without merit, to be sure, but it needs to be enlarged by putting it into a dynamic setting."

Still, one of the most startling results that have emerged in empirical studies is that entry by firms into an industry is apparently not substantially deterred or even deterred at all in capital-intensive industries in which scale economies play an important role (Audretsch, 1995).[15] While studies have generally produced considerable ambiguity concerning the impact of scale economies and other measures traditionally thought to represent a *barrier to entry*, Audretsch (1995) found conclusive evidence linking the technological regime to startup activity. New-firm startup activity tends to be substantially more prevalent under the entrepreneurial regime, or where small enterprises account for the bulk of the innovative activity, than under the routinized regime, or where the large incumbent enterprises account for most of the innovative activity.[16] These findings are consistent with the view that differences in beliefs about the expected value of new ideas are not constant across industries but rather depend on the knowledge conditions inherent in the underlying technological regime.

Survival

Geroski (1995) and Audretsch (1995) point out that one of the major conclusions from studies about entry is that the process of entry does not end with entry itself. Rather, it is what happens to new firms subsequent to entering that sheds considerable light on industry dynamics. The early studies (Mansfield, 1962; Hall, 1987; Dunne et al. 1989; Audretsch, 1991) established not only that the likelihood of a new entrant surviving is quite low, but that the likelihood of survival is positively related to firm size and age. More recently, a wave of studies have confirmed these findings for diverse countries, including Portugal (Mata et al., 1995; Mata, 1994), Germany (Wagner, 1994), and Canada (Baldwin and Gorecki, 1991; Baldwin, 1995; Baldwin and Rafiquzzaman, 1995).

Audretsch (1991), Audretsch and Mahmood (1995) shifted the relevant question away from *Why does the likelihood of survival vary systematically across firms?* to *Why does the propensity for firms to survive vary systematically across industries?* The answer to this question suggests that what had previously been considered to pose a barrier to entry may, in fact, constitute not a barrier to entry barrier but rather a barrier to survival. The answer to these questions suggests that what had previously been considered to pose a barrier to entry may, in fact, constitute not an entry barrier but rather a barrier to survival.

Growth

What has become known as *Gibrat's Law*, or the assumption that growth rates are invariant to firm size, has been subject to numerous empirical tests (Sutton, 1997). Studies linking firm size and age to growth have also produced a number of stylized facts (Wagner, 1992). For small and new firms there is substantial evidence suggesting that growth is negatively related to firm size and age (Hall, 1987; Wagner, 1992, 1994; Mata, 1994; Audretsch, 1995). However, for larger firms, particularly those having attained the MES level of output, the evidence suggests that firm growth is unrelated to size and age.

An important finding of Audretsch (1991, 1995) and Audretsch and Mahmood (1995) is that although entry may still occur in industries characterized by a high degree of scale economies, the likelihood of survival is considerably less. People will start new firms in an attempt to appropriate the expected value of their new ideas, or potential innovations, particularly under the entrepreneurial regime. As entrepreneurs gain experience in the market they learn in at least two ways. First, they discover whether they possess the right stuff, in terms of producing goods and offering services for which sufficient demand exists, as well as whether they can produce the goods more efficiently than their rivals. Second, they learn whether they can adapt to market conditions as well as to strategies engaged in by rival firms. In terms of the first type of learning, entrepreneurs who discover that they have a viable firm will tend to expand and ultimately survive. But what about those entrepreneurs who discover that they are either not efficient or not offering a product for which there is a viable demand? The answer is that it depends on the extent of scale economies as well as on conditions of demand. The consequences of not being able to grow will depend, to a large degree, on the extent of scale economies. Thus, in markets with only negligible scale economies, firms have a considerably greater likelihood of survival. However, where scale economies play an important role, the consequences of not growing are substantially more severe, as evidenced by a lower likelihood of survival.

Dynamic contribution of SMEs

What emerges from the new evolutionary theories and empirical evidence on the economic role of new and small firms is that markets are in motion, with many new firms entering the industry and many firms exiting out of the industry. But is this motion horizontal, in that the bulk of firms exiting are composed of firms that had entered relatively recently, or vertical, in that a significant share of the exiting firms had been established incumbents that were displaced by younger firms? In trying to shed some light on this question, Audretsch (1995) proposes two different models of the evolutionary process of industries over time.

Some industries can be best characterized by

the model of the conical revolving door, where new businesses enter, but where there is a high propensity to subsequently exit from the market. Other industries may be better characterized by the metaphor of the forest, where incumbent establishments are displaced by new entrants. Which view is more applicable apparently depends on three major factors: the underlying technological conditions, scale economies, and demand. Where scale economies play an important role, the model of the revolving door seems to be more applicable. While the rather startling result just discussed that the startup and entry of new businesses is apparently not deterred by the presence of high scale economies, a process of firm selection analogous to a revolving door ensures that only those establishments successful enough to grow will be able to survive beyond more than a few years. Thus the bulk of new entrants that are not so successful ultimately exit within a few years subsequent to entry.

There is at least some evidence also suggesting that the underlying technological regime influences the process of firm selection and therefore the type of firm with a higher propensity to exit. Under the entrepreneurial regime new entrants have a greater likelihood of making an innovation. Thus, they are less likely to decide to exit from the industry, even in the face of negative profits. By contrast, under the routinized regime the incumbent businesses tend to have the innovative advantage, so that a higher portion of exiting businesses tend to be new entrants. Thus, the model of the revolving door is more applicable under technological conditions consistent with the routinized regime, and the metaphor of the forest, where the new entrants displace the incumbents, is more applicable to the entrepreneurial regime.

Why is the general shape of the firm-size distribution not only strikingly similar across virtually every industry – that is, skewed with only a few large enterprises and numerous small ones – but has persisted with tenacity not only across developed countries but even over a long period? The evolutionary view of the process of industry evolution is that new firms typically start at a very small scale of output and are motivated by the desire to appropriate the expected value of new economic knowledge. But, depending on the extent of scale economies in the industry, the firm may not be able to remain viable indefinitely at its startup size. Rather, if scale economies are anything other than negligible, then the new firm is likely to have to grow to survival. The temporary survival of new firms is presumably supported through the deployment of a strategy of compensating factor differentials that enables the firm to discover whether or not it has a viable product.

The empirical evidence supports such an evolutionary view of the role of new firms in manufacturing, because the post-entry growth of firms that survive tends to be spurred by the extent to which there is a gap between the MES level of output and the size of the firm. However, the likelihood of any particular new firm surviving tends to decrease as this gap increases. Such new suboptimal scale firms are apparently engaged in the selection process. Only those firms offering a viable product that can be produced efficiently will grow and ultimately approach or attain the MES level of output. The remainder will stagnate, and depending on the severity of the other selection mechanism – the extent of scale economies – may ultimately be forced to exit out of the industry. Thus, the persistence of an asymmetric firm-size distribution biased toward small-scale enterprise reflects the continuing process of the entry of new firms into industries and not necessarily the permanence of such small and suboptimal enterprises over the long run. Although the skewed size distribution of firms persists with remarkable stability over long periods, a constant set of small and suboptimal scale firms does not appear to be responsible for this skewed distribution. Rather, by serving as agents of change, new firms provide an essential source of new ideas and experimentation that otherwise would remain untapped in the economy.

3. Determinants of SME dynamism

Enabling environment

As Table VIII shows, the evidence revealing small enterprises to be the engine of innovative activity in certain industries, despite an obvious lack of formal R&D activities, raises the question, *Where do new and small firms get the innovation producing inputs; that is, the knowledge?* The answer proposed by Audretsch (1995) is from other, third-party, firms or research institutions, such as universities. Economic knowledge may *spill over* from the firm or research institution creating it for application by other firms (Acs et al., 1992).

That knowledge spillover is barely dispute. However, the geographic range of such knowledge spillovers is greatly contested. In disputing the importance of knowledge externalities in explaining the geographic concentration of economic activity, Krugman (1991) and others do not question the existence or importance of such knowledge spillovers.[17] In fact, they argue that such knowledge externalities are so important and forceful that there is no compelling reason for a geographic boundary to limit the spatial extent of the spillover. According to this line of thinking, the concern is not that knowledge does not spill over but that it should stop spilling over just because it hits a geographic border, such as a city limit, state line, or national boundary.

A recent body of empirical evidence clearly suggests that R&D and other sources of knowledge not only generate externalities, but studies by Audretsch and Feldman (1996), Almeida and Kogut (1997), Jaffe (1989), Audretsch and Stephan (1996), Feldman (1994a, b), and Jaffe et al. (1993) suggest that such knowledge spillovers tend to be geographically bounded within the region where the new economic knowledge was created. That is, new economic knowledge may spill over but the geographic extent of such knowledge spillovers is limited (Prevenzer, 1997).

Krugman (1991, p. 53) has argued that economists should abandon any attempts at measuring knowledge spillovers because ". . . knowledge flows are invisible, they leave no paper trail by which they may be measured and tracked." But as Jaffe et al. (1991, p. 578) point out, "knowledge flows do sometimes leave a paper trail," in particular in the form of patented inventions and new product introductions.

The innovations from Table VIII can be classified according to the four-digit SIC industry of the new product and the city where the innovating establishment was located. We adapt either the Consolidated Metropolitan Statistical Area (CMSA) or the Metropolitan Statistical Area (MSA) as the spatial unit of observation. The analysis here is based on 3969 new manufacturing product innovations for which the address of the innovating establishment could be identified.

The most innovative city in the United States was New York. Seven hundred and thirty-five, or 18.5 percent, of the total number of innovations in the country were attributed to firms in the greater New York City area. Four hundred and seventy-seven (12.0 percent) were attributed to San Francisco, California, and 345 (8.7 percent) to the Boston, Massachusetts, area and 333 (8.4 percent) to the Los Angeles, California, area. In total, 1,890, or 45 percent of the innovations, took place in those four consolidated metropolitan areas. In fact, all but 150 of the innovations included in the data base are attributed to metropolitan areas. That is, less than 4 percent of the innovations occurred outside of metropolitan areas. This contrasts with the 70 percent of the population that resided in those areas.

Of course, simply comparing the absolute amount of innovative activity across cities ignores the fact that some cities are simply larger than others. Cities vary considerably in size, and we expect that city scale will have an impact on innovative output. Table IX presents the number of innovations normalized by the size of the geographic unit. Population provides a crude but useful measure of the size of the geographic unit. Cities in Table IX are ranked in descending order by innovation rate or the number of innovations per 100,000 population. While New York has the highest count of innovation, it has the third highest innovation rate. The most innovative city in the United States, on a per capita measure of city size, was San Francisco, with an innovation rate of 8.90, followed by Boston, with an innovation rate of 8.69. By contrast, the mean innovation rate for the entire country is 1.75 innovations per 100,000 population. The distribution of innovation rates is considerably skewed. Only 14 cities are more innovative than the national average. Clearly, innovation appears to be a large city phenomenon.

Studies identifying the extent of knowledge spillovers are based on the knowledge production function. Jaffe (1989), and Audretsch and Feldman (1996), and Feldman and Audretsch (1999) modified the knowledge production function approach to a model specified for spatial and product dimensions:

$$I_{si} = IRD^{\beta_1} * UR_{si}^{\beta_2} * (UR_{si} * GC_{si}^{\beta_3}) * \varepsilon_{si} \qquad (1)$$

where I is innovative output, IRD is private cor-

TABLE IX
Counts of innovation normalized by population

Consolidated metropolitan statistical area	Innovations (1982)	1980 population (thousands)	Innovations per 100,000 population
San Francisco – Oakland	477	5368	8.886
Boston – Lawrence	345	3972	8.686
New York – Northern New Jersey	735	17539	4.191
Philadelphia – Wilmington	205	5681	3.609
Dallas – Fort Worth	88	2931	3.002
Hartford	30	1014	2.959
Los Angeles – Anaheim	333	11498	2.896
Buffalo – Niagara	35	1243	2.816
Cleveland – Akron	77	2834	2.717
Chicago – Gary	203	7937	2.558
Providence – Pawtucket	25	1083	2.308
Portland – Vancouver	25	1298	1.926
Cincinnati – Hamilton	30	1660	1.807
Seattle – Tacoma	37	2093	1.768
Pittsburgh	42	2423	1.733
Denver – Boulder	28	1618	1.731
Detroit – Ann Arbor	68	4753	1.431
Houston – Galveston	39	3101	1.258
Miami – Fort Lauderdale	13	2644	0.492

Source: 1980 Population is from the Statistical Abstract. Innovation data from Feldman and Audretsch (1999).

porate expenditures on R&D, *UR* is the research expenditures undertaken at universities, and *GC* measures the geographic coincidence of university and corporate research. The unit of observation for estimation was at the spatial level s, a state, and industry level i. Estimation of equation (1) essentially shifted the knowledge production function from the unit of observation of a firm to that of a geographic unit.

Implicitly contained within the knowledge production function model is the assumption that innovative activity should take place in those regions where the direct knowledge-generating inputs are the greatest, and where knowledge spillovers are the most prevalent. Audretsch and Feldman (1996) and Audretsch and Stephan (1996) link the propensity for innovative activity to cluster together to industry specific characteristics, most notably the relative importance of knowledge spillovers.

To actually measure the extent to which innovative activity in a specific four-digit SIC industry is concentrated within a geographic region, Audretsch and Feldman (1996) calculate gini coefficients for the geographic concentration of innovative activity. The gini coefficients are weighted by the relative share of economic activity located in each state. Computation of weighted gini coefficients enables us to control for size differences across states. The gini coefficients are based on the share of activity in a state and industry relative to the state share of the national activity for the industry. Of course, as Jaffe, Trajtenberg, and Henderson (1993) point out, one obvious explanation why innovative activity in some industries tends to cluster geographically more than in other industries is that the location of production is more concentrated spatially. Thus, in explaining why the propensity for innovative activity to cluster geographically varies across industries, we need first to explain, and then control for, the geographic concentration of the location of production.

There are three important tendencies emerging. First, there is no obvious simple relationship between the gini coefficients for production and innovation. Second, the gini coefficient of the number of innovations exceeds that of value added and employment in those industries exhibiting the greatest propensity for innovative activity to cluster spatially. By contrast, the gini coefficients of innovative activity for most industries is less than that for value added and employment.

Third, those industries exhibiting the greatest propensity for innovative activity to cluster are high-technology industries. There are, however, several notable exceptions. For example, in motor vehicle bodies, which is certainly not considered to be a high-technology industry, the geographic concentration of production of innovative activity is the seventh greatest. One reason may be the high degree of geographic concentration of production, as evidenced by gini coefficients for value added (0.9241) and employment (0.8089) that actually exceed that of innovative activity (0.6923). This points to the importance of controlling for the geographic concentration of production in explaining the propensity for innovative activity to spatially cluster. And finally, the gini coefficient for value added exceeds that for employment in virtually every industry.

Audretsch and Feldman (1996) measure three different types of new economic knowledge: industry R&D, university R&D, and skilled labor. A key assumption they make in examining the link between knowledge spillovers in an industry and the propensity for innovative activity to cluster is that knowledge externalities are more prevalent in industries where new economic knowledge plays a greater role.

One obvious complication in testing for this link is that innovative activity will be more geographically concentrated in industries where production is also geographically concentrated, simply because the bulk of firms are located within proximity. Even more problematic, though, is the hypothesis that new economic knowledge will tend to shape the spatial distribution of production as well as that of innovation. Indeed, we found that a key determinant of the extent to which the location of production is geographically concentrated is the relative importance of new economic knowledge in the industry. But even after controlling for the geographic concentration of production, the results suggest that industries in which knowledge spillovers are more pervasive – that is where industry R&D, university research and skilled labor are the most important – have a greater propensity for innovative activity to cluster than industries where knowledge externalities are less important.

A growing literature suggests that *who* innovates and *how much* innovative activity is undertaken is closely linked to the phase of the industry life cycle. Audretsch and Feldman (1996) suggest an additional key aspect to the evolution of innovative activity over the industry life cycle: *where* that innovative activity takes place. The theory of knowledge spillovers, derived from the knowledge production function, suggests that the propensity for innovative activity to cluster spatially will tend to be the greatest in industries where *tacit knowledge* plays an important role, and because it is tacit knowledge, as opposed to *information*, which can only be transmitted informally, and typically demands direct and repeated contact. The role of tacit knowledge in generating innovative activity is presumably the greatest during the early stages of the industry life cycle, before product standards have been established and before a dominant design has emerged.

The stage of the industry life cycle has been typically measured by tracking the evolution of an industry starting with its incipiency, based on a wave of product innovations. But the measures of geographic concentration and dispersion, for both innovation and the location of production, documented in the previous section, are available only for one point of time. That is, these measures provide a snapshot at a single point in time for each industry. Thus, the life cycle stage of each industry at this point in time needs to be measured. More specifically, industries that are highly innovative and where that innovative activity tends to come from small firms are better characterized as being in the introduction stage of the life cycle. Industries that are highly innovative and where the large firms tend to generate that innovative activity are better characterized by the growth stage of the life cycle. Industries that are low innovative and where large firms have a higher propensity to innovate are better characterized by the mature stage of the life cycle. And finally, industries that are low innovative and where small firms have a higher propensity to innovate are best characterized by the declining stage of the life cycle. The higher propensity to innovate of small enterprises vis-à-vis their larger counterparts may reflect the seeds of the introductory phase of the life cycle of new products emerging in what would otherwise be a declining industry.

This framework was used to classify 210 four-digit SIC industries into those four stages of the life cycle. High innovative industries were rather arbitrarily defined as those industries exhibiting innovative activity in excess of the mean. Low innovative industries were similarly defined as those industries with innovative rates less than the mean. The innovation rate is defined as the number of innovations divided by the number of employees in the industry (measured in thousands). The innovation rate is used rather than the absolute number of innovations to control for the size of the industry. That is, if two industries were to exhibit the same number of innovations but one industry were twice as large as the other, then it will have an innovation rate one-half as large as the other industry. To measure the relative innovative advantage of large and small firms, the small-firm innovation rate is compared to the large-firm innovation rate, where the small-firm innovation rate is defined as the number of innovations made by firms with fewer than 500 employees divided by small-firm employment and the large-firm innovation rate is defined as the number of innovations made by firms with at least 500 employees divided by large-firm employment.

By using this classification system, 62 of the industries were classified as being in the introductory stage of the life cycle (defined as highly innovative, and the small firms have the innovative advantage), 32 industries were classified as being in the growth stage of the life cycle (defined as highly innovative, and the large firms have the innovative advantage), 64 industries were defined in the mature stage of the life cycle (defined as low innovative, and the large firms have the innovative advantage), and 52 were defined in the declining stage of the life cycle (defined as low innovative, and the small firms have the innovative advantage).

The results provide considerable evidence suggesting that the propensity for innovative activity to spatially cluster is shaped by the stage of the industry life cycle. On the one hand, new economic knowledge embodied in skilled workers tends to raise the propensity for innovative activity to spatially cluster throughout all phases of the industry life cycle. On the other, certain other sources of new economic knowledge, such as university research, tend to elevate the propensity for innovative activity to cluster during the introduction stage of the life cycle but not during the growth stage, but then again during the stage of decline.

Perhaps most striking is the finding that greater geographic concentration of production actually leads to more, and not less, dispersion of innovative activity. Apparently, innovative activity is promoted by knowledge spillovers that occur within a distinct geographic region, particularly in the early stages of the industry life cycle, but as the industry evolves toward maturity, decline may be dispersed by additional increases in concentration of production that have been built up within that same region. That is, the evidence suggests that what may serve as an *agglomerating influence* in triggering innovative activity to spatially cluster during the introduction and growth stages of the industry life cycle may later result in a *congestion effect*, leading to greater dispersion in innovative activity. In any case, the results of this paper suggest that the propensity for an innovative cluster to spatially cluster is certainly shaped by the stage of the industry life cycle.

Despite the general consensus that has now emerged in the literature that knowledge spillovers within a given location stimulate technological advance, there is little consensus as to exactly how this occurs. The contribution of the knowledge production function approach was simply to shift the unit of observation away from firms to a geographic region. But does it make a difference how economic activity is organized within the black box of geographic space? Political scientists and sociologists have long argued that the differences in the culture of a region may contribute to differences in innovative performance across regions, even holding knowledge inputs such as R&D and human capital constant. For example, Saxenian (1994) argues that a culture of greater interdependence and exchange among individuals in the Silicon Valley, California, region has contributed to a superior innovative performance than is found around Boston's Route 128, where firms and individuals tend to be more isolated less interdependent.

In studying the networks in California's Silicon Valley, Saxenian (1990, pp. 96–97) emphasizes that it is the communication between individuals that facilitates the transmission of knowledge across agents, firms, and even industries, and not just a high endowment of human capital and knowledge in the region: "It is not simply the concentration of skilled labor, suppliers and information that distinguish the region. A variety of regional institutions – including Stanford University, several trade associations and local business organizations, and a myriad of specialized consulting, market research, public relations, and venture capital firms – provide technical, financial, and networking services which the region's enterprises often cannot afford individually. These networks defy sectoral barriers: individuals move easily from semiconductor to disk drive firms or from computer to network makers. They move from established firms to startups (or vice versa) and even to market research or consulting firms, and from consulting firms back into startups. And they continue to meet at trade shows, industry conferences, and the scores of seminars, talks and social activities organized by local business organizations and trade associations. In these forums, relationships are easily formed and maintained, technical and market information is exchanged, business contacts are established, and new enterprises are conceived. . . . This decentralized and fluid environment also promotes the diffusion of intangible technological capabilities and understandings."[18]

While many social scientists tend to avoid attributing differences in economic performance to cultural differences, there has been a series of theoretical arguments suggesting that differences in the underlying structure between regions may account for differences in rates of growth and technological change. In fact, a heated debate has emerged in the literature about the manner in which the underlying economic structure within a geographic unit of observation might effect economic performance. One view, which Glaeser and others (1992) attribute to the Marshall-Arrow-Romer externality, suggests that an increased concentration of a particular industry within a specific geographic region facilitates knowledge spillovers across firms. This model formalizes the insight that the concentration of an industry within a city promotes knowledge spillovers between firms and therefore facilitates innovative activity. An important assumption of the model is that knowledge externalities with respect to firms exist, but only for firms within the same industry. Thus, the relevant unit of observation is extended from the firm to the region in the tradition of the Marshall-Arrow model, and in subsequent empirical studies, but spillovers are limited to occur within the relevant industry.

By contrast, restricting knowledge externalities to occur only within the industry may ignore an important source of new economic knowledge: inter-industry knowledge spillovers. Jacobs (1969) argues that the most important source of knowledge spillovers are external to the industry in which the firm operates and that cities are the source of considerable innovation because the diversity of these knowledge sources is greatest in cities. According to Jacobs it is the exchange of complementary knowledge across diverse firms and economic agents that yields a greater return on new economic knowledge. She develops a theory that emphasizes that the variety of industries within a geographic region promotes knowledge externalities and ultimately innovative activity and economic growth.

The extent of regional specialization versus regional diversity in promoting knowledge spillovers is not the only dimension over which there has been a theoretical debate. A second controversy involves the degree of competition prevalent in the region, or the extent of local monopoly. The Marshall-Arrow-Romer model predicts that local monopoly is superior to local competition because it maximizes the ability of firms to appropriate the economic value accruing from their innovative activity. By contrast, Jacobs (1969) and Porter (1990) argue that competition is more conducive to knowledge externalities than is local monopoly.[19] It should be emphasized that by local competition Jacobs does not mean competition within product markets as has traditionally been envisioned within the industrial organization literature. Rather, Jacobs is referring to the competition for the new ideas embodied in economic agents. Not only does an increased number of firms provide greater competition for new ideas, but, in addition, greater competition across firms facilitates the entry of a new firm specializing in some particular and new product niche. This is because the necessary complementary inputs and services are likely to be available from small specialist niche firms but not necessarily from large vertically integrated producers.

The first important test of the specialization

versus diversity theories to date has focused not on the gains in terms of innovative activity, but rather in terms of employment growth. Glaeser and others (1992) employ a data set on the growth of large industries in 170 cities between 1956 and 1987 to identify the relative importance of the degree of regional specialization, diversity, and local competition ply in influencing industry growth rates. The authors find evidence that contradicts the Marshall-Arrow-Romer model but is consistent with the theories of Jacobs. However, their study provided no direct evidence as to whether diversity is more important than specialization in generating innovation.

Feldman and Audretsch (1999) identify the extent to which the organization of economic activity is either concentrated, or alternatively consists of diverse but complementary economic activities, and how this composition influences innovative output. We ask the question, *Does the specific type of economic activity undertaken within any particular geographic concentration matter?* To consider this question they link the innovative output of product categories within a specific city to the extent to which the economic activity of that city is concentrated in that industry or, conversely, diversified in terms of complementary industries sharing a common science base.

To systematically identify the degree to which specific industries share a common underlying science and technology base, we rely upon a deductive approach that links products estimated from their closeness in technological space. They use the responses of industrial R&D managers to a survey by Levin and others (1987). To measure the significance of a scientific discipline to an industry, the question was asked, *How relevant were the basic sciences to technical progress in this line of business over the past 10–15 years?* The survey uses a Likert scale of 1 to 7, from least important to most important, to assess the relevance of basic scientific research in biology, chemistry, computer science, physics, math, medicine, geology, mechanical engineering, and electrical engineering. Any academic discipline with a rating greater than 5 is assumed to be relevant for a product category. For example, basic scientific research in medicine, chemistry, and chemical engineering is found to be relevant for product innovation in drugs (SIC 2834).

They then used cluster analysis to identify six groups of industries that rely on similar rankings for the importance of different academic disciplines. Those six groups reflect distinct underlying common scientific bases.

Table X presents the prominent cities within each science-based industrial cluster. Again, the listing of prominent cities recalls the well known association between cities and industries. For example, Atlanta, Georgia, was a prominent center for innovation that used the common science base of agra-business. While the national innovation rate was 20.34 innovations per 100,000 manufacturing workers, agra-business in Atlanta was almost five times as innovative. A chi-squared test of the independence of location of city and science-based industrial activity reveals that neither the distribution of employment nor the distribution of innovation is random. Industries that rely on a common science base exhibit a tendency to cluster together geographically with regard to the location of employment and the location of innovation. We conclude that the distribution of innovation within science-based clusters and cities appears to reflect the existence of science-related expertise.

To test the hypothesis that the degree of specialization, or alternatively diversity, as well as the extent of local competition within a city shapes the innovative output of an industry, we estimate a model where the dependent variable is the number of innovations attributed to a specific four-digit SIC industry in a particular city. To reflect the extent to which economic activity within a city is specialized, we include as an explanatory variable a measure of industry specialization, which was used by Glaeser and others (1992) and is defined as the share of total employment in the city accounted for by industry employment in the city, divided by the share of U.S. employment accounted by that particular industry. This variable reflects the degree to which a city is specialized in a particular industry relative to the degree of economic activity in that industry that would occur if employment in the industry were randomly distributed across the United States. A higher value of this measure indicates a greater degree of specialization of the industry in that particular city. Thus, a positive coefficient would indicate that increased specialization within

TABLE X
Innovation in science-based industry clusters

Cluster	Prominent cities	Mean industry innovations per 100,000 workers
Agra-business	Atlanta	92.40
	Dallas	41.15
	Chicago	33.03
	St. Louis	91.74
Chemical engineering	Dallas	38.09
	Minneapolis	66.67
	San Francisco	43.89
	Wilmington	85.47
Office machinery	Anaheim-Santa Ana	92.59
	Minneapolis	31.86
	Rochester	72.20
	Stanford	68.40
Industrial machinery	Anaheim-Santa Ana	54.95
	Cincinnati	66.01
	Cleveland	141.51
	Passaic, NJ	90.90
High-tech computing	Boston	73.89
	Houston	62.08
	San Jose	44.88
	Minneapolis	181.74
Biomedical	Boston	38.71
	Cleveland	68.76
	Dallas	35.22
	New York	188.07

a city is conducive to greater innovative output and would support the Marshall-Arrow-Romer thesis. A negative coefficient would indicate that greater specialization within a city impedes innovative output and would support Jacobs' theory that diversity of economic activity is more conducive to innovation than is specialization of economic activity.

To identify the impact of an increased presence of economic activity in complementary industries sharing a common science base on the innovative activity of a particular industry within a specific city, a measure of the presence of science-based related industries is included. This measure is constructed analogously to the index of industry specialization and is defined as the share of total city employment accounted for by employment in the city in industries sharing the science base divided by the share of total U.S. employment accounted for by employment in that same science base. This variable measures the presence of complementary industries relative to what the presence would be if those related industries were distributed across the United States. A positive coefficient of the presence of science-based related industries would indicate that a greater presence of complementary industries is conducive to greater innovative output and would lend support for the diversity thesis. By contrast, a negative coefficient would suggest that a greater presence of related industries sharing the same science base impedes innovation and would argue against Jacobs' diversity thesis.

The usual concept of product market competition in the industrial organization literature is typically measured in terms of the size-distribution of firms. By contrast, Jacobs' concept of *localized competition* emphasizes instead the extent of competition for the ideas embodied in individuals. The greater the degree of competition among firms, the greater will be the extent of specialization among those firms and the easier it will be for individuals to pursue and implement new ideas. Thus the metric relevant to reflect the degree of localized competition is not the size of the firms in the region relative to their number (because, after all, many if not most manufacturing product markets are national or at least inter-regional in nature) but rather the number of firms relative to the number of workers. In measuring the extent of localized competition we again adopt a measure used by Glaeser and others (1992), which is defined as the number of firms per worker in the industry in the city relative to the number of firms per worker in the same industry in the United States. A higher value of this index of localized competition suggests that the industry has a greater number of firms per worker relative to its size in the particular city than it does elsewhere in the United States. Thus, if the index of localized competition exceeds one then the city is locally less competitive than in other U.S. cities.

In Feldman and Audretsch (1999) the regression model is estimated on the basis of the 5,946 city-industry observations for which data could be collected. The Poisson regression estimation method is used because the dependent variable is a limited dependent variable with a highly skewed distribution. By focusing on innovative activity for particular industries at specific locations, we find compelling evidence that specialization of economic activity does not promote innovative output. Rather, the results indicate that diversity across complementary economic activities sharing a common science base is more conducive to innovation than is specialization. In addition, the results indicate that the degree of local competition for new ideas within a city is more conducive to innovative activity than is local monopoly.

Public policy measures that affect SMEs

Globalization combined with the telecommunications revolution has drastically reduced the cost of transporting not just material goods but also information across geographic space. High wages are increasingly incompatible with information-based economic activity, which can be easily transferred to a lower cost location. By contrast, the creation of new ideas on the basis of tacit knowledge cannot easily be transferred across distance. Thus, the comparative advantage of the high-cost countries of North America and Western Europe is increasingly based on knowledge-driven innovative activity. The spillover of knowledge from the firm or university creating that knowledge to a third-party firm is essential to innovative activity. Such knowledge spillovers tend to be spatially restricted. Thus, an irony of globalization is that even as the relevant geographic market for most goods and services becomes increasingly global, the increased importance of innovative activity in the leading developed countries has triggered a resurgence in the importance of local regions as a key source of comparative advantage.

As the comparative advantage in Western Europe and North America has become increasingly based on new knowledge, public policy toward business has responded in two fundamental ways. The first has been to shift the policy focus away from the traditional triad of policy instruments essentially constraining the freedom of firms to contract; that is, regulation, competition policy, or antitrust in the United States and public ownership of business. The policy approach of constraint was sensible as long as the major issue was how to restrain footloose multinational corporations in possession of considerable market power. This is reflected by the waves of deregulation and privatization along with the decreased emphasis of competition policy throughout the Organisation for Economic Co-operation and Development (OECD). Instead, a new policy approach is emerging that focuses on enabling the creation and commercialization of knowledge. Examples of such policies include encouraging R&D, venture capital, and new-firm startups.

The second fundamental shift involves the locus of such enabling policies, which are increasingly at the state, regional, or even local level. The downsizing of federal agencies charged with the regulation of business in the United Sates has been interpreted by many scholars as the eclipse of government intervention. But to interpret deregulation, privatization, and the increased irrelevance of competition policies as the end of government intervention in business ignores an important shift in the locus and target of public policy. The last decade has seen the emergence of a broad spectrum of enabling policy initiatives that fall outside of the jurisdiction of the traditional regulatory agencies. Sternberg (1996) documents how the success of a number of different high-technology clusters spanning a number of developed countries is the direct result of enabling policies, such as the provision of venture capital or research support. For example, the Advanced Research Program in Texas has provided support for basic research and the strengthening of the infrastructure of the University of Texas, which has played a central role in developing a high-technology cluster around Austin (Feller, 1997). The Thomas Edison Centers in Ohio, the Advanced Technology Centers in New Jersey, and the Centers for Advanced Technology at Case Western Reserve University, Rutgers University, and the University of Rochester have supported generic, precompetitive research. This support has generally provided diversified technology development involving a mix of activities encompassing a spectrum of industrial collaborators.

Such enabling policies that are typically implemented at the local or regional level are part of a silent policy revolution currently underway. The increased importance of innovative regional clusters as an engine of economic growth has led policy makers to abandon the policy cry frequently heard two decades ago, *Should we break up, regulate, or simply take over General Motors, IBM, and U.S. Steel*, for a very different contemporary version, *How can we grow the next Silicon Valley?*

One of the most important policies to promote SMEs at the federal level has been the Small Business Innovation Research (SBIR) program. The U.S. Congress enacted the SBIR in 1984. The Program provides a mandate that each participating government agency must spend a share of its research budget on contracts to small firms. This includes the major federal agencies, such as the Department of Defense, the National Institutes of Health, the National Science Foundation, Department of Energy, and the National Aeronautics and Space Administration. The Small Business Innovation Development Act of 1982[20] required that agencies with extramural R&D budget of $100 million or more set aside not less than 0.2 percent of that amount for the SBIR program. In addition, the Act provided for annual increases up to a ceiling of not less than 1.25 percent of the agencies' budgets. The amount of awards will total over $1.4 billion in 1999.

The SBIR consists of three phases. Phase I is oriented toward determining the scientific and technical merit along with the feasibility of a proposed research idea. Phase II extends the technological idea and emphasizes commercialization. Phase III involves additional private funding for the commercial application of a technology. Under the Small Business Research and Development Enhancement Act of 1992, funding in Phase I was increased to $100,000, and in Phase II to $750,000.

The SBIR was an offshoot of the Small Business Investment Company (SBIC) program, which provided more than $3 billion to young firms between 1958 and 1969. During this period this amounted to more than three times the total amount of private venture capital.

The SBIR represents about 60 percent of all public SME finance programs. Taken together, the public SME finance is about two-thirds as large as private venture capital. In 1995 the sum of equity financing provided through and guaranteed by public programs financing SMES was $2.4 billion, which amounted to more than 60 percent of the total funding disbursed by traditional venture funds in that year. Equally as important, the emphasis on SBIR and most public funds is on early stage finance, which is generally ignored by private venture capital. Some of the most innovative American companies received early stage finance from SBIR, including Apple Computer, Chron, Compaq, and Intel.

While systematic evidence has been compiled indicating that SMEs receiving SBIR support exhibit greater rates of growth than those that do not, there is also evidence suggesting that the SBIR alters the career choices of scientists and engineers. In particular, the evidence suggests that (1) a significant number of the firms would not have been started in the absence of SBIR, (2) a significant number of other firms are started because of the demonstration effect by the efforts of scientists to commercialize knowledge, (3) as a result of the demonstration effect by SBIR-funded commercialization, a number of other scientists alter their careers to include commercialization efforts, and (4) technology-based entrepreneurs start firms because they have ideas that they think are potentially valuable and not start firms and then search for useful ideas or products. This is reflected by the fact that not a single respondent on either the survey or from the case studies suggested that they would have tried to start the firm with a different idea in the absence of SBIR funding. However, once the firm exists, one-quarter of the respondents and one-sixth of the case studies indicated that they would have tried to continue the firm with a different idea in the absence of SBIR funding. These different results may suggest that the SBIR has a greater impact on commercializing ideas that otherwise would not find their way into the market on potential entrepreneurs than on existing small firms.

4. Conclusions

When viewed through the static lens provided by industrial organization, small firms place an efficiency burden on the economy. Their small scale of production inflicts a substantial loss in terms of higher production costs. However, when viewed through a more evolutionary lens, such static losses in production efficiency are more than offset in gains in dynamic efficiency. The greatest contribution to economic efficiency by small firms is dynamic and evolutionary in nature: Small firms serve as agents of change.

In the current debate on the relationship between employment and wages, it is typically argued that the existence of small firms that are suboptimal within the organization of an industry represents a loss in economic efficiency. However, this argument is based on a static analysis. When viewed through a dynamic lens a different conclusion emerges. One of the most striking results in the new literature is the finding of a positive impact of firm age on productivity and employee compensation, even after controlling for the size of the firm. Given the strongly confirmed stylized fact linking both firm size and age to a negative rate of growth (that is, the smaller and younger a firm the faster it will grow but the lower is its likelihood of survival), this new finding linking firm age to employee compensation and productivity suggests that not only will some of the small and suboptimal firms of today become the large and optimal firms of tomorrow, but there is at least a tendency for the low productivity and wage of today to become the high productivity and wage of tomorrow.

The public policies emerging in the post-war period dealing with business have been shaped by the static view of industrial organization and therefore are essentially constraining in nature. There were three general types of public policies towards business: antitrust (competition policy), regulation, and public ownership. All three of those policy approaches toward the firm in the market restricted the firm's freedom to contract. While specific policy approaches tended to be more associated with one country than with others, such as antitrust in the United States or public ownership in France and Sweden, all developed countries shared a common policy approach of intervening to restrain what otherwise was perceived as too much market power held by firms. Public policies constraining the freedom of the firm to contract were certainly consistent with the *Weltanschauung* emerging from the theories and empirical evidence regarding the firm in the market during the post-war period. Left unchecked, the large corporation in possession of market power would allocate resources in such a way as to reduce economic welfare. Through state intervention the Williamsonian tradeoff between efficiency on the hand and fairness on the other would be solved in a manner that presumably would be more socially satisfying.

More recently the relevant policy question has shifted away from *How can the government constrain firms from abusing their market power?* to *How can governments create an environment fostering the success and viability of firms?* The major issues of the day have shifted away from concerns about excess profits and abuses of market dominance to the creation of jobs, growth, and international competitiveness. The concern about corporations is now more typically not that they are too successful and powerful but that they are not successful and powerful enough. Thus, the government policies of the 1990s have increasingly shifted away from *constraining* to *enabling*. Public policy in the United States is increasingly fostering efforts to create new firms to promote job creation and economic growth within their jurisdictions. While this policy emphasis on small and new firms as engines of dynamic efficiency may seem startling after decades at looking to the corporate giants to bestow efficiency is anything but new. Before the country was even half a century old, Alexis de Tocqueville, in 1835, reported, "What astonishes me in the United States is not so much the marvelous grandeur of some undertakings as the innumerable multitude of small ones."[21]

Acknowledgements

I am particularly grateful for the insightful suggestions made on draft versions of this paper by Farrukh Iqbal, Shujiro Urata, Migara De Silva, Al Berry, Christina Boari, Jeff Nugent, Bee Aw Roberts and Hideki Yamawaki.

Notes

[1] Lester Thurow, "Losing the Economic Race," *New York Review of Books*, September 1984, pp. 29–31.

[2] W.W. Restow, "Here Comes a New Political Chapter in America," *International Herald Tribune*, 2 January 1987.

[3] For example, U.S. News and World Report (16 August 1993) reported, "What do Bill Clinton, George Bush and Bob Dole have in common? All have uttered one of the most enduring homilies in American political discourse: That small businesses create most of the nation's jobs."

[4] Cited from Davis, Haltiwanger, and Schuh (1996b, p. 298).

[5] Representative Robert Michel, House Minority Leader, in the Republican Response to the 1993 State of the Union Address, cited from Davis et al. (1996, p. 298).

[6] While it was acknowledged that small firms were able to avoid direct competition by occupying strategic niches, Weiss (Audretsch and Yamawaki, 1991, p. 404) observed that, "The survival of smaller plants within any given industry may be due to their specialization in items with short production runs or to their service of small geographic markets within which their relatively small national market share is irrelevant. To the extent that such explanations hold, small plants are not necessarily suboptimal. However, such explanations seem unlikely to hold for a number of the industries where the percentage of suboptimal capacity is larger."

[7] Quotation from p. xiv of the Introduction in Audretsch and Yamawaki (1991).

[8] Coase (1937, p. 23) himself asked, "A pertinent question to ask would appear to be (quite apart from the monopoly considerations raised by Professor Knight), why, if by organizing one can eliminate certain costs and in fact reduce the cost of production, are there any market transactions at all? Why is not all production carried on by one big firm?"

[9] See for reviews of this literature Baldwin and Scott (1987), Scherer (1991), and Dosi (1988).

[10] See for example Scherer (1991), Cohen and Klepper (1991, 1992), and Arrow (1962).

[11] Cohen and Klepper (1991, 1992).

[12] See Baldwin and Scott (1987).

[13] A similar startup size for new manufacturing firms has been found by Dunne et al. (1989) for the United States, Mata (1994) and Mata and Portugal (1994) for Portugal and Wagner (1994) for Germany.

[14] For example, Weiss (1976, p. 126) argues that, "In purely competitive long-run equilibrium, no suboptimal capacity should exist at all."

[15] The country studies included in Geroski and Schwalbach (1991) also indicate considerable ambiguities between measures reflecting the extent of scale economies and capital intensity on the one hand, and entry rates on the other.

[16] While the concept of technological regimes does not lend itself to precise measurement, the major conclusion of Acs and Audretsch (1988, 1990) was that the existence of these distinct regimes can be inferred by the extent to which small firms are able to innovate relative to the total amount of innovative activity in an industry. That is, when the small-firm innovation rate is high relative to the total innovation rate, the technological and knowledge conditions are more likely to reflect the entrepreneurial regime. The routinized regime is more likely to exhibit a low small-firm innovation rate relative to the total innovation rate.

[17] Macki (1996) points out that these views are not original with Krugman (1991).

[18] Saxenian (1990, pp. 97–98) claims that even the language and vocabulary used by technical specialists is specific to a region, ". . . a distinct language has evolved in the region and certain technical terms used by semiconductor production engineers in Silicon Valley would not even be understood by their counterparts in Boston's Route 128."

[19] Porter (1990) provides examples of Italian ceramics and gold jewelry industries in which numerous firms are located within a bounded geographic region and compete intensively in terms of product innovation rather than focusing on simple price competition.

[20] Public Law 97–219, 22 July 1982.

[21] Quoted from *Business Week*, Bonus Issue, 1993, p. 12.

References

Acs, Zoltan J. and Catherine Armington, 1998, 'Longitudinal Establishment and Enterprise Microdata (LEEM) Documentation', Center for Economic Studies, U.S. Department of Commerce, Discussion Paper, 98-9 July 1998.

Acs, Zoltan J., Catherine Armington and Alicia Robb, 1999, 'Measures of Job Flow Dynamics in the U.S.', Center for Economic Studies, U.S. Department of Commerce, Washington DC, Discussion Paper 99-1 January 1999.

Acs, Z. J. and David B. Audretsch, 1987, 'Innovation, Market Structure and Firm Size', *Review of Economics and Statistics* **69**(4), 567–575.

Acs, Z. J. and David B. Audretsch, 1990, *Innovation and Small Firms*, Cambridge, Mass.: MIT Press.

Acs, Z. J. and David B. Audretsch, 1993, *Small Firms and Entrepreneurship: An East-West Perspective*, Cambridge, U.K.: Cambridge University Press.

Acs, Z. J. and David B. Audretsch, 1998, 'Innovation in Large and Small Firms: An Empirical Analysis', *American Economic Review* **78**(4), 678–690.

Acs, Z. J., David B. Audretsch and Maryann P. Feldman, 1992, 'Real Effects of Academic Research', *American Economic Review* **82**(1), 363–367.

Almeida, P. and B. Kogut, 1997, 'The Exploration of Technological Diversity and the Geographic Localization of Innovation', *Small Business Economics* **9**(1), 21–31.

Arrow, Kenneth J., 1962, 'Economic Welfare and the Allocation of Resources for Invention', in R. R. Nelson (ed.), *The Rate and Direction of Inventive Activity*, Princeton: Princeton University Press.

Audretsch, David B., 1991, 'New Firm Survival and the Technological Regime', *Review of Economics and Statistics* **73**(3), 441–450.

Audretsch, David B., 1995, *Innovation and Industry Evolution*, Cambridge, Mass.: MIT Press.

Audretsch, David B. and Maryann P. Feldman, 1996, 'R&D Spillovers and the Geography of Innovation and Production', *American Economic Review* **86**(3), 630–640.

Audretsch, David B. and Talat Mahmood, 1995, 'New-Firm Survival: New Results Using a Hazard Function', *Review of Economics and Statistics* **77**(1), 97–103.

Audretsch, David B. and Paula E. Stephan, 1996, 'Company-Scientist Locational Links: The Case of Biotechnology', *American Economic Review* **86**(3), 641–652.

Audretsch, David B. and Hideki Yamawaki (eds.), 1991, *Structure, Conduct and Performance: Leonard Weiss*, New York: New York University Press.

Baily, Martin Neil, Eric J. Bartelsman and John Haltiwanger, 1996, 'Downsizing and Productivity Growth: Myth or Reality?' *Small Business Economics* **8**(4), 259–278.

Baldwin, John R., 1995, *The Dynamics of Industrial Competition*, Cambridge, U.K.: Cambridge University Press.

Baldwin, John R. and Paul K. Gorecki, 1991, 'Entry, Exit, and Production Growth', Iin P. Geroski and J. Schwalbach (eds.), *Entry and Market Contestability: An International Comparison*, Oxford: Basil Blackwell.

Baldwin, John R. and M. Rafiquzzaman, 1995, 'Selection Versus Evolutionary Adaptation: Learning and Post-Entry Performance', *International Journal of Industrial Organization* **13**(4), 501–523.

Baldwin, W. L. and J. T. Scott, 1987, *Market Structure and Technological Change*, New York: Harwood.

Brown, Charles, James Hamilton and James Medoff, 1990, *Employers Large and Small*, Cambridge, Mass.: Harvard University Press.

Caves, Richard E., 1998, 'Industrial Organization and New Findings on the Turnover and Mobility of Firms', *Journal of Economic Literature* **36**(4), 1947–1982.

Coase, R. H., 1937, 'The Nature of the Firm', *Economica* **4**(4), 386–405.

Cohen, W. M. and S. Klepper, 1991, 'Firm Size Versus Diversity in the Achievement of Technological Advance', in Z. J. Acs and D. B. Audretsch (eds.), *Innovation and Technological Change: An International Comparison*, Ann Arbor: University of Michigan Press.

Cohen, W. M. and S. Klepper, 1992, 'The Tradeoff Between Firm Size and Diversity in the Pursuit of Technological Progress', *Small Business Economics* **4**(1), 1–14.

Davis, Steven J., John Haltiwanger and Scott Schuh, 1996a, *Job Creation and Destruction*, Cambridge, Mass.: MIT Press.

Davis, Steven J., John Haltiwanger and Scott Schuh, 1996b, 'Small Business and Job Creation: Dissecting the Myth and Reassessing the Facts', *Small Business Economics* **8**(4), 297–315.

Dertouzos, Michael L., Richard K. Lester, Robert M. Solow and the MIT Commission on Industrial Productivity, 1989, *Made in America: Regaining the Productive Edge*, Cambridge, Mass.: MIT Press.

Dosi, G., 1982, 'Technological Paradigms and Technological Trajectories: A Suggested Interpretation of the Determinants and Directions of Technical Change', *Research Policy* **13**(1), 3–20.

Dosi, G., 1988, 'Sources, Procedures, and Microeconomic Effects of Innovation', *Journal of Economic Literature* **26**(3), 112–117.

Dunne, T., M. J. Roberts and L. Samuelson, 1989, 'The Growth and Failure of U.S. Manufacturing Plants', *Quarterly Journal of Economics* **104**, 671–698.

Feldman, M., 1994a, 'Knowledge Complementarity and Innovation', *Small Business Economics* **6**(3), 363–372.

Feldman, M., 1994b, *The Geography of Innovation*, Boston: Kluwer.

Feldman, Maryann P. and David B. Audretsch, 1999, 'Innovation in Cities: Science-Based Diversity, *Specialization and Localized Competition', European Economic Review* **43**, 409–429.

Feller, Irwin, 1997, 'Federal and State Government Roles in Science and Technology', *Economic Development Quarterly* **11**(4), 283–296.

Galbraith, John Kenneth, 1956, *American Capitalism*, Boston: Houghton Mifflin.

Geroski, Paul A., 1991, 'Some Data-Driven Reflections on the Entry Process', in Paul Georski and Joachin Schwalbach (eds.), *Entry and Market Contestability: An International Comparison*, Oxford: Basil Blackwell.

Geroski, Paul A., 1995, 'What Do We Know About Entry', *International Journal of Industrial Organization* **13**(4), 421–440.

Geroski, Paul A. and Joachim Schwalbach (eds.), 1991, *Entry and Market Contestability: An International Comparison*, Oxford: Basil Blackwell.

Glaeser, E., H. Kallal, J. Scheinkman and A. Shleifer, 1992, 'Growth of Cities', *Journal of Political Economy* **100**, 1126–1152.

Griliches, Zvi, 1979, 'Issues in Assessing the Contribution of R&D to Productivity Growth', *Bell Journal of Economics* **10** (Spring), 92–116.

Hall, Bronwyn H., 1987, 'The Relationship Between Firm Size and Firm Growth in the U.S. Manufacturing Sector', *Journal of Industrial Economics* **35** (June), 583–605.

Hannan, Michael T. and John Freeman, 1989, *Organizational Ecology*, Cambridge, Mass.: Harvard University Press.

Hirschman, Albert O., 1970, *Exit, Voice, and Loyalty*, Cambridge, Mass.: Harvard University Press.

Jacobs, J., 1969, *The Economy of Cities*, New York: Random House.

Jaffe, A., 1989, 'Real Effects of Academic Research', *American Economic Review* **79**, 957–970.

Jaffe, A., Trajtenberg, M. and Henderson, R., 1993, 'Geographic Localization of Knowledge Spillovers as Evidenced by Patent Citations', *Quarterly Journal of Economics* **63**, 577–598.

Jovanovic, Boyan, 1982, 'Selection and Evolution of Industry', *Econometrica* **50**(2), 649–670.

Krugman, Paul, 1991, *Geography and Trade*, Cambridge, Mass.: MIT Press.

Levin, R. C., A. K. Klevorick, R. R. Nelson and S. G. Winter, 1987, *Appropriating the Returns From Industrial Research and Development. Brooking Papers on Economic Activity*, Washington, D.C., pp. 783–820.

Malecki, E. J., 1996, *Technology and Economic Development*, London: Longman.

Mansfield, Edwin, 1962, 'Entry, Gibrat's Law, Innovation, and the Growth of Firms', *American Economic Review* **52**(5), 1023–1051.

Mata, Jose, 1994, 'Firm Growth During Infancy', *Small Business Economics* **6**(1), 27–40.

Mata, J. and P. Portugal, 1994, 'Life Duration of New Firms', *Journal of Industrial Economics* **27**(3), 227–246.

Mata, Jose, Pedro Portugal and Paulo Guimaraes, 1995, 'The Survival of New Plants: Start-Up Conditions and Post-Entry Evolution', *International Journal of Industrial Organization* **13**(4), 459–482.

Nelson, Richard R. and Sidney G. Winter, 1982, *An Evolutionary Theory of Economic Change*, Cambridge, Mass.: Harvard University Press.

Neumann, Manfred, 1993, 'Review of Entry and Market Contestability: An International Comparison', *International Journal of Industrial Organization* **11**(4), 593–594.

Porter, M., 1990, *The Comparative Advantage of Nations*, New York: Free Press.

Pratten, C. F., 1971, *Economies of Scale in Manufacturing Industry*, Cambridge, U.K.: Cambridge University Press.

Prevenzer, M., 1997, 'The Dynamics of Industrial Clustering in Biotechnology', *Small Business Economics* **9**(3), 255–271.

Saxenian, A., 1990, 'Regional Networks and the Resurgence of Silicon Valley', *California Management Review* **33**, 89–111.

Saxenian, Anna Lee, 1994, *Regional Advantage*, Cambridge, Mass.: Harvard University Press.

Scherer, F. M., 1973, 'The Determinants of Industry Plant Sizes in Six Nations', *Review of Economics and Statistics* **55**(2), 135–175.

Scherer, F. M., 1991, 'Changing Perspectives on the Firm Size Problem', in Z. J. Acs and D. B. Audretsch (eds.), *Innovation and Technological Change. An International Comparison*, Ann Arbor: University of Michigan Press.

Schumpeter, Joseph A., 1942, *Capitalism, Socialism and Democracy*, New York: Harper and Row.

Sternberg, Rolf, 1996, 'Technology Policies and the Growth of Regions', *Small Business Economics* **8**(2), 75–86.

Sutton, John, 1997, 'Gibrat's Legacy', *Journal of Economic Literature* **35**(1), 40–59.

Thurow, Lester C., 1985, 'Healing with a Thousand Bandages', *Challenge* **28**, 19–28.

Tyson, Laura, Tea Petrin and Halsey Rogers, 1994, 'Promoting Entrepreneurship in Eastern Europe', *Small Business Economics* **6**(3), 165–184.

Wagner, Joachim, 1992, 'Firm Size, Firm Growth, and Persistence of Chance: Testing Gibrat's Law with Establishment Data from Lower Saxony, 1978–1989', *Small Business Economics* **4**(2), 125–131.

Wagner, Joachim, 1994, 'Small Firm Entry in Manufacturing Industries: Lower Saxony, 1979–1989', *Small Business Economics* **6**(3), 211–224.

Weiss, L. W., 1964, 'The Survival Technique and the Extent of Suboptimal Capacity', *Journal of Political Economy* **72**(3), 246–261.

Weiss, L. W., 1976, 'Optimal Plant Scale and the Extent of Suboptimal Capacity', in R. T. Masson and P. D. Qualls (eds.), *Essays on Industrial Organization in Honor of Joe S. Bain*, Cambridge, Mass.: Ballinger.

Weiss, Leonard W., 1979, 'The Structure-Conduct-Performance Paradigm and Antitrust', *University of Pennsylvania Law Review* **127**, 1104–1140.

Winter, Sidney G., 1984, 'Schumpeterian Competition in Alternative Technological Regimes', *Journal of Economic Behavior and Organization* **5**, 287–320.

Entry of Small and Medium Enterprises and Economic Dynamism in Japan

Hiroki Kawai
Shujiro Urata

ABSTRACT. In examining the evolution of small and medium enterprises in Japan in the postwar period, this paper shows that entry rates for new firms have declined sharply in the last quarter century or so, a trend observed across most sectors of the economy as well as across most firm-size categories. To explain this pattern, the paper investigates the determinants of entry in Japan. Among other factors, it finds that cost disadvantages owing to small scale and the shortage of technical resources are significant deterrents to entry. It also finds that the availability of government-directed credit deters entry which suggests that, in their current form, such credit programs protect incumbents. Among positive factors, it finds that subcontracting opportunities promote entry which suggests that the subcontracting system in Japan is open to newcomers and helps give them a foothold in the economy.

1. SMEs in the Japanese economy

Small and medium enterprises (SMEs) have many important roles in the economy. One of the crucial roles in promoting economic growth is to promote dynamism in the economy. Being flexible and versatile, SMEs can adjust to changing business environments better than large firms. In many cases it is SMEs that enter new markets first, and some of them become large as a result of successful operation. Indeed, there have been a number of such cases in the post-WW II period in Japan. For example, in the electronics industry, there were 120 large firms as of March 1979, whose paid-in capital exceeded 1 billion yen. Out of these 120 large firms, 54 firms, or 45 percent of the total, were SMEs in March 1955. And six large firms were established as an SME between March 1955 and March 1979.[1] These figures indicate that more than 50 percent of large electronics firms existing in March 1979 had grown from the level of SMEs during the post WW II period.

The share of Japan's SMEs in the total number of establishments has been remarkably constant for the last four decades, fluctuating between a high of 99.7 percent in 1957 and a low of 98.8 percent in 1996. A similar pattern can be observed for the share of employment, although that fluctuates over a slightly larger range. Within this overall constancy, however, one can detect much variation across sectors, enterprise size groups, and periods (see Table I).[2]

For example, the number of SMEs declined in manufacturing and distribution (wholesale and retail sales) after 1989 but continued to grow in services, construction, real estate, and transportation and communications. This pattern mostly reflects the changes in the production structure from manufacturing and distribution to other services in the Japanese economy. These changes in production structure in turn can be explained by the corresponding changes in demand patterns and industrial policies. One specific example is revision of the large retail store law in the late 1980s. The large retail store law had protected SMEs by limiting the scope of operation of large retail stores. However, faced with pressure from the U.S. government, which was interested in promoting entry of large U.S. retail stores in the Japanese market, the Japanese government relaxed the law. As a result of liberalization, inefficient small retail stores had to exit from the market,

Hiroki Kawai
Faculty of Economics
Keio University
2-15-45 Mita Minato-ku
Tokyo 108-8345, Japan

Shujiro Urata
Waseda University
Tokyo
Japan

Small Business Economics **18**: 41–51, 2002.

TABLE I
Small and medium enterprises in the Japanese economy

		Number of establishments			Number of employees		
		Number (1,000)	Share of total establishments (%)	Share of non-primary total (%)	Number (1,000)	Share of total employment (%)	Share of non-primary total (%)
Manufacturing	1957	541	99.4	15.6	5,475	73.5	33.7
	1969	733	99.4	15.9	8,680	69.0	31.7
	1981	868	99.5	13.9	9,551	74.3	25.7
	1986	874	99.5	13.3	9,921	74.4	25.1
	1996	768	99.4	11.7	9,576	74.1	21.5
Wholesale and retail	1957	1,804	99.8	52.2	5,635	94.4	34.7
	1969	2,287	99.6	49.5	9,010	86.9	32.9
	1981	3,011	99.5	48.3	12,978	87.4	34.9
	1986	3,045	99.4	46.3	13,635	87.0	34.5
	1996	2,805	99.1	42.7	15,146	83.2	34.0
Services	1957	773	99.4	22.3	2,318	88.8	14.2
	1969	973	98.9	21.0	3,664	74.5	13.4
	1981	1,335	98.5	21.4	5,580	69.2	15.0
	1986	1,519	98.3	23.1	6,448	67.1	16.3
	1996	1,746	97.2	26.6	8,449	61.2	19.0
Construction	1957	176	99.9	5.0	1,097	88.3	6.7
	1969	345	99.8	7.5	2,931	89.3	10.7
	1981	550	99.9	8.8	4,714	95.3	12.7
	1986	595	99.9	9.1	4,597	96.0	11.6
	1996	647	99.9	9.9	5,527	95.7	12.4
Real estate	1957	23	100.0	0.6	60	98.3	0.3
	1969	127	100.0	2.7	294	95.7	1.1
	1981	238	100.0	3.8	610	97.6	1.6
	1986	280	100.0	4.3	694	98.0	1.8
	1996	292	100.0	4.4	896	96.5	2.0
Transporation and communications	1957	67	100.0	1.9	799	82.3	4.9
	1969	84	99.3	1.8	1,549	81.9	5.7
	1981	133	99.6	2.1	2,083	88.8	5.6
	1986	151	99.5	2.3	2,446	88.1	6.2
	1996	189	99.5	2.9	3,033	87.6	6.8
Nonprimary total	1957	3,452	99.7	100.0	16,222	82.8	100.0
	1969	4,624	99.4	100.0	27,414	78.3	100.0
	1981	6,230	99.4	100.0	37,206	81.4	100.0
	1986	6,572	99.2	100.0	39,506	80.6	100.0
	1996	6,562	98.8	100.0	44,493	77.6	100.0

Notes: SMEs are those firms with fewer than 299 employees, except for those in wholesale (fewer than 99 employees), and for those in retail and services (fewer than 49 employees).
Source: Management and Coordination Agency, Establishment Census, various years.

leading to a decline in the number of establishments. Despite a relative decline in recent years, the manufacturing and distribution sectors still account for a large share of total, as their combined share in 1996 was 54 percent.

Looking at employment changes, it is interesting to note that manufacturing is the only sector that lost employees, as the number of employees in manufacturing declined from 9.9 million in 1989 to 9.6 million in 1996. This decline in the number of employees in manufacturing SMEs is attributable not only to a decline in the level of production but also partly to an increase in labor productivity, resulting from introduction of labor-saving technologies.

There have been significant changes in the size distribution of SMEs over time. Among SMEs of different sizes, SMEs of the smallest size group (one to four employees) saw a decline in their number starting in the mid-1980s after a continuous increase, while the larger SMEs continued to increase in their number (Table II). Specifically, the number of very small SMEs, declined from 4.4 million in 1986 to 4.1 million in 1996, while the number of relatively larger SMEs with 5–299 employees increased from 2.1 million to 2.4 million during the same period.

Observing the contrasting changes in the number of establishments between micro SMEs and relatively larger SMEs in recent years, one should note that the relative weight of SMEs in terms of the number of establishments has been shifting from micro SMEs to relatively larger SMEs throughout the post-WW II period. Specifically, the share of micro SMEs in total number of establishments declined steadily from 83 percent in 1951 to 63 percent in 1996, while the shares of larger SMEs increased their shares. In particular, the share of SMEs with five to nine employees increased significantly from 9 percent to 19 percent during the 1951–1996 period.

SMEs also playan important role as subcontractors. According to a survey by the SME Agency, in 1987, 55.9 percent of SMEs were engaged in subcontracting. Most large firms depend on SMEs for the supply of parts and components. It is well known that the competitiveness of Japanese automobile, electronics, and other machinery production comes from an efficient subcontracting system involving SMEs. SMEs also have an important position in a number of regional production networks, or clusters, that are an integral part of regional economic activities in many parts of Japan. Indeed, it is often the case that subcontracting arrangements take place within clusters.

2. Entry and exit of SMEs

The previous section examined the position of SMEs in the Japanese economy and its changes in the post-war period. In particular, the examination focused on the changes in the number of establishments over time. This section examines the changing patterns of entry and exit of firms, especially those of SMEs, which are reflected in the changes in the number of firms.

The entry rate declined substantially from the mid-1960s to the mid-1990s (Figure 1).[3] From the late 1960s through the late 1970s (1978–1981), the average annual entry rate for the private nonprimary sector remained around 6–7 percent, then it started to decline notably to register 2.82 percent in the first half of the 1990s.[4] The average annual

TABLE II
Number of enterprises by employment size: Non-primary sector

Year	Total	1–4	5–9	10–29	30–49	50–99	100–299	300–
				Number of enterprise (1,000)				
1957	3461	2715	433	237	38	22	12	4
1969	4650	3360	687	431	84	54	27	7
1981	6269	4349	1056	640	113	70	33	8
1986	6494	4428	1118	705	124	75	36	8
1996	6503	4080	1230	886	156	94	46	10
				Compositional shares (%)				
1957	100	78.45	12.51	6.85	1.10	0.64	0.35	0.12
1969	100	72.26	14.77	9.27	1.81	1.16	0.58	0.15
1981	100	69.37	16.84	10.21	1.80	1.12	0.53	0.13
1986	100	68.19	17.22	10.85	1.90	1.16	0.56	0.12
1996	100	62.74	18.92	13.63	2.40	1.45	0.70	0.16

Source: Management and Coordination Agency, Establishment Census, various years.

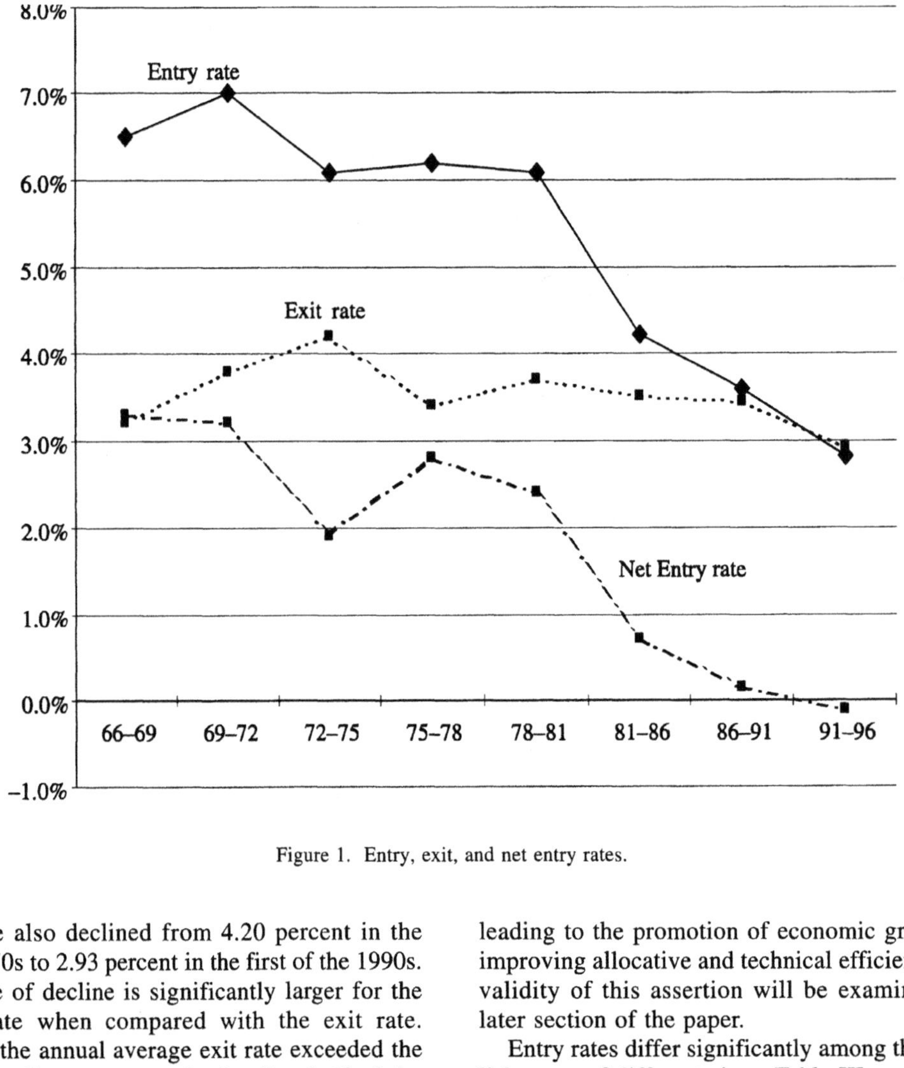

Figure 1. Entry, exit, and net entry rates.

exit rate also declined from 4.20 percent in the mid-1970s to 2.93 percent in the first of the 1990s. The rate of decline is significantly larger for the entry rate when compared with the exit rate. Indeed, the annual average exit rate exceeded the corresponding entry rate in the first half of the 1990s, resulting in the decline in the number of firms.

The observed patterns of the changes in entry and exit rates above seem to indicate that they are correlated. A study by the Small and Medium Enterprise Agency (1999) found both entry and exit rates are closely correlated to the rate of economic growth. While high economic growth would increase business opportunities, inducing entry, high rate of entry results in high exit rates, since the probability of exit is high for new firms.[5] During the boom period, turnover of the firms through entry and exit becomes high, probably leading to the promotion of economic growth by improving allocative and technical efficiency. The validity of this assertion will be examined in a later section of the paper.

Entry rates differ significantly among the establishments of different sizes. Table III reveals that entry rates are high for the firms with five to nine employees and 10–19 employees. Firms with five to nine employees register the highest entry rate. The entry rate declines steadily with the size of firms, and the entry rate is the lowest for large firms with more than 300 employees. The relationship between the entry rates and the firm size observed above can be found for most sectors shown in the table. The exit rate declines with the firm size, similar to the pattern observed for the entry rate.[6] One difference is that unlike the entry rate, whose value for the smallest firms (firms with one to four employees) is not the highest

TABLE III
Rate of entry by industry and by establishment size in 1986–1991

	Employment Size (number of employees)									
	Average	1–4	5–9	10–19	20–29	30–49	50–99	100–199	200–299	300–
All sectors	6.2	5.9	*7.3*	*6.8*	6.0	5.3	4.4	3.6	3.4	2.6
Agric. forst. fishery	4.1	*4.3*	*4.5*	*4.2*	3.5	2.7	1.2	2.1	0.0	0.0
Mining	2.7	*4.1*	2.6	2.0	1.0	1.7	2.6	0.0	0.0	*5.6*
Construction	4.9	4.1	*6.2*	*5.4*	4.4	4.0	3.3	3.0	3.3	4.1
Manufacturing	4.3	3.8	*5.1*	*5.3*	*4.8*	*4.4*	3.8	3.2	2.4	1.4
Utilities	4.0	2.8	*6.0*	*5.8*	*4.6*	3.9	3.6	3.0	2.4	2.4
Transp. and communication	5.9	5.4	*9.2*	*7.1*	4.8	4.3	3.5	2.8	3.2	2.3
Wholesale and retail	6.6	6.4	*7.5*	*7.3*	6.4	5.6	4.9	3.9	4.5	4.5
Finance and insurance	7.7	*8.9*	*10.0*	7.1	6.3	5.3	4.4	4.1	4.5	3.6
Services	6.8	6.2	*8.6*	*8.3*	*8.0*	7.2	5.3	4.5	4.5	3.7

Note: The figures in italic are greater than the average for the sector.
Source: Management and Coordination Agency, Establishment Census, various years.

among all size groups, the exit rate for the smallest firms is the highest, resulting in the steady decline in exit rate with firm size. High entry and exit rates observed for small firms appear to reflect the fact that entry and exit barriers such as required investment in physical and human capital, or sunk cost, are low for small firms. High exit rates for small firms may also be due to a lack of competitiveness, which in turn is due to limited amount of financial and human resources.

Differences in the rates of turnover among the firms of different sizes observed above are reflected in the age structure of the firms of different sizes. From the figures in Table IV one observes that small firms are young, while large firms are old. Specifically, for the firms with 5–19 employees, more than 50 percent of them were established after 1975, while the corresponding value for the firms with 300 or more employees is much lower at 29.1 percent. By contrast, 30 percent of the firms with 300 or more employees were established before 1954, while the corresponding value for the firms with 5–19 employees is significantly lower at 13 percent. In addition to the differences in the entry and exit rates among the firms of different sizes noted above, the fact that surviving firms tend to increase their size in terms of employment explain the high proportion of old firms among large firms.[7]

TABLE IV
Age structure of establishment (%): 1996

Size of establishment by employment	Year of establishment							
	–54	55–64	65–74	75–84	85–86	87–89	90–	Total
Total	15.7	12.0	21.3	26.6	6.7	11.6	6.2	100.0
1–4	16.9	12.2	21.1	26.4	6.5	10.8	5.9	100.0
5–9	13.3	11.0	20.6	27.2	7.1	13.5	7.3	100.0
10–19	12.3	11.1	22.1	27.4	7.1	13.2	6.8	100.0
20–29	13.2	12.1	23.4	26.4	6.7	12.3	6.0	100.0
30–49	14.8	13.2	23.7	25.4	6.2	11.4	5.3	100.0
50–99	17.2	14.9	24.5	23.5	5.7	9.9	4.4	100.0
100–199	19.8	16.6	24.8	21.6	5.2	8.4	3.6	100.0
200–299	23.1	16.4	24.9	19.4	4.9	7.9	3.4	100.0
300–	30.6	17.3	23.1	15.8	4.5	6.2	2.6	100.0

Source: Management and Coordination Agency, Establishment Census, various years.

3. Entry motives and impediments

In this section we examine the motives of entry and the barriers to entry of Japanese SMEs by mainly using the results of a questionnaire survey conducted on the founders of SMEs by the Small and Medium Enterprise Agency of the Japanese government.[8] In the next section we attempt to identify the determinants of entry in the Japanese manufacturing sector by analyzing statistically the factors encouraging and discouraging entry.

According to the results of the survey, the most popular motive, which was noted by 47 percent of the respondents, was to pursue their dreams. Other motives that received high response rates, include "try out their potential (36.3 percent)" and "work independently (22.6 percent)." Behind these noneconomic and somewhat spiritual motives comes the profit-seeking motive (21.6 percent). A large number of entrepreneurs with noneconomic motives may explain the high failure rate, or exit rate, among the new entrants, as their business plans may not be well prepared from the financial aspect. It is interesting to note that "admiration for successful entrepreneurs" and "acquaintance with entrepreneurs" are the two more popular reasons for acquiring an interest in starting business among business-oriented students.[9]

Potential entrants face various obstacles. According to the results of a survey conducted by the Small and Medium Enterprise Agency, the three most serious obstacles are lack of financial resources, lack of human resources, and difficulty in developing distribution network[10] Young entrants find these obstacles to be particularly serious. Below we examine some of the problems faced by the entrants in obtaining financial and human resources in more detail.

A large proportion of potential entrants of small business has limited financial resources. According to the survey by the Small and Medium Enterprise Agency, approximately 70 percent of potential entrants of small and medium size had an income of 5 million yen or less.[11] In 1998 for as many as 79 percent of startups the initial amount of financial expenses was at least 5 million yen, and for 67 percent the amount was more than 10 million yen. In light of these observations, those who are interested in starting business with their own funds are likely to have difficulty in obtaining necessary financial resources. However, personal savings is most commonly used means of obtaining initial financial resources for SMEs, because lack of market credibility and small size make it difficult for entrepreneurs to borrow or raise funds from external sources. Indeed, for 80 percent of newly established SMEs, personal saving was a source of finance. Family members and friends are also important sources of finance, because approximately 30 percent of new SMEs relied on them as a source of loans or investments.

Approximately 40 percent of startup SMEs obtained loans from financial institutions, but they faced difficulty in obtaining loans and in many cases the amount of loans they obtained was significantly lower than the amount they requested. The results of a survey by People's Finance Corporation reveals that problems potential entrants of small size face include lack of collateral (73 percent of the firms surveyed), low credit worthiness (59 percent), and lack of guarantor (29 percent).[12] To obtain loans in Japan, collateral and guarantor are generally required. Lack of clear distinction between personal property and firm's property results in loss of personal property, which is often used as collateral, in case of business failure. Indeed, the concern over such possibility makes potential entrepreneurs hesitate to start new business. Public financial assistance in the form of loans and subsidies for startup firms has been provided. However, SMEs are not so interested in loans from public institutions because those loans are not much different from private loans with respect to the conditions on borrowing and repayment.

In light of the difficulty in obtaining financing, it is desirable for SMEs to expand the sources of funds to other sources such as capital markets, venture capital, and angel funds. However, it is not easy for SMEs to do so, because they have to provide detailed information, such as a balance sheet, which the investors use for making investment decisions. Realizing such a difficulty, a large number of SMEs are more interested in the extension of the upper limit of the loan that is covered by the Credit Guarantee Association, and the increase of the subsidies for startups.[13]

Difficulty in recruiting capable personnel is another problem often encountered by potential entrants. A survey by the Small and Medium Enterprise Agency showed that 40 percent of the entrants surveyed were successful in recruiting personnel who turned out to be capable at the time of startup.[14] The respondents noted that an inability to pay a high salary and an inability to provide a desirable working environment was a major contribution in the success or failure in recruiting qualified personnel. Furthermore, a strong interest in working for established and large firms on the part of Japanese workers makes it difficult for new and small firms to attract capable workers.

4. Determinants of entry: A quantitative analysis

Entry occurs when the expected profit from entry is positive. The expected profit is in turn determined by the difference between the expected value of sales and the cost of starting and running business. As was pointed out earlier in the results of the survey on the obstacles to startup, the cost of starting a business, which depends on the height of entry barriers, has an important impact on entry. Obviously, entry takes place when the value of expected sales is high and entry barriers are low. Even if the expected sales are high, then entry is not likely to take place when entry barriers are high.

Several studies have examined the determinants of entry for the Japanese manufacturing sector.[15] Yamawaki (1991) estimated the net entry equation for 135 Japanese three-digit industries over the 1979–1984 period. He found that net entry is positively and significantly affected by lagged profitability (price-cost margin, PCM), lagged industry growth, and the growth rate of GNP, and negatively and significantly affected by the price of investment goods and the discount rate. Because the price of investment goods and the discount rate are used as a proxy for the cost of capital, his finding indicates that high cost of capital is an effective barrier to net entry.

Odagiri and Honjo (1995) estimated the net entry equation for 98 industries by using a panel data covering 1988–1990. They found that profitability (PCM) and sales growth had a positive and significant impact on net entry, while both economies of scale and capital-output ratio had a negative and significant impact. The coefficient on market size was positive but it was not significant. In a separate estimation, they tested the impact of concentration on net entry and found that concentration had a negative impacton net entry but the relationship is not statistically significant. Morikawa and Tachibanaki (1997) analyzed the gross entry rate for 561 industries between 1990 and 1993. They found that gross entry rate is positively and significantly affected by sales growth and negatively and significantly affected by the average number of employees per establishment and capital-labor ratio. In addition, they found that a regulation dummy had a negative and significant impact on gross entry.

These studies on entry in the Japanese manufacturing sector have confirmed the positive impact of demand-side factors and the negative impact of entry barriers on entry for Japanese firms. We will examine the determinants of entry by extending the previous analyses in several ways. One is to incorporate additional explanatory variables, and another is to examine entry for the firms of different sizes.

Following the previous studies of the determinants of entry, we use three variables to test the impact of entry inducing factors on entry (price-cost margin, market size, and sales growth), and four variables to test the impact of entry barriers on entry (minimum efficient scale, MES), minimum capital requirement, technological requirement, and product differentiation). We expect the impact of entry-inducing factors to have a positive impact on entry, and we expect the impact of entry barriers on entry to be negative.

A few words on the variables representing entry barriers are in order. Two types of entry barriers are considered in our analysis, economies of scale and cost disadvantage, that are closely related to each other as will be shown below. In an industry where scale economies play an important role in production or sales, an entrant with a limited scale of production faces a cost disadvantage vis-à-vis the incumbents who have already achieved the MES of production and therefore are able to produce at low cost. We use MES as an indicator of economies of scale and measure MES by taking the ratio of average value of shipment of the plants supplying the upper half of industry shipments and total value of shipment of the industry.

Cost disadvantage faced by an entrant may be captured by three different types of investment required for entry; that is, investment in physical capital, technologies, and marketing or advertising. Well-performing incumbents, against whom entrants have to compete, have already constructed factories and installed machinery and other necessary equipment. Moreover, not only have they already developed necessary technologies and human resources through R&D but also have established brand names through advertising. The greater the amount of investment required for entry, the larger becomes the risk of investment, thereby becoming an effective entry barrier. Because investment in physical capital, technologies, and advertisement has a characteristic of fixed cost, cost disadvantage is closely related to scale economies. Recognizing this point, we include capital-output ratio, R&D-sales ratio, and advertisement expenditure-sales ratios to examine the impact of three different types of entry barriers. We expect these entry barriers to be particularly effective to deter entry of small firms.

In addition to these variables, we include three other variables: concentration, subcontracting, and policy loans. Market concentration may have two contrasting impacts on entry.[16] One hypothesis is that incumbents can retaliate against entry more easily in concentrated industries than in non-concentrated industries, because incumbents in concentrated industries can easily detect entry. According to this hypothesis, concentration discourages entry. Alternatively, one can hypothesize that high profits resulting from concentration would induce entry. Considering that entry by small firms would be of only little threat to incumbents, one would expect that concentration would have a positive impact on entry.

Many firms, especially SMEs, are involved with other firms through subcontracting in Japan. They have been engaged in subcontracting because it has brought benefits to the firms involved. The benefits may be gained by avoiding coordination failure by adjusting production levels through close contact. Subcontractors also gain benefits from obtaining technical and financial assistance from subcontractees, or parent firms.

As to the impact of subcontracting system on entry, one may argue that it acts as an entry barrier, because the subcontracting system is built on a long-term business relationship between the firms involved in the subcontracting system. Alternatively, one may argue that subcontracting encourages entry, because subcontracting practiced in Japan is generally open to outsiders. Indeed, parent firms encourage competition among subcontractors by making the subcontracting system open to obtain benefits in the form of low priced and high quality services provided by subcontractors. Specifically, parent firms do not hesitate to reduce or stop the business with the subcontractors that do not perform as expected, and they recruit actively new subcontractors with high performance.

Another factor associated with subcontracting that promotes entry is that there have been many cases where former employees of parent firms start business as a subcontractor to their former employers. Parent firms often encourage their employees to start new business and to be engaged in subcontracting relationship with them, because subcontracting would bring the benefits just discussed and at the same time would reduce the cost of operation. Finally, one may argue that subcontracting facilitates entry of new firms, because under the subcontracting system new firms can avoid substantial initial investment because it allows them to specialize in a particular process that they have competitiveness in. On the basis of these discussions, one cannot assign expected impact of subcontracting on entry, a priori.

Policy loans from public financial institutions have important position as a source of financing for SMEs. At the end of 1997, policy loans account for approximately 25 percent of outstanding balance of the loans to SMEs.[17] Policy loans have been given to entrants, but a dominant part of them have been given to incumbent firms. Although policy loans would be helpful to potential entrants, who suffer from the shortage of the fund, policy loans to incumbents would lead to the creation of entry barriers as they would help the incumbents improve their competitiveness.

The results of the regression analysis on the determinants of entry rates are shown in Table V. The dependent variable is the average annual rate of gross entry. The explanatory variables used in the analysis explain 60–90 percent of the variations of the entry rates. Examining the results for the establishments of all sizes, which are shown

TABLE V
Determinants of gross entry rates for Japanese manufacturing by size: 1986–1991 (two-digit industrial classification)

	1–4 employees		5–9 employees		10–19 employees		20–29 employees		30–49 employees	
	Coefficients	*t*-value	Coefficients	*t*-value	Coefficients	*t*-value	Coefficients	*t*-value	Coefficients	*t*-value
PCM	0.054	1.147	0.021	1.562	0.024	1.721	0.015	1.393	0.015	1.272
Market size	0.001	0.558	0.000	0.002	0.000	–0.264	0.001	0.307	0.000	–0.043
Sales growth	0.376	2.735	0.274	2.519	0.294	2.979	0.223	1.937	0.107	0.654
MES	–0.020	–1.867	–0.004	–1.222	–0.003	–1.210	–0.011	–0.593	–0.022	–0.827
Capital/output	–0.005	–0.172	–0.005	–0.224	–0.034	–1.605	–0.055	–2.223	–0.049	–1.414
Concentration	–0.004	–1.437	–0.002	–1.721	–0.002	–1.751	–0.001	–1.280	0.000	–1.070
R&D	–0.004	–2.263	–0.002	–1.783	–0.002	–1.719	0.000	–1.016	–0.002	–1.661
Advertise/sales	0.001	0.247	0.002	0.457	0.000	0.100	0.001	0.247	0.000	–0.005
Subcontracting	0.000	1.961	0.000	1.809	0.000	1.887	0.000	1.972	0.000	1.787
Policy loan	–0.002	–2.079	–0.002	–1.915	–0.002	–1.050	–0.001	–1.588	–0.003	–1.031
constant	0.037	1.071	0.036	1.332	0.046	1.898	0.041	1.414	0.043	1.049
R^2	0.758		0.7796		0.8211		0.7763		0.6174	
nob	20		20		20		20		20	

	50–99 employees		100–199 employees		200–299 employees		300– employees		Total	
	Coefficients	*t*-value	Coefficients	*t*-value	Coefficients	*t*-value	Coefficients	*t*-value	Coefficients	*t*-value
PCM	0.018	1.461	0.005	1.131	0.012	1.271	0.013	1.293	0.070	6.416
Market size	0.002	0.937	0.003	1.618	0.004	1.875	0.002	0.883	0.006	2.268
Sales growth	0.189	1.633	0.228	2.017	0.103	0.798	0.101	0.799	0.052	2.788
MES	0.000	–1.015	–0.023	–1.214	–0.014	–1.635	–0.003	–1.122	–0.010	–3.019
Capital/output	–0.068	–2.777	–0.054	–2.230	–0.041	–1.485	–0.021	–0.776	0.000	–2.991
Concentration	–0.001	–1.344	0.001	0.444	0.001	0.287	0.003	0.046	–0.002	–1.475
R&D	–0.003	–1.123	–0.001	–0.416	–0.002	–0.721	0.000	0.137	–0.004	–3.386
Advertise/sales	0.002	0.439	0.002	0.617	–0.001	–0.202	0.001	0.309	0.001	–1.955
Subcontracting	0.000	0.722	0.000	–0.767	0.000	0.136	0.000	–0.401	0.000	4.258
Policy loan	–0.001	–0.482	–0.001	–1.733	–0.001	–0.572	0.002	0.731	–0.002	–2.878
Constant	0.031	1.093	–0019	–0.683	–0.012	–0.361	–0.032	–1.035	0.012	1.122
R^2	0.7358		0.7192		0.664		0.4723		0.9559	
nob	20		20		20		20		20	

Note: The definitions of variables and their data sources are shown in Appendix 1.

under total establishments, one observes that entry inducing factors, profitability (PCM), market size, and sales growth are significantly positive, while entry barriers, minimum efficient scale, capital-output ratio, R&D, and advertisement-sales ratio are significantly negative. These findings are consistent with our expectation. The estimated coefficient on concentration, here measured by the Herfindahl index, is negative, but not statistically significant. Subcontracting is shown to have a positive impact on entry. This result suggests that not only subcontracting relation is open to outsiders, but also it may offer an opportunity for SMEs to specialize in the process in which they are competitive and to obtain financial, technical, and other assistance from their parent firms. The impact of policy loans on entry is estimated to be negative, suggesting that policy loans protect incumbents.

An examination of the results for the establishments of different sizes reveals that the explanatory variables used in the analysis explain the entry rates for SMEs better than for larger establishments. Indeed, none of the estimated coefficients is statistically significant for establishments with more than 300 employees. Among the factors inducing entry, sales growth turns out to be positive and significant for the establishments of different sizes, but profitability and market size are revealed to be insignificant in most cases. Scale economies (MES) is found to be an effective entry barrier only for the establishments of very small size, while capital constraint is shown to be an effective entry barrier for the establishments of medium sizes (those with 20–199 employees). Technical barrier (R&D) is shown to be effective for the establishments of relatively small sizes, while subcontracting is shown to promote entry for small and medium establishments. Provision of policy loans to incumbents appears to be an effective deterrent to entry by very small establishments.

5. Conclusions

The entry rate in Japan has been declining more or less steadily since the early 1980s. We have identified several structural barriers to entry from our cross-sectional analysis of the determinants of entry. Specifically, cost disadvantage owing to small scale and shortage of financial and technical resources are shown to be effective deterrents to entry. To reduce technical barriers, the government can provide technical education and training to prospective SME entrants and provide financial assistance to reduce financial or capital requirement barriers. Recognizing that financial assistance to incumbents could protect them from entry, it is important that financial assistance be given to potential entrants and the incumbents with high potentiality.

Acknowledgements

The authors are grateful for helpful comments and discussions from the participants of the project entitled The Role of Small and Medium Enterprises in Development organized by the World Bank Institute.

Appendix 1. Variable definition and sources of data used for estimating the determinants of entry

Variable name	Definition	Source
Price-cost margin (PCM)	(sales-material costs-capital costs)/sales	MITI, *Kogyo Tokei Hyo (Census of Manufacturing)*
Market size	Sales	MITI, *Kogyo Tokei Hyo (Census of Manufacturing)*
Sales growth	Growth rate of sales	MITI, *Kogyo Tokei Hyo (Census of Manufacturing)*
Minimum efficient scale (MES)	See the main text	MITI, *Kogyo Tokei Hyo (Census of Manufacturing)*
Capital-output ratio	Value of tangible assets/output	MITI, *Kogyo Tokei Hyo (Census of Manufacturing)*
Market concentration	Herfindahl index	Fair trade commission, *Annual Survey of Market Concentration*
R&D	R&D expenditure/sales	MITI, *Input-output tables*
Advertisement-sales ratio	Advertisement expenditure/Sales	MITI, *Input-output tables*
Subcontracting	Shares of firms engaged in subcontracting in total number of firms	SME Agency, *Kogyo Jittai Kihon Chosa [Basic Survery of Manufactures]*
Policy loan	Outstanding balance of public loan/ Outstanding balance of total loan	SME Agency, *Kogyo Jittai Kihon Chosa [Basic Survery of Manufactures]*

Note: MITI (Ministry of International Trade and Industry).

Notes

[1] Small and Medium Enterprise Agency (1979, p. 336).

[2] The analysis in this section is based on information on establishments rather than firms, because of data availability. In this paper, the terms indicating "firms" such as SMEs and "establishments" are used interchangeably in many cases, although most of the information used are those on establishments. The following definitions of SMEs are used in Japan. In terms of employees, SMEs in manufacturing are defined as those with 299 or fewer employees. SMEs in wholesale on the one hand, and retail and other services on the other, are defined as those with 99 or fewer, and 49 or fewer employees, respectively. In addition to the definitions in terms of employees, definitions based on the size of paid-in capital are also used. In terms of paid-in capital, SMEs in manufacturing are those with paid-in capital worth less than 100 million yen. SMEs in wholesale are those with paid-in capital worth less than 30 million yen, while those in retail and other services are those with paid-in capital worth less than 10 million yen.

[3] The rate of entry (exit) is defined as the number of entering firms (exiting firms) divided by the number of firms at the beginning of the period.

[4] One should note that the average annual rates of entry and exit for the period before 1981 and those after 1981 shown in Figure 1 are not strictly comparable. This is because the length of the period compared is different between those two periods owing to the differences in the timing of the data compilation. For the period before 1981 data are compiled every three years, while for the period after 1981 they are compiled every five years. The average annual rates of entry and exit tend to be lower for the period after 1981 when compared with those for the period before 1981. This is because the number of firms that entered and subsequently exited within the period and thus are not recorded tends to be higher when the period of data compilation is longer.

[5] Caves (1998) makes this argument.

[6] See Small and Medium Enterprise Agency (1999, p. 217) on this point. This observation is consistent with the findings on other countries. See Caves (1998) for a review of previous studies.

[7] Small and Medium Enterprise Agency (1999, p. 234) found that the number of surviving firms increasing in their employment size is greater than those reducing in their size.

[8] Chusho Kigyo Sozoteki Katsudo Jittai Chosa [Survey of Creative Activities by SMEs], October 1998.

[9] Small and Medium Enterprise Agency (1999, p. 281).,

[10] Small and Medium Enterprise Agency (1999, p. 284). Itoh and Urata (1994) found that in Japan the public sector played a useful role in providing financial, technical, and marketing support for the firms in the early stages of development.

[11] Small and Medium Enterprise Agency (1999, p. 288).

[12] People's Finance Corporation (1997).

[13] Small and Medium Enterprise Agency (1999, p. 289).

[14] Small and Medium Enterprise Agency (1999, p. 290).

[15] In addition to those studies on Japanese economy, various studies on other economies have been conducted. For review of previous studies, see Acs and Audretsch (1991), Caves (1998), and Martin (2001).

[16] Acs and Audretsch (1991) presents a good discussion on this point.

[17] The Bank of Japan, Monthly economics statistics.

References

Acs, Zoltan J. and David B. Audretsch, 1989, 'Births and Firm Size', *Southern Economic Journal* **56** (October), 467–475.

Acs, Zoltan J. and David B. Audretsch, 1991, *Innovation and Small Firms*, Cambridge, Mass.: MIT Press.

Baily, Martin N., Charles Hulten and David Campbell, 1992, 'Productivity Dynamics in Manufacturing Plants', Brookings Paper on Economic Activity: Microeconomics. Brookings Institution, Washington, D.C.

Caves, Richard E., 1998, 'Industrial Organization and New Findings on the Turnover and Mobility of Firms', *Journal of Economic Literature* **36** (December), 1947–1982.

Haltiwanger, John. 1997, 'Measuring and Analyzing Aggregate Fluctuations: The Importance of Building from Microeconomic Evidence', *Bank of St. Louis Federal Reserve Bank Economic Review* **79**(3), 55–77.

Itoh, M. and S. Urata, 1994, 'Small and Medium-Size Enterprise Support Policies in Japan', Policy Research Working Paper 1403. World Bank, Policy Research Department, Washington, D.C.

Liu, Lili and James R. Tybout, 1996, 'Productivity Growth in Chile and Colombia: The Role of Entry, Exit, and Learning', in Mark J. Roberts and James R. Tybout (eds.), *Industrial Evolution in Developing Countries*, New York: Oxford University Press.

Martin, Stephen, 2001, *Advanced Industrial Economics*, 2nd ed., Cambridge, Mass.: Basil Blackwell.

Morikawa, Masayuki and Toshiaki Tachibanaki, 1997, 'Sannyu-Taishutsu and Koyo Hendo [Entry-Exit and Employment Variation]', Discussion Paper 97-DOJ-85, Research Institute of International Trade and Industry, Ministry of International Trade and Industry, the Government of Japan, Tokyo [in Japanese].

Odagiri, Hiroyuki and Yuji Honjo, 1995, 'Seizogyo heno Sannyu no Keiryo Bunseki [An Econometric Analysis of Entry in Manufacturing]', Discussion Paper 95-DOJ-55, Research Institute of International Trade and Industry, Ministry of International Trade and Industry, the Government of Japan, Tokyo [in Japanese].

People's Finance Corporation, 1997, 'Shinki Kaigyo Hakusho', Whitepaper on New Openings, Tokyo.

Small and Medium Enterprise Agency, 1979, 'Chuso Kigyo Hakusho', White Paper on Small and Medium Enterprises, Tokyo.

Small and Medium Enterprise Agency, 1999, 'Chuso Kigyo Hakusho', White Paper on Small and Medium Enterprises, Tokyo.

Yamawaki, Hideki, 'The Effects of Business Conditions on Net Entry: Evidence from Japan', in Paul A. Geroski and Joachim Schwalbach (eds.), *Entry and Market Contestability: An International Comparison*, Cambridge Mass.: Basil Blackwell.

Technological Progress by Small and Medium Enterprises in Japan

Shujiro Urata
Hiroki Kawai

ABSTRACT. This paper examines various aspects of total factor productivity across different firm sizes in Japan. It shows that larger firms have higher total factor productivity levels and growth than smaller firms. There are, however, some exceptions to this pattern especially in the electric machinery sector where small firms tend to have the edge. The paper also finds that two distinctive characteristics of small and medium firms, the practice of subcontracting and the use of external patents, are positively related to total factor productivity growth while the availability of subsidized public loans is not.

1. Introduction

Technological progress contributed significantly to the remarkable economic growth of the Japanese economy in the post-WW II period. According to an estimate by Nishimizu and Hulten (1978), as much as 30 percent of Japan's economic growth in the 1955–1971 period was attributable to technological progress (as measured by growth in total factor productivity, TFP). While the rate of economic growth declined substantially in the early 1970s, technological progress continued to contribute significantly to economic growth. Indeed, the contribution of technological progress increased after the mid-1970s, accounting for more than 50 percent of economic growth from 1975 to 1985 (Kawai, 1999). However, in the 1990s, during which economic growth stagnated, the rate of technological progress has been negative. Because of demographic and economic maturity, there is a small likelihood of rapid expansion of capital and labor inputs in the Japanese economy in the future. Accordingly, the importance of technological progress for achieving economic growth will be greater.

One special characteristic of the Japanese economy is a large and important position held by small and medium enterprises (SMEs). In 1957, 99.7 percent of establishments in the nonprimary sector were SMEs, and 82.8 percent of workers were employed by SMEs. Although the shares of SMEs on these indicators declined over time to register 98.8 and 77.6 percent in 1996, respectively, SMEs still hold a dominant and important position in the Japanese economy. These numbers alone point to the importance of SMEs in the Japanese economy, but their importance would be increased if one considers their close relationships with large enterprises through various channels such as subcontracting relationships.

In light of these observations, this paper examines technological progress achieved by SMEs in the manufacturing sector. Specifically, we first estimate the rate of technological progress, here measured by growth of TFP, of establishments of different sizes for the 1966–1996 period. The analysis covers the final part of the rapid economic growth period (1966–1972), the lower but steady growth period (1972–1991) including a sub-period affected by two oil crises (1972–1981) and a sub-period characterized as a bubble economy (1985–1991), and the period of prolonged recession (1991–1996). We then examine differences in the levels of TFP among establishments of different sizes. We also analyze the determinants of technological progress and technological levels. In addition to statistical analysis, we examine technological progress by SMEs by utilizing information obtained from various surveys.

Shujiro Urata
School of Social Sciences
Waseda University
1-6-1 Nishiwaseda
Shinjuku-ku
Tokyo, 169-50
Japan

Hiroki Kawai
Keio University
Japan

Small Business Economics **18**: 53–67, 2002.

The structure of the paper is as follows. Section 2 briefly describes the methodology for estimating TFP. Section 3 examines technological progress by SMEs from the mid-1960s to the mid-1990s, and Section 4 analyzes the determinants of technological progress by considering technological capability, interfirm relationships, and government policy. Finally, in Section 5 some concluding remarks and policy implications are presented.

2. Methodology[1]

The methodology of estimating technological progress in this paper is based on the standard model of production.[2] The production function for each sector is assumed to give output (O) as a function of labor (L), capital (K), intermediate inputs (M) and the level of technology (T).

$$O = f(L, K, M, T) \quad (1)$$

Production technology is described as exponential function of the logarithms of inputs, or translog production function. Production is assumed to follow constant returns to scale. Furthermore, necessary conditions for producer equilibrium are assumed to be satisfied.

With these assumptions, one can derive the average rate of technological change (v_T) between time periods t and $t - 1$, which is unobservable, as the difference between successive logarithms of output and a weighted average of the differences between successive logarithms of inputs where the weights are the corresponding average value shares (equation (2)).

$$v_T = [\ln O(t) - \ln O(t-1)] - v_L[\ln L(t) - \ln L(t-1)] - v_K[\ln K(t) - \ln K(t-1)] - v_M[\ln M(t) - \ln M(t-1)] \quad (2)$$

where

$v_L = [v_L(t) + v_L(t-1)]/2$
$v_K = [v_K(t) + v_K(t-1)]/2$
$v_M = [v_M(t) + v_M(t-1)]/2$
$v_L + v_K + v_M = 1$

v_L: share of compensation to labor in the value of output
v_K: share of compensation to capital in the value of output
v_M: share of payments to intermediate inputs in the value of output

Since equation (2) measures the difference in output between two periods less the corresponding difference in combined inputs, the resulting measure is called the change in TFP.

Some comments on the meaning of technological progress, which is estimated by equation (2), are in order.[3] First, the results of the estimation by using equation (2) are usually interpreted as efficiency gains caused by adoption of new technology. Such an interpretation is appropriate if the firms can achieve maximum amount of output given the level of inputs and technology in both time $t - 1$ and t, for which the estimation is performed. In other words, one may attribute the results of the estimation to technological change in the framework of long run equilibrium. However, in the short to medium run, firms are generally constrained by immobility of inputs, so that they may not achieve most efficient allocation of inputs. As a consequence, under-utilization of inputs occurs. Because of this problem, estimation of equation (2) does not necessarily indicate technological progress, but it is influenced by changes in utilization of inputs.

Second, somewhat related to the problem discussed above, firms may not be able to obtain maximum amount of output because of inefficient management or inappropriate incentive systems. If such a situation arises, our TFP estimates not only reflect the change in technological level but also the change in management style or other elements affecting production. In broad terms, an improvement in management skills or production environment is also characterized as technological progress.

Finally, there is a possible problem related to the characteristics of production function. Although the methodology described above is derived with an assumption of constant returns to scale, true production technology may be subject to increasing returns to scale. Under such circumstances, our estimates would include the effect arising from scale economies.

3. Technological progress by small and medium enterprises

This section provides the results of estimation of TFP for the manufacturing establishments of different sizes. Before examining TFP estimates in the next section, this section will briefly examine the changing patterns of economic growth in Japan by referring to the changes in output, capital, labor, and intermediate inputs over time, to set the stage for the analysis of TFP.[4]

Changing patterns of economic growth from the mid-1960s through the 1990s

The 1966–1996 period, for which the analysis is undertaken, encompasses different phases of economic growth and performance for the Japanese economy. The 1966–1972 period captures the final part of rapid economic growth in the post-WW II period in Japan. The rate of economic growth declined significantly in the following periods. Two oil shocks, one in 1973 and the other in 1979, resulted in serious economic recession in Japan, which depended on foreign sources for almost 100 percent of its oil supply. Emergence of several structural problems also contributed to slowing of Japanese economic growth. Shortage of labor, as a result of rapid economic growth, made it difficult for the Japanese economy to realize economic growth based on expansion of labor inputs. The situation was particularly serious for SMEs, which were in a disadvantageous position vis-à-vis large firms for attracting workers. Narrowing of the technological gap between Japan and the Western economies, as a result of successful catching up by Japan, also contributed to the decline in economic growth rate, because it reduced the scope for economic growth based on technological progress.

Despite the unfavorable effect of the two oil shocks, the Japanese economy performed rather well through the 1980s when compared with other developed economies. In particular, the Japanese economy recorded a remarkably high growth rate in the latter half of the 1980s, resulting mainly from expansionary fiscal and monetary policies, which were adopted to deal with recessionary impact of the steep yen appreciation in the mid-1980s. Indeed, during this period, a "bubble" economy, characterized by sharply increased asset prices, emerged as a result of active investment based on optimistic future projections. The bubble economy contributed to rapid economic growth, but it did not last long.

The bubble burst in the early 1990s. Since a large part of investment in land and other assets was financed by bank loans, the collapse of the bubble resulted in a huge number of bad loans. Faced with unfavorable balance sheet problems owing to bad loans, the banks reduced their lending, especially to SMEs. Coupled with other problems such as an unfavorable demographic situation and a delay in required structural reforms, the Japanese economy experienced a prolonged period of stagnation during the 1990s, a period that will be looked back upon as Japan's lost decade.

The preceding discussions present a cursory overview of Japan's overall economic performance from the mid-1960s through the current period. In the remaining part of this section, we examine the changes in outputs and inputs in the manufacturing sector by focusing on the differences for the establishments of different sizes.

After recording a very high average annual growth rate of 12.2 percent for the 1966–1972 period, the average annual rate of output growth for the manufacturing sector declined to 3.5 percent in 1972–1981, mainly because of the two oil shocks and several structural factors discussed earlier (Table I). The average annual growth rate recovered somewhat to 4.6 percent for the 1981–1991 period, but it declined significantly to 0.9 percent in the following 1991–1996 period.

An examination of the growth rates of output for the establishments of different sizes reveals that the establishments with 30–49 employees, the smallest cohort in the sample, recorded the lowest growth rate for the four periods under study. For the 1991–1996 period, the smallest establishments experienced the average annual growth rate of –0.5 percent. By contrast to relatively unfavorable output performance of small establishments, large establishments performed better in output growth. In particular, the largest establishments with 300 or more employed registered the highest output growth in the 1966–1972 and 1991–1996 periods. For the 1972–1981 period the establishments with 50–99 employees recorded the highest growth rate, while for the 1981–1991 those with 100–199 employees recorded the highest growth rate.

As a result of the differences in the rate of output changes for the establishments of different

TABLE I
Changes in output, inputs, and TFP in the Japanese economy

	(Average annual growth rate: %)					
	Size of establishments in terms of employees					
	Total	30–49	50–99	100–199	200–299	300–
Output						
1966–1996	5.2	4.2	5.0	5.2	5.1	5.4
1966–1972	12.2	11.2	12.0	11.2	12.3	12.6
1972–1981	3.5	3.2	4.2	3.8	3.3	3.4
1981–1991	4.6	3.2	4.0	5.0	4.5	4.9
1991–1996	0.9	–0.5	0.4	0.7	1.1	1.2
Labor inputs						
1966–1996	0.0	–0.3	0.3	0.4	0.3	–0.4
1966–1972	2.1	1.0	2.0	2.1	2.6	2.4
1972–1981	–1.4	–1.0	–0.3	–0.7	–1.2	–2.2
1981–1991	0.8	0.4	1.0	1.5	1.2	0.5
1991–1996	–2.0	–2.2	–2.1	–1.6	–1.7	–2.2
Capital inputs						
1966–1996	5.3	6.4	6.7	6.3	6.0	4.6
1966–1972	12.2	13.2	13.8	12.4	12.2	11.8
1972–1981	0.6	2.3	2.4	1.5	1.5	–0.2
1981–1991	5.4	6.1	6.7	6.9	5.5	4.8
1991–1996	5.3	6.2	6.0	6.3	7.4	4.5
Intermediate inputs						
1966–1996	4.9	3.9	4.7	4.7	4.7	5.1
1966–1972	12.2	11.7	12.1	10.7	12.2	12.7
1972–1981	3.2	2.7	4.0	3.3	3.0	3.2
1981–1991	4.3	2.9	3.4	4.7	3.9	4.5
1991–1996	0.1	–1.1	–0.4	0.0	0.6	0.3
Total factor productivity						
1966–1996	0.8	0.7	0.8	0.8	0.7	0.8
1966–1972	1.0	0.9	1.4	1.1	0.8	0.9
1972–1981	0.7	0.7	0.6	0.7	0.6	0.7
1981–1991	0.8	0.6	0.6	0.7	0.8	0.8
1991–1996	0.7	0.4	0.6	0.6	0.5	0.8

Source: Authors' estimates.

sizes from 1966 to 1996, the distribution of output shares shifted from small establishments to large establishments. Specifically, the share of output for large establishments with 300 or more employees in total output increased from 57.9 percent in 1966 to 61.0 percent in 1996. In contrast, the share of output for smaller establishments with 299 or fewer employees declined. Among the sub-groups of smaller establishments, smallest establishments with 30–49 employees lost the largest share from 8.3 percent to 6.1 percent, while the remaining sub-groups of relatively larger establishments experienced a smaller decline.

Turning to output growth for different sectors, one observes wide variations. Roughly speaking, light and traditional manufacturing sectors such as textiles and material-intensive manufacturing sector such as chemicals and metal products exhibited low growth rates, while high-tech sectors such as electric machinery and transport machinery achieved high growth rates. These sectoral differences in the patterns of output growth are also found for the establishments of different sizes.

Turning to the changes in inputs, one finds that the changes in labor inputs showed sizeable fluctuations over the 1966–1996 period. During the high growth period of 1966–1972, labor inputs increased significantly at the average annual rate of 2.1 percent. However, during the low growth period of 1972–1981, labor inputs declined. Labor inputs increased slightly again from 1981 to 1991 in response to an upturn in economic growth, but from 1991 to 1996 labor inputs declined again at the average annual rate of 2.0 percent. Examining the rate of change in labor inputs for the establishments of different sizes over time, one observes greater fluctuations in the use of labor inputs by large establishments when compared with small establishments. This finding indicates that large establishments are more active in adjusting labor inputs to deal with economic situation. To put it differently, one may argue that small establishments contributed to the stability of employment. This pattern changed during the prolonged recession of the 1990s, because small establishments did reduce labor inputs as much as large establishment in terms of percentage from 1991 to 1996. Serious business situations faced by small establishments forced them to cut down labor inputs.

Capital inputs increased notably in the high growth period at the average annual rate of 12.2 percent. After recording a low rate of 0.6 percent during the 1972–1981 period, the average annual rate of growth of capital inputs increased to 5.4 percent in 1981–1991 and remained at around the similar level through 1991–1996. It is important to note that the smaller establishments showed a higher rate of increase in capital inputs than large establishments for the entire 1966–1996 period.

The changes in the use of intermediate inputs show a very similar pattern observed for outputs, indicating that the production relationship between intermediate inputs and outputs was more or less fixed over time. Intermediate inputs increased at an average annual rate of 12.2 percent during the rapid economic growth period of 1966–1972, then the rate of their growth declined sharply through the mid-1990s, registering at 0.1 percent for 1991–1996. Similar to the pattern observed for output growth, the rate of growth in the use of intermediate inputs is greater for large establishments when compared with smaller establishments.

In sum, over the 1966–1996 period output growth declined significantly, indicating a transition from a high growth period in the earlier stage of economic development to a low growth period in the matured stage of economic development. Output of smaller establishments grew less than that of large establishments, leading to a shift in output structure from smaller establishments to large establishments. We observe an interesting contrast between small establishments and large establishments in the use of labor and capital inputs. Small establishments expanded capital inputs faster than large establishments, while small establishments expanded labor inputs more slowly than large establishments. As a result of these changes, the gap in capital-labor ratio between small and large establishments narrowed over time.

These differences in the growth rates of labor and capital inputs reflect the differences in the availability of resources for small and large establishments. As a result of rapid economic growth and sectoral shift in production from manufacturing to services, recruitment of workers for the manufacturing sector became difficult. The situation was particularly acute for small establishments, because working condition such as wage rates and fringe benefits for small establishments was in general less favorable than that for large establishments. Faced with the shortage of labor, small establishments resorted to the increase in capital inputs through active fixed investment to expand or maintain their business. To undertake fixed investment, small establishments could utilize financial resources provided by various financial lending institutions. Thanks to SME promotion policies pursued by the government, public SME lending institutions were actively supplying the fund for fixed investment to SMEs. Moreover, the availability of financial resources to SMEs from the private financial institutions increased as large firms shifted from borrowing from financial institutions to self-financing such as issuing bonds for acquiring financial resources.[5]

Technological progress: TFP growth

The results of the computation of TFP growth by using equation (2) are shown in Tables I and II. An examination of the computed TFP for overall manufacturing shown at the bottom of Table I points out relatively small variations in TFP among the four periods under study. For the high growth period of 1966–1972, TFP increased at the average annual rate of 1.0 percent, while the corresponding rates for the following three periods are lower at 0.7–0.8 percent. Observing a substantial decline in output growth rates from the mid-1960s to the mid-1990s, one finds that the contribution of TFP growth to output growth increased during the period. Specifically, for 1966–1972, only 8 percent of output growth was attributable to TFP growth, while for 1991–1996 as much as 78 percent of output growth was accounted for by TFP growth.

The differences in the TFP growth rates among the establishments of different sizes are very small for the 1972–1991 period, during which the output growth rate was averaged about 4 percent. However, one observes noticeable differences for the 1966–1972 period of high economic growth and the 1991–1996 period of prolonged recession. For the 1966–1972 period medium-sized establishments with 50–99 employees performed best with 1.4 percent TFP growth, and both small and large establishments recorded TFP growth at 0.9 percent. For the 1991–1996 period large estab-

TABLE II
Annual growth rate of TFP (%)

	1966–1972	Size of establishments in terms of employees					1972–1981	Size of establishments in terms of employees				
	Total	30–49	50–99	100–199	200–299	300–	Total	30–49	50–99	100–199	200–299	300–
0. Total	0.97	0.94	1.40	1.05	0.83	0.88	0.70	0.68	0.63	0.70	0.65	0.72
1. Food	1.21	0.38	2.74	1.02	0.92	0.85	0.06	0.36	0.12	0.32	–0.10	–0.10
2. Textile and apparel	0.72	0.67	0.73	0.56	0.72	0.78	0.96	1.00	0.97	1.00	1.04	0.76
3. Chemical	1.13	1.23	1.07	1.33	0.59	1.03	0.40	0.71	0.73	0.62	0.83	0.27
4. Metal prod	0.96	1.01	0.85	1.03	1.10	0.88	0.53	0.50	0.45	0.35	0.23	0.61
5. General machinery	1.28	1.55	1.81	1.33	1.53	1.09	0.85	1.09	0.71	1.02	0.90	0.81
6. Elec machinery	1.37	1.57	1.47	1.34	0.82	1.38	1.46	1.71	1.65	1.72	1.85	1.38
7. Trans machinery	0.33	1.14	0.99	0.86	0.45	0.24	1.04	1.16	1.03	0.95	0.81	1.04
8. Precision machinery	1.25	1.51	1.40	1.24	1.37	1.17	1.71	2.10	1.91	2.10	1.90	1.54
9. Other manuf	0.97	0.97	0.93	1.04	0.54	1.17	0.22	0.23	0.23	0.29	0.27	0.20

	1981–1991	Size of establishments in terms of employees					1991–1996	Size of establishments in terms of employees				
	Total	30–49	50–99	100–199	200–299	300–	Total	30–49	50–99	100–199	200–299	300–
0. Total	0.76	0.63	0.60	0.71	0.77	0.81	0.69	0.44	0.61	0.57	0.51	0.77
1. Food	–0.50	–0.52	–0.23	–0.64	–0.31	–0.68	–0.13	–0.03	–0.12	–0.10	–0.07	–0.17
2. Textile and apparel	0.36	0.39	0.39	0.38	0.19	0.32	0.46	0.44	0.34	0.56	0.16	0.59
3. Chemical	0.43	0.81	0.87	1.12	0.53	0.08	0.23	0.14	0.93	0.41	0.21	0.08
4. Metal prod	0.33	0.26	0.23	0.51	0.63	0.23	0.43	0.25	0.47	0.11	0.04	0.72
5. General machinery	0.38	0.50	0.50	0.34	0.35	0.33	–0.23	–0.38	–0.27	–0.25	–0.25	–0.18
6. Elec machinery	1.28	1.49	1.45	1.28	1.36	1.25	1.04	1.62	1.61	1.43	1.17	0.91
7. Trans machinery	0.06	0.40	0.53	0.38	0.52	–0.02	0.06	–0.09	–0.40	–0.05	–0.17	0.10
8. Precision machinery	0.61	0.87	0.82	0.35	0.59	0.60	0.43	–0.08	0.67	0.71	–0.10	0.26
9. Other manuf	0.28	0.26	0.29	0.21	0.48	0.21	0.09	0.07	0.04	0.11	–0.12	0.11

Note: Originally, the figures are computed for 19 sectors and then aggregated; 19 sectors are food, textiles, apparel, wooden products, furniture, paper and pulp, printing, chemicals, petroleum, rubber, leather, glass, iron and steel, nonferrous metals, fabric metals, general machinery, electric machinery, transport machinery, and precision machinery.
Source: Authors' computation.

lishments achieved highest TFP growth at 0.8 percent, while the small establishments fared worse at 0.4 percent. An examination of the changes in TFP growth rates for the groups of different sizes over time reveals that the TFP growth rate declined sharply for small establishments, while the corresponding rate for large establishments stayed more or less at the same level. Despite relatively low growth rate of TFP for small establishments, the contribution of TFP growth to output growth was significantly higher for small establishments than large establishments.

Wide variations in TFP growth rates are observed for different manufacturing sub-sectors and for different periods (Table II). Accordingly, it is difficult to discern consistent patterns regarding sectoral TFP performance throughout the 1966–1996 period. However, one may observe that the machinery sectors, especially electric machinery, registered relatively high TFP growth, while resource intensive sectors such as food, chemicals, and metal products, and traditional sectors such as wooden products and leather products (included in other manufacturing) recorded low TFP growth. It is interesting to find that for electric machinery, which recorded the highest TFP growth among manufacturing sub-sectors, small establishments exhibited better TFP performance than large establishments, in contrast to the patterns observed for other sectors. One may argue that good performing small establishments contributed to high TFP performance of the electric machinery sector, in which many small establishments are involved with other establishments through subcontracting arrangements.

So far we have examined the change in TFP for the Japanese manufacturing sector from the mid-1960s to the mid-1990s. In the remainder of this section, we analyze the differences in the level of TFP among the establishments of different sizes.

The methodology for the computation is basically the same as the one used for the TFP growth accounting. The only difference is that instead of taking the difference of outputs and inputs between the two periods the corresponding differences between the establishments of different sizes are measured.

The results of the computation for 1966 and 1996 are shown in Table III. In the computation the level of TFP for the establishments of the average size for 1966 are used as an criterion for comparison, that is, the TFP level of the establishments of the average size for 1966 is set to unity. According to our computation, in 1966 large establishments show the highest TFP level at 1.013, while the establishments with 50–99 employees show the lowest level at 0.978. Putting it differently, the gap in TFP levels between large establishments and those with 50–99 employees was 3.6 percent. In 1996 the TFP level of manufacturing sector increased by 26.1 percent from the 1966 level. Large establishments fared more favorably than small establishments. The TFP level of large establishments increased by 26.7 percent from 1.013 in 1966 to 1.284 in 1996, while small establishments with 30–49 employees performed unfavorably by increasing the TFP levels by 22.4 percent from 0.982 to 1.202 over the same period. As a result of these changes, the TFP gap between large establishments and small establishments widened to 6.8 percent in 1996.

Generally, small establishments are shown to have lower TFP levels than large establishments, as the average TFP levels for larger establishments are higher than the corresponding values for smaller establishments in 1966 and 1996. But in several sectors, such as the machinery sectors, small establishments show higher TFP levels than large establishments in 1996. One reason for this may be that in the machinery sectors there are a number of small but innovative establishments engaged in parts and components production. By contrast, in metal production such as iron and steel, for which large-scale facilities are required for production, TFP levels of large establishments are higher, probably indicating that computed TFP levels captured not only technological factors but also scale economies.

4. Determinants of technological progress by SMEs

In the previous section we examined technological progress measured by TFP growth and the level of TFP for establishments of different sizes from the mid-1960s to the mid-1990s. In this section we investigate the factors determining TFP growth and TFP levels. Before conducting a statistical analysis of the determinants of TFP growth and TFP levels, we examine R&D activities of

TABLE III
The level of TFP by establishment size (1966 average = 1.0)

	Size of Establishments in terms of employees					
	Total	30–49	50–99	100–199	200–299	300–
1966						
0. Total	1.00	0.98	0.98	0.98	0.99	1.01
1. Food	1.00	0.97	0.95	0.96	0.98	1.06
2. Textile and apparel	1.00	1.01	1.01	1.00	1.00	0.99
3. Chemical	1.00	0.97	0.97	0.97	1.01	1.01
4. Metal prod	1.00	1.01	1.00	1.00	0.99	1.00
5. General machinery	1.00	1.00	1.00	1.00	0.98	1.00
6. Elec machinery	1.00	0.97	0.96	0.97	0.98	1.01
7. Trans machinery	1.00	0.99	0.98	0.98	0.99	1.00
8. Precision machinery	1.00	0.99	1.00	1.01	1.01	1.00
9. Other manuf	1.00	0.98	0.99	0.98	1.00	1.02
1996						
0. Total	1.26	1.20	1.23	1.23	1.23	1.28
1. Food	1.02	0.97	1.11	0.98	1.00	1.03
2. Textile and apparel	1.21	1.22	1.21	1.21	1.18	1.19
3. Chemical	1.20	1.22	1.27	1.28	1.22	1.15
4. Metal prod	1.17	1.16	1.15	1.16	1.15	1.19
5. General machinery	1.20	1.25	1.23	1.21	1.19	1.18
6. Elec machinery	1.48	1.57	1.53	1.49	1.47	1.47
7. Trans machinery	1.13	1.22	1.18	1.17	1.14	1.12
8. Precision machinery	1.37	1.42	1.44	1.41	1.37	1.32
9. Other manuf	1.12	1.09	1.10	1.11	1.10	1.14

Note: See the note in Table II.
Source: Authors' computation.

SMEs, because R&D is considered to play an important role in achieving technological progress.

R&D activities by SMEs

The results of the survey conducted by the Small and Medium Enterprise Agency in 1968 bring out interesting observations on the patterns of R&D activities by SMEs (Table IV). The results show that the smaller the firm, the less concerned with R&D activities. At least two reasons may be given for the observation. One is that very small firms are not engaged in production activities requiring R&D, and the other is that small firms have no resources, human as well as financial resources, to be spent on R&D activities, even if they were interested in such activities.

R&D takes various forms, that is, in-house activities and joint-research among others. There are significant differences in the patterns of R&D activities among the firms of different sizes. In-house R&D has an important role in R&D activities for large firms. Among the SMEs, in-house R&D is important for the firms with 50–299 employees; 30.3 percent of the firms in that group conduct in-house R&D.[6] For the smaller SMEs, participation in R&D seminars is an important form of R&D activity for acquiring technologies. For medium to large SMEs (20–299 employees), technological assistance provided by parent firms is an important source of technologies.[7] Although not shown in Table IV, other useful sources of technologies for SMEs include competitors in the same industry, material and equipment suppliers, and foreign firms.[8]

It is somewhat a surprise to find that SMEs are as active as large firms in conducting R&D jointly with the public research institutes and other types of research institutes such as those belonging to the universities and industry associations. Wide

TABLE IV
Research and Development by SMEs: 1968

	Firm size (number of employees)			
	1–19	20–49	50–299	300–
In-house R&D with full-time researchers	3.5	9.8	30.3	44.1
Collaborative R&D with universities and other research institutes	5.5	7.1	6.8	8.9
Use of public R&D institutes	7.8	9.0	7.3	8.4
Technical assistance from parent firms	5.5	10.6	10.3	7.9
Participating in seminars	34.9	37.9	44.8	40.6
Other R&D activities	5.0	4.9	5.9	5.9
Not considering R&D activities	19.8	14.9	6.1	3.0

Source: *Chushokigyo Keiei Jittai Chosa* [*Survey on the Current Management Conditions of Small and Medium Firms*], Small and Medium Enterprise Agency, September 1968.

use of public testing and R&D research institutes by SMEs was particularly notable for light manufacturing sectors, as more than 40 percent of SMEs in wood products, textiles, ceramics, and casting surveyed by the Small and Medium Enterprise Agency used the public testing and research institutes.[9]

Reliance on external institutions for R&D is rational for SMEs. Since R&D activities are subject to scale economies, it is not profitable for a small firm with limited resources and limited market power to conduct R&D alone. Joint-research activity is more attractive. Recognition of this point indicates the importance of the availability of public R&D institutes to SMEs, which are interested in improving technological capability.

Determinants of technological progress by SMEs: A statistical analysis

In the statistical analysis the following four variables are tested for the effect on cross-sectoral and time-series variations in TFP: the number of industrial patents held per establishment (PAH), the number of industrial patents introduced/acquired from external sources per establishment (PAI), the share of public loans in total amount of loans (PUB), and the share of establishments engaged in subcontracting in total number of establishments (SUB). All of the data are taken from a series of *Kogyo Jittai Kihon Chosa Hokoku Sho (Report on Comprehensive Survey of Manufacturers)* 1971, 1976, 1981, and 1987.

Possession of industrial patents indicates technological capability. Thus PAH is expected to have a positive impact on TFP growth and TFP levels. Table V shows PAH for different sectors and for establishments of different sizes in 1987. As expected, large establishments possess a substantially greater number of patents compared to small establishments. In 1987 the average number of industrial patents held by large establishments was 174.1, while the corresponding number for small establishments (10–49 employees) was much smaller at 3–4. There are wide variations in PAH among different sectors. Electric machinery had the highest number, while food and textiles had very low numbers. These sectoral differences in PAH are consistent with our expectations that the production of electric machinery requires technology intensive methods, while the production of food and textiles does not. Having observed sectoral differences in PAH, one notices that these differences are mainly due to the differences in the number of patents held by large establishments, and the number of patents held by a small establishment is not so different among different sectors.

Acquisition of technologies from external sources is an important means of improving technological capability of the firms. This is particularly true for small firms, because they cannot rely on their own technological capability because of shortage of human and financial resources. Indeed, we saw in the previous section that SMEs utilize external R&D sources to supplement their own technological capability. We would expect the

TABLE V
The number of patents developed by establishments (number per establishment)

	Total	10–29	30–49	50–99	100–199	200–299	300–
1987							
0. Total	48.6	3.9	4.5	5.8	9.3	13.7	174.1
1. Food	7.4	1.6	3.8	3.0	5.1	10.4	29.4
2. Textile and apparel	14.3	1.7	3.3	2.0	3.1	4.4	56.0
3. Chemical	68.6	8.2	6.4	10.1	12.9	22.7	175.0
4. Metal prod	46.3	5.1	3.7	4.2	6.1	7.6	108.2
5. General machinery	46.3	4.1	7.6	7.4	17.1	14.6	128.9
6. Elec machinery	212.1	4.4	2.9	3.8	7.7	14.5	448.9
7. Trans machinery	51.6	1.7	4.9	6.7	6.6	8.3	88.6
8. Precision machinery	21.9	3.0	5.8	6.1	9.5	18.0	143.6
9. Other manuf	16.0	2.5	2.3	3.8	6.1	10.4	65.1

Source: MITI, *Kogyo Jittai Kihon Chosa Hokoku Sho* [Report on Comprehensive Survey of Manufacturers], 1971 and 1987.

impact of PAI on TFP to be positive. According to Table VI, large establishments are more active in acquiring external technologies than smaller establishments. Although this observation is similar to that observed for industrial patents developed in-house, the gap in the number of patents acquired from external sources between large establishments and smaller establishments is significantly smaller when compared with the case of patents developed in-house. These findings indicate that smaller establishments rely more on external sources than internal source for the supply of industrial patents and for the acquisition of technological capability. Sectoral differences in PAI are not substantial, compared to PAH, although generally larger numbers are reported for chemicals and machinery sectors, where technology plays a greater role in the production.

One of the problems that SMEs face in conducting business is a lack of financial resources to be used for fixed investment or working capital. The Japanese government has actively provided financial resources to SMEs to modernize their equipment and achieve high productivity. To test the importance of this, we include the proportion of policy loans in total amount of loans (PUB) as an explanatory variable. If the policy were effective, we would expect a positive impact of PUB on TFP growth. According to Table VII, the value of PUB is high for small- and medium-sized estab-

TABLE VI
The number of patents acquired from external sources (number per establishment)

	Size of establishments in terms of employees						
	Total	10–29	30–49	50–99	100–199	200–299	300–
1987							
0. Total	3.8	1.9	1.5	2.8	2.1	1.9	5.0
1. Food	3.3	1.5	2.0	10.6	1.0	0.0	1.3
2. Textile and apparel	1.8	4.9	0.6	0.6	1.3	1.3	1.8
3. Chemical	4.8	1.1	1.6	1.3	4.2	1.3	5.0
4. Metal prod	3.2	0.6	1.0	4.2	0.6	1.6	3.4
5. General machinery	3.3	2.4	1.7	1.4	1.7	2.2	6.1
6. Elec machinery	6.5	1.7	1.3	1.0	1.8	1.6	5.8
7. Trans machinery	4.1	0.0	0.0	1.0	1.0	1.0	3.3
8. Precision machinery	2.4	1.0	2.5	3.4	1.2	3.0	2.8
9. Other manuf	3.8	0.3	0.3	1.5	2.9	1.0	3.0

Source: MITI, *Kogyo Jittai Kihon Chosa Hokoku Sho* [Report on Comprehensive Survey of Manufacturers], 1971 and 1987.

TABLE VII
Policy loans and subcontracting by size of firm

	Size of establishments in terms of employees						
	Total	10–29	30–49	50–99	100–199	200–299	300–
Share of policy loans in total loans (%)							
1971	11.6	20.9	22.8	22.4	18.9	17.1	8.6
1987	13.1	16.4	19.2	19.0	17.5	13.3	9.1
Proportion of firms engaged in subcontracting (%)							
1971	58.7	55.3	57.2	47.4	47.2	42.3	0.0
1987	55.8	48.3	47.7	47.2	45.7	41.5	30.3

Source: MITI, *Kogyo Jittai Kihon Chosa Hokoku Sho* [Report on Comprehensive Survey of Manufacturers], 1971 and 1987.

lishments with the values ranging between 13 and 23 percent in 1971 and 1987. For large establishments PUB is much smaller at less than 10 percent.

Japanese industrial organization is distinctive in having well-developed subcontracting arrangements, and it is often argued that the subcontracting system provides an environment conducive to improving technological efficiency. Subcontracting enables a parent firm to specialize in one or several operations in which that firm has a competitive edge. Specialization, in turn, leads to an improvement in productivity.

Being a subcontractor to one or several parent firms provides a subcontracting firm with an environment under which technological progress is enhanced. As was noted in the previous section, many SMEs acquire technologies from their parent firm. As such, subcontractors are in a better position to improve technological capability by acquiring new technologies from their parent firms. It is not uncommon to exchange technical personnel between subcontractors and parent firms to transfer technologies from parent firms to subcontractors. Moreover, parent firms often put pressure on subcontractors to improve their technological capability by having flexible relations, in which subcontracting arrangement may be cut if subcontractors do not perform to fulfill parent firms' expectations.[10] The preceding discussions suggest that SUB should have a positive effect on TFP.

A few observations may be warranted on the values of SUB in Table VII. Smaller establishments exhibit high incidence of participation in subcontracting arrangement. It is interesting to note that the proportion of establishments engaged in subcontracting declined slightly from 1971 to 1987, indicating a gradual breaking up of a traditional long-term business relationships in Japan.[11]

Results

A statistical analysis is performed to identify the determinants of TFP growth and TFP levels of the Japanese manufacturing sector with a focus on the impact associated with the differences in the establishment size. The data sample that we used for the analysis consists of 19 manufacturing sectors, seven establishment size groups, and five years (1972, 1975, 1978, 1981, and 1986), and four periods (1972–1975, 1975–1978, 1978–1981, and 1981–1986).[12] Although we computed TFP levels for nine years (1966, 1969, 1972, 1975, 1978, 1981, 1986, 1991, and 1996) and TFP growth rates for eight periods encompassing the nine years just stated, we reduced the sample period because of the availability of the information on the explanatory variables, which we use for the statistical analysis. The values for the explanatory variables, PAH, PAI, PUB, and SUB, are taken from *Kogyo Jittai Kihon Chosa Hokoku Sho*, as explained in the previous section. Since this survey was conducted only for 1971, 1976, 1981, and 1987, the necessary data for the analysis were derived by interpolation.

We first analyze the determinants of TFP growth, and then turn to the determinants of TFP levels. For both analyses we proceed as follows. First, we conduct OLS estimation with and without time dummy variables. Then we apply estimation methods specially developed for analyzing panel data. Specifically, we first test the presence of the individual effect. If the presence of the individual effect is detected, we then test if the individual effect can be regarded as random or fixed. We tested the validity of the specification of the random effect model, and in all the cases we could reject the hypothesis by using the BP's LM test, and we could support the use of the fixed effect model by applying the Hausman test, as shown in Table VIII. Therefore, we examine the results obtained from the application of the fixed effect model.

The results of the regression analysis are shown in Table VIII. To begin with the results on the determinants of TFP growth, we obtained positive and significant impact of PAI and SUB, as expected. These findings indicate that the sectors characterized by active patent introduction and active participation in subcontracting are likely to promote technological progress. Contrary to our expectation, active patent generation is not shown to promote technological progress, because the estimated coefficient on PAH is negative and statistically insignificant. The effectiveness of policy loans on technological progress was not detected, since the estimated coefficient on PUB is negative and statistically insignificant. In addition to these variables, we tested if catching up in terms of technological capability occurred during the period under investigation by including the initial gap in the levels of TFP among the establishments of different sizes as an explanatory variable (GAP). GAP captures the difference in the TFP levels for the establishments of different sizes. For each sector the size group of establishments with the highest TFP is given unity for the value of GAP, and for the remaining size groups the values of GAP reflect their TFP gap with the highest TFP. The estimated coefficient on GAP turns out to be positive and statistically significant. This finding that the technological gap among the establishments of different size groups narrowed over time indicates successful catching up.

To test the presence of size-specific effect on TFP growth, we included size dummy variables and their interaction terms with other variables.[13] The estimation results show that TFP growth was particularly high for the establishments with 50–99 employees (d6), and the catching up was particularly notable for the larger establishments (GAP*d8 and GAP*d9, 200 or more employees). The results on the interaction of PAH and size dummies show that holding patent or possession of technological capability is important to promote technological progress for the establishments with 100–199 employees (d7). Though not statistically significant, use of patents obtained from external sources (PAI) is likely to be effective in promoting technological capability for the establishments of small size, since the coefficients on size dummy variables are all negative.

A lack of effectiveness of policy loans for technological progress is particularly notable for the establishments with 50–99 employees. (PUB*d6) Indeed, for the establishments with 50–99 employees, policy loans are shown to retard technological progress. It is possible that provision of policy loans reduce incentives to improve technological capability, because it enables the establishments to maintain business without making much effort. Recognizing that there are various objectives of policy loans, ranging from modernization of equipment to employment protection, one has to conduct a more detailed analysis on the impact of policy loans by relating their objectives and their impacts to examine their effectiveness. Participation in subcontracting relationships is shown to promote technological progress for small establishments (SUB). Indeed, when compared with small establishments, subcontracting relationships are shown to play only a limited role in promoting technological progress for larger establishments, as the estimated coefficients on SUB*d7, SUB*d8, and SUB*d9 turned out to be negative and the coefficient on SUB*d9 is statistically significant.

Turning to the results on the determinants of TFP levels, we come up with more or less similar findings to those obtained for TFP growth. The results from the panel estimation with the fixed effect show that patent holding (PAH), patent introduction (PAI), and participation in subcontracting (SUB) have a significantly positive impact on improving technological level. The impact of policy loans (PUB) is shown to be negative and

TABLE VIII
The determinants of TFP

OLS Estimates	Dependent variable: TFP growth		Dependent variable: TFP levels	
	Without dummies	With time dummies	Without dummies	With time dummies
GAP	0.032899***	0.03033***		
PAH	0.000227*	0.000204*	0.003908***	0.003747***
PAI	5.91E-05**	6.82E-05**	0.001148***	0.001063***
PUB	–0.0003	–0.00216	–0.031	–0.03159
SUB	0.008796***	0.009517***	0.066728***	0.060297***
C	–0.00161		1.075465***	
r^2	0.1212	0.148	0.1091	0.1475
no	511	511	641	641
Panel estimates	Random effect	Fixed effect	Random effect	Fixed effect
GAP	0.036033***	0.090519***		
PAH	0.000209*	–4E-05	0.001111*	0.000792*
PAI	5.95E-05**	1.76E-05**	0.001061***	0.000964***
PUB	–0.00032	–0.00198	–0.01733	–0.01495
SUB	0.008591***	0.005042**	0.068599***	0.075172***
C	–0.00169	-1.657	1.081893***	
BP's LM test: chi^2 = 5.67 ***			BP's LM test: chi^2 = 517.95 ***	
Hausman test: chi^2 = 179.28 ***			Hausman test: chi^2 = 10.76 **	
OLS estimates with establishment size dummies				
d6	0.006232*		0.029118	
d7	–0.00364		0.008521	
d8	0.003897		0.065682**	
d9	0.001095		0.105771***	
GAP	0.047856***			
GAP*d6	0.03274**			
GAP*d7	0.007742			
GAP*d8	0.028609*			
GAP*d9	0.025971**			
PAH	-1.8E-05		–0.00028	
PAH*d6	0.000153		0.004056*	
PAH*d7	0.000533*		0.007177*	
PAH*d8	0.000259		0.003278	
PAH*d9	–0.00013		0.000743	
PAI	0.000709		0.006122	
PAI*d6	–0.00076		–0.00964**	
PAI*d7	–0.00049		–0.0084**	
PAI*d8	–0.00065		–0.00608	
PAI*d9	–0.00066		–0.00571	
PUB	–0.00108		–0.0126	
PUB*d6	–0.0422*		0.103517	
PUB*d7	0.014895		0.107127	
PUB*d8	–0.0255		–0.01286	
PUB*d9	0.00557		–0.01296	
SUB	0.005256**		0.177368***	
SUB*d6	0.004776*		–0.0682*	
SUB*d7	–0.00152		–0.04934*	
SUB*d8	–0.00309		–0.11041**	
SUB*d9	–0.01099**		–0.12685**	
r^2	0.452		0.5425	
nob	511		641	

Notes: GAP: Gap in TFP levels, PAT: Patent holding, PAI: Use of external patents, PUB: Policy loans, SUB: Subcontracting; d6: establishments with 50–99 employees, d7: establishments with 100–199 employees, d8: establishments with 200–299 employees, d8: establishments with 300+ employees ***, **, and * indicates statistical significance of 1, 5, and 10 percent by the two-tail test.

statistically insignificant. This finding may be interpreted in such a way that the sectors suffering from low TFP levels tend to receive policy loans.

The results of the estimation with size dummy variables and their interaction with other explanatory variables reveal several interesting observations, which are mostly consistent with the findings on TFP growth. Small establishments are found to register lower TFP levels compared with larger establishments, as the estimated coefficients on d8 and d9 are positive and statistically significant. This observation is consistent with the results in Table III. In-house technological capability indicated by patent holding (PAT) is shown to increase TFP levels for the establishments with 50–199 employees, while the use of industrial patents from external sources (PAI) is shown to prove effective in raising TFP levels for the small establishments with 30–49 employees. Subcontracting (SUB) is shown to provide an environment conducive to improve technological levels for small establishments with 30–49 employees.

5. Conclusions

Our analysis of TFP growth and TFP levels by establishment size reveals that small firms on average have lower TFP growth rates and lower TFP levels when compared with larger ones. However, there are several important exceptions to these patterns. In several machinery sectors, small establishments have not only higher TFP growth rates but also higher TFP levels. These observations indicate large variations in technological performance among small establishments in different sectors.

The results on the determinants of TFP growth and TFP levels showed that the use of external patents play important roles in promoting technological progress. These findings argue in favor of public support for improving technological capability and for facilitating the use of patents. Subsidies for R&D and for the purchase of patents appear to be justified on this ground. These policies should prove particularly effective for small- and medium-sized establishments. It is important to note that public assistance should be given directly to promote technological activities and not to support other kinds of activities through multi-purpose policy loans. Indeed, our results indicate that provision of policy loans has a negative impact on technological progress.

Acknowledgements

For helpful comments and discussions the authors thank Al Berry, Bee Yan Aw, and other participants of the project entitled The Role of Small and Medium Enterprises in Development organized by the World Bank Institute.

Notes

1 Since the methodology used in this analysis is basically the same as that used by a number of studies, our discussion on the methodology is brief. See, for example, Jorgenson and Nishimizu (1978) and Jorgenson et al. (1987) for detailed discussion.

2 A large number of studies examined the change in technology level and the difference in the level of technology for a variety of countries and for different time periods. For the case of Japan, see, for example, Jorgenson and Nishimizu (1978), Jorgenson et al. (1987), and Jorgenson and Kuroda (1990).

3 Nishimizu and Page (1991) provides concise discussion on the interpretation of technological change measured by the methodology applied here.

4 The data for the analysis are taken from MITI, *Kogyo Tokei Hyo* [*Census of Manufacturers*], which are deflated to be expressed in real terms. Specifically, values of output, material inputs, labor compensation, and the value of tangible assets are used for output, material inputs, labor inputs, and capital inputs, respectively. These data are deflated to make the comparison between the different time periods sensible by using the following price indices. The price indices of output and material inputs are taken from *SNA Input-Output Table* (Economic Planning Agency). The price index of hourly labor service is taken from *Monthly Survey* (Ministry of Labor). The price index of capital services, p_K, is estimated by using the following formula, $p_K = p_I(r + \delta - (p_I - p_{I-1})/p_I)$, where p_I is the price index of capital goods reported in *Fixed Capital Formation Matrix* (MITI), r is nominal rate of return, and δ is the depreciation rate (= depreciation/$(p_I K)$).

5 See Itoh and Urata (1994) for detailed discussion on this point.

6 Various types of support for in-house R&D have been provided by the central and local governments. They include preferential tax treatment and preferential loans. See Itoh and Urata (1994) for the details.

7 A study of SMEs in silverware, textiles, and machinery parts industries by Itoh and Urata (1994) reveals that in the early stages of industry development public technical assistance proved useful to the SMEs. But once the industry attained a certain level of development, technical assistance from public sources lost its effectiveness, and instead technical assistance from parent firms and equipment suppliers became quite useful.

[8] Small and Medium Enterprise Agency (1968).

[9] See the results from the survey conducted by the Science and Technology Agency in 1961, which was reported in Small and Medium Enterprise Agency (1963).

[10] Itami and others (1988) points out that severe competition among subcontractors was induced by parent firms in the Japanese automobile sector.

[11] The value of SUB for the establishments with more than 300 employees are shown to be zero in 1971. This is because the survey was conducted on SMEs and it excluded large firms.

[12] See Table II for the 19 manufacturing sectors. Seven establishment size groups include the employees with following sizes: 30–49, 50–99, 100–199, 200–299, 300–499, 500–999, and 1000–.

[13] In the estimation we included time dummy variables and industry dummy variables, but because of space we do not report the estimated results on these dummy variables.

References

Itami, Hiroyuki, Tadao Kagono, Takao Kobayashi, Kiyonori Sakakibara and Motoshige Itoh, 1988, *Kyoso to Kakushin: Jidosha Sangyo no Kigyo Seicho (Competition and Innovation: Growth of Automobile Industry)*, Tokyo: Toyo Keizai Shimpo-Sha. [In Japanese.]

Itoh, Motoshige and Shujiro Urata, 1994, 'Small and Medium Enterprise Support Policies in Japan', Policy Research Working Paper 1403. World Bank, Washington, D.C.

Jorgenson, Dale W. and Mieko Nishimizu, 1978, 'U.S. and Japanese Economic Growth 1952–1974: An International Comparison', *Economic Journal* **88**, 707–726.

Jorgenson, Dale W. and Masahiro Kuroda, 1990, 'Productivity and International Competitiveness in Japan and the United States', in C. R. Hulten (ed.), *Studies in Income and Wealth*, Chicago, Ill.: University of Chicago Press.

Jorgenson, Dale W., Masahiro Kuroda and Mieko Nishimizu, 1987, 'Japan-U.S. Industry-Level Productivity Comparisons 1960–1979', *Journal of the Japanese and International Economies* **1**, 1–30.

Kawai, Hiroki, 1999, 'Kigyo Dotai to Seisansei Henka (Firm Dynamics and Productivity Change)', Mimeo. Keio University. [In Japanese.]

Nishimizu, Mieko and Charles R. Hulten, 1978, 'The Sources of Japanese Economic Growth: 1955–1971', *Review of Economics and Statistics* **40**, 351–361.

Nishimizu, Mieko and John Page, 1991, 'Trade Policy, Market Orientation, and Productivity Change in Industry', in Jaime de Melo and Andre Sapir (eds.), *Trade Theory and Economic Reform: North, South, and East: Essays in Honor of Bela Balassa*, London: Basil Blackwell.

Small and Medium Enterprise Agency, 1963, *Chusho Kigyo Hakusho (White Paper on Small and Medium Enterprises)*, Tokyo: Small and Medium Enterprise Agency. [In Japanese.]

Small and Medium Enterprise Agency, 1968, *Chushokigyo Kindaika Chosa (Survey of Modernization by SMEs)*, Tokyo: Small and Medium Enterprise Agency. [In Japanese.]

Productivity Dynamics of Small and Medium Enterprises in Taiwan

Bee-Yan Aw

ABSTRACT. Using firm level data from Taiwan, this paper examines the link between firm size, growth and productivity. It shows that firms grow because they are more productive and not because they are larger in size. Indeed, the statistical analysis shows that while employment growth among Taiwanese firms was positively related to initial levels of total factor productivity, it was negatively related to initial size. The paper also shows that the productivity-size relationship has a virtuous cycle built in. More productive firms get larger and, in the process, obtain access to resources and information which enables them to become more productive. One implication of these results is that public policies should target productivity rather than size and should support reforms that make it possible for market mechanisms to weed out low productivity firms while facilitating the entry or growth of high productivity firms. Taiwan's ability to keep entry and exit costs low is one reason why productivity gains there have been high.

1. Introduction

Taiwan's real gross national product grew at an average of over 8 percent per year for three decades beginning in the early 1960s to the early 1990s. Two key features characterize this rapid and sustained growth: an export-oriented trade regime and a market structure based predominantly on small and medium enterprises (SMEs). The former has been part of Taiwan's industrial strategy since the late 1950s while the preponderance of SMEs began around the same time period and persists through the present day. A significant amount of research has focused on the roles of Taiwanese exporters and SMEs in the successful performance of the economy in general. However, the bulk of this research is either at the aggregate level or anecdotal in nature.

Department of Economics
The Pennsylvania State University
501 Kern Graduate Building
University Park
PA 16802
U.S.A.

The primary goal in this paper is to analyze the dynamic role of SMEs by using micro level data in the cross section as well as in the panel data. We quantify the magnitude and nature of turnover among SMEs as well as their level and growth of total factor productivity relative to large firms. It is a well known fact from research using micro data in both developed and developing countries that the levels and growth of productivity are positively correlated with firm size. We examine if this is also true of Taiwanese firms. For the purpose of policy, the critical issue is which comes first: higher productivity (leading to the growth in firm size) or large firms (leading to higher productivity). The first suggests that larger firm size reflects the self selection of more efficient producers that survive over time. The second indicates that larger firms, by virtue of their size and the advantages associated with greater resources or access to more resources, are able to adopt better techniques that result in higher productivity. Both explanations are consistent with the positive correlation between productivity and firm size in the cross section. In this paper we exploit our ability to track firms over time to address the issue of whether high levels of productivity precedes or proceeds from firms that grow significantly in size.

More specifically, we focus on the relationship between productivity and the movement of producers in and out of larger firm size categories. It is productivity differences between producers with different transition patterns, rather than just different firm size status, that are crucial to separating the selection versus size-specific advantage explanations. If self selection is shown to be more important, then policies that strengthen market selection forces are likely to result in the survival of the relatively more efficient producers and thus higher aggregate productivity. Alternatively, if the

Small Business Economics **18**: 69–84, 2002.

results suggest that producers' choice to be "large" leads directly to improvements in productivity over time, then there is some justification for policies supporting the entry and survival of such "large" firms.

In section 2 we report the results of a cross-sectional analysis of several key features that characterize SMEs in the Taiwanese manufacturing sector. In section 3 we use panel data to focus on the interaction of firm size with total factor productivity to arrive at a more complete understanding of the role of SMEs in economic development. Finally, we conclude with policy implications of our results in section 4. In the data appendix at the end of the paper, we describe the data set on which this study is based.

2. SMEs: Cross-sectional features

General characteristics

First, we document information on some general statistics of the manufacturing sector to provide the context for our analysis of SMEs. In Table I we note that while the number of firms increased by about 25 percent in each of the two five-year periods between census years, employment per firm has fluctuated from 20 in 1981 to 24 and 18 in 1986 and 1991, respectively. The aggregate data suggest that if firm size is measured in terms of employment, then average firm size underwent a small decline over the 10-year period. However, over the first five-year period, average capital stock doubled while average sales rose by 67 percent. Growth rate in sales per firm in the second five-year period remain positive although at about a third of the level of the 1981–1986 period. In this latter period there was a 50 percent growth in the capital stock per firm. It is interesting to note that the rate at which the average firm subcontracted out part of their production increased by 198 percent between 1981 and 1986 and 116 percent between 1986 and 1991.

The general impression from the figures in Table I suggests that while in terms of employment firm size has not changed dramatically, in terms of other variables, such as sales, capital stock, and subcontracting activities, the average firm appears to be "bigger" by the end of the 10-year period under study. Nevertheless, even at its largest, whether in terms of average employment or sales, those measures of firm size are smaller than the corresponding figures for other countries at similar levels of development.

Though the standard definition of SMEs are firms that employ 300 or fewer workers, over 90 percent of firms in Taiwan are SMEs by this criteria. In the analysis that follows we find it useful to decompose SMEs into micro (fewer than five workers), small (5–99 workers), and medium (100–299 workers) enterprises. Table II reports several key shares in each of the nine major industries in the manufacturing sector: those relating to total manufacturing firms, total manufacturing employment, and total value of output by the above firm size categories and year.

Four features stand out in the table. First, the overall average size distribution in each industry is relatively time invariant. The stability of the firm size distribution is especially apparent in several industries. Throughout the decade of the 1980s, the fabricated metals and nonelectrical industries have the highest concentration of micro-sized firms while chemicals and electric and electronics industries have among the lowest. Second, on average across all nine industries in the manufacturing sector for all three census years, about 30 percent of the firms are micro enterprises

TABLE I
General characteristics of manufacturing sector in Taiwan, 1981–1991

	1981	1986	1991
Number of firms	88,450	110,818	137,428
Employment per firm	20.12	24.0	18.89
Sales per firm (NT$'000)	17,300	28,800	34,400
Subcontracting expenditure per firm (NT$'000)	116	341	736
Subcontracting revenue per firm (NT$'000)	551	739	1,210
Capital stock per firm (NT$'000)	4,900	9,500	14,000

TABLE II
Distribution of firms among Taiwan's SMEs and their output and employment share in total manufacturing

Industry	1981			1986			1991		
	Micro	Small	Medium	Micro	Small	Medium	Micro	Small	Medium
Textiles:									
Firm share	0.27	0.58	0.10	0.21	0.65	0.10	0.24	0.68	0.03
Output share		0.45			0.56			0.63	
Labor share		0.52			0.66			0.70	
Clothing:									
Firm share	0.29	0.60	0.08	0.16	0.71	0.10	0.21	0.72	0.06
Output share		0.70			0.68			0.79	
Labor share		0.67			0.72			0.81	
Chemicals:									
Firm share	0.22	0.69	0.05	0.26	0.67	0.04	0.21	0.72	0.04
Output share		0.34			0.28			0.28	
Labor share		0.37			0.33			0.35	
Plastics:									
Firm share	0.37	0.55	0.06	0.25	0.67	0.06	0.30	0.68	0.02
Output share		0.59			0.61			0.67	
Labor share		0.74			0.73			0.84	
Basic metal:									
Firm share	0.29	0.66	0.05	0.26	0.69	0.04	0.26	0.70	0.03
Output share		0.83			0.64			0.59	
Labor share		0.87			0.76			0.72	
Fabricated metal:									
Firm share	0.57	0.42	0.01	0.50	0.49	0.01	0.48	0.51	0.01
Output share		0.90			0.88			0.88	
Labor share		0.94			0.92			0.94	
Nonelectrical mach:									
Firm share	0.48	0.51	0.01	0.37	0.62	0.01	0.35	0.64	0.01
Output share		0.81			0.82			0.83	
Labor share		0.88			0.90			0.90	
Electrical mach:									
Firm share	0.28	0.62	0.06	0.18	0.71	0.07	0.19	0.74	0.04
Output share		0.32			0.38			0.42	
Labor share		0.40			0.47			0.55	
Transportation:									
Firm share	0.33	0.60	0.05	0.23	0.71	0.05	0.24	0.72	0.04
Output share		0.39			0.43			0.38	
Labor share		0.70			0.65			0.66	

Note: Definition of size categories: micro ≤ 5 workers; small = 5–99 workers; medium = 100–299 workers.

employing fewer than five workers. Between 1981 and 1991, however, the highest gains have been made by firms classified as small firms (5–99 employees). With the exception of the fabricated metals industry, the share of firms in that size category alone ranged from 64 to 74 percent of all firms by 1991. Thus, for Taiwanese firms it is important that we keep in perspective the use of the standard definition of SMEs as firms employing fewer than 300 workers.

Third, SMEs in Taiwan, unlike those in more developed countries like the United States, make significant contributions to employment and total sales in the manufacturing sector. On average, more than 50 percent of total manufacturing employment, and at least one-third of total sales in every two-digit manufacturing industry, come from SMEs. The higher figures for employment share relative to output share that come from SMEs in each of the nine two-digit industry indicate that when compared with their larger counterparts, SMEs are relatively more labor intensive in production. Finally, both output and employment shares of this group of firms are increasing over time, implying their increasing importance over the period from 1981 to 1991.

It is clear from Table II that over 90 percent of firms in all principal manufacturing industries in Taiwan employ fewer than 100 workers. This feature is a result of very rapid turnover of firms in general and firms in these size categories in particular. Table III summarizes the size distribution of the entrants and exits into and out of the manufacturing sector, respectively.

Over the decade between 1981 and 1991, between three-quarters and four-fifths of the total number of entering and exiting firms in Taiwan are SMEs. Aw et al. (2001) document that the pattern of turnover in Taiwan's manufacturing sector is closely reflected in systematic productivity differences across firms and conclude that, unlike the finding in other countries, the turnover of Taiwanese enterprises through entry and exit play a significant role in explaining the increase in aggregate productivity growth generally because there are significant productivity differences between entering and exiting firms. Those groups account for a substantial share of total industry output. These results together with the observed high concentration of SMEs among entrants and exits imply that the productivity dynamics of the manufacturing sector in Taiwan is driven significantly by the contribution of a constantly evolving group of small businesses.

The dominance of small scale firms in Taiwan allows firms to enter production with relatively small amounts of capital, thus lowering the sunk costs of entry. Absent from the manufacturing landscape are large companies with big advertising budgets. In fact, there is little emphasis among Taiwan manufactures on brand or product differentiation thus reducing the need for such sunk advertising or R&D expenditures by entering firms (Hobday, 1995).[1] Anecdotal evidence emphasize the infinitely flexible characteristic of Taiwan's SMEs, adapt at switching businesses as market conditions dictate. This evidence further documents the fact this group of SMEs, by their sheer numbers, can collectively create a critical mass by exploiting the niches in a particular industry and, by so doing, compensate for the marketing inefficiencies of each undersized member. The specific feature that much of the evidence points to as being responsible for the flexible and efficient response to global shocks in demand and supply in Taiwan is the preponderance of its dense network of SME subcontractors.[2] The subcontracting activity itself is related closely with the ease of entry and exit and therefore low barriers to entering and exiting the business of producing in an industry.[3]

Thus in our analysis of the relationship between firm size and the growth in total factor productivity (TFP) in section 4, we incorporate information on firm level subcontracting activity into the regressions to proxy the flexibility of these firms over time.

Firm size and total factor productivity

To measure productivity at the firm level we use a modification of the multilateral index developed by Caves et al. (1981). In appendix 2, we describe the measure in detail both for the firm and for the

TABLE III
Size distribution of entering, exiting, and surviving firms, 1981–1986, 1986–1991

Share of	1981–1986			1986–1991		
	Micro/small	Medium	Large	Micro/small	Medium	Large
Total entrants	0.77	0.19	0.04	0.79	0.17	0.04
Total exits	0.79	0.17	0.05	0.78	0.17	0.05

Note: Micro/small: 1–99; medium: 100–299; large: > 300.

industry. We construct this index of firm-level TFP for each firm in each of the three census years 1981, 1986, and 1991.[4]

Table IV reports the results of the regression of firm productivity on year and firm size dummies for each of the nine two-digit industries. We also include a variable that measures the age of the firm. This variable accounts for the length of time that the firm has been in the market. Older firms have more experience in production and have also survived competition from other firms. Both those factors imply that age is positively correlated with TFP. However, younger firms may have higher productivity levels if those firms were to have newer and better technology, which would result in a negative correlation between age and TFP level. The net effect will depend on which of these forces is stronger. In Table IV, the figures in the second to last column indicate that in every industry productivity is positively and significantly correlated to firm age.

The intercept in column 1 of the table represents the mean productivity of the base group of firms; that is, those that employ fewer than five workers (micro-sized). The remaining coefficients from columns 2–4 measure the percentage difference in average productivity between those micro-sized firms and small (5–99 workers), medium

TABLE IV
Mean productivity differences across firms based on firm size[b]

Industry	Firm size categories[a]				Age	Test results[c]
	Intercept	Small	Medium	Large		
Textiles	–0.277* (0.008)	0.222* (0.007)	0.409* (0.012)	0.438* (0.018)	0.001** (0.0005)	1
Clothing	–0.245* (0.010)	0.197* (0.009)	0.376* (0.016)	0.389* (0.027)	0.001 (0.0007)	1
Paper/publishing	–0.187* (0.005)	0.151* (0.004)	0.370* (0.019)	0.471* (0.032)	0.001* (0.0003)	1, 2
Chemicals	–0.227* (0.016)	0.163* (0.013)	0.278* (0.029)	0.271* (0.033)	0.002** (0.0008)	1
Plastics	–0.188* (0.005)	0.146* (0.004)	0.304* (0.009)	0.337* (0.017)	0.004* (0.0003)	1
Basic Metal	–0.215* (0.009)	0.137* (0.007)	0.217* (0.018)	0.232* (0.038)	0.002* (0.0005)	1
Fabricated metal	–0.165* (0.003)	0.138* (0.003)	0.296* (0.013)	0.313* (0.030)	0.001* (0.0002)	1
Machinery	–0.115* (0.004)	0.137* (0.004)	0.304* (0.016)	0.338* (0.034)	0.002* (0.0003)	1
Electric/electronics	–0.214* (0.006)	0.145* (0.005)	0.226* (0.010)	0.238* (0.012)	0.004* (0.0004)	1
Transportation equipment	–0.196* (0.008)	0.158* (0.007)	0.287* (0.015)	0.382* (0.027)	0.002* (0.0005)	1, 2

* Statistically significant at 1%.
** Statistically significant at 5%.
[a] Definition of size categories: small = 5–99; medium = 100–299; large = 300+.
[b] All regressions include year dummies.
[c] 1. Reject equality of small and medium sized firms' coefficients at $\alpha = 0.05$ level.
2. Reject equality of medium and large sized firms' coefficients at $\alpha = 0.05$ level. Even at the cross-sectional level of analysis, the above results present a nonlinear relationship between productivity and firm size. There is a steep increase in total factor productivity from micro to small firms, which in turn are only slightly less productive than medium firms. Large firms do not have productivity levels that are significantly different from medium firms.

(100–299 workers) and large (300+ workers) firms, respectively. The positive and significant coefficients on the firm-size dummies for all nine industries indicate clearly higher levels of productivity of small, medium, and large firms relative micro-sized firms. What is more interesting is that the largest increase in efficiency is in the movement from micro to small firms, ranging from a 13.7 percent gain in nonelectrical machinery and basic metals to a 22.2 percent gain in textiles. The difference between small and medium firms is slightly less, ranging from an 8 percent gain in basic metal and electric/electronics to a 21.9 percent gain in paper and publishing. The difference is even less between medium and large firms. In the last column of the table we report the results of the tests of equality between the coefficients between small and medium sized firms and then between medium and large firms. For all nine industries we reject that the coefficients of small firms equal to those of medium firms; and for seven of the nine industries it is not possible to reject the hypothesis that average productivity is the same across the medium and large. Thus, the gains in productivity, at least in the cross section, flattens out significantly after firms reach medium size.

To summarize, the productivity advantage of increasing firm size is significant only among SMEs that employ fewer than 100 workers. Given that firm size is endogenous to various government policies as well as market selection mechanisms, a firm classified as a micro-sized firm today may very quickly exit/fail or grow into a medium/large firm tomorrow. As such, rather than treat firm size as given and examining how performance of firms vary with size at a given point, it is important to understand the interaction of firm size with productivity as well as the interaction of firm size with employment generation over time.

In the next section of this paper, we exploit information in the panel data to separate the sources higher levels and growth of total factor productivity more precisely, taking into account firms that not only continue production but those that fail and those that are new entrants into production.

3. Productivity dynamics of SMEs

Recent theoretical models of industry dynamics all begin with the assumption that producers within the same industry are heterogeneous in their productive efficiency. Another common thread running through the models is that differences in the evolution of productivity over time result in divergent paths of growth and failure of producers within the same industry. These models provide a very useful way in which to organize and view firm-level productivity and its interaction with firm size. We begin with a simple analysis of relating firm growth as measured by changes in employment at the firm-level with the productivity and size of the firm as measured in the initial time period. We then use the results obtained from this exercise to explore further the pattern of relationship between firm size and productivity change.

Table V displays the results of the regression of employment growth on productivity level and firm size in the initial period and a year dummy. The results indicate that initial levels of TFP are positively related to firm growth, and the relationship is statistically significant in all but two of the nine industries. Initial firm size is negatively correlated to firm growth, implying that larger firms have smaller growth in employment. Given that the regression focuses on growth rates in employment as the dependent variable, the regression does not include firms that are new entrants or exits in the industry. To have a clearer understanding of the relationship among the variables, we incorporate information on firms that enter and exit the industry into the analysis.

We make use of some of the cross-sectional results reported in section 3 as a basis of our analysis of how the relationship between firm size and productivity varies in the panel data. To organize the analysis, we separate firms into six cohorts based on the size of the firm as measured by employment between year t and year $t + 1$:

Firm Status	Year t	Year $t + 1$
Stay micro	<5 workers	<5 workers
Grew	<5 workers	≥5 workers
Stay SML	≥5 workers	≥5 workers
Entered micro	Does not exit	<5 workers
Entered SML	Does not exist	≥5 workers
Exit	<5 workers	ceased production

Note: SML: small, medium, or large firms.

TABLE V
Regression of employment growth by industry

	Constant	Initial firm size	Initial TFP	Year dummy
Textiles	1.775**	–0.378**	0.665**	–0.405**
	(0.128)	(0.032)	(0.166)	(0.094)
Apparel	2.111**	–0.388**	0.787	–0.642**
	(0.249)	(0.066)	(0.336)	(0.184)
Chemicals	1.359**	–0.250**	0.367	–0.424**
	(0.194)	(0.049)	(0.296)	(0.157)
Plastics	1.908**	–0.400**	0.782**	–0.674**
	(0.077)	(0.023)	(0.123)	(0.061)
Basic metals	1.740**	–0.342**	0.735*	–0.425**
	(0.199)	(0.053)	(0.291)	(0.147)
Fabricated metals	1.398**	–0.395**	1.266**	–0.284**
	(0.047)	(0.019)	(0.082)	(0.082)
Machinery	1.262**	–0.359**	0.485**	–0.075
	(0.055)	(0.021)	(0.090)	(0.045)
Electric/electronics	2.920**	–0.500**	2.114**	–1.093**
	(0.167)	(0.041)	(0.250)	(0.138)
Transportation	1.841**	–0.332**	0.125	–0.574**
	(0.155)	(0.043)	(0.241)	(0.116)

* Statistically significant at 1%.
** Statistically significant at 5%.

Given that the largest increase in TFP, as found in the regression of mean productivity levels on categories of firms of different sizes (Table III), is between firms that have fewer than 5 workers (micro) and small firms (5–99 workers), we define a firm as having grown in size as one that was observed to employ fewer than five workers in year t and more than five workers by year $t + 1$. Moreover, in many countries micro-sized firms are usually defined as those with fewer than five workers. The literature with respect to these micro-sized firms also suggests that micro firms are often distinctive in their organizational structure. For all these reasons the choice of five workers as the cutoff between firms that grew and those that did not is of most interest. Later in the paper, we will show that the regression results are independent of the exact definition of what constitutes micro-sized firms.

Firms in cohort 1 are those that stayed at employment levels of fewer than five workers (stay micro). Similarly, those that employed five workers or more in both year t and year $t + 1$ are classified under cohort 3 (stayed small or medium or large). New entrants are firms that observed for the first time in year $t + 1$ and are classified under cohort 4 if they started production with fewer than five workers (entered micro), but are under cohort 5 if they started production at levels of employment greater than five workers (entered small, medium, or large). Cohort 6 consists of firms that employed fewer than five workers in year t but ceased production five years later.

Several of the cohorts consist of firms that are likely to be very heterogeneous. For example, firms that we observe for the first time in 1991 could vary from one to four years old given the five-year intervals in our observations in the census data. To control for this dimension of the heterogeneity problem we include the age variable in the relative productivity regressions.

In Table VI we begin by comparing the productivity of the first five transition groups in year $t + 1$ to see, after accounting for firm age, if the transition patterns of firms is reflected in underlying productivity differences. The base category are the firms that stayed micro-sized throughout the period; that is, category 1 firms. The constant

TABLE VI
Mean productivity differences across firms based on transitions in and out of firm size

Categories	Differential					Age
	Constant	Grew	Stay[a]	Micro entrants	SML entrants	
Textiles	–0.193*	0.192*	0.343*	0.074*	0.284*	0.003*
	(0.018)	(0.028)	(0.018)	(0.018)	(0.017)	(0.001)
Clothing	–0.281*	0.080**	0.273*	0.032	0.250*	0.003*
	(0.027)	(0.040)	(0.027)	(0.028)	(0.026)	(0.001)
Paper/publishing	–0.209*	0.110*	0.193*	0.025*	0.167*	0.002*
	(0.008)	(0.012)	(0.008)	(0.008)	(0.008)	(0.000)
Chemicals	–0.088**	0.164*	0.267*	0.066	0.229*	0.002*
	(0.038)	(0.056)	(0.038)	(0.038)	(0.037)	(0.001)
Plastics	–0.118*	0.120*	0.222*	0.044*	0.187*	0.004*
	(0.010)	(0.014)	(0.010)	(0.010)	(0.009)	(0.000)
Basic metal	–0.140*	0.200*	0.245*	0.061*	0.191*	0.002*
	(0.023)	(0.034)	(0.024)	(0.023)	(0.023)	(0.001)
Fabricated metal	–0.146*	0.117*	0.182*	0.016*	0.148*	0.001*
	(0.005)	(0.008)	(0.005)	(0.005)	(0.004)	(0.000)
Machinery	–0.104*	0.095*	0.184*	0.020**	0.149*	0.001*
	(0.008)	(0.012)	(0.009)	(0.008)	(0.008)	(0.000)
Electric/electronics	–0.134*	0.100*	0.206*	0.030**	0.176*	0.004*
	(0.015)	(0.022)	(0.015)	(0.016)	(0.015)	(0.000)
Transportation equipment	–0.275*	0.097*	0.225*	0.035**	0.187*	0.002*
	(0.021)	(0.029)	(0.029)	(0.021)	(0.021)	(0.001)

* Statistically significant at 1%.
** Statistically significant at 5%.
Note: All regressions include year dummies.
[a] This represents small (5–99 workers), medium (100–299 workers), and large (300+ workers) firms.

term represents the average productivity of this base group of firms. Columns 2–5 measure the percentage deviation in average productivity between the base group and each of the other four categories. Not surprisingly, firms that stayed micro-sized over time is also the group with the lowest productivity. The magnitudes range from –0.281 in the clothing industry to –0.088 in chemicals. These are followed, in order of increasing productivity, by firms that are micro-sized entrants, firms that graduated from micro to SML enterprises, firms that entered as (larger than micro-sized) SML enterprises, and firms that remained SMLs over time.

Column 4 indicates that in only two of the nine industries micro-sized entrants were, on average, not significantly different than the firms that stayed micro-sized over time. In the other industries they were marginally (1.6–7.4 percent) more efficient than firms in the base category. In contrast, firms that made the transition from micro to one of the larger size categories (cohort 2) had average productivity levels that were 8–20 percent higher than those that stayed as micro-sized firms. The figures in the second to last column of the table represent firms that entered as SML enterprises (cohort 5). On average, these firms were about 15–28 percent more productive than firms that stayed micro. One possible explanation for the similarity in these magnitudes with firms that grew from micro to SML firms is that firms lumped together under cohort 5 are likely to be heterogeneous in characteristics, even after accounting for when they began business. In particular, some of the firms that technically entered as SML firms may be very similar to the ones that "grew" from the smallest size category by the time this latter group is first observed.

The size category that records the highest difference in productivity levels from the base category are those in cohort 3 (Stay SML). The figures in column 3 indicate that the average productivity of this group range from gains of 18–34 percent when compared with firms in the base category of firms.

To show that these results are insensitive to the specific cutoff size in employment used to determine firms that grow and those that do not, the above regressions were repeated by using the higher threshold levels of 10 as well as 20 workers in firm employment rather than five workers to determine which firms stayed the same size and which firms grew. With the cutoff at 10 or 20, the results essentially remains qualitatively unchanged.[5] In the case of the 20-worker cutoff, with the sole exception of the chemicals industry, the magnitude of the intercept terms for the other eight industries average about 10 percent higher when compared with the five worker cutoff. Given the higher cutoff this is reasonable and consistent with the strong positive relationship between size and productivity in the cross-section. The same qualitative results continue to hold in all nine industries under study: that firms that grew from micro/small size to medium/large firms have average productivity levels significantly higher than those that stayed micro/small and that these magnitudes in turn are only slightly smaller than the cohort of firms that either entered as medium/large firms or stayed in those size categories.

Though the information from examining Table VI reinforces the cross-sectional results that micro-sized firms suffer the greatest productivity disadvantage, it is also clear that those that survived and grew into larger firms have productivity levels significantly higher than those that did not. The important question from these results is, *Does higher productivity precede or proceed from a larger firm size?* We address this issue by focusing on firms that are micro-sized in year t and compare the average productivity in t and t + 1 between those that grew larger (cohort 2) and those that stayed micro-sized (cohort 1). If self-selection were important, then a producer's transition into or out of a larger size category should be reflected in initial productivity. If being in a larger size category were important, then those that grew should have subsequent productivity changes that are different from producers that do not grow. As before, to account for the degree of heterogeneity within each cohort, we include the age variable in the regression results reported in Table VII.

The second column in the table provides the percentage difference between these two groups in year t and column 3 reports the changes in the productivity differential in year $t + 1$. In every industry those firms that eventually grew from micro to small, medium, or large firms have significantly higher average productivity prior to this growth than those that did not grow and stayed micro. The differential varies from 6.5–17 percent across the nine industries. These deviations are statistically significant in all but one industry. In fact, if we were to compare the magnitudes in column 2 with those in column 2 of Table VI, then we find that, with the exception of the basic metal industry, the coefficients are not significantly different. This suggests that the bulk of the productivity advantage that the firms that grew larger existed in the pre-growth period. This result is consistent with the self-selection hypothesis.[6] Column 3 shows that the initial difference between the two groups does not widen in all the industries. This latter result indicates that there is little evidence that being "larger" per se leads to higher productivity.

Table VIII summarizes the difference in productivity between micro firms that fail (cohort 6) and those that survived but stayed micro (cohort 1). The second column reports the productivity differential in year t when all micro-sized firms are in production. A negative and significant coefficient indicates that firms that fail (exit production after year t) are less productive than their counterparts that survived but stayed the same size, a pattern consistent with productivity-driven selection on the exit side of the market. We observe this pattern in three major industries in Taiwanese manufacturing (textiles, plastics, and electric/electronics). The productivity gap varies from 3 to 7 percent. The coefficient is not significantly different than zero in the rest of the other industries. We conclude that the selection mechanism on the exit side is rather industry-specific.

TABLE VII
Mean productivity differences in initial productivity and subsequent productivity of firms that grew and those that stayed micro (<5 workers)

	Intercept	Before growth	After growth	Age	Year dummy
Textiles	–0.126*	0.169*	–0.058	–0.002	–0.013
	(0.024)	(0.032)	(0.045)	(0.002)	(0.027)
Clothing	–0.158*	0.073	–0.046	–0.003	–0.066
	(0.035)	(0.047)	(0.067)	(0.002)	(0.043)
Paper/publishing	–0.206*	0.103*	–0.007	–0.001	0.008
	(0.009)	(0.012)	(0.018)	(0.001)	(0.011)
Chemicals	–0.045	0.144**	–0.042	0.0002	–0.028
	(0.066)	(0.074)	(0.106)	(0.005)	(0.069)
Plastics	–0.126*	0.094*	–0.033	0.003*	0.042**
	(0.012)	(0.015)	(0.022)	(0.001)	(0.014)
Basic metal	–0.128*	0.114**	0.066	0.0003	0.017
	(0.034)	(0.040)	(0.057)	(0.003)	(0.037)
Fabricated metal	–0.131*	0.092*	–0.016	0.0002	–0.003
	(0.005)	(0.008)	(0.011)	(0.0004)	(0.006)
Machinery	–0.127*	0.086*	–0.033	0.0002	0.053*
	(0.009)	(0.012)	–(0.017)	(0.001)	(0.011)
Electric/electronics	–0.074*	0.071**	–0.005	0.004*	–0.023
	(0.020)	(0.024)	(0.035)	(0.002)	(0.025)
Transportation equipment	–0.236*	0.065**	–0.040	–0.005*	0.037
	(0.025)	(0.030)	(0.043)	(0.002)	(0.030)

* Statistically significant at 1%.
** Statistically significant at 5%.

In summary, one of the key sources of the low productivity of micro firms that we observed in the cross section in Table IV is that the figure is an average of four different types of micro firms in that year: those that failed in year $t + 1$, those that survived but stayed micro, those that entered as micro-sized firms, and, finally, those that grew bigger. Tables V–VII imply that those micro firms that failed have the lowest productivity followed, in order of increasing productivity, by those that survived but stayed micro to those that entered as micro firms and those that grew. More important, our results indicate very clearly that the higher productivity of firms that grew relative to those that did not existed in the period before growth occurred. This pattern is exactly what one would expect in the context of strong self-selection forces, suggesting that it is not their size per se that dooms a micro firm to low productivity. Those that are more productive among them survive and are more likely to grow larger and have average productivity levels that converge to those of larger firms. We next analyze the relationship between firm size and productivity growth.

4. TFP growth and firm size

One of our key findings in this paper provides further insight into the nature of the interaction between firm size and productivity growth. That is, good performance in the form of high levels (and growth) of productivity is clearly not the prerogative of large firms, a very common result in numerous countries for which micro-level analysis have been performed. Micro-sized producers (fewer than five workers) that eventually cross this employment threshold are shown to have, in the pre-growth time frame, levels of productivity that are only at a small disadvantage to their larger and more resource-filled counterparts. The same holds

TABLE VIII
Mean productivity differences in initial productivity of firms that exited and firms that stayed micro (<5 workers)

	Intercept	Before exit	Age	Year 75
Textiles	–0.203*	–0.046**	–0.003*	0.116*
	(0.029)	(0.027)	(0.001)	(0.019)
Clothing	–0.229	0.006	–0.002	–0.007
	(0.048)	(0.044)	(0.002)	(0.024)
Paper/publishing	–0.216*	0.011	–0.0003	0.016
	(0.012)	(0.012)	(0.001)	(0.010)
Chemicals	–0.209**	0.032	0.001	0.185*
	(0.091)	(0.086)	(0.004)	(0.044)
Plastics	–0.165*	–0.025**	0.003*	0.092*
	(0.016)	(0.014)	(0.001)	(0.010)
Basic metal	–0.210*	0.023	–0.003**	0.136*
	(0.051)	(0.049)	(0.002)	(0.020)
Fabricated metal	–0.156*	–0.002	–0.0002	0.032*
	(0.007)	(0.007)	(0.001)	(0.006)
Machinery	–0.187*	–0.007	0.001	0.068*
	(0.013)	(0.012)	(0.001)	(0.009)
Electric/electronics	–0.151*	–0.067**	0.003**	0.129*
	(0.027)	0.025)	(0.002)	(0.015)
Transportation equipment	–0.226*	0.038	–0.001	–0.025
	(0.034)	(0.033)	(0.002)	(0.017)

* Statistically significant at 5%.
** Statistically significant at 10%.

true for small firms employing from 5 to 100 workers. A related point is that, of the heterogeneous group of producers in both these size categories, the ones with low productivity levels generally end up exiting the industry, leaving behind the relatively more efficient firms. As was pointed out in section 2, the reason for the apparent strong market selection forces is likely to be related to low sunk costs of entry and exit owing to the dense network of subcontractors in the economy.

For subcontracting to play an important role in lowering the sunk costs of entry for potential entrants into an industry, it must be the case that potential entrants into an industry can start up production at a small scale as subcontractors for other firms; that is, making some component in the middle of a long chain of supply. Alternatively, the network of subcontract services available must be available to all firms, large and small, so that it is feasible for potential entrants to start production with very small investments of their own; that is, relying on other firms for part of the production process. These views are consistent with our findings that entrants (and exits) are concentrated among micro to small firms and that the rapid growth of the value of subcontract services in the manufacturing sector of Taiwan between 1981 and 1991 is also increasingly concentrated among firms in the same size category.

In the TFP growth regression, in addition to the firm size dummies, we also include firm age and the share of firm revenue that comes from the firm's subcontracting activity. The age of the firm not only reflects the firm's experience in production but also the vintage of the firm's capital and technology. Clearly, productivity growth and firm access and use of modern technology are likely to be positively correlated. Table IX reports the results of this regression. As before, the base category are continuing micro-sized firms, and columns 2–4 display the coefficients as deviations

TABLE IX
Regression of TFP growth on firm size, age, and subcontracting activity by industry

	Constant	Small	Medium	Large	Year dummy	Age	Subcontracting
Textiles	–0.141*	0.174*	0.313*	0.324*	0.012	–0.006*	–0.357**
	(0.070)	(0.064)	(0.068)	(0.074)	(0.032)	(0.002)	(0.164)
Apparel	–0.548*	0.425*	0.484*	0.545*	0.109**	0.001	–0.304
	(0.108)	(0.108)	(0.111)	(0.122)	(0.045)	(0.004)	(0.269)
Chemicals	0.197	0.132	–0.141	0.013	–0.205	–0.001	-1.673
	(0.411)	(0.312)	(0.462)	(0.320)	(0.314)	(0.016)	(5.299)
Plastics	–0.145	0.089	0.099	0.125	0.098*	–0.002	0.194
	(0.070)	(0.063)	(0.072)	(0.086)	(0.038)	(0.003)	(0.237)
Basic metals	0.367**	–0.218	–0.050	–0.064	–0.145**	–0.001	0.316
	(0.153)	(0.140)	(0.154)	(0.174)	(0.067)	(0.004)	(0.613)
Fabricated metals	–0.109**	0.064**	0.055	0.277**	–0.006	–0.0004	–0.020
	(0.046)	(0.032)	(0.058)	(0.110)	(0.038)	(0.002)	(0.166)
Machinery	–0.104	0.008	–0.013	–0.042	0.021	0.003	0.059
	(0.62)	(0.042)	(0.092)	(0.179)	(0.049)	(0.003)	(0.192)
Electric/electronics	–0.075	0.089	0.177**	0.173**	0.135**	–0.005	0.237
	(0.073)	(0.062)	(0.071)	(0.079)	(0.043)	(0.003)	(0.254)
Transportation	–0.161	–0.017	0.152	0.296**	0.069	–0.004	0.285
	(0.092)	(0.075)	(0.091)	(0.151)	(0.071)	(0.004)	(0.283)

Note: The definition of size are as follows: small (5–99 workers), medium (100–299 workers), and large (300+ workers) firms.

of average TFP growth of continuing firms in the small-, medium-, and large-size categories from the average TFP growth of continuing micro firms.

The results on the correlates of TFP growth are much more mixed than the ones relating to levels of productivity. They indicate that, conditional on survival, in four of the nine industries (chemicals, plastics, basic metals, and machinery) there is no statistically significant relationship between TFP growth and firm size. The productivity growth of micro-sized firms are not significantly different from their larger counterparts. However, in the other five industries there is a positive relationship between firm size and productivity growth. In textiles and apparel this relationship is monotonic with TFP growth progressively increasing with each firm size category. In the remaining industries the positive relationship is statistically significant only in firms employing 100 or more workers (electric/electronics) or 300 or more workers (fabricated metals and transportation equipment). Except for the textiles industry, firm age and the degree of subcontracting activity by the firm are not significantly correlated with TFP growth. It is very possible that the share of subcontracting in firm revenue is too aggregate a measure to proxy for the degree of flexibility possessed by the firm in responding to exogenous changes.

5. Conclusions

There are two main findings from this study on SMEs in the manufacturing sector in Taiwan. The first is that firms with higher initial levels of productivity are more likely to survive and grow in size. This pattern is consistent with models of self selection. Our findings indicate that it is the process of survival and growth rather than the absolute size to which firms grow into that appears to be important. For example, firms that graduate from micro to small firms are just as likely to achieve productivity levels that converge toward those of large firms as firms that graduate from small to medium firm size.

The second finding is that the growth in productivity in several of Taiwan's major industries is positively related to firm size, suggesting that in these industries micro firms that survive and grow bigger have higher growth in TFP.

It is quite clear that in general incentives that target a specific firm size are likely to be ineffective in encouraging higher productivity. The highest levels of productivity are achieved by firms that survive and grow in size over time. This observation applies equally to firms that employ fewer than five workers as to those with many times more employees. The results reflect strong market selection forces that are in place in Taiwan where we find that these forces are clearly important in explaining high aggregate productivity growth. For Taiwan, further strengthening market selection forces may require reducing the imperfections in the capital market to allow all firms access to loans at market interest rates.

For other countries, strengthening the process of market selection may involve reducing barriers to entry into and exit from an industry in production as well as in the export market. This process of creative destruction requires that the economy be flexible in the sense that it is easy for new companies to start up and existing ones that are no longer competitive to fail. Our finding of extremely high turnover among firms in Taiwan, especially among small businesses, is consistent with low costs of entering and exiting production and the export market. Part of the explanation for these low costs rests with the small scale, low – capital-intensive industries in which firms often cluster around. Entrants can easily start up business as subcontractors for other firms and in so doing have a ready market for their output without developing brands of their own. This reduces the need for expensive advertising and research.

Our findings also indicate that even small businesses are able to subcontract the production of many of their components. This means that they do not need to spend much on fixed assets, such as machinery, which, in turn, reduces the costs of exiting the market. Thus the low costs of entry and exit made possible by this dense network of subcontracting relationships among firms in a given industry means that the economy is in a good position to respond to demand and supply shocks in the global economy. For instance, during a boom in demand, firms are likely to use more subcontractors, which, in turn, encourage more firms to enter the industry. Conversely during recessions, firms cut down on the amount of subcontracting work, encouraging some firms to exit the market. Thus, the subcontracting network can be a great absorber of domestic and global shocks and allows the economy to adjust to both rapid growth as well as to sudden economic contraction.

Acknowledgements

The author is grateful for helpful comments from David Audretsch, Albert Berry, Hiroki Kawai, Carl Liedholm and other participants of the project entitled The Role of Small and Medium Enterprises in Development, organized by the World Bank Institute.

Appendix 1

Our database is a compilation of the last three Industrial and Commercial Census collected by the Statistical Bureau of Taiwan's Executive Yuan. It covers the years 1981, 1986, and 1991. The Statistical Bureau collects detailed data on each of the firms in operation in the manufacturing sector, which was more than 88,000 firms in 1981 and more than 100,000 manufacturing firms in each of the latter two census years. The firm observations not only provide complete cross-sectional coverage of the manufacturing sector but are matched across the censuses so that individual firms can be followed over time, allowing measurement of firm turnover and firm growth. The panel data are unbalanced so that we have information on cohorts of firms that survive across census years, enter as new firms, or exit the industry in a given census year.

All three Industrial Censuses provide information on the output and input variables necessary to measure total factor productivity at the firm-level: sales, employment, book value of the capital stock, and expenditures on labor and different types of intermediate inputs.[7]

Firm output is defined as total firm sales deflated by a wholesale price index defined at the two-digit industry level. There are two weaknesses to this measure. First, we are not able to measure the firm's inventories of final output in each census year so we are not able to distinguish firm sales from firm production in the year. The latter is preferable in productivity studies. The second weakness is that there is no information on firm-level output prices to use in deflating firm sales. Though this is a limitation of virtually all productivity studies, it does create the possibility that TFP estimates at the firm level will be biased in a way that is related to firm size. If large firms were to have lower (higher) output prices than small firms, then the use of a common industry price deflator would underestimate (overestimate) the real output of large producers and overestimate (underestimate) the output of small firms, leading to a systematic bias in firm TFP across the firm size distribution. In a separate project (Aw et al., 2001) we have been able to analyze firm-level output prices for Taiwan's electronics producers, and, though prices do vary across firms, we have found no systematic relationship between output price and firm size or the output market, export versus domestic, in which the output is sold.

We model each firm as using four inputs in production: labor, capital, materials, and subcontracting services. The labor input is measured as the number of production plus nonproduction workers. We do not have information on the mix of worker skills in the firm and so are not able to account for improvements in labor quality over time. Total payments to labor are measured as total salaries to both groups. We do not have data on nonwage benefits paid by the firm.

The measure of capital input is the book value of capital stock of the firm. To attempt to control for price level changes in new capital goods that will cause the book value of firms to change over time as they invest in new equipment, we deflate the change in each firm's book value by a price index for new capital goods. For example, to convert the firm capital values in 1991 to the same basis as reported in 1986, we calculate the change in each firm's reported book value between 1986 and 1991, deflate this using an industry-specific price index for new capital goods, and then add this deflated value to the firms reported book value in 1986. Though much cruder than constructing perpetual inventory capital stocks, this procedure does recognize both the level differences in the firms' capital, which are important in the cross-section, and the fact that later additions to each firm's capital stock partly reflect general price level increases. A similar procedure is used to scale the 1981 book values to the 1986 basis. Finally we note that price changes for new capital goods are generally small, averaging less than one percent per year for most industries, so that comparisons of book values over time probably do not greatly distort the growth in capital stocks. The firm's expenditure share on capital is calculated as the residual after subtracting the expenditure on labor, material inputs, and subcontracting from the firm's sales.

The material input includes the raw materials, fuel, and electricity used by the firm. Expenditures on these categories are converted to 1986 dollars. Raw material expenditures are deflated by a general producer price index that covers both manufacturing and nonmanufacturing output in the country. Fuel and electricity expenditures are deflated by an energy price index. These deflators are the same for all industries. The subcontracting input is included as a separate factor because, while small as a share of a typical firm's total cost, it has risen in importance over the time period we study. This input is not used by all firms, although it has become more widely used over time, and failing to account for it would mean that we systematically underestimate the inputs used by firms that hired subcontractors relative to those that did everything internally. The would lead us to overestimate TFP for firms that used subcontractors relative to those that did not. In the census data a firm that out-sources some of the production steps to a subcontractor generally transfers material inputs to the subcontractor. The value of those transferred material inputs are not reported separately but are included with the hiring firm's expenditure on materials. The hiring firm also reports its payments to subcontractors, which effectively represents the cost to the hiring firm of using the labor and equipment services of the subcontractors as well as the latters' expenses for fuel and electricity. To construct a subcontracting input, we deflate the firm's payments to subcontractors by the output price of the industry in which the firm operates. If we had information on the precise step of the production process in which the subcontractor was involved and more disaggregated price deflators, then it might be possible to use a more accurate price deflator for the subcontracting input. Neither of those pieces of information is available. Our correction, however, attempts to recognize that the inputs of firms that subcontract some of the production steps to others need to be increased, and thus their TFP reduced, relative to the firms that do not subcontract.[8]

Appendix 2

Measurement of firm and industry total factor productivity

By using the Taiwanese manufacturing data, we construct an index of firm-level TFP for each firm in each of the three census years 1981, 1986, and 1991.[9] A multilateral index useful for measuring inputs, outputs, and TFP in firm-level panel data sets was developed by Caves et al. (1982). It has been used to measure productivity in U.S. airlines by Caves et al. (1981) and to measure import prices by country-of-origin by Aw and Roberts (1988). The multilateral index relies on a single reference point that is constructed as a hypothetical firm with input revenue shares that equal the arithmetic mean revenue shares over all observations and input levels that equal the geometric mean of the inputs (which is equivalent to the arithmetic mean of the log of the inputs) over all observations. Each firm's output, inputs, and/or productivity in each year is measured relative to this hypothetical firm, and the multilateral index provides transitive comparisons between any subset of the observations.

Good et al. (1997) discuss an extension of the multilateral index that uses a separate hypothetical-firm reference point for each cross-section of observations and then chain-links the reference points together over time in much the same way as the conventional Tornqvist index of productivity growth. This productivity index is particularly useful in our application because it provides a consistent way of summarizing the cross-sectional distribution of firm productivity, using only information specific to that time period, and how the distribution moves over time.

Let each firm f produce a single output Y_{ft} by using the set of inputs X_{ift} where $i = 1, 2, \ldots n$. The total factor productivity index for firm f in year t is defined as

$$ln\ \mathrm{TFP}_{ft} = (ln\ Y_{ft} - \overline{ln\ Y_t}) + \sum_{s=2}^{t} (\overline{ln\ Y_s} - \overline{ln\ Y_{s-1}})$$

$$\sum_{i=1}^{n} \frac{1}{2} (S_{ift} + \overline{S_{it}}) (ln\ X_{ift} - \overline{ln\ X_{it}})$$

$$\sum_{s=2}^{t} \sum_{i=1}^{n} \frac{1}{2} (\overline{S_{is}} + \overline{S_{is1}}) (\overline{ln\ X_{is}} - \overline{ln\ X_{is1}}). \quad (1)$$

In this formula the input weights S_{ift} are the share of the firm's total revenue attributable to input X_i. The overbars denote the average value over all firms in year *t*. The index provides a measure of the proportional difference in TFP for firm *f* in year *t* relative to the hypothetical firm in the base time period. In our application we will use 1981 as the base time period.

Industry productivity is defined as the market-share weighted sum of the firm productivity levels:

$$ln\ \mathrm{TFP}_t = \sum_f \theta_{ft}\ ln\ \mathrm{TFP}_{ft}$$

where firm productivity is defined in equation (1) and θ_{ft} is the value of firm *f* sales relative to total industry sales in year *t*.

Notes

[1] This is evidenced by the common observation that most would be hard pressed to name a single Taiwanese firm. The bulk of Taiwanese producers operate in small, young, and often inconspicuous firms making seemingly obscure products, such as small metal fittings or machine tools, that eventually end up as a branded product sold by large enterprises in the international market.

[2] In a field survey, Levy and Kuo (1991) find evidence that firms entering the electronics industry are often characterized by modest up-front investment and that the companies subcontract the manufacturing of a substantial number of components of the finished product. They find that it is not uncommon for firms to have as many subcontractors as employees. In fact, it is believed that the business network in Taiwan is so dense that local subcontractors can usually be found for everything a particular firm needs to begin production of its specialty, enabling firms to horizontally integrate across the entire industry.

[3] The other side of the coin to a firm's spending on subcontracting out some component in the middle of a long supply chain is the firm's providing subcontract services that earns the firm revenue.

[4] Tybout (1996a) discusses alternative productivity measures based on econometric estimation of production functions and summarizes the literature on the sources of productivity differences across producers. Olley and Pakes (1996) develop an econometric methodology for estimating production functions consistent with a dynamic, stochastic model of industry development and use it to study productivity growth in the U.S. telecommunications industry.

[5] We do not report any of these results in detail, but they are available from the author.

[6] Aw, Chung, and Roberts (2000) find that the key explanation for the higher productivity of Taiwanese exporters relative to nonexporters is the selection of more productive forms into the export market.

[7] The type of data collected in the Taiwan manufacturing census is very similar to what is collected in the United States (see Baily et al. (1992) for its use in productivity measurement) or in the developing countries analyzed in Roberts (1996) and Tybout (1996a).

[8] The firms that engage in subcontracting are not included in the set of firms whose productivity we study. The census data report a zero value of sales for these firms. Also, most of the material inputs they use are not reported by the subcontracting firm but instead are reported as material purchases by the firm that hires the subcontractor. Thus there is no way to construct productivity measures for subcontractors that are comparable to the measures we construct for the firms we analyze.

[9] Tybout (1996a) discusses alternative productivitymeasures based on econometric estimation of production functions and summarizes the literature on the sources of productivity differences across producers. Olley and Pakes (1996) develop an econometric methodology for estimating production functions that is consistent with a dynamic, stochastic model of industry development and use it to study productivity growth in the U.S. telecommunications industry.

References

Aw, Bee-Yan and Mark J. Roberts, 1988, 'Price and Quality Comparisons for U.S. Footwear Imports: An Application of Multilateral Index Numbers', in Robert C. Feenstra (ed.), *Empirical Methods for International Trade*, Cambridge, Mass.: MIT Press.

Aw, Bee-Yan, Geeta Batra and Mark J. Roberts, 2001, 'Firm Heterogeneity and Export-domestic Price Differentials: A Study of Taiwanese Electronics Products', *Journal of International Economics* **54**, 149–169.

Aw, Bee-Yan, Xiaomin Chen and Mark J. Roberts, 2001, 'Firm-Level Evidence on Productivity Differentials and Turnover in Taiwanese Manufacturing', *Journal of Development Economics* **66**, 51–86.

Aw, Bee-Yan, Sukkyun Chung and Mark J. Roberts, 2000, 'Productivity and Turnover in the Export Market: Micro-Evidence From Taiwan and South Korea', *World Bank Economic Review* **14**, 65–90.

Baily, Martin Neil, Charles Hulten and David Campbell, 1992, 'Productivity Dynamics in Manufacturing Plants', Brookings Papers on Economic Activity: Microeconomics 1992. Brookings Institution, Washington, D.C.

Caves, Douglas W., Laurits Christensen and Erwin Diewert, 1982, 'Output, Input, and Productivity Using Superlative Index Numbers', *Economic Journal* **92**, 73–96.

Caves, Douglas W., Laurits Christensen and Michael Tretheway, 1981, 'U.S. trunk Air Carriers, 1972–1977: A Multilateral Comparison of Total Factor Productivity', in Thomas Cowing and Rodney E. Stevenson (eds.), *Productivity Measurement in Regulated Industries*, New York: Academic Press.

Good, David H., M. Ishaq Nadiri and Robin Sickles, 1997, 'Index Number and Factor Demand Approaches to the Estimation of Productivity', in Hashem Pesaran and Peter Schmidt (eds.), *Handbook of Applied Econometrics*, Vol. II: *Microeconometrics*, Oxford: Basil Blackwell.

Hobday, Michael, 1995, *Innovation in East Asia: The Challenge to Japan*, Hampshire, U.K.: Edward Elgar.

Levy, Brian and Wen-Jeng Kuo, 1991, 'Strategic Orientations of Firms and the Performance of Korea and Taiwan in

Frontier Industries: Lessons from Comparative Case Studies of Keyboard and Personal Computer Assembly', *World Development* **19**(4), 363–374.

Olley, G. Steven and Ariel Pakes, 1996, 'The Dynamics of Productivity in the Telecommunications Equipment Industry', *Econometrica* **64**, 1263–1297.

Pack, Howard, 1992, 'New Perspectives on Industrial Growth in Taiwan', in Gustav Ranis (ed.), *Taiwan From Developing to Mature Economy*, Boulder, Colo.: Westview Press.

Roberts, Mark J., 1996, 'Colombia, 1977–1985: Producer Turnover, Margins and Trade Exposure', in Mark J. Roberts and James R. Tybout (eds.), *Industrial Evolution in Developing Countries: Micro Patterns of Turnover, Productivity, and Market Structure*, Oxford: Oxford University Press.

Tybout, James R., 1996a, 'Chile, 1976–1986: Trade Liberalization and its Aftermath', in Mark J. Roberts and James R. Tybout (eds.), *Industrial Evolution in Developing Countries: Micro Patterns of Turnover, Productivity, and Market Structure*, Oxford: Oxford University Press.

Tybout, James R., 1996b, 'Heterogeneity and Productivity Growth: Assessing the Evidence', in Mark J. Roberts and James R. Tybout (eds.), *Industrial Evolution in Developing Countries: Micro Patterns of Turnover, Productivity, and Market Structure*, Oxford: Oxford University Press.

Small and Medium Enterprises in Korea: Achievements, Constraints and Policy Issues

Jeffrey B. Nugent
Seung-Jae Yhee

ABSTRACT. This paper provides an overview of the evolution of the small and medium enterprise sector in Korea during the past quarter century. It shows how the industrial structure of Korea has changed dramatically over this period reflecting much greater shares in employment and value added by SMEs. It reviews the evidence on SME dynamism showing that SMEs have contributed to the enormous transformations that have taken place in the Korean economy since 1975, especially with regard to exports, foreign investment and productivity performance. It discusses the role of subcontracting as well as that of government and non-governmental institutions in supporting SME development. Finally, it examines the link between variations in the economic importance of SMEs, as measured by their shares in employment, and aspects of growth and inequality to assess whether SMEs function as business cycle shock absorbers and inequality-reducing mechanisms.

Introduction

Virtually nowhere has the relative role of small and medium enterprises (SMEs) in the country changed as much over time as in South Korea (henceforth Korea). The role of its SMEs has gone through at least two very distinct phases, one of sharp decline (from the early 1960s to about 1976), and one in which that role has been gradually increasing (from 1976 to at least quite recently). With the currency and monetary crisis of 1997–99, and a relative decline in investment in SMEs since the mid-1990s, however, it is quite possible that the latter trend has been stalled and beginning to be reversed once again. Whether this is only a temporary stall or a turning point to another period of relative SME decline remains to be seen and may hinge on the way in which the crisis is resolved.

SMEs dominated the manufacturing sector of the economy in the early 1960s but by the mid-1970s, Korea had become known for the extreme dominance in economic and public policy of its large *chaebol* (conglomerate) firms in the economy. Indeed, it had become so much large firm and *chaebol*-oriented that Korea has often been contrasted with other East Asian economies like Japan and Taiwan where SMEs have continued to play a comparatively much more important role.[1] Less well known is that since the mid-to-late 1970s there has been a steady decline in the dominance of large firms and a corresponding rise in the role of SMEs in all aspects of manufacturing activity. The dramatic rise of the *chaebol* and the Korean economy as a whole has been closely linked to an especially cozy relation between government and business and to the country's development strategy.

Whether Korea's economic development has been helped or hurt by the country's development strategy is still hotly debated, as is of course the extent to which the financial and currency crisis of the last two years can be attributed to the excessive power and international borrowing of the *chaebol*. Even more controversial is what, if anything, should be done to correct the widely perceived excesses of the *chaebol* and government policies in support of them. Meanwhile, gradually and especially since the early 1980s, the Korean government has instituted a whole host of policies designed to assist SMEs. But, there is little evidence to date as to whether these policies have had any significant effects and, if so, whether or not these policies have been cost-effective in

Department of Economics
University of Southern California
University Park
Los Angeles, CA 80089
U.S.A.
E-mail: nugent@rcf.usc.edu

Small Business Economics **18**: 85–119, 2002.

social terms. Coinciding with the resurgence in SME shares in manufacturing employment and exports, as will be demonstrated in Section 7, there has been a decline in income inequality. If it could be shown that SME support policies were effective and that the trends in SME shares and income inequality were related, lower inequality could indeed be one social benefit of such policies.

The purpose of this study is to identify achievements, problems, and policy issues concerning Korea's SMEs. Attempts are made to deal with dynamic issues despite the lack of access to a panel dataset well suited for analyzing such issues. The Korean experience is bound to have important lessons for other developing countries for several reasons. First, because of the extremely rapid growth of the South Korean economy (averaging over 8 percent per annum in the last 35 years). Second, because of the country's tremendous success in penetrating international markets in manufacturing and in acquiring and developing new technology. Third, because the aforementioned success has been accomplished without an appreciable increase in income inequality. Fourth, because of the several changes in role and importance of SMEs in the economy. Finally, the Korean experience is useful because of the country's important changes in policy regimes.

This study is divided into seven sections. Section 1 provides an overview of the changing importance and roles of SMEs over time. Section 2 treats productivity and growth therein over time by size of establishment (or firm) and by sector. Section 3 is devoted to firm dynamics and dynamic issues. Sections 4 and 5 are devoted to external sources of support for SMEs: Section 4 to support available through subcontracting relationships with private firms, and Section 5 to support from governmental and other nonprofit institutions, sectoral associations, and government policies. The possible roles of SMEs as shock absorbers in business cycle fluctuations and in mitigating income inequality are discussed in Section 6. Finally, our conclusions, including the lessons for other developing countries, are given in Section 7.

1. Changing importance and roles of SMEs over time

In virtually all dimensions, the role of SMEs in the Korean economy has been ever-changing. In general, and in most dimensions, there have been at least two and possibly three or four distinct and opposing trends. First, an upward trend (in the share of SMEs in both establishments and employment at least) in the 1950s; second, a declining trend in the SME share from the early 1960s to the mid-to-late 1970s; third, an again rising trend until the mid-1990s; and, since then, a stalling or even possibly a reversal in that trend. Evidence for the first and the last of these possible trends, however, is much weaker than for the others.

The basic trends can be observed in Table I. This table presents the size shares of both SMEs and large establishments (LEs)[2] in terms of number of establishments, employment, value added, and production in the manufacturing sector. As noted by the break in the table and as explained in the note to the table, the official size cutoff between SMEs and LEs changed from 200 employees to 300 after 1973, making the top part of the table not exactly comparable to the bottom part.[3] There are also some differences in the years of the turning points among the different dimensions. For example, in the case of number of establishments, the first turning point occurred only in 1966, whereas for employment it occurred in 1960. Similarly, the second turning point occurred only in 1975 for both numbers of establishments and employment but in 1970 for both value added and production. In the case of both value added and production, moreover, a new trend reversal of declining SME shares seems to have occurred since 1993 or 1994 but not yet for employment. If, as before, the turning points in the SME shares of value added and production precede that in employment, these declines in SME shares in value added and production could presage a decline in the SME share of employment by the turn of the century.

Another shortcoming of the figures presented in Table I is that they exclude very small plants with one to four workers. The omission of this size class of plants has to be considered throughout this study as well as in comparisons with SME statistics for those countries that include very small

TABLE I
SME shares in number of establishments, employment, value added, and gross production in manufacturing 1952–96, in percent

	Manufacturing establishments		Manufacturing employment		Manufacturing value-added		Manufacturing production	
	Small and medium (5–300)	Large (300+)	Small and medium (5–300)	Large (300+)	Small and medium (5–300)	Large (300+)	Small and medium (5–300)	Large (300+)
1952	95.8	4.2	61.5	38.5				
1955	97.2	2.8	63.3	36.7				
1960	97.6	2.4	67.7	32.3	57.0	43.0		
1966	98.3	1.7	60.3	39.7	42.5	57.5	45.6	54.4
1970	97.1	2.9	49.0	51.0	28.5	71.5	30.3	69.7
1973	97.0	3.0	46.3	53.7	33.9	66.1	33.8	66.2
1975	96.2	3.8	45.7	54.3	31.7	68.3	30.7	69.3
1980	96.6	3.4	49.6	50.4	35.2	64.8	31.9	68.1
1985	97.5	2.5	56.1	43.9	37.6	62.4	35.4	64.6
1990	96.1	3.9	61.7	38.3	44.3	55.7	42.7	57.3
1991	98.5	1.5	63.5	36.5	45.8	54.2	44.6	55.4
1992	98.6	1.4	65.8	34.2	47.6	52.4	45.8	54.2
1993	98.9	1.1	68.9	31.1	50.3	49.7	47.8	52.2
1994	99.0	1.0	69.1	30.9	49.2	50.8	47.9	52.1
1996	99.1	0.9	69.2	30.8	47.2	52.8	46.8	53.2
1997	99.1	0.9	69.3	30.7	46.5	53.5	46.3	53.7

Note: Definition of small and medium-sized enterprise changed: 5–200 workers before 1973 and 5–300 thereafter.
Source: National Statistics Office, Report of the Mining and Manufacturing Census and Survey, various years, Korean Federation of Small Business, Central Cooperative.

establishments. Only very occasionally (e.g., in the 1973 Manufacturing Census) have the Korean statistical agencies tried to capture this segment of manufacturing. One reason for this is that many such plants appear to be in reality closer to repair and other services than manufacturing. Another reason for the omission is that the share of economic activity accounted for by establishments of one to four workers is fairly small (about 2 percent of manufacturing value added according to Ho (1980)) and believed to have remained fairly constant over time. In any case, Nugent (1989) demonstrated (on the basis of the very limited information available on very small plants) that their inclusion would not have changed the aforementioned overall trends in the size distribution of Korean manufacturing establishments.[4]

Yet, despite these qualifications, the first three of the aforementioned trends are much in evidence. For example with respect to employment, the SME share rose from 61.5 percent in 1952 to 67.7 percent in 1960, then fell to 45.7 percent in 1975, and finally rose again to 69.3 percent in 1997. These are remarkably strong shifts in employment structure: a decline of more than 20 percent in manufacturing employment between 1960 and 1975, followed by a rise of almost 25 percent by 1997. Much of the decline in the SME share between 1960 and 1975 could have been due to the growth or graduation of SMEs into LEs (especially since the number of enterprises was only slightly growing during this period).[5] After 1975, there is no evidence that LEs decreased in size sufficiently to become SMEs, but instead evidence of an acceleration in the growth rate of new firms.[6] Hence, the post-1975 trend seems to have been a genuine shift in employment to SMEs, many of which are new.

In principle, the aforementioned trends could have been due to substantial changes in the size shares of firms near the cutoff between SMEs and LEs. Yet, as mentioned in footnote 3, in fact, the trends are not sensitive to the choice of cutoff. Table II shows why. In particular, the shares of the two largest size classes of SMEs in the total employment of SMEs (i.e., those with 100–199 and 200–299 employees, respectively) were also falling between 1978 and 1997 (from 25.5 percent

TABLE II
Size shares of employment among SMEs in manufacturing over time, in percent

Year/Size	5–9	10–19	20–49	50–99	100–199	200–299	Total
1960	17.69	20.57	27.52	14.14	14.08	6.00	100
1966	20.48	18.04	20.99	15.80	15.54	9.15	100
1973	14.08	12.40	18.07	17.80	22.43	15.22	100
1978	7.35	9.22	19.32	19.81	25.55	18.74	100
1986	6.68	11.44	24.07	22.14	22.10	13.58	100
1992	9.96	15.68	28.25	19.56	16.88	9.67	100
1993	12.16	17.15	27.85	18.70	15.48	8.66	100
1994	12.34	17.17	27.67	18.65	15.44	8.72	100
1996	14.28	17.66	26.83	17.76	14.97	8.50	100
1997	15.11	16.94	26.23	17.79	15.48	8.47	100

Source: Economic Planning Board, Report of the Mining and Manufacturing Census and Surveys, various years.

and 18.7 percent in 1978 to 15.1 percent and 8.5 percent, respectively, in 1997). Also, the size classes whose shares in employment have been rising the most have been those in establishments with 5–49 employees. Since 1978 the share of this group (i.e., the three smallest size groups in Table II) rose from 35.9 percent of the SME total in 1978 to 58.7 percent in 1996. Hence, it is clear that the upward trend in the SME share in manufacturing employment since 1978 is primarily due to the rising share of small SMEs (those with fewer than 50 employees) rather than to the growth of relatively small SMEs into medium sized ones. Consistent with the virtual disappearance of any trend in the share of SMEs in total employment between 1996 and 1997, even within SMEs there was an increase in the share of establishments of 100 or more workers between 1996 and 1997.

Prior to 1978 the shares within SMEs of the two largest size classes (i.e., those with 100 or more workers) increased sharply from 20 percent in 1960 to 44.2 percent in 1978. Within the two smallest size classes, however, there was considerable volatility in the pre-1978 period.

What about the SME share in exports? Unfortunately, data on exports are not contained in the Reports on the Mining and Manufacturing Census (or Survey) from which all the data reported in the preceding tables are taken. There is also a conceptual problem in exports in the Korean context, given that much of the exporting by SMEs is done indirectly through subcontracting relationships with other manufacturing firms and trading firms. Because the distinction between direct exports and indirect exports is far from sharp, different managers in the same objective circumstances may well respond differently to questions regarding the amount of exports in total sales.[7]

The only data over time on the SME share in exports are presented in Table III. Note that the

TABLE III
SME share of Korean commodity exports (1965–95), in percent

Year	1965	1970	1975	1980	1981	1982	1983	1984	1985	1986
SME share	23	32.2	34.5	32.1	31	22.3	20.2	25.5	27.8	35.2

Year	1987	1988	1989	1990	1991	1992	1993	1994	1995
SME share	37.7	38.1	38.6	45.5	39.4	40	42.8	42.4	39.6

Source: Korean Federation of Small Business (81–92), Korea Trade Association (65–80), Annual Report on SMEs, each year, SME Department, Ministry of Commerce and Industry, and Monthly Bulletin, 1997/99, Bank of Korea (93–95).

data for 1965–80 and 1981–95 come from different sources (which could possibly be inconsistent), and, even were they to come from the same source, for reasons given above, managers may not respond consistently one to another or even over time to a request for exports. From Table III one can see much more in the way of fluctuations of SME shares than in the case of employment and value added. Yet, even so, one can detect several reversals in trends: a rising share of SMEs in exports from 1965–75, a sharp decline 1975–83, a sharp rise until 1990, and fluctuations but also probably another decline after that.

What is the composition of SME exports? Table IV presents a breakdown of SME exports into product groups. Though such information is provided here only for 1993–95, even during these few years, one can see considerable change. By 1995 electronics had become the most important export, followed closely by textiles. Other rapidly growing exports are chemicals, primary metals, and metal products and machinery. Going back further, one should realize that even in the late 1960s, electronics, chemicals, and machinery exports were essentially nonexistent. Instead, exports were concentrated on light manufactures such as wigs, plywood, and very simple textiles. Manufactures as a whole accounted for but 6 percent of total exports in 1960, but 76 percent by 1970 and 96 percent in 1996.

While good time series data on such investment abroad does not exist and in any case is of relatively recent origin, Table V shows that foreign direct investment (FDI) by Korean SMEs has been quite significant and rising not only absolutely but also relative to LEs. Between 1990 and 1994, for example, both the number of "cases" (i.e., all firms making direct investment abroad and the value of such FDI) more than tripled. Yet, FDI by SMEs rose by well over five times in both numbers and values during the same period. As a result, the proportion of cases of outward FDI made by SMEs rose to almost two-thirds and that in value terms to over one-fifth.[8] This rapid growth in FDI, especially by SMEs, is significant in two important respects: (1) It represents another dimension (outward capital flows) in which Korea has begun to assume the characteristics of a highly developed country. (2) It is also representative of the way in which the country's productive structure (including its increasingly important SME sector) has been allowed to adjust to its rapidly changing comparative advantage.

TABLE IV
Exports of SMEs by sector (in million $US)

	1993	1994	1995
Food, beverage products	2,313	2,593	2,971
Chemical	1,403	2,091	2,593
Plastic, rubber, and fur	2,249	2,648	3,308
Nonmetal minerals	761	887	876
Textiles	10,885	12,353	13,561
Other light industry	2,842	2,837	2,878
Primary metal and metal products	1,612	2,089	3,176
Electronics and electric equipment	9,330	10,981	14,371
Machinery	3,243	3,655	5,003
Others	560	639	767

Source: Annual Report on SMEs, each year, SME Department, Ministry of Commerce and Industry.

TABLE V
Foreign direct investment of all firms and SMEs (in million $US)

		1990	1991	1992	1993	1994
Total (all firms)	Number	2,297	3,324	4,421	5,432	7,497
	Cases	1,226	1,646	2,109	2,725	4,132
SMEs	Number	286	483	721	1,027	1,517
	Cases	455	731	1,086	1,596	2,715
% of SMEs	Number	12.5	14.5	16.3	18.9	20.2
	Cases	37.1	44.4	51.5	58.6	65.7

Source: Annual Report on SMEs, each year, Federation of SME Cooperation.

TABLE VI
Productivity growth rates and other indexes of SMEs and LEs compared, 1979–97 (in percent)

Growth indicator		1979	1980	1981	1982	1983	1985	1989	1990	1991	1992	1993	1994	1995	1996	1997
Growth rate of value added per capita	SMEs	30.1	12.5	15.02	20.59	–4.17	11.4	18.2	21.1	17	9.7	12.04	14.86	10.36	8.76	3.34
	LEs	25.86	21.23	38.4	6.8	17.23	8.5	18.7	17.9	17.2	11.8	15.17	18.9	21.93	–2.08	5.67
Growth rate of employmentcost per capita	SMEs	33.85	13.14	13	19.71	0.5	7.27	21.2	19.9	17.9	15.4	9.88	13.41	11.05	11.9	5.37
	LEs	22.56	23.2	23.87	11.09	16.27	6.03	25.7	18.7	19.4	10.5	11.1	16.62	13.48	12.19	3.85
Growth rate of capital per capita	SMEs	2.23	2.71	3.39	4.83	3.47	4.78	9.8	12.15	13.66	16.15	20.29	23.92	26.03	30.32	37.71
	LEs	4.56	6.61	9.78	11.03	12.42	14.45	26.43	32.96	40.46	49.02	64.2	68.89	78.02	89.37	113.31
Growth rate of total assets per capita	SMEs	6.99	8.96	10.21	14.2	10.78	14.46	29.72	34.9	39.37	46.59	54.47	64.4	72.87	85.62	111.66
	LEs	12.6	18.21	26.37	28.16	32.17	39.64	69.04	88.3	114.01	137.61	167.73	182.59	216.4	250.05	322.43
Ratio of gross value added to total assets	SMEs	41.3	36.2	36.5	31.8	40	36.7	36.2	35.1	35.5	34.1	33.47	33.75	32.93	30.91	27.08
	LEs	29.5	24.8	23.7	23.7	24.3	23.9	27.9	25.2	24.2	22.4	21.69	23.15	24.7	20.84	17.32
Ratio of gross value added to total sales	SMEs	25.9	23.9	22.8	22.4	24.4	23.7	25.2	25.8	26	26.3	26.84	26.07	24.93	24.83	23.06
	LEs	25	20.1	20.2	20.8	20.8	21	27.3	26.2	26.3	25.6	25.78	26.43	27.01	24.17	21.32
Ratio of employment costs to gross value added	SMEs	61.3	61.7	60.6	60.1	63.1	61	61.5	61.9	64.6	67.4	64.95	62.59	64.64	64.57	62.58
	LEs	47.8	48.6	43.5	45.3	44.9	44.7	48.4	48.8	49.4	49.5	46.85	46.54	41.71	48.27	47.04

Source: Analysis of Firm's Management, each year, Bank of Korea.

2. Productivity change and its analysis

Simple measures of productivity growth such as output or value added per worker are easy to carry out and not controversial. Table VI presents some comparisons between SMEs and LEs engaged in manufacturing for the years 1979–97. Despite the fact that capital per worker (capital intensity) was about three times as high among LEs as among SMEs at the beginning of the period, LEs tended to accumulate capital per capita at about three times the rate of SMEs throughout these years. This is reflected in the much higher growth rates of capital (i.e., equity capital) per capita and total assets per capita among LEs than among SMEs. Despite facing somewhat lower wage rates than LEs, and some fluctuations from year to year, the average growth rates of wage rates (employment costs per capita) were quite similar between SMEs and LEs. The greater labor intensity of production in SMEs is reflected in a 15–22 percent differential in the share of labor costs in value added in favor of SMEs. Despite the higher capital intensity and hence also labor productivity of LEs at the beginning of the period, the growth rates of labor productivity (value added per capita) of SMEs actually exceeded those of LEs in several years, especially in the early part of the period (1979, 1982, and 1985). The table also shows that, because of the greater labor-intensity of SMEs, capital productivity (i.e., value added per unit of total assets) of SMEs consistently exceeded that of LEs.

The somewhat poorer relative performance of SMEs in the 1990s compared to the 1980s in value added per capita and assets per capita could well presage a future reversal of the rise in the SME shares in manufacturing sales, value added, and employment that has been occurring since the mid-to-late 1970s.

While labor productivity was growing relatively rapidly in both SMEs and LEs, in both cases this growth was to a large extent the result of rising capital intensity. The concept of total factor productivity (TFP) permits a distinction to be made between the growth of capital and technological change. Yet, inasmuch as numerous assumptions and judgments have to be employed in the calculation of TFP, such results are often quite controversial. In the case of Korea, the calculations have been especially controversial, in part because the wide variations in TFP growth rates for manufacturing have been obtained in different studies. Among these are Nishimizu and Robinson (1984), Chenery and others (1986), Kim and Lau (1994), Kim (1995), Young (1995), Hong and Kim (1996),[9] Kwack (1997), and Nam (1999). One of these (Kim, 1995) has estimated TFP growth over a 20-year period to be *negative* while others have found TFP growth rates for virtually the same period to be as high as 6 percent per annum.

The widely varying results have to be attributed to differences in one or more of the following points: (1) sources of output data and price deflators; (2) the measure of output (gross production or value added) in the former case including materials and energy as an inputs;[10] (3) the assumed form of the production function (Cobb-Douglas, CES, translog); (4) the nature of any adjustments made for the quality of labor or capital; (5) the extent to which economies of scale are accounted for; (6) the assumed character of technological change (neutral or otherwise, embodied or not); (7) adjustments in working hours, capital utilization rates, price markups, etc.; and (8) the level of aggregation. Not surprisingly, the studies that most seriously attempt to correct for changing quality of labor and capital, allow for price markups, and incorporate economies of scale are those in which TFP growth tends to be lowest and those which make no such adjustments tend to be among the highest. Whether or not one should make such adjustments and corrections depends of course on the purpose of the study.

Table VII presents several of the estimates of the average annual rate of TFP growth for these sectors obtained by these different authors. Several observations can be made. First, as expected, the extremes obtained were those of Nishimizu and Robinson (1984) on the high end, who made no adjustment for changes in input quality, and Kim (1995) "adjusted" at the low end who did make such adjustments.[11] Second, there is universal agreement that TFP growth was highest in metal products and machinery, a sector in which SMEs have been consistently under-represented. Third, according to a majority (three of the five) of studies, the simple average of TFP growth rates in sectors in which SMEs were over-represented (given in the top part of Table VII) is lower than

TABLE VII
Estimates of average annual rates of sectoral TFP growth by different authors in sectors in which SMEs are over represented and under represented compared

Source of estimates	Coverage	Textiles, apparel, leather	Wood and wood products	Paper, printing, publishing	Nonmetallic minerals	Average of SME over-represented sectors
Nishimizu and Robinson (1984)	1960–1977	2.98	5.25	4.52	4.53	4.32
Hong and Kim (1996)	1967–1993	1.78	1.36	1.74	2.28	1.79
Nam (1999)	1971–1996	2.45	–1.09	2.58	n.a.	1.33
Kim (1995) unadjusted[a]	1966–1988	1.41	1.23	1.58	1.59	1.45
Kim (1995) adjusted[b]	1966–1988	0.70	0.39	–1.50	0.28	–0.03
Source of estimates		Chemicals	Basic metals	Metal products and machinery		Average of SME under-represented
Nishimizu and Robinson (1984)	1960–1977	2.54	1.87	6.02		3.48
Hong and Kim (1996)	1967–1993	1.52	1.02	2.48		1.67
Nam (1999)	1971–1996	1.21	3.23	5.81		3.42
Kim (1995) unadjusted[a]	1966–1988	1.56	0.75	2.34		1.55
Kim (1995) adjusted[b]	1966–1988	0.57	–0.30	1.02		0.43

Notes: Where subsectors had to be aggregated to obtain the sectors reported here, this was done by taking unweighted means.
[a] Unadjusted" estimates have been corrected for changes in the quality of labor, working hours, and in effective rates of depreciation not taken into consideration in the other studies.
[b] Adjusted also for economies of scale and for imperfection in competition (markup).

that of the SME under-represented sectors (given in the bottom half of the table). The variation in estimates is particularly disconcerting in the case of wood and wood products, a sector in which one would not expect to have much measurement error and the assignment of the contributions of different factors to growth relatively straightforward.

Despite the variability, especially at the subsectoral, most of the estimates for Korea have been in the 2.5 percent to 3 percent per annum range, still putting Korea ahead of most other countries in TFP growth. Notably, such an estimate was also obtained by Young (1995), who is best known for pointing out that TFP growth was generally much lower in East Asia than had been presumed in earlier studies.[12] Hence, despite some disagreements, and as long as one does not attempt to control for quality of labor and other inputs as in Kim (1995), there would seem to have been a near general consensus that TFP growth in Korean manufacturing has been relatively high when compared with other countries.

Because these results are still far from representing the growth path of TFP in individual enterprises, in Tables VIII and IX we report results generated by taking advantage of the largest known available dataset on individual SMEs, namely, the aforementioned SME Survey carried out by KIET in 1990. Our work with this dataset follows two stages. First, we estimate sector-specific Cobb-Douglas production functions for light industry, heavy industry, and electronics and also for manufacturing as a whole. Second, the sector-specific parameter estimates for these functions α and β are then used to generate firm-specific indexes of technical efficiency or TFP (via frontier production functions) based on aggregate or sectoral production functions. The TFP indexes are calculated from the formula: $Y/(K^{\alpha}N^{\beta})$

In the top part of Table VIII are the mean, median, and trimmed mean values of TFP based on the aggregate function for each of four size classes of SMEs in that survey. As is well known, the means are rather sensitive to outliers, which may be of dubious reliability. Hence, the values shown for the median and trimmed means are

TABLE VIII
Total factor productivity of sampled SMEs, 1989

	Number of observations	Mean	Median	Trimmed mean[a]
Size group (INXMAN)				
1. 5–49	414	3.500	0.910	1.180
2. 50–99	195	1.962	1.078	1.273
3. 100–199	147	2.908	1.157	1.385
4. 200–299	164	1.262	0.913	1.012
Industry type				
1. Light industry	318	2.170	0.974	1.126
2. Heavy industry	453	3.245	1.083	1.349
3. Electronics	148	2.046	0.740	0.920

[a] Trimmed mean is the mean without upper and lower 5 percent of the TFP indexes in the sample.
Source: Korea Institute for Industrial Economics and Trade (KIET) SME Survey.

TABLE IX
Regression estimates of TFP indexes by sector

	Light industry		Heavy industry		Electronic industry	
	R-square	0.1867	*R*-square	0.1393	*R*-square	0.1055
	Adj *R*-sq	0.1625	Adj *R*-sq	0.1217	Adj *R*-sq	0.0468
Variable	Parameter estimate	*t*-value	Parameter estimate	*t*-value	Parameter estimate	*t*-value
INTERCEP	−1.3444	−4.075	−0.4681	−1.689	−0.4927	−0.978
FIRMAGE	0.0310	2.364	0.0545	3.793	0.0336	1.391
FIMAGESQ	−0.0007	−2.532	−0.0012	−3.428	−0.0005	−1.035
EQU	0.8358	6.228	0.6387	5.866	0.2557	1.189
DFPART	−0.5013	−1.682	−0.0127	−0.066	0.1705	0.694
INXMAN	0.3280	1.143	−0.5527	−2.193	−0.1620	−0.398
INXMANSQ	−0.1094	−1.947	0.0699	1.337	0.0000	0
SITUFUND	0.2077	3.009	0.2151	3.785	0.2053	2.049
YOUNGCHN	0.0680	0.508	−0.2804	−2.684	−0.1006	−0.574
HOKANG	−0.0038	−0.026	−0.3159	−2.527	−0.5268	−2.399

Source: Based on KIET Sample SME Survey of 1990.

probably more reliable than the means. While there is no distinct pattern in the results across size classes for the untrimmed mean TFP indexes, for both the median and trimmed mean there are. In particular, TFP rises with size through the 101–200 size class but then declines with size after that. In the lower portion of the table are the same calculations by industry, once again based on the aggregate production function. By all three measures, TFP is lower in electronics than in the other sectors, quite the opposite of most of the findings concerning TFP growth.

If the three sectors have different TFP indexes, they might also have different production functions, which is the rationale for estimating the sector-specific production functions. In Table IX we present the results of regressions of the sector-specific TFP on a number of different firm characteristics, including the age of the firm (FIRMAGE) and its square (FIMAGESQ), size (measured in terms of numbers of workers according to the INXMAN index defined in Table VIII) and its square,[13] a dummy variable for corporate form (EQU), a dummy variable for having a foreign partner (DFPART), the degree of satisfaction with the funding situation

(SITUFUND),[14] and, finally, dummy variables for the two least developed regions (labeled YOUNGCHN and HOKANG).

Note that there are in fact considerable differences in these relationships between sectors. While age and its square both have highly significant effects on TFP in the light and heavy industries, they do not in electronics. The same holds true for the EQU and to a lesser extent the size variables INXMAN and INXMANSQ. DFPART, on the other hand, plays a role only in light industry. Location of the plant in the lesser developed regions has no influence on TFP in light industry but has significant negative influences on TFP in the other sectors. By contrast, SITUFUND is positively and significantly related to TFP in each sector and indeed has a positive coefficient of almost the same magnitude in each case. While this could be interpreted as revealing the pervasive influence of freedom from financial constraints (due in part to the fungibility of money), as was noted previously, it may not be entirely exogenous.[15] Since as a firm ages it also tends to grow, a typical firm in both light and heavy industries would derive the initially positive but diminishing effects of both age and size.

A study of TFP based on the more compete census data by using the production frontier methodology is Yoo (1991, 1992). That study used sector-specific production functions to estimate sector-specific production frontiers and indexes of technical inefficiency. It did so separately for each year between 1978 and 1988 on the basis of actual census tapes and empirically estimated the determinants of variations in technical efficiency across industries. Disappointingly, however, Yoo's results showed (1) little stability in the results over time, (2) considerable sensitivity of the results to the use of different measures of technical efficiency/inefficiency, and (3) lower explanatory power of the hypothesized determinants of technical efficiency than in other studies (e.g., Caves and Associates, 1992; Caves and Barton, 1990). In the latter respect, Yoo found technical efficiency to be *positively* related to industrial concentration, the fuel-intensity of production, the degree of product specialization by firms in the industry, and the relative size of plants in the industry. He also found it to be *negatively* related to an index of input price inefficiency and the relative importance of both multi-plant shipments in the industry and the subcontracting of inputs. The latter finding was opposite to that found in a comparable Japanese study.[16] He also showed that technical efficiency was higher if plants with fewer than twenty employees were excluded, thereby confirming the hypothesis that very small firms have lower technical efficiency than all others.

A related study is that of Pai Kim (1996), which goes into greater detail for fewer (11) industries and years (two) with somewhat improved methodology (a full frontier production function with gamma density and estimated with maximum likelihood following the approach of Greene (1980)). It focuses on differences in the cross-section results for technical efficiency between 1978 and 1989. In particular, the study found that the heavily interventionist LE-oriented HCI policy of the 1970s had the effect of raising the production frontier of HCI sectors (and especially of LEs in those sectors) but also the degree of technical inefficiency of these sectors relative to the more sector-neutral economic policies of the 1980s. While the HCI policy allowed LEs to increase their production frontiers, the large amounts of credit and other resources provided on a discriminatory basis to the HCI sector and especially to LEs in the sector allowed more inefficient firms to survive.

These studies underscore the conclusion of endogenous growth theory that TFP growth does not simply arrive as "manna from heaven" but as a result of appropriate choices with respect to organizational form and product variety,[17] national and international competition, intersectoral resource allocation, labor training, and R&D. Attention at present is confined (and necessarily very briefly) to the latter four factors.

The extent to which increasing openness or international competition has contributed to TFP growth, like many other issues in Korean growth and public policy, remains very controversial. Several studies, such as Nishimizu and Robinson (1984), Dollar and Sokoloff (1990), and Nam (1999) have found positive and significant effects on TFP growth of their openness or international competition measures (export growth), thus supporting the hypothesis that TFP growth is positively affected by trade liberalization. Yet, the authors of these studies did nothing to remove possible endogeneity in their openness measures. Hence, their results could be due to reversed causality or to common causation by another variable. Notably, those studies, such as Kim (1995), that use more exogenous measures of openness (e.g., measures of protection)[18] obtain weaker and more mixed results for openness.

The contributions of the intersectoral allocation of resources to aggregate TFP growth and the role of government policy in such allocation have been equally controversial. Many have criticized the government's HCI strategy as being premature and hence detrimental to growth, suggesting that Korean growth would have been even greater without this heavy-handed policy. Others,[19] however, have argued that, in hindsight, the priority to HCI policy has been very successful in raising TFP growth because it expanded the sectors with the highest TFP growth, namely, electronics, machinery, and chemicals (as was previously noted). One way to test for this is to compare the weighted average of the sectoral TFP growth rates with the aggregate TFP growth rate. Nam (1999) makes such a comparison and finds that the former substantially exceeded the latter, suggesting that intersectoral resource allocation was inefficient.

Of greater relevance to TFP growth in SMEs relative to LEs are the last two factors, namely, R&D and labor training and expertise. Because of their greater difficulty in recruiting skilled labor and in internalizing externalities arising from either R&D and labor training (because of their smaller size and aforementioned higher labor turnover rates), SMEs are clearly at a distinct disadvantage in both these means of raising TFP. In particular, despite having less total manpower than SMEs, LEs had five times as many Ph.D.s, over seven times as many M.A.s, and over four times as many research technicians and R&D expenditures as SMEs in 1990. SMEs, nevertheless, have made at least some progress in both respects. Indeed, as shown in Table X, by 1990 over 10 percent of SMEs had established programs of R&D. Yet, the table also shows that between 1990 and 1997 the percentage of firms with R&D expenditures fell significantly to 8 percent. This reduction would seem to be the result of two factors. First, there was a change in the size structure of firms in favor of very small SMEs (with fewer than 20 employees) that only rarely engage in R&D and away from the largest SMEs among whom R&D programs are relatively common. Second, there were some significant declines in the propensity to engage in R&D within some of the size groups, namely, those with 5–9, 10–19, and 200–299 workers.[20]

Of particular interest are two recent studies. One by Chang et al. (1994) shows the social rate of return to R&D expenditures to be far higher than the private rate of return in several sectors including electronics. This is not surprising in view of the fact that many of the benefits may take the form of externalities. The other by Lee (1995) is more surprising in finding that the effect of R&D expenditures on labor productivity appears to be greater for SMEs than for LEs. The latter finding could have several explanations, for example, diminishing returns to R&D or the beneficial effects of cooperation between LEs and SMEs, perhaps through the extensive subcontracting relations to be discussed in Section 5.

Given the obvious disadvantages of SMEs relative to LEs in training, acquiring skilled personnel and R&D, and new more sophisticated equipment, how is it that Korean SMEs have managed to do as well as they have in productivity growth? The answer is that much of the technology acquisition in SMEs has come from imitation and the advantages of being a follower. For example, if the technology is relatively simple, SMEs can reverse-engineer, copy, or purchase second-hand equipment from LEs at home or abroad. With increasing compliance by Korea with international property rights conventions, and the increasing complexity of technology, however, these simple processes of technology acquisition are becoming less feasible, suggesting that future productivity growth of SMEs may depend more heavily on external sources of support, the subject of Sections 4 and 5.

3. Firm dynamics

By linking the plant identifiers in the different Manufacturing Censuses (or Surveys) produced formerly by the Economic Planning Board, it is in principle possible to follow individual plants and their behavior over time, and in particular to measure entry and death rates of plants by size,

TABLE X
The incidence of R&D plans and expenditures across different sizes of SMEs in manufacturing, selected years 1990–97

	1990			1993			1995			1996			1997		
Firm size	*N*	R&D %	R&D costs	*N*	R&D %	R&D costs	*N*	R&D %	R&D costs	*N*	R&D %	R&D costs	*N*	R&D %	R&D costs
Total	64,365	10.5	188,874	73,364	7.7	441,782	78,797	8.3	436,810	84,374	8.4	500,490	85,947	8.0	476,227
5–9	19,537	3.2	7,753	26,994	2.1	25,042	29,492	2.6	11,228	33,807	1.8	13,687	37,870	1.6	6,197
10–19	18,909	7.9	11,506	21,236	3.3	19,501	24,312	5.9	66,903	25,064	7.4	68,028	24,657	7.7	34,514
20–49	16,801	11.9	60,329	16,958	12.5	117,483	17,537	14.3	145,571	17,451	14.0	120,879	16,194	14.8	94,685
50–99	5,651	23.8	46,250	5,243	23.3	117,211	5,087	19.4	66,165	5,201	22.2	101,905	4,427	22.4	82,382
100–199	2,621	33.9	38,333	2,234	32.4	93,928	1,867	32.7	90,402	2,195	33.6	118,998	2,130	34.8	132,327
200–299	846	50.8	24,702	699	43.6	68,617	502	41	56,542	656	45.7	76,992	669	39.5	126,123
Small	38,446	5.5	19,260	48,230	2.6	44,542	71,341	6.6	223,702	76,322	6.4	202,595	78,721	6.2	135,395
Medium	25,919	17.9	169,614	25,134	17.4	397,239	7,456	24.2	213,108	8,052	27.2	297,895	7,226	27.6	340,832

Notes: R&D % is the percentage of SMEs with R&D programs; R&D costs are in millions of won.
Source: Survey of Small and Medium Enterprises, each year, Small and Medium Enterprise Authority and the Federation of Small and Medium Enterprises.

sector, and vintage cohort. Nevertheless, the statistical authorities in Korea have proved very resistant to providing researchers with the necessary identifiers. Fortunately, there has been one notable exception, reflected in the unpublished Ph.D. dissertation of Chung (1998). Even in this case the identifiers and data were made available for only three censuses, namely, for 1983, 1988, and 1993, all somewhat after the major growth phase of the Korean economy.

Table XI shows the exit, entry, and net entry rates calculated by Chung for 17 individual sectors and for manufacturing as a whole. The rates are calculated according to the formulas given in the notes to this table. From the bottom row of the table, it can be seen that 53 percent of the manufacturing plants operating and reporting in 1983 did not report in 1988, but on the other hand 69 percent of those reporting in 1988 did not report in 1983. The former is identified as the exit rate and the latter as the entry rate. Since there could be other reasons why a plant might not report in a given year, these rates may represent overestimates of the true exit and entry rates. The corresponding exit and entry rates for the period 1988–93 were even higher, 61 percent and 74 percent, respectively. The net entry rate of 53 percent, however, was slightly higher in the first period than that in the second period (49 percent).

The table also shows that there is considerable variation from sector to sector, exit and entry rates both being especially high in apparel, leather, fabricated metals, electronics, and furniture.[21] Net entry rates were high in electric machinery, nonelectric machinery transport equipment, and precision instruments in both periods and high in leather and electronics between 1983 and 1988 but not between 1988 and 1993. By contrast, net entry rates were high in fabricated metals in the 1988–93 period but not in the 1983–88 period. Net

TABLE XI
Exit, entry, and net entry rates of manufacturing plants between 1983 and 1988 and 1988 and 1993

Sector	1983–88			1988–93		
	Exit	Entry	Net entry	Exit	Entry	Net entry
15. Food	0.36	0.39	0.05	0.41	0.52	0.25
17. Textiles	0.49	0.65	0.46	0.59	0.68	0.28
18. Apparel	0.63	0.78	0.67	0.71	0.79	0.38
19. Leather	0.64	0.80	0.84	0.73	0.78	0.23
20. Wood products	0.47	0.53	0.14	0.54	0.65	0.31
21. Paper, printing	0.46	0.64	0.50	0.57	0.72	0.52
24. Chemicals	0.63	0.60	–0.09	0.47	0.62	0.40
25. Plastics	0.57	0.76	0.82	0.62	0.75	0.54
26. Nonmetals	0.44	0.52	0.18	0.48	0.63	0.41
27. Basic metals	0.56	0.69	0.42	0.62	0.70	0.27
28. Fabricated metals	0.64	0.76	0.50	0.64	0.83	1.07
29. Nonelectric machinery	0.56	0.77	0.96	0.63	0.80	0.85
30. Electronics	0.57	0.84	1.59	0.70	0.78	0.38
31. Electric machinery	0.54	0.78	1.07	0.66	0.82	0.86
33. Precision instruments	0.55	0.77	0.99	0.65	0.80	0.77
34. Transport equipment	0.57	0.79	1.03	0.65	0.80	0.76
36. Furniture	0.59	0.76	0.70	0.70	0.76	0.27
Total	0.53	0.69	0.53	0.61	0.74	0.49

Notes:
1. The exit rates are calculated as the number of plants that reported in census year t but not reporting in census year $t + 1$ divided by the total number of plants reporting in census year t.
2. The entry rates are calculated as the number of plants reporting in year $t + 1$ but not reporting in year t divided by the total number of plants in year $t + 1$.
3. The net entry rates are calculated as the number of entrants in year $t + 1$ less the number of exits in year $t + 1$ divided by the total number of plants reporting in year t.

Source: Chung (1998, Table 3.1).

entry rates were relatively low in food, textiles, wood products, basic metals, and chemicals, and in the latter case even negative between 1983 and 1988.

Table XII shows the corresponding calculations for exit, entry, and net entry rates when the entries and exits are weighted by the number of employees. While the patterns are rather similar across sectors and over time, they are rather consistently lower than those shown in Table XI, suggesting that both entry and exit rates are higher among smaller plants. This is consistent with the evidence for the United States and many other countries provided in the studies surveyed by Caves (1998). Note that whereas there was only one instance (chemicals in 1983–88) with a negative net entry rate with the unweighted data of Table XI, when the employment-weighted data are used, small declines are observed for 1988–93 in textiles, apparel, leather, electronics, and furniture, all relatively early developed labor-intensive industries.

Chung (1998) also calculates indexes of total factor productivity based on the somewhat more sophisticated version of the TFP indexes computed in Section 2 provided by Good, Nadiri, and Sickles (1996). He does so for both the new entrants and incumbents in each sector for both 1988 and 1993 on the basis of data for gross output, materials inputs, and productive factors. These calculations yield industry-specific TFP distributions for both entrants and incumbent plants. From these distributions, various measures of the characteristics of the distributions can be constructed. For new entrants he calculates the standard error (a commonly used measure of dispersion). For incumbent plants, he calculates the change in the TFP index in period $t + 1$ conditional on that in period t. Finally, he also calculates for each of the 17 sectors the median capital-labor ratio at the beginning of each period.

In each case, he finds relatively consistent differences across sectors from one period to another. For example, in each year the probability that a plant characterized by a low quartile TFP index in period t would be able to make the transition to a relatively higher quartile productivity index in period $t + 1$ is relatively high in nonmetals, food, wood products, and chemicals but low in leather, electronics, plastics, transport equipment,

TABLE XII
Employment shares of entrants, exits, and net entrants by sector and period

Sector	1983–88			1988–93		
	Exit	Entry	Net entry	Exit	Entry	Net entry
15. Food	0.22	0.28	0.13	0.24	0.35	0.08
17. Textiles	0.27	0.41	0.21	0.33	0.40	–0.02
18. Apparel	0.41	0.60	0.36	0.56	0.61	–0.11
19. Leather	0.29	0.50	0.38	0.62	0.54	–0.36
20. Wood products	0.43	0.45	0.02	0.47	0.55	0.08
21. Paper, printing	0.33	0.47	0.33	0.37	0.47	0.15
24. Chemicals	0.42	0.33	–0.08	0.19	0.37	0.25
25. Plastics	0.41	0.56	0.56	0.42	0.55	0.19
26. Nonmetals	0.26	0.39	0.21	0.27	0.47	0.26
27. Basic metals	0.21	0.33	0.21	0.25	0.31	0.05
28. Fabricated metals	0.46	0.59	0.33	0.49	0.64	0.25
29. Nonelectric machinery	0.42	0.56	0.56	0.44	0.60	0.26
30. Electronics	0.25	0.44	0.73	0.33	0.36	–0.03
31. Electric machinery	0.33	0.49	0.49	0.41	0.57	0.24
33. Precision instruments	0.35	0.56	0.71	0.51	0.64	0.06
34. Transport equipment	0.29	0.37	0.34	0.23	0.38	0.25
36. Furniture	0.38	0.53	0.40	0.48	0.53	–0.09
Total	0.32	0.46	0.32	0.38	0.47	0.05

Notes: For definitions of entry, exit, and net entry rates see notes to Table XI.
Source: Chung (1998, Table 3.3).

precision instruments, and electrical machinery. Likewise, the dispersion of TFP indexes of new entrants tends to be consistently higher in textiles, food, chemicals, apparel, and nonmetals than in sectors such as wood products, basic metals, plastics, transport equipment, and electrical machinery. Finally, capital intensity is consistently high over time in food, chemicals, basic metals, machinery, and transport equipment but low in apparel, leather, furniture, electronics, and precision instruments.

Naturally, some of these industry characteristics could be expected to affect the entry and exit rates of plants across industries. In particular, Caves (1998) and others have suggested that greater capital intensity would represent higher sunk costs, thereby lowering both entry and exit rates. Similarly, the higher the rate of growth in output (a proxy for favorable demand conditions), the higher would be the entry rate and the lower the exit rate. The greater the likelihood that incumbent plants would experience increases in their relative TFP indexes, the lower the entry and exit rates should be. Finally, the greater the dispersion of TFP among entrants, reflecting perhaps less complete information on appropriate technology, the lower the entry and exit rate that might be expected.

Table XIII from Chung (1998) provides some simple tests of these suppositions in the form of the simple correlation coefficients between the entry and exit rates and each of these other measures. Some, but by no means all, of these hypotheses receive some support from these results. For example, capital intensity is (as hypothesized) negatively related to most of the measures of both entry and exit rates. Similarly, again as expected, output growth is positively related to most measures of entry rates but negatively related to exit rates.[22] While the likelihood of improvement in relative TFP scores has (as expected) consistently negative effects on entry and exit rates, none of these correlations is statistically significant. Finally, as expected the correlation between the dispersion (standard error) of the productivity indexes and both entry and exit rates is consistently negative.

Another issue of relevance to firm dynamics is the nature of the frequently observed positive relation between exports and productivity. This is of special relevance to Korean manufacturing plants and firms, given the importance of exports to the development of Korean manufacturing industries. Does higher productivity or growth in productivity lead to exports or does experience in exporting lead to improved productivity? The same dataset is of course suitable for answering these questions. To this end, Aw et al. (1999) show that, in each of five sectors (textiles, apparel, plastics, electrical machinery and electronics, and transport equipment) and for each of the three years (1983, 1988, and 1993), the average pro-

TABLE XIII

Simple correlation coefficients (and Spearman rank correlations in second row) between exit and entry rates and the average age of exiting firms and each of four possible determinants

	Capital intensity	Productivity improvement of incumbents	Productivity dispersion of entrants	Output growth rate
Entry rate (un-weighted)	–0.25*	–0.91	–0.34	0.31
	–0.29	–0.84	–0.32	0.33
Employment-weighted entry rate	–0.29	–0.55	–0.23*	0.05*
	–0.22*	–0.54	–0.20*	–0.11*
Exit rate (un-weighted)	–0.21*	–0.68	–0.24*	–0.13*
	–0.18*	–0.49	–0.11*	–0.08*
Employment-weighted exit rate	–0.32	–0.45	–0.14*	–0.41
	–0.23	–0.41	–0.21*	–0.28*
Average age of exiting firms	0.44	0.70	0.28*	–0.16
	0.52	0.67	0.17*	–0.20

Source: Chung (1998, Table 3.9).
Note: * indicates statistical significance at the 5 per cent level.

ductivity of exporting firms is significantly higher than that of nonexporters. The difference is greatest for textiles, followed by apparel and transport equipment. With a few exceptions, however, there are no such significant differences in productivity between firms of different export propensities (low, medium, and high). Only in the textile and transport equipment sectors is there evidence that plants exporting more than 75 percent of their total production have significantly higher productivity than plants that export less, and even in these cases the productivity differentials are rather narrow.[23]

Unlike Taiwan where these authors found significantly higher productivity among plants that enter export markets than among those that do not in all five sectors, for Korean manufacturing plants, the differentials exist but are statistically significant only in textiles and transport equipment. They also find some year *t* productivity differentials between plants that exit the export market in the next period ($t + 1$) and those that remain in the market. These differences are in favor of the export survivors in four of the five sectors, and the differences are statistically significant in three of them (textiles, plastics, and electrical machinery). Finally, comparing continuous exporters with continuous nonexporters, they find sizable and statistically significant differences in favor of continuous exporters in four of the five sectors (all except electrical machinery) but neither significant widening nor narrowing of these differentials over time. In general, while there is strong evidence of a correlation between productivity and export experience in Korea as in Taiwan, the evidence in support of either high productivity inducing subsequent export entry or export experience raising subsequent productivity is weaker in Korea than in Taiwan.

Over time, besides increasing in size, surviving SMEs change in a number of other respects. Table XIV presents the means of various other characteristics and performance indicators for SMEs of different age groups. The results show that the longer the firms are in existence, the more likely they are to (1) be of corporate form (EQU), (2) have a foreign partner (DFPART), (3) be larger in size (no matter whether measured in terms of labor (MAN89), capital (ASS89), or sales (SAL89), (4) export more (EXP89) or be more likely be an exporter (DEXP), and (5) have greater R&D expenditures (RSH89), more researchers on the

TABLE XIV
Average firm characteristics and performance indicators variables by firm age

Variable	Label	First quartile		Second quartile		Third quartile		Fourth quartile	
		N	Mean	*N*	Mean	*N*	Mean	*N*	Mean
FIRMAGE	Firm age in 1989	275	3.269	276	7.467	275	13.556	276	25.257
EQU	Corporate	275	0.564	276	0.612	275	0.651	276	0.728
DFPART	Foreign partner	275	0.033	276	0.047	275	0.04	276	0.094
RFPART	Foreign share in equity	275	1.422	276	2.688	275	1.6	276	4.514
CAP89	Equity capital (billion won)	241	0.048	253	0.155	255	0.124	254	0.285
ASS89	Total asset(billion won)	201	0.188	235	0.645	243	0.502	243	1.295
MAN89	Number of workers	272	62.14	272	90.82	270	124.94	270	286.95
SAL89	Sales (billion won)	215	3.452	248	6.301	253	12.205	257	18.596
EXP89	Export (million U.S.$)	275	0.526	276	1.545	275	2.065	276	3.311
DEXP	Export dummy	275	0.164	276	0.417	275	0.415	276	0.486
RSH89	R&D costs (billion won)	275	0.026	276	0.03	275	0.038	276	0.095
NORSH	Numbers of researchers	275	1.142	276	1.645	275	2.36	276	6.243
RANDDD	R&D department	275	0.204	276	0.243	275	0.269	276	0.413
RESINS	Research institute	275	0.04	276	0.036	275	0.065	276	0.159
NOPATENT	Number of patents	275	1.76	276	1.674	275	1.669	276	1.547
LIGHT	Light industry	275	0.382	276	0.388	275	0.313	276	0.355
HEAVY	Heavy industry	275	0.473	276	0.467	275	0.513	276	0.486
ELECT	Electronics	275	0.145	276	0.145	275	0.175	276	0.156

Source: Korean Institute for Industry and Trade (KIET) SME sample survey of 1990.

staff (NORSH), or a research institute. A somewhat surprising finding, however, is that the number of patents (NPATENT) declines with firm age. One explanation for this might be that patenting is more common in high tech firms which also might be typically younger.

Additional insights as to firm dynamics can be gained from case studies. Linsu Kim (1997) provides several interesting ones of SMEs that have successfully managed to fill leading positions in niche markets. One of these is of an SME paper board manufacturer founded and managed by an ex naval engineer. In contrast to the typical LE manager, the manager of this SME did not acquire a modern turnkey plant designed and developed abroad, but rather designed his own plant after considerable reading of technical literature and several visits to Japanese factories. He then bought used equipment for the plant from Japan. Although very cheap, the used equipment was missing parts that the new SME had to design and make. Yet, after much trial and error, being himself the master of his chosen technology, this entrepreneur was in a better position than his competitors to increase his capacity, improve the technology to overcome its observed shortcomings, and modify it to adjust to changing circumstances. After 15 years of experience like this and through extra knowledge gained through membership in an American technical institute for paper, he decided to start a new plant based on equipment designed jointly with local machine producers. In each of these steps, the use of his experience reduced his investment costs to a fraction of the cost of new imported machinery. At no time did this paperboard manufacturer have to rely on licensing of foreign technology or machinery. Since the learning was done by the entrepreneur himself, none of the benefits of this learning leaked out to others, thereby avoiding an important disincentive for investments in training and R&D by SMEs.

Another of Kim's case studies of successful SMEs is that of a metal pipe manufacturer which made its big technological breakthrough by hiring one superb, experienced engineer from an existing LE in the country, having him train others on the job, and then buying the machinery he recommended from abroad. Yet, within a year of its introduction, the team of engineers was able to improve on the imported (Japanese) model. Its success was attributed to the way its engineering team and others in the firm learned from their own experience.

Still another case is that of the Medison Company, a producer of ultrasonic scanners used in hospitals and medical laboratories. Medison was formed when a team of university and government researchers hooked up with a venture capitalist. The government played three key roles in Medison's success. First, it provided four years of sponsored R&D funding to the researchers before the company's establishment. Second, it provided government-backed venture capital financing. Finally, it provided temporary tariff protection allowing the firm to penetrate domestic markets (rural hospitals which could not afford to buy imported scanners inclusive of the tariffs). Working under the time pressure to be competitive in a relatively short period of time and learning from their experience to date, the research team soon managed to design and produce scanners of much higher quality for export markets.

Even these few case studies illustrate a variety of ways in which, by learning from experience, internalizing its benefits, hiring foreign or other experienced consultants, taking advantage of the expertise of equipment suppliers and hard work by conscientious and talented entrepreneurs, SMEs can overcome the various constraints on their development. From the technical side, this may be getting more difficult, suggesting that government or other external support may be needed in the future, especially in high-tech sectors. In the case of marketing and finance, however, there is little reason to see why these difficulties should get more serious over time, except perhaps in the case in which a relatively young and capital-intensive SME attempts to pioneer in the penetration of international markets in that activity.[24]

4. External sources of support: private firms through subcontracting

Especially for SMEs in countries like Korea that are rapidly moving up the technology scale and enforcing intellectual property rights, access to successful LEs and other firms can be an important means of overcoming the various constraints on their development, at least under the right circumstances.

The purpose of this section is to examine the role of subcontracting relationships in SMEs, both currently and over time. How pervasive is subcontracting? How does it vary in extent and character across subsectors of manufacturing? To what extent do these relationships satisfy the SMEs participating in them? What problems arise? These are among the questions to be addressed. Subcontracting relations can go in either or both of two directions: "in" when a firm receives orders and "out" when the firm places or gives out orders.

To examine the extent to which SMEs are engaged in subcontracting of any type and the direction of these subcontracting relations by size of firm, turn to Table XV. Note that the overall incidence of subcontracting increases moderately by size (calculated by subtracting the entries in the last column "no contracting" from 100 percent). Specifically, 65.6 percent of firms with five to nine workers are involved in subcontracting of some kind, compared with 83.2 percent of those of size 200–299. This moderate increase, however, is the resultant of two opposing trends with respect to size: first, the percentage of firms involved in "subcontracting in only," which falls with size; and, second, the percentage of firms that either "subcontract out only" or "subcontract both in and out," which rises with size. Contrary to popular perception, Korean SMEs do about as much contracting out as they do contracting in. The smallest ones, however, are considerably more likely to contract in than out.

Generally speaking, Korea is a relatively latecomer to subcontracting, except in a few relatively old industries such as the aforementioned case of woven textiles. Korea has long aspired to have a deeper, more multi-tiered subcontracting system than the one it has, the Japanese automobile industry serving as a model.[25] Such a system is believed to be transaction cost-efficient in that, at each level, the principal needs to contract with only a few contractors, each of which, in turn, can contract with a small number of others (subcontractors), etc., down the various tiers in the overall contractual structure. With only a few firms with which to relate directly, more attention can be devoted to detail, the monitoring of performance is facilitated, and the basis for cooperation between the two parties is believed to be enhanced (less likelihood of the benefits of this cooperation leaking out in externalities). Levy (1991) compared the character of subcontracting in Korea with that in Taiwan. Just as in the case of comparisons to Japan, Taiwan's subcontracting system was found to be both deeper and more transaction cost-efficient than that of Korea in the footwear industry. Levy (1991) attributed this to Taiwan's stronger family networks, higher income, and greater length of experience in production and exports.

Table XVI shows how the importance of subcontracting has changed over time. The biggest change was between the 1980s and the 1990s, in large part due to the rise of auto parts and other suppliers of assembling industries. Since 1991, the percentage of SMEs engaged in subcontracting has fluctuated somewhat around a mean of a little over 70 percent. Of the firms engaged in subcontracting, their dependence on subcontracting for

TABLE XV
Incidence of subcontracting by SMEs in manufacturing by direction and by size, 1997

Firm size group (by number of workers)	Number of SMEs	Subcontracting out only (%)	Subcontracting in only (%)	Either or both directions (%)	No subcontracting (%)
All sizes	85,947	14.1	19.7	37.9	28.3
5–9	37,870	12.9	22.4	30.3	34.4
10–19	24,657	10.2	20.7	43.2	25.9
20–49	16,194	18.0	15.6	44.6	21.8
50–99	4,427	24.9	12.4	45.6	17.1
100–199	2,130	28.5	7.7	42.5	21.3
200–299	669	29.9	7.2	46.1	16.8

Source: Small and Medium Enterprise Authority and Federation of Small and Medium Enterprises (1998).

TABLE XVI
Variations in the incidence of subcontracting over time and across size groups of SMEs in manufacturing

Year	Any subcontracting	0–20%	20–40%	40–60%	60–80%	80–100%
1986	42.5	4	5.4	5.4	6.1	79.1
1991	73.6	1.6	1.6	3	5.4	88.4
1992	73.4	1.6	1.5	3.3	4.1	89.5
1993	65.4	3.2	3.8	4.1	5.4	83.5
1995	72.1	3.8	3.4	4.8	7.1	80.9
1996	73.6	2.7	2.7	5.1	11.8	77.7
1997	71.7	6.1	4.1	3	7.2	79.6

Source: The Survey of Small & Medium Enterprises, each year, Small & Medium Enterprise Authority, Federation of Small & Medium Enterprises.

orders is quite high, though perhaps declining slightly since 1992. Many SMEs engaged in "subcontracting in" like the technological support and other benefits of subcontracting, but, on the other hand, would like also to develop their own sales channels so as to obtain higher prices for their products if they can get them.

Tables XVII and XVIII reveal the ways in which both the benefits and the problems of the subcontracting from the perspectives of the SMEs, themselves, have varied over time. From Table XVII it can be seen that the provision of raw materials, technology, and product design are by far the most frequently cited types of support received. Of these, the provision of raw materials (typical of light industries, such as textiles and leather) is of declining importance while technology is of rising importance. Also on the rise are management and to a lesser extent financial support. Other forms of support mentioned by a minority of SMEs involved in contracting in are equipment loan, loan guarantees, manpower, capital, and joint development of parts.

Table XVIII, on the other hand, reports the frequencies of various problems encountered in these relationships for SMEs which contract in. The most frequently identified of these problems is too low a price for the work. Korean contractors, like their counterparts in Japan, are notorious for insisting that the subcontractors each year produce the product for less (forcing firms to increase productivity). Note, moreover, that the frequency of such reports has increased between 1986 and 1997 from 40 percent to over 60 percent. The second and even more rapidly growing problem is delay in payment, having risen from 18.5 percent of the firms in 1986 to 53.3 percent in 1997. Other increasingly cited problems are "demand for too high quality," "inconvenient timing of orders," and "too short delivery times."

TABLE XVII
Percentages of subcontracting in SMEs reporting support received in their subcontracting relations, by type for selected years between 1993 and 1997

Year	Type of support received									
	Technology	Management	Financial	Loan guarantee	Raw materials	Loan of equipment	Product design	Capital	Loan of manpower	Joint development of parts
1993	37.2	11.5	9.2	5.3	56.4	9.4	37.2	3.4	7.6	n.a.
1995	43.7	15.7	13.4	8.7	53.8	12.8	40.7	1.9	5.0	10.0
1996	44.1	16.9	14.8	7.2	47.9	19.4	33.4	2.1	4.2	11.0
1997	50.4	24.7	12.4	6.8	34.2	9.4	32.6	2.8	5.8	n.a.

Note: Multiple entries were possible for each respondent.
Source: Survey of Small and Medium Enterprises, Table 47 for each year, Small and Medium Enterprise Authority and Federation of Small and Medium Enterprises.

TABLE XVIII
Percentages of subcontracting in SMEs reporting problems in their subcontracting relations, by type for selected years between 1986 and 1997

Year	Type of problem							
	Demand for too high quality	Delay in receiving goods	Too low price for work	Delay in payment	Inconvenient time of order	Too short delivery time	Change in the contracting enterprise	Others
1986	13.9	n.a.	40.0	18.2	15.5	10.9	n.a.	1.5
1991	11.7	n.a.	39.7	22.9	17.3	5.8	n.a.	2.6
1993	25.7	3.6	74.6	41.6	35.1	32.9	20.5	1.7
1995	30.8	6.7	75.4	40.7	44.5	35.0	23.1	2.8
1996	32.0	7.0	68.4	44.9	48.3	34.2	26.2	4.2
1997	33.1	6.9	61.3	53.3	41.5	29.6	22.7	5.7

Note: Multiple entries were possible for each respondent.
Source: Survey of Small and Medium Enterprises, Table 48 for each year, Small and Medium Enterprise Authority and Federation of Small and Medium Enterprises.

Since as yet we have not attempted to examine the possible effects of subcontracting on performance, in Table XIX, we relate TFP to "subcontracting in" by using the same KIET sample of SMEs in 1990 used previously. Table XIX compares the sector-specific trimmed means of TFP of SMEs with and without "subcontracting in" for 11 sectors and for the full sample.[26] For eight of the 11 subsectors as well as for them all combined, the trimmed mean TFP index is higher with subcontracting than without it. Moreover, for five of the eight subsectors in which the TFP score is higher with subcontracting than without it, the difference is statistically significant at the 5 percent level. Only in clothing, fur, leather, and shoes is the mean TFP index for the SMEs *without* subcontracting significantly higher than for those *with* subcontracting.[27]

5. External sources of support: government and nongovernmental institutions

Private firms through subcontracting relationships are of course by no means the only source of

TABLE XIX
The relation between "Contracting In" and TFP in the KIET sample of SMEs in 1990 in different subsectors of manufacturing

Subsector of manufacturing	Number Subcontracting in		Subcontracting in	
	N	TFP Index (trimmed mean)	*N*	TFP Index (trimmed mean)
Food manufacturing	42	0.140	22	0.144
Textiles	17	0.142	27	0.125
Clothing, fur, and leather, shoes	15	0.181	27	0.098
Wood and wood products	25	0.291	25	0.206
Paper and printing	19	0.166	17	0.227
Chemicals, petroleum, rubber, and plastics	74	0.210	45	0.229
Nonmetallic minerals	11	0.150	21	0.185
Basic metals	32	0.129	27	0.188
Metal structures and products	19	0.136	19	0.215
Machinery and transport equipment	54	0.164	70	0.620
Electrical machinery and other	47	0.113	91	0.114
Total manufacturing	356	0.167	392	0.242

Source: Computed from KIET SME Survey.

external support for SMEs. Indeed, in Korea there has been a proliferation of institutions and policies aimed at providing technical, marketing, financial, or other forms of assistance to SMEs. As was already mentioned, there has been considerable change in the orientation of government policies with respect to SMEs over time. In the 1960s and early 1970s, in the pursuit of rapid economic development, and in the absence of market and other institutions capable of providing access to small and new firms, SMEs were relatively neglected. Policy was directed to providing the credit and other support to the "winners," those firms, perhaps originally small, but which had managed to succeed in export markets and hence which had grown to be very large. Firms and sectors were assigned ambitious growth quotas. Failure to meet these quotas could result in the loss of access to highly subsidized policy loans or other penalties. SMEs, on the other hand, had access primarily only to credit on the informal or curb market at interest rates perhaps double those in the formal credit market.

When in the 1970s the government's development plan assigned top priority to heavy and chemical industries or HCI (industries usually characterized as having economies of scale and capital-intensive) and exports, SMEs were put in an even more unfavorable position. An SME bank had been set up, but loan repayment rates were quite low, transaction costs very high and hence making little difference for SMEs in general. Even in the late 1960s, however, some seeds were set for the beginnings of an effective SME support system. The Korean Credit Guarantee Fund (KCGF) was created to facilitate the provision of bank credit to SMEs. A special trading corporation was set up for assisting SMEs in export marketing. The beginnings of the SME reservation scheme and of another to foster vertical integration (subcontracting) with LEs were established in the mid-1970s, and in 1979 the Small and Medium Industry Promotion Corporation (SMIPC) was established for the purpose of providing technical assistance and training programs to SMEs.

In the 1980s the shift toward a stronger SME support system and policies aimed at overcoming the earlier neglect of SMEs accelerated. The new constitution stipulated that the protection and promotion of SMEs should be included among the basic responsibilities of the government. A series of laws was passed to turn this broad objective into a body of law. Many specific-purpose credit funds were set up, for example, to help rural industries, to foster venture capital designed to assist small high tech startups, to foster collective or cooperative activities among SMEs, to help older SMEs update their technology, and, as was mentioned previously, even to help existing SMEs to relocate some of their operations abroad. An ambitious system for identifying and providing various kinds of support for "promising SMEs" was established, and, even more important, both commercial banks (city banks) and rural local banks were required to allocate minimum specified percentages of their loans to SMEs. Such quotas were even forced on nonbank financial institutions, such as insurance companies. Various tax breaks to SMEs (accelerated depreciation allowances, deductions from taxable income, tax moratoria, and tax rate reductions) for special purposes were also implemented.[28]

The 1980s and 1990s have also seen a proliferation of technical research centers, institutes, standards centers, productivity centers, and a design and packaging center organized as either government or nonprofit agencies. Although not developed exclusively for use by SMEs, several of these agencies were in fact fairly heavily used by SMEs. Moreover, as the internal capabilities of LEs increased with accumulated experience and staff additions, LEs had less need to rely on those external agencies, such as the Korean Overseas Trading Association (KOTRA), which had earlier catered almost exclusively to LEs. Some of the new centers have also proliferated into networks of either regional general-purpose agencies or national but highly specialized ones.

Nevertheless, because of the large number of programs and agencies, the lack of data on both their benefits and costs, and the likelihood that their effects would appear only in the relatively long run and leak out in the form of externalities, the proper evaluation of these programs and organizations is quite a challenge. Kim and Nugent (1999), as part of a broader multi-country study designed and led by Brian Levy of the World Bank, made a serious, though largely qualitative, attempt to evaluate the usefulness of these programs in a relatively small sample (122) of mostly exporting SMEs. Four different subsectors were chosen to reflect different environmental conditions, stages in the product cycle, and other subsector characteristics. While no attempt was made to obtain cost of program data, the use by and usefulness to the sample firms of each of three different types of SME support was investigated. For each general type of support an attempt was made to distinguish those specific forms and specific delivering agencies that were more highly evaluated from those that were not.

In general, the following conclusions were obtained:

1. When and where somewhat comparable support was available from both private commercial sources and from government or other nonprofit agencies, the services of the commercial services were more highly evaluated. Among the reasons were that the support from nonprofit agencies was often too general to be of great use or too difficult to access.
2. The use of nonprofits would be less and the services less well evaluated when there existed reasonably accessible support from subcontracting arrangements.
3. Subcontracting arrangements tended to be used most frequently and evaluated most highly by relatively small SMEs. The best subcontracting arrangements were those that had evolved relatively slowly in communities where informational networks were especially strong, such as the aforementioned Taegu area for woven textiles. In this case, contracting firms (both LEs and SMEs) were a frequently used and highly evaluated source of each major type of support. In the case of the more recently developed and government-encouraged subcontracting relations in the auto parts subsector, contracting firms (generally LEs) were a frequently used and highly evaluated source of technology support but of neither financial nor marketing support. Since subcontracting arrangements were not especially highly evaluated by sample SMEs in the electronic parts and components subsector, even when created and well established, subcontracting relations need not be a cure-all for the constraints that SMEs face.
4. Since use of collective support (especially in the case of technical support) rises with size and other indicators of internal capabilities of SMEs, it is clear that inadequate capabilities within the firm can make it difficult for SMEs to access collective support.
5. Both foreign and domestic equipment suppliers are important and highly evaluated sources of ideas about product and process improvement. Individual consultants and university researchers are another potentially useful though somewhat less frequently used private source of technological information and support.
6. In the case of marketing, foreign buyers are another important source of external support. Yet, foreign buyers may not be available to SMEs until the country has become a relatively important source of subsector exports. Hence, it is relatively early in the subsector's export experience in sectors without dense subcontracting networks (as exist in woven textiles) and for relatively large firms that have the ability to access collective sources of support that nonprofit agencies have played a well-evaluated role. As in the case of technology support, the principal shortcoming of such support is its excessive generality.
7. While financial support from public agencies tends to come at a substantially lower interest rates, nevertheless, its usefulness is rarely indicated to be superior to that from commercial sources. Two reasons for this seem to be the narrow scope and eligibility requirements of such programs and delays in obtaining the funds.
8. In good times and in the absence of the severe financial repression of the nonbank and other financial markets that took place in the early 1970s, Korean SME exporters have had access to a relatively wide range of financial support. This reflects the high priority that was given to exports in the country's economic development plans. In bad times, SMEs are likely to be the first to be squeezed financially, with nonrenewal of loans, and lengthening delays in payment by their clients. As is the case elsewhere, however, external sources of financial support are rarely available to SMEs at startup.

9. The low use and usefulness evaluations of support from nonprofit agencies are frequently attributed to the excessively general character of such support or to its irrelevance or inaccessibility to SMEs. Hence, increased use and usefulness of nonprofit sources of support will clearly depend on improvements in the ability of nonprofit agencies to supply the type of services needed and in an easily accessible and timely manner. This requires that the supplying agencies have good governance systems. The ingredients of good governance seemed to be (1) a well-functioning system of performance evaluation by principals, (2) a strong human resource base allowing the agencies to supply high quality services, (3) "voice"[29] or other means of participation by the SME clients of such agencies, and (4) a market test.[30] In many agencies, one or more of these crucial ingredients seemed to be missing. In general, those agencies coming closest to satisfying all four of these ingredients were the most highly evaluated.
10. An especially low cost and widely used and highly evaluated source of support, typically supplied by external, largely nonprofit, sources, was trade fairs, especially international ones.

The sample from which these findings emerged is not only small but also, being limited to largely exporting firms in a small number of subsectors, is clearly far from representative of Korean SMEs in general. For this reason, to compare the use and usefulness of subcontracting and noncommercial sources of external support in a larger and more representative sample of Korean SMEs, in Tables XX and XXI we make use of the same 1990 SME Survey carried out by KIET that has been used in several of the preceding tables.

Table XX provides the means of the support variables from both subcontracting and nonprofit agencies for each of four age-of-firm groups. As can be seen from the entries for FIRMAGE in the top row of the table, the youngest group of SMEs has an average of a little over three years, and the oldest an average of a little more than 25 years. Two rows of entries are given for the subcontracting relations, DSUBIN, a dummy variable for being involved in subcontracting in, and DHELPFPA, a dummy variable from receiving any form of help from that relation. While DSUBIN declines only ever so slightly with age, DHELPFPA declines more sharply and more regularly with age. Clearly, the likelihood of help is smaller than that for subcontracting in, suggesting that in only about half the cases do recipient firms feel that they have received help from the relation. Nevertheless, about a quarter of all the youngest firms receive such help, and half of those who are involved in subcontracting. Among the oldest group less than one-sixth of the sample SMEs received such help, which is only one-third of the number engaged in subcontracting in.

For government and other nonprofit agencies quite a few different agencies and types of support are listed. Only a few of them have ever been used by more that 10 percent of the firms. The most frequently used have been special government policy loans (POLFIN), general bank finance (GENFIN), credit guarantees (CREDIGU), the Korea Productivity Center (HPROD), the SME Promotion Corporation (SMEBSEV), and several types of tax incentives, deductions for specific purposes (ITAXDUD), tax incentives on prefunds such as feasibility studies (PREFUND), and special depreciation allowances (SPEDEP). Notice that, regardless of frequency of use, or the specific program or supplying agency, use tends to rise with age of the firm. There are but two exceptions to this rule, CREDIGU and KOTRADE, for which there is no consistent pattern. Since the natural thing would be for the likelihood of use to increase with the time the firm has been in existence, these two exceptional cases would seem to indicate that these two agencies have been especially successful in becoming accessible and useful to newer firms. In only a few cases have we put usefulness scores, those variable names beginning with the letter "E."[31] The scores for EKOTRA indicate that the youngest firms found KOTRA to be slightly more useful than the older firms, though in general the averages (based on a five point) scale were not very high and, indeed, considerably lower than those for EGENFIN (general bank credit). For the more policy-dictated funds (POLFIN), although use rises sharply with age, the usefulness of such funds (as indicated by EPOLFIN) shows that those relatively new SMEs that did use such funds found them just as useful as did older SMEs.

TABLE XX
Use of external support by source and by age of SME firm group, 1990

Variable	Label	Means for variables by firm age							
		First quartile		Second quartile		Third quartile		Fourth quartile	
		N	Mean	*N*	Mean	*N*	Mean	*N*	Mean
FIRMAGE	Firm age in 1989	275	3.269	276	7.467	275	13.556	276	25.257
Support from contractor through subcontracting relations									
DSUBIN	Subcontract-in	275	0.513	276	0.467	275	0.52	276	0.446
DHELPFPA	Help from contractor	275	0.247	276	0.196	275	0.167	276	0.156
Support from government and other nonprofit agencies									
SUBSIDY		275	0.029	276	0.029	275	0.047	276	0.087
POLFIN	Policy funds	275	0.258	276	0.551	275	0.818	276	1.033
EPOLFIN	Effectiveness of policy funds	50	3.277	84	3.153	116	3.223	131	3.253
GENFIN	General funds	275	0.207	276	0.322	275	0.455	276	0.5
CREDIGU	Use of credit guarantee	255	1.98	245	2.253	263	2.384	251	2.096
TAXDED	Tax deductions	275	0.255	276	0.446	275	0.705	276	1.033
ITAXDUD	Other tax benefits	275	0.069	276	0.188	275	0.258	276	0.239
PREFUND	Tax incentive on prefunds	275	0.091	276	0.315	275	0.553	276	0.801
SPEDEP	Special depreciation	275	0.065	276	0.181	275	0.338	276	0.46
GEYUL	Vertical Integration	275	0.011	276	0.011	275	0.047	276	0.047
SMEBSEV	SME Promotion Corp.	275	0.269	276	0.417	275	0.76	276	0.721
SMECP	SME Federation	275	0.036	276	0.054	275	0.08	276	0.116
HPROD	Korea Product Center	275	0.116	276	0.145	275	0.215	276	0.373
HDISIGN	Korea Design Center	275	0	276	0.022	275	0.025	276	0.047
EKOTRA	Effective:KOTRA	10	2.85	15	3.033	28	2.75	36	2.861
KOTRADE	Korea Trade Promotion Corp.	275	0.044	276	0.033	275	0.033	276	0.051
KIET	KIET	275	0.073	276	0.098	275	0.185	276	0.225
PROTEC	Institute product technology	275	0.051	276	0.033	275	0.036	276	0.094

Source: Korea Industry and Trade Institute (KIET) Sample SME Survey of 1990.

Table XXI provides the corresponding means on many of the same variables (and a few others) for each of four firm size groups. With respect to subcontracting, note that DHELPFPA tends to rise with size, even though it fell with FIRMAGE. This presumably reflects the fact that some of the larger SMEs are auto parts producers that receive considerable technical assistance from the large auto assemblers. Since as noted in the top row of the table, firm size and age are positively related, this implies that subcontracting help is most frequently received by young firms regardless of size even though young firms tend to be small. As with firm age, use of all the support variables except the credit guarantee system (CREDIGU) and KOTRADE rise fairly sharply with age. In both of the latter cases, the pattern is of the Inverted-U (nonlinear) form. Once again there is little systematic variation in the usefulness scores by size. There is considerable variation in usefulness across types of support, from a low of 0 for the Quality Testing Office to well over 3.0 for the financial support variables CREDIGU and GENFIN. Given the multiplicity of different sources and types of SME support in Korea, of particular interest may be the scores given to the overall evaluations SATISSUP and EFFSUP. The scores for EFFSUP indicate that the supports offered are generally viewed as useful (with well above average score, rising with size of firm). At the same time, however, the relatively low scores for SATISSUP indicate that not all SME needs are satisfied by the programs.

From both the small sample of exporting SMEs and the larger sample of all SMEs, it is clear that financial support of virtually every type, but

TABLE XXI
Use of external support by size of SME

Variable	Label	Means of variables by number of employees							
		< 50		50–99		100–200		200–299	
		N	Mean	*N*	Mean	*N*	Mean	*N*	Mean
FIRMAGE	Firm age in 1989	537	9.657	222	11.982	164	14.89	179	18.832
Support from contractor through subcontracting relations									
DSUBIN	Subcontract-in	554	0.458	225	0.507	167	0.545	180	0.533
DHELPFPA		554	0.157	225	0.209	167	0.251	180	0.233
Support from government and other nonprofit agencies									
KNOWSUP	Know of SME support?	547	2.771	223	3.13	167	3.275	178	3.242
MUCHSUP	How much use of SME support?	544	2.063	222	2.554	166	2.651	174	2.575
SATISSUP	Satisfied with SME support?	502	2.315	213	2.61	164	2.646	163	2.706
EFFSUP	SME support effective?	512	3.012	216	3.37	163	3.509	170	3.618
SUBSIDY		554	0.02	225	0.062	167	0.072	180	0.094
POLFIN	Policy funds	554	0.247	225	0.733	167	1.066	180	1.456
GENFIN	General funds	554	0.132	225	0.409	167	0.557	180	0.878
EGENFIN	Effectiveness of GENFIN	55	3.145	62	3.401	61	3.417	100	3.318
CREDIGU	Use of credit guarantee	498	1.902	206	2.505	161	2.516	171	2.281
ECREDIGU	Effectiveness of CREDIGU	440	3.155	188	3.479	156	3.481	160	3.431
TAXDED	Tax deductions	554	0.184	225	0.631	167	0.976	180	1.55
ITAXDUD		554	0.054	225	0.249	167	0.311	180	0.411
TAXRED	Tax reductions	554	0.141	225	0.276	167	0.437	180	0.506
PREFUND	Tax incentive on prefunds	554	0.092	225	0.396	167	0.743	180	1.289
SPEDEP	Special depreciation	554	0.076	225	0.249	167	0.413	180	0.694
GEYUL	Vertical Integration	554	0.005	225	0.027	167	0.066	180	0.067
DEMANSUP	iyang+uniqsme+useofsme+collcon	554	0.034	225	0.053	167	0.066	180	0.061
SMEBSEV	SME Promotion Corp.	554	0.298	225	0.684	167	1	180	0.75
EXPERI	Quality test office	554	0.058	225	0.12	167	0.138	180	0.128
EEXPERI	Effectiveness of EXPERI	32	0	27	0	23	0	23	0
SMECP	SME Federation	554	0.025	225	0.08	167	0.15	180	0.144
HPROD	Korea Product Center	554	0.042	225	0.187	167	0.425	180	0.561
HDISIGN	Korea Design Center	554	0.004	225	0.018	167	0.042	180	0.072
KOTRA	KOTRA	554	0.056	225	0.178	167	0.228	180	0.233
KOTRADE	Korea Trade Promotion Corp.	554	0.022	225	0.062	167	0.054	180	0.05
KIET	KIET	554	0.083	225	0.142	167	0.257	180	0.25
PROTEC	Institute product technology	554	0.009	225	0.107	167	0.096	180	0.1

Source: Korea Industry and Trade Institute (KIET) Sample SME Survey of 1990.

especially general commercial bank loans, are very highly evaluated and widely used. Some of these are made possible by guarantees on loans to SMEs from the Korean Credit Guarantee Fund (KCGF) and other smaller and more specialized agencies. The KCGF whose guarantees go almost exclusively to SMEs grew rapidly; its outstanding guarantees grew (in nominal terms) by 10-fold between 1976 and 1984 and by almost another 15-fold by 1998. Expansion of the KCGF has been heavily dependent on new infusions of government funds since the fees have generally been insufficient to cover losses and other sources of funds have been quite small. The time path of KCGF expansion indicates rather clearly that its expansion is financial problem-driven. The two most severe recessions during the period were between 1979 and 1981 and again 1997 and 1998. The guarantees accepted almost tripled between 1979 and 1981 and more than tripled between 1996 and 1998. Defaults also exploded as a percentage of outstanding guarantees on both these occasions from 1.1 percent in 1979 to 4 percent in 1981 and almost 9 percent in 1982, and from 7 percent in 1996 to almost 20 percent in 1998. As a result, with fees held constant throughout the period, the compensation ratio, defined as the amount of fees collected in a particular year divided by the defaults for which the KCGF must compensate the banks, plummeted from around 150 percent in the mid-1970s to 11 percent in 1982. After that, with good times, the compensation ratio recovered to about 30 percent by 1990 but since then has fallen farther, hitting a new low of about 7.5 percent in 1998.

Another important factor contributing to the availability of external finance to SMEs has been the policy of the government to impose gradually increasing minimal credit allocations to SMEs on commercial and regional banks, and to a lesser extent on some other financial institutions. As shown in Table XXII, the result of these two measures has been a strong upward trend (at least until 1996) in the percentage of commercial bank loans allocated to SMEs. But since bank loans are but one of several important external sources of enterprise finance, by no means does this tell the whole story. Other important sources are various kinds of nonbank financial institutions. Since these (less regulated) institutions have been increasingly bought up and controlled by chaebol, the bulk of such funds has been directed to LEs. Bond markets and equity markets have also developed, but again almost exclusively for the benefit of LEs.[32]

To conclude, when times are good SMEs can obtain technological or marketing help from subcontracting relations with private firms, and especially when technology is simple, can obtain external support from private consultants, observation, reverse engineering, equipment suppliers, and local networks. When there is a recession or financial crisis, however, SMEs may be the first firms screened out by banks. Whereas LEs can usually borrow long-term even in bad years, if they can borrow at all, SMEs have to borrow short-term often at high interest rates from nonbank financial institutions. Moreover, also in bad times, they tend to get squeezed from lengthening delays in payment by their customers, against which they are quite powerless to act.

Over time, as technology gets more complex and SMEs enter into product niches in which there is less accumulated experience, they are also likely to become more dependent on external sources of marketing and technological support. Attempts by nonprofit agencies to supply such support are often plagued by difficulties in access, and by a mismatch between the kinds of services provided and those desired by users. With the right incentive structure and governance characteristics, such agencies are capable of providing such assistance quite efficiently. Despite the proliferation of programs in support of SMEs, and the ostensible change in government priorities in favor of SMEs, in view of the continuing close relationship between chaebol and the government, many analysts doubt that the change really amounts to anything very substantial.[33] Because of its fungibility and the lengthening payment delays that SMEs are subjected to in recessions, access to finance is especially highly evaluated though often unavailable to SMEs in such times.

6. SMEs as business cycle shock absorbers and inequality-reducing devices

Two interesting claims have been made concerning the benefits of SMEs in an economy. First,

TABLE XXII
Share of SME loans in total credit extended by commercial banks, 1979–95

	1979	1985	1988	1989	1990	1991	1992	1993	1994	1995.6
Total loans	71.7	257.9	356.2	462	540.2	649	745	834.1	992.9	1,054.4
Loans to SMEs	27	111	171.3	231.3	300	368.5	419.7	494.2	583.4	632.2
SME Share (%)	37.7	43.1	48.1	50.1	55.5	56.3	56.3	59.3	58.8	60.0

Unit: Won 100 million

Source: Annual Report on SME, each year, Federation of SME Cooperation Annual Report on Regional Economy, each year, Bank of Korea.

the claim that SMEs serve as shock absorbers, without which business cycles would be more serious and without which necessary structural adjustments would not have been made. Second, that the greater the relative importance of SMEs in the economy, the lower income inequality is likely to be. Does the Korean experience lend any credibility to such claims?

Shock absorber hypothesis

The shock absorber hypothesis applied to the Korean case would go something like this: Business cycle adjustments in fast growing economies such as Korea involve structural adjustments. If these structural adjustments are made quickly and smoothly, business cycle swings may be rather small and the downward phases not very painful to the economy as a whole. On the other hand, if the needed structural adjustments are postponed or undertaken only very slowly, business cycle troughs might last for some time and be rather deep. Since SMEs typically experience both higher failure rates and (among surviving SMEs) higher labor turnover rates than LEs, if the firm structure is heavily tilted to SMEs, such adjustments are likely to occur more smoothly and quickly than if the firm structure were tilted to LEs and *chaebol*.

When Korean SME entrepreneurs are faced with changed circumstances and severe financial or other crises, and therefore have to close their businesses promptly, they may already have ideas of other types of business better suited to the changed circumstances. Instead of engaging in collective action to protect their old businesses (if it is not already too late), as might be more typical of LEs, they are more likely to start new businesses. In the latter case, therefore, as soon as conditions improve, new firms are created that can be expected to go through the various phases of growth outlined before. The failure of individual SMEs is unlikely to gain much attention of policy makers to offer protection. Even if many SMEs were to fail at the same time, then the large size and heterogeneous character of their group and other factors make it unlikely that they would be able to succeed in the kind of collective action that would bring them protection in their old activities. Typically also, SME entrepreneurs have invested much less capital per unit of activity than their LE counterparts, and hence face lower costs of "exit" than LEs. On the other hand, even when only one or two *chaebol* are threatened with bankruptcy, especially those in the same industry, they might be expected to push for, and to be more successful in obtaining, protection of that industry, impeding the necessary adjustments. While in Korea such protection has only been very temporary, at the very least such an event induces a considerable debate in and out of government about the best way to cope with the crisis. Government has often been involved in bringing about mergers and selectively granting credit allowing the most important of such firms to survive the crisis, but thereby postponing or totally avoiding meaningful structural adjustment.

Is this plausible in the Korean context? In preceding sections we have seen that Korean SMEs have indeed experienced high failure rates, high labor turnover rates, and no evidence of SMEs engaging in collective action. The one notable special concession made to SMEs in the two most severe recessions has been substantial infusions of government capital to the KCGF. Yet, in view of the substantial number of startups that also occur in these recessions, some of these infusions can be interpreted as helping the new businesses to get started instead of only allowing troubled SMEs to survive. The process can be facilitated if Korean SME entrepreneurs have the foresight to originally invest in the type of capital that could be converted easily to the new business. Yet, this is precisely the type of strategy that many SME entrepreneurs adopt. What is probably not true, however, is that there has been any *large* difference in this respect between SMEs and *chaebol* and LEs. This is because, quite frequently, the Korean government has used bankruptcies in LEs as an opportunity to obtain greater rationalization of the industry, pushing *chaebol* firms to swap assets so as to concentrate more on those business activities for which they are best suited and experienced.[34] Even so, however, there is likely to be an important difference in the speed of adjustment in the two cases, necessarily rapid for SMEs, but more deliberate in the case of LEs.

On the side of the workers also, because of the historically higher labor turnover rates and lower asset specificity of the human capital in SMEs, any increase in turnover caused by SME bankruptcies should not increase structural unemployment to the extent that it would if the bankruptcies occurred in LEs. In general, therefore, the hypothesis would seem plausible qualitatively but unlikely to have a large quantitative effect.

Because of Taiwan's greater SME orientation relative to Korea, one might be tempted to use a Taiwan–Korea comparison of business cycle variability to provide evidence. In the East Asian currency and financial crisis of 1997 and 1998, Korea suffered a much greater recession than did Taiwan, thus strongly supporting the hypothesis. But, since Taiwan did not have the currency crisis that Korea did, it would be dangerous to make much of such a comparison without first trying to account for other differences between the two countries.

Alternatively, could one make use of the different business cycle episodes of Korea itself to see whether the intensity of business cycles varied with the SME shares in manufacturing or other activity? Unfortunately, a test of this sort would be equally difficult to carry out. It would require a full-fledged model of the business cycle with the SME share a critical variable interacting with others and from which it would be possible to conduct a counterfactual simulation. The empirical validity of such a model would require a number of observations on both business cycle severity and SME shares. The fact that Korea has enjoyed such sustained and rapid growth that business cycles have been relatively few and mild (until 1997) further impedes such a test. Hence, despite the fact that the shock absorber hypothesis seems plausible in the Korean context, it is probably weak and empirical evidence on it very difficult to obtain.

The best that can be done in this respect is some very casual empiricism. The quicker than expected seeming recovery of the Korean economy from the currency and financial crisis of 1997 might be at least *partly* attributed to the greater role that SMEs play in the economy now relative to 15 years before in the crisis of 1979–81. Something of an anomaly is the fact that between 1996 and 1997 the exit rate among LEs was actually greater than that among SMEs. To some extent, the anomaly might be explained by the crisis-stimulated pressure of an outside agency (the International Monetary Fund) to provide special funds in support of SMEs. It would appear highly likely, however, that, when the 1998 data on SMEs become available, both the failure rate and the new firm creation rate will be found to be higher among SMEs than among LEs by a considerable margin.

Income inequality-dampening hypothesis

Again applied to the Korean case, the inequality-dampening hypothesis would be something like what follows. SMEs are more labor intensive than LEs and have narrower wage differentials across workers. Wages are also distributed more equally than profits, rent, and other components of national income. Hence, as the SME sector expands relative to the LE sector of the economy, ceteris paribus, (1) the share of labor in national income should rise, (2) inequality among wage earners should decrease, and (3) overall income inequality should decrease.

Is the hypothesis plausible for Korea? It is generally the case that the wage bill is higher relative to other components of value added in SMEs than in LEs and SMEs exhibit greater labor intensity. Nugent (1989) showed that the dispersion of wages across workers is also lower in SMEs than in LEs.[35] Likewise, virtually all studies in Korea or anywhere else have shown wage income to be more equally distributed than other components of national income. For this reason, the conditions for the hypothesis to be valid seem to be satisfied. Is there any evidence?

Comparable time series data on measures of income inequality are notoriously hard to come by. Among the factors limiting comparability are changes over time or from one survey to another in the questionnaires used, response rates, the timing of the survey within a calendar year, various factors contributing to under-reporting such as changes in income tax rates or fears that the responses will be turned over to tax authorities, and assumptions for converting income in kind into value terms or for dealing with open-ended income groups. There is also the issue of the best measure to use of income inequality and the sensitivity of inequality rankings to the choice of measure. The existing literature on income distribution in Korea shows clearly that the validity and comparability of various estimates of income inequality are at least as full of controversy in Korea as elsewhere.

Though the results of many alternative income distribution studies are sometimes cited, the most widely cited and perhaps the most comparable time series on income inequality are the observations on the Gini coefficients for Korea contained in Deininger and Squire (1996). Although another index might be preferable since the Gini coefficient puts more weight on observations in the middle of the distribution than other measures, this is probably the best that can be done and for this reason are presented in Table XXIII. Also shown in the table are the shares of SMEs in manufacturing. At least in rough terms, the data would seem to support the hypothesized relationship. While the SME share in manufacturing employment was rising between 1952 and 1960, the Gini coefficient was rising. Then, between 1960 and 1975 while the SME share was falling, the Gini coefficient measure of income inequality was rising quite sharply. After 1975 when, as we have seen, the SME share was rising, the Gini coefficient was falling. Hence, not only is the hypothesis plausible for Korean conditions, but also there is at least some empirical evidence to support the hypothesis.[36]

Clearly, however, such a simple test does not rule out the possibility that there may have been other factors responsible for these two different trends in income inequality. Indeed, one distinct alternative would be a version of the Ranis-Fei-Lewis model concerning surplus labor. This model assumes a dual economy with different incomes per capita or wage rates in the two sectors.[37] According to this hypothesis, at first, growth of the manufacturing sector increases income inequality since it pulls people out of the low but homogeneous income sector into the high income, high variance sector. Over time, however, as more and more people enter the high income sector, intersectoral income differentials decline. Moreover, when the surplus labor in the traditional (non-manufacturing) sector disappears, the wage rate will rise in the traditional sector, further reducing income inequality. Kuznets (1955) also emphasized the role of human capital growth on income inequality. The rapid expansion of education (with the demand structure for labor of different skills held constant) should at some point tend to decrease income inequality within the high income, high variability sector. Since all these processes would seem to have been occurring in Korea simultaneously, without further research it is unclear as to which of these three explanations best explains the changes over time in Korea's income inequality.

7. Conclusions and lessons for other developing countries

In many respects, the South Korean experience with SMEs in manufacturing has been somewhat similar to other countries. For example, many of the constraints on their development seem to have been similar. Their strategies for overcoming these difficulties would also seem to have been similar in many respects. For example, developing subcontracting relationships and conserving on capital requirements by using used, borrowed, or rented capital and land are two such strategies. Their comparative characteristics vis-à-vis LEs are also rather similar; for example, their use of more labor intensive technologies, similar sectoral composition of output, concentration on a single product, the dominance of single-establishment firms, the relatively high level of education of SME entrepreneurs, and means of technology acquisition (through imitation, backward engineering, etc.).

TABLE XXIII
Relation between SME shares in manufacturing employment and Gini coefficient (based on household income)

	1952	1960	1966	1970	1975	1980	1985	1988	1996
Share of SMEs in manufacturing employment	61.5	67.7	60.3	49.0	45.7	49.6	56.1	60.0	69.2
Gini coefficient	34.0 (1953)	32.0 (1961)	34.2	33.3	39.1	38.6	34.5	33 .6	n.a.

Source: SME shares in manufacturing employment from Table I; Gini coefficients from Deininger and Squire (1996)

Although the data on dynamic patterns are unfortunately quite limited, they too seem to be similar to those in other countries. For example, the failure rates would appear to be very high in the first few years, declining gradually thereafter, and be higher for small SMEs than for large ones. Also, technical efficiency or TFP growth of SMEs would seem to have lagged substantially behind that of LEs.

Nevertheless, there are also some distinctive features of the Korean experience. One of these is the several trend reversals in the relative importance of SMEs over time and the determinants and effects of these changes. Another is the extremely rapid growth of the manufacturing sector, and lying behind this, the high rates of accumulation of both physical and human capital. Korea was also one of the earliest countries to make a substantial transition from a strategy of import substitution to increasing openness and export-led development. Two other very distinctive features are the unusually great importance of *chaebol* or conglomerate firms (with their many subsidiaries), and the increasingly large network of government and other nonprofit sources of external support to SMEs in marketing, technology, and finance. Indeed, it is the experience of Korea with respect to these somewhat distinguishing features that is of greater use in drawing lessons for other developing countries and for future research. For this reason in what follows we concentrate on these.

Changing trends in the importance of SMEs and their determinants and effects

As was already mentioned, since the 1950s the share of SMEs in manufacturing employment and value added first rose until the mid 1960s, then fell substantially to a low in the mid 1970s, then rose again to a high in the mid-1990s, and perhaps may have been declining since then. There is no single explanation for these changes but rather a combination of factors, including variations in the degree of financial repression, in mandatory minimum credit allocations to SMEs, in exports, in the various support mechanisms, and to some extent also in the sectoral composition of output, some of which was the result of interventionist government policies.[38]

While the generally high and sustained growth of the economy and differences relative to other countries make it difficult to sharply distinguish the effects of these various trend reversals in the relative importance of SMEs, two possibilities would seem to be (1) variations in the overall degree of income inequality that vary inversely with the SME shares in manufacturing employment and value added, and (2) the fact that the financial crisis of 1997–98 was less severe than expected because the greater importance of SMEs at this time relative to earlier years (i.e., the shock absorber hypothesis). Both of these hypotheses deserve further investigation.

Especially rapid growth of capital and human capital in general and manufacturing in particular

The considerably more rapid growth of physical and human capital in the Korean economy has implied both a rapidly changing structure of the economy, including a rising share of manufacturing, and changing comparative advantage from labor intensive to human capital and technology intensive goods. As a result, labor markets have progressively tightened, causing wage rate growth rates among the highest in the world. The increasing tightness of labor and rapidly rising wage rates have forced even SMEs to adjust in various ways, most important, by technology upgrading, but also in some cases by relocating their labor intensive operations to lower income countries of the region through outward flows of FDI. Support from government financial institutions and to a lesser extent from technological centers has helped SMEs in both types of adjustment. Even more important has been government discipline to limit the duration of protection and to see to it that support was offered primarily to those firms that could prove their competitiveness by exporting. Likewise, the priority given to exports in the drive for rapid growth meant that SMEs had to find ways of penetrating international markets. In some cases, this could be accomplished through subcontracting with LEs or with large trading firms. In other cases, it required the efforts of the firms themselves to increase their marketing expertise, and in still other cases, to access to nonprofit marketing organizations.

Relative importance of the chaebol

Although to some extent the relative importance of *chaebol* varied inversely with that of SMEs, throughout the period conglomerate-type firms have been relatively more important than in other countries. At first, this may have been the result of government policies aimed at maximizing growth at the expense of virtually all other goals. In particular, the *chaebol* organizational form made it possible for LEs to be as or even more flexible than SMEs, allowing LEs to enter new sectors and acquire new technologies even faster than SMEs, one of whose advantages is usually said to be greater flexibility. Later on, however, as government policy changed to one of greater concern for excessive concentration of industry and interest in promoting SMEs, more emphasis was placed on establishing complementarities between SMEs and LEs (and *chaebol*) through the promotion of subcontracting and other linkages between SMEs and LEs. In recent years, however, government policy has been increasingly oriented toward assuring SMEs of access to finance, markets, and technology independent of *chaebol* and LEs.

Transition to increasing openness of the economy

Though it is sometimes said that liberalization of product and other markets is a *sine qua non* for a healthy SME sector, the initial period of greater liberalization in the Korean economy coincided with the decreasing importance of the SME sector. During this period since credit and other resource allocations were heavily biased in favor of firms whose production and exports had grown rapidly, this encouraged mergers and buyouts of SMEs and was reflected in a sharply increasing LE share in manufacturing activity. Yet, as expertise in exports grew, and somewhat more neutral economic policies were adopted after the mid-1970s, the effect of increasing openness was no longer the same. Additional external sources of support from both private and public sources for SMEs in their efforts to sell abroad became available over time. Given that LEs increasingly had their own expertise and experience to assist them, over time existing agencies became more interested and able to help SMEs.

Proliferation of external support mechanisms from nonprofit sources

The steady growth and proliferation of Korea's external support systems has posed two problems for evaluation. First, since many of the programs have been developed simultaneously, it is difficult to attribute results to any particular program. Second, a comprehensive and comparative evaluation of their effectiveness is made (perhaps prohibitively) expensive. This study reports the results of some recent surveys based on the subjective evaluations of the programs of the various agencies by SME entrepreneurs. For the most part, nonprofit sources of support are rated as less effective than private commercial sources of support. Among the reasons for this are (1) the excessive generality of the information, training, and other support provided; (2) difficulties that SMEs may have in accessing such support or taking advantage of it effectively; and (3) the deficient characteristics of good governance by these support providers. All three of these shortcomings are interrelated. In the case of Korea, some components of good governance (e.g., competitive recruitment, managerial oversight, monitoring, and clearly defined objectives) are generally well provided for. Yet, the provision of "voice" or some other mechanism for ensuring that the support providers supply primarily those services that SMEs most want was generally rather weak. In qualitative terms, the agencies whose programs received the highest subjective evaluation scores were those with the best governance characteristics. This underscores the importance of governance in government and other nonprofit support providers. Several of the most consistently highly evaluated services of support providers are international trade fairs (in the case of marketing), easily accessible information on technical and other standards in foreign markets, financial support of various kinds (because of its fungibility), and credit guarantees that in turn have increased the access and improved the timeliness of that access to bank loans. In the past the most important sources of technical support have been informal mechanisms of consultants, university professors, equipment suppliers, imitation, and reverse engineering.

Problems and future prospects

Both private (subcontracting) relations with *chaebol* and other firms and government and other nonprofit agencies have helped SME achieve a growing importance in manufacturing employment, sales, value added, and exports over the last 20 years. Nevertheless, evidence has been presented in the form of recent SME share data and productivity trends to suggest that the relative importance of SMEs in many of these respects may now be reversing. It would seem that SMEs are currently facing increasing problems in a number of respects.

First, the increasing technological sophistication of production for foreign as well as domestic markets in the face of increasing openness of the economy and rapidly rising labor costs implies that the traditional means of technological acquisition and basis for comparative advantage for SMEs are no longer viable. This may require more in the way of public provision of quite specific kinds of technological information and training that will be a challenge to supply on a cost-effective basis.

Second, because of the rapid changes in the composition of output even within the SME sector itself, today's and tomorrow's SMEs are less likely to have experience in marketing.

Third, given the importance of healthy financial institutions and of SME access to them, the recent financial crisis has greatly clouded the future prospects of SMEs. Bankruptcies among both LEs and SMEs have rendered many financial institutions sick or totally nonviable. Even worse for SMEs is that because the fee structure of credit guarantees has remained constant despite the rapidly increasing loan default rates, the country's credit guarantee system that almost exclusively serves SMEs is no longer viable. Changes in the fee structure are urgently needed.

Fourth, given the time-consuming nature of court actions in defense of contracts and the continuously increasing delays in payment experienced by SMEs, SMEs seem increasingly powerless to take actions that would assure themselves of timely payment for the products and services they provide, often to LEs through subcontracting relations. The most effective solution to this problem would seem to be the provision of an electronic system for reporting payment arrears by individual companies and greater competition among contractors so that reputation for timely payment could be considered by SMEs in choosing their contracting partners.

Acknowledgements

The authors are deeply indebted and extremely grateful to Junkyu Lee and Sandra Manickam for able research assistance, to Be Yan Aw for gaining access to the results of yet unpublished work based on panel data, to numerous Korean officials, but especially Dr. Sung-No Choi, for assistance in obtaining information used in this study, and to Linsu Kim who had been a valued co-author in earlier joint work on South Korean SMEs for his many insights. They are also extremely grateful for the many useful comments and suggestions of Carl Liedholm, David Audretsch and various other participants of the project on The Role of Small and Medium Enterprises in Development, organized by the World Bank Institute.

Notes

1 One of the most well-known studies of this sort is Scitovsky (1986).

2 Since the vast majority of firms in Korea are single-establishment firms, the same trends apply as far as firms are concerned. What is rather special about Korea, however, is that conglomeration of firms is quite common, some of the largest conglomerates (known as *chaebol*) controlling large portions of GDP.

3 As demonstrated in Nugent (1989), however, the same trends would appear regardless of the particular size cutoff used between 100 and 500 workers.

4 The patterns within the food sector, however, where such establishments are plentiful might have been affected.

5 Between 1966 and 1975 the number of manufacturing establishments with five or more employees grew only from 22,718 to 22,787.

6 Between 1975 and 1996 the number of manufacturing establishments with five or more employees more than quadrupled from 22,787 to 98,119. (See Table V.)

7 Part of the ambiguity arises from the following points: While direct exports are those taken from the factory gate to the port of embarkation for export, in many cases these exports are channeled to a contractor who actually does the exporting. The contractor may be an assembling firm, such as an automobile assembling firm, which buys parts and then exports the car. The parts may therefore be an indirect export and the automobile a direct export, but this also introduces double counting. The parts producers may also think of themselves

as exporting by virtue of their receiving certain tax or credit preferences for exporting.

[8] Most of this FDI by SMEs has been to low wage countries in the region, such as China, Vietnam, and Indonesia. Despite many political barriers, in recent years, there has even been some investment in North Korea.

[9] These authors measured TFP growth in each of 36 manufacturing sectors and for various time periods. Nevertheless, over the period 1967–93 TFP averaged well over 2 percent per annum.

[10] The use of value added instead of gross production requires the additional assumption that time, capital, labor, and any other inputs are separable from raw material and intermediate inputs, an assumption which was rejected in most sectors for the United States (Jorgenson, Gollop and Fraumeni, 1987).

[11] They also made allowances for imperfect competition and markup whereas the former authors did not.

[12] Young (1995) showed, however, that manufacturing was something of an exception for Korea, the rate of TFP growth for the whole economy, being quite low.

[13] The reason for introducing this quadratic term is of course to capture the non-linearity in the relationship suggested by the results given in top portion of Table XVIII.

[14] While this factor might also depend on TFP, the purpose of its introduction is to control for short-run differences in the flow of funds or financial constraints.

[15] As a result, the direction of causation could in this case be going from TFP to SITUFUND rather than the other way around.

[16] See Uekusa and Torii (1987).

[17] For an interesting exploration of the effect of differences in sector- and time-specific product differentiation or variety on comparative sectoral TFP growth between Taiwan and Korea see Feenstra and others (1997).

[18] From the point of view of endogenous policy or political economy even these measures may not be exogenous and hence these, too, could yield biased results. Such measures, moreover, may capture only one dimension of openness, ignoring other components that could be more important (such as offsetting policies to support exports).

[19] See especially Pack and Westphal (1986) and Lim (1998).

[20] See Korea Industrial Technology Promotion Association (1991), Lim (1998).

[21] Both entry and exit rates were relatively low in food, wood products, and nonmetals in both periods.

[22] Note, however, that some of these relationships are rather sensitive to the particular measures of entry and exit.

[23] See Aw, Chung and Roberts (1999, Tables I and II).

[24] Clearly, in such a case the firm would not be able to take advantage of the experience of other more pioneering firms.

[25] See especially Kang and Park (1990) and Kim (1991).

[26] These TFP indexes are those computed separately for each sector, thereby allowing the production functions (from which the TFP indexes were constructed) to vary from one sector to another.

[27] The reader is cautioned that these results do not necessarily imply that causality is one way, going from subcontracting to the TFP index.

[28] For further details of the government programs and policies in support of SMEs see Seong (1995), Kim (1997), and Kim and Nugent (1999)

[29] "Voice" occurs in this context when both a client can complain to the supplier agency when the services are deemed to be of low quality or not relevant to the SME's needs and the complaint may result in corrective action by the agency.

[30] By market test is meant that a cost of service is paid for in a fee so that continued use of the service by the client SME suggests that the value of the service exceeds its cost.

[31] The reason for the exclusion of the others was the lack of variation across age groups.

[32] Indeed, as the currency and financial crisis of 1997–98 emerged, the share of LEs in corporate bond issues rose from 89 percent in 1996 to 99 percent by 1998 (International Monetary Fund, 1998).

[33] For example, critics point to the fact that, even after the financial crisis, *chaebol* firms are allegedly stronger than ever before and that the new Small and Medium Enterprise Authority does not have a budget to match its responsibilities.

[34] Moreover, the IMF program for Korea broke new ground by putting considerable emphasis on *chaebol* restructuring, setting up a broad Corporate Restructuring Agreement among 200 financial institutions, including the *chaebol*-owned nonbank financial institutions. The Coordinating Committee of this institution , moreover, was empowered to impose debt workout programs on firms and banks (International Monetary Fund, 1998).

[35] Berry and Mazumdar (1991) and Mazumdar (1998) have shown this to be the case rather generally for a number of countries.

[36] Needless to say, in view of the large number of alternative sources of data on income distribution in Korea, the use of alternative data sources could well lead to a quite different relationship than that depicted here.

[37] See Ranis and Fei (1961) for an exposition of the model and Berry and Urrutia (1976) for a careful application of the model to income distribution over time.

[38] For more details see Nugent (1996).

References

Aw, Bee Yan, Sukkyun Chung and Mark J. Roberts. 1999. 'Productivity and Turnover in the Export Market: Micro Evidence from Taiwan and South Korea', paper prepared for the Far Eastern Meetings of the Econometric Society in Singapore, July 1999.

Berry, Albert and Dipak Mazumdar, 1991, 'Small-Scale Industry in the Asian-Pacific Region', *Asian Pacific Economic Literature* **5**(2), 35–67.

Bank of Korea, 1998, *Statistical Monthly Bulletin*, Seoul: Bank of Korea.

Berry, Albert and Miguel Urrutia, 1976, *Income Distribution in Colombia*, New Haven: Yale University Press.

Caves, Richard E., 1998, 'Industrial Organization and New Findings on the Turnover and Mobility of Firms', *Journal of Economic Literature* **36** (December), 1947–1982.

Caves, Richard E. and David R. Barton, 1990, *Efficiency in*

U.S. Manufacturing Industries, Cambridge, MA: MIT Press.

Caves, Richard E. and Associates, 1992, *Industrial Efficiency in Six Nations*, Cambridge, MA: MIT Press.

Chang, J. K., S. C. Chung and K. K. Kim, 1994, *Economic Effect Analysis of R&D Investment*, Seoul: STEPI. [In Korean.]

Choi, Sung No, 1998, *Korean Conglomerates and Business Data Base*, Seoul: Center for Free Enterprise, Korean Federation of Industry.

Chung, Sukkyun, 1998, *Plant Turnover and Productivity Dynamics in Production and Export Markets: South Korea, 1983–1993*, unpublished Ph.D. Dissertation. Pennsylvania State University, State College, PA.

Deininger, Klaus and Lyn Squire, 1996, 'A New Data Set Measuring Income Inequality', *World Bank Economic Review* **10**, 565–591.

Dollar, David and Kenneth Sokoloff, 1990, 'Patterns of Productivity Growth in South Korean Manufacturing Industries, 1963–1979', *Journal of Development Economics* **33**, 309–328.

Economic Planning Board, 1995, *Report on the Mining and Manufacturing Census*, Seoul: Economic Planning Board.

Feenstra, Robert C., Dorsati Madani, Tzu-Han Yang and Chi-Yuan Liang, 1997, "Testing Endogenous Growth in South Korea and Taiwan', Working Paper 6028, National Bureau of Economic Research, Cambridge, MA.

Good, David H. M., Ishaq Nadiri and Robin Sickles, 1996, 'Index Number and Factor Demand Approaches to the Estimation of Productivity', Working Paper 5790. National Bureau of Economic Research, Cambridge, MA.

Greene, William H., 1980, 'Maximum Likelihood Estimation of Econometric Frontier Production Functions', *Journal of Econometrics* **13**, 170–188.

Ho, Sam P. S., 1980, 'Small-Scale Enterprises in Korea and Taiwan', Staff Working Paper 384. World Bank, Washington, DC.

Hong, Sung-Duk and Jung-Ho Kim, 1996, *Long Term Changes in Total Factor Productivity in Manufacturing 1967–93*, Seoul: Korea Development Institute.

International Monetary Fund, 1998, *Staff Report on the Third Quarterly Review Under the Stand-by Agreement*, Washington, DC: International Monetary Fund.

Jorgenson, Dale, W. F. M. Gollop and B. Fraumeni, 1987, *Productivity and U.S. Economic Growth*, Amsterdam: North-Holland.

Kim, Euysung, 1995, 'Trade Liberalization and Productivity Growth in Korean Manufacturing Industries: Price Protection, Market Power, and Scale Efficiency', mimeo. San Diego University, San Diego, CA.

Kim, Jong-Il and Lawrence Lau, 1994, 'The Sources of Growth of the East Asian Newly Industrialized Countries', *Journal of Japanese and International Economies* **8**, 235–271.

Kim, Joo Hoon, 1991, *Liberalization, Subcontracting and Reorganization*, Seoul: Korea Development Institute.

Kim, Kwang-suk and Joon-kyung Park, 1985, *Sources of Economic Growth in Korea 1963–1982*, Seoul: Korea Development Institute.

Kim, Linsu, 1997, *Imitation to Innovation: The Dynamics of Korea's Technological Learning*, Cambridge, MA: Harvard Business School Press.

Kim, Linsu and Jeffrey B. Nugent, 1999, 'Korean SMEs and Their Support Systems', in Brian Levy, Albert Berry and Jeffrey B. Nugent (eds.), *Fulfilling the Export Potential of Small and Medium Firms*, Boston: Kluwer.

Kim, Sun Koon et al., 1994, *R&D and Technical Manpower of Technology Intensive SMEs*, Seoul: STEPI.

Korea Development Institute, 1997, *Long-Term Change of Industrial Structure and Suggestions on SME Development*, Seoul: Korea Development Institute.

Korea Industrial Technology Promotion Association, 1991, *Report on Survey of Industrial Technology Development*, Seoul: Korea Industrial Technology Promotion Association.

Krugman, Paul, 1994, 'The Myth of Asia's Miracle', *Foreign Affairs* **73**(6), 62–78.

Kuznets, Simon, 1955, 'Economic Growth and Income Inequality', *American Economic Review* **45**(March), 1–28.

Kwack, Sung Yeung, 1997, *An Analysis of Factors and Determinants of Productivity Growth in Korean Manufacturing Sector*, Seoul: Korea Institute for Industrial Economics and Trade (KIET).

Lee, Byungki, 1995, *Technology Policy and Technology Development Effects of the Government and Private R&D*, Seoul: Korea Economic Research Institute.

Lee, Kyu-Uck and Sung Soon Lee, 1985, 'Business Integration and Concentration of Economic Power', Research Report 85-02. Korea Development Institute, Seoul.

Levy, Brian, 1991, 'Transaction Costs, the Size of Firms and Industrial Policy: Lessons from a Comparative Case Study of the Footwear Industry in Korea and Taiwan', *Journal of Development Economics* **34** (November), 151–178.

Lim, Youngil, 1998, *Technology and Productivity: Korean Way of Learning and Catching Up*, Cambridge, MA: MIT Center for International Studies.

Mazumdar, Dipak, 1991, 'Import Substituting Industrialization and Protection of Small Scale: The Indian Experience in Textile Industry', *World Development* **19**(9), 1197–1213.

Mazumdar, Dipak, 1998, 'Size Structure of Manufacturing Establishments and the Productivity Differentials Between Large and Small Firms: A Comparative Study of Asian Economies', mimeo.University of Toronto, Toronto.

Nam, Sang-yirl, 1999, 'Total Factor Productivity in Korean Industry', paper prepared for the PEO Structure Meeting in Osaka, Japan, March 1999.

National Statistical Office, 1998, *Korea Statistical Yearbook*, Seoul: National Statistical Office.

Nishimizu, Michio and Sherman Robinson, 1984, 'Trade Policies and Productivity Change in Semi-Industrialized Countries', *Journal of Development Economics* 16, 177–206.

Nugent, Jeffrey B., 1989, 'Variations in the Size Distribution of Korean Manufacturing Establishments Across Sectors and Over Time', working paper. Korea Development Institute, Seoul.

Nugent, Jeffrey B., 1996, 'What Explains the Trend Reversal in the Size Distribution of Korean Manufacturing

Establishments?', *Journal of Development Economics* **48**, 225–251.

Pack, Howard and Larry E. Westphal, 1986, 'Industrial Strategy and Technological Change: Theory Versus Reality', *Journal of Development Economics* **22**(1), 87–128.

Paek, Nak Ki, 1992, *Analysis of Actual Usage and Effect of SME Support System*, Seoul: Korea Institute for Industrial Economics and Trade.

Pai Kim, Mi-Kyung, 1996, 'The Variations in the Technical Efficiency of Korean Manufacturing Establishments Under Two Distinctive Industrial Policies: A Cross-Sectional and Intertemporal Approach', unpublished Ph.D. Dissertation. University of Southern California, Los Angeles, CA.

Ranis, Gustav and John C. H. Fei, 1961, 'A Theory of Economic Development', *American Economic Review* **51** (September), 533–565.

Rodrik, Dani, 1995, 'Getting Interventions Right: How South Korea and Taiwan Grew Rich', *Economic Policy* **20**, 146–171.

Scitovsky, Tibor, 1986, 'Economic Development in Taiwan and South Korea, 1965–1981', in Lawrence J. Lau (ed.), *Models of Development: A Comparative Case Study of Economic Growth in South Korea and Taiwan*, San Francisco, CA: ICS Press.

Seong, Somi, 1995, 'Small and Medium-Sized Enterprises and the Structural Adjustment of the Korean Economy', in Eul Yong Park (ed.), *Small and Medium-Sized Enterprises and Economic Development*, Seoul: Korea Development Institute.

Small and Medium Enterprise Authority and Federation of Small and Medium Enterprises, 1998, *Survey of Small and Medium Enterprises*, Seoul: Federation of Small and Medium Enterprises.

Uekusa, Masu and Akio Torii, 1987, 'The Determinants of the Level of Technical Inefficiency in Japanese Industries', mimeo. Yokohama National University, Yokohama. [In Japanese.]

Yoo, Seong Min, 1991, 'Technical Efficiency in Korea', Working Paper 9106, Korea Development Institute, Seoul.

Yoo, Seong Min, 1992, 'Technical Efficiency over Time in Korea, 1978–88: Exploratory Analysis', in Richard A. Caves and Associates (eds.), *Industrial Efficiency in Six Nations*, Cambridge, MA: MIT Press.

Young, Alwyn, 1995, 'The Tyranny of Numbers: Confronting the Statistical Realities of the East Asian Growth Experience', *Quarterly Journal of Economics* **110** (August), 641–680.

The Evolution and Structure of Industrial Clusters in Japan

Hideki Yamawaki

ABSTRACT. This paper focuses on two aspects of the evolution and structure of clusters in Japan, namely, what gives rise to clusters and what benefits are acquired by small firms from participating in clusters. The determinants of clustering are discussed by way of a review of the history of 14 industrial clusters which cover a wide range of industries and locations in Japan. It is noted that different factors dominate in different cases. Among the more important ones are the existence of leading large firms, the availability of a pooled labor market, and the presence of public research and testing facilities. The four most important benefits from clusters reported by small firms are : (i) specialization; (ii) ease of procurement; (iii) diffusion of technology, and (iv) public policy support. Access to skilled workers is not reported to be a significant benefit. This may be explained by the fact that the dominant source of skills acquisition among Japanese workers is on-the-job training and such skills may be too firm-specific to be useful to others, even within a geographically concentrated cluster.

1. Introduction

It is a well established fact that Japan hosts the largest number of small- and medium-sized enterprises (SMEs) among industrialized countries. When SMEs are broadly defined as those enterprises with fewer than 300 employees or less than Yen 100 million in capital, more than 99 percent of all enterprises in Japanese manufacturing were classified as SMEs in 1994. Further, 67 percent of total employees in manufacturing worked for SMEs in 1994.[1]

An equally important feature of Japan's industrial organization is that Japan's SMEs often form clusters. According to the 1996 survey of the Small and Medium Enterprise Agency, a total of 537 clusters are reported to exist throughout Japan.

The Peter F. Drucker Graduate School of Management
Claremont Graduate University
1021 North Dartmouth Avenue
Claremont, CA 91711
U.S.A.
E-mail: h.yamawaki@cgu.edu

While the economic significance of these clusters varies widely from clusters producing primarily for exports to clusters producing indigenous goods little known outside Japan, an important question common to these clusters arise: Where do these clusters come from? What are the key drivers for the birth and growth of these clusters in Japan? What competitive advantage do they have? The purpose of this paper is to address these issues. Specifically, the paper first identifies factors that are important in shaping the evolution of clusters in Japan. Second, it describes the structure of Japan's clusters and examines their sources of competitive advantage.

While clusters are defined generally as geographic concentrations of interconnected companies and institutions in a particular business field (Porter, 1990, 1998), each cluster varies greatly in terms of key features such as geographic locations, products, functions, and patterns of inter-firm linkages. Clusters differ from each other because of differences in historical circumstances, demand conditions, supporting industries, and competitive conditions that underlie their evolution. Some clusters arise from peculiar historical conditions, yet others may develop through the confluence of various economic conditions. The initial economic conditions that shaped a cluster, however, do not necessarily remain constant beyond certain periods. Rather, economic conditions surrounding clusters may change over time because of changes in domestic and international competitive conditions.

On the basis of information provided in the previous surveys on Japan's manufacturing clusters (People's Finance Corporation, 1987, 1995; MITI, 1996; SMEA, 1997; Ito and Urata, 1997, 1998), this paper examines a sample of 14 major cases of manufacturing clusters in Japan that have shown high propensities to export. After

Small Business Economics **18**: 121–140, 2002.

providing a brief description on the historical development of each of these clusters, the paper extracts key driving forces for the evolution of a cluster. The 14 clusters studied manufacture a wide range of products including silk, cotton, and synthetic fabrics; apparel; ceramic goods; general machinery; automobile parts; binoculars; silverware and cutlery; hand tools; and eyeglass frames.

The remainder of this paper is organized as follows. In the next section, evolutionary patterns of this sample of 14 clusters are qualitatively examined to derive a certain set of factors that contributed to the birth of clusters. This analysis identifies historical circumstances, prior existence of related industries in the region, prior existence of related clusters in neighboring regions, technology transfers from other clusters and foreign countries, and regional government policy as most important drivers of the birth and growth of clusters. Section 3 describes structural features of these clusters and examines various sources of advantage that they create. The analysis finds that the existence of small and medium enterprises with specialized skills in an industry in a geographic space is likely to create agglomeration in Japanese clusters. Section 4 examines the development of technological and human assets in Japanese clusters. Section 5 sheds some light on the issues of cluster performance. Finally, Section 6 summarizes the key findings and concludes the paper.

2. Evolution of industrial clusters in Japan

A sample of 14 clusters in Japan was selected from the clusters previously studied by the People's Finance Corporation (1987, 1995), MITI (1996), SMEA (1997), and Ito and Urata (1997, 1998). The 14 clusters were chosen rather subjectively by using the following criteria: (1) The cluster is distinctive in that interconnected firms are located in a geographically concentrated area and produce a particular class of products; (2) the cluster has been important in terms of the size of economic activity; (3) the cluster has been competitive in international markets with significantly high export share; and (4) the evolution pattern of the cluster is unique. The locations of these clusters are not concentrated in one particular area but dispersed widely across Japan. In what follows, each of these clusters is briefly described focusing on its history, key conditions for birth, and interfirm linkages.

Brief histories of Japan's clusters[2]

Kiryu (Gumma)

Kiryu City, located in Gumma prefecture, is an old town that specializes in silk and man-made silk and other synthetic fabrics. Its roots can be traced back to the Edo period (the 1600s) when the city became famous as a prime production location of high-quality silk (*habutae*) and specialty silk weaves such as *kinrandonsu*. The cluster's modern history starts in 1878 when the city imported Jacquard looms to produce silk fabrics with sophisticated weaves. After just four years since its introduction of this new technology, Kiryu's firms started to export silk fabrics to the U.S. market. Its major product shifted from silk to man-made silk fabrics during the 1920s and further to synthetic fabrics (e.g., acetate and polyester). While the cluster hosts more than 600 weavers with 2,000 employees, the majority of them are very small (90 percent of firms with fewer than five workers) and operate as subcontractors who receive fees on consigned production. Surrounding these weavers are small firms that have highly specialized yet complementary skills in different production stages such as threading, design, dyeing, and embroidery. The cluster exported more than 35 percent of sales to foreign markets through the 1980s.[3]

Fukui and Ishikawa

Fukui and Ishikawa prefectures, two neighboring prefectures facing the Sea of Japan, form a large cluster of textile manufacturers. The cluster in Fukui arose in the early 1900s when the prefecture imported the silk weaving technology from Kiryu in Gunma. Later, the cluster grew rapidly as many new firms followed to enter the industry. The prefecture government helped nurture the region's rayon textile industry by introducing new technology through the government-managed technical centers during the 1910–30 period. After WW II, new materials such as nylon and polyester were introduced in this region through private licensing agreements between Japanese and U.S. firms. Fukui is the largest cluster of synthetic fabric in Japan in terms of shipment, and exports more than 70 percent of products abroad.

The synthetic fabric industry in Ishikawa grew rapidly during the mid-1960s to fill the large demand increase in polyester fabric. The prefecture government provided assistance for local firms during this period as a policy to develop the region's economy. The cluster's export share is very high ranging between 70 and 85 percent during the 1980s. The two clusters' weavers are typically characterized as small- and medium-sized firms and operate, on average, with fewer than 50 looms.[4] The distinctive feature of inter-firm relationship in this cluster is that the majority of weaving firms function as subcontractors for chemical firms (or major textile firms), trading companies, and local wholesalers. Local weavers receive fees and margins based on the quantity of products consigned by chemical firms and trading companies that in turn supply yarns. Subcontractors engage in different activities such as threading, weaving, and dyeing in the production process according to their skills and competencies.

Komatsu (Ishikawa)

Komatsu City is an old city in Ishikawa prefecture that evolved from a major manufacturing location of silk weaves to the industrial supply base for the world's second largest construction machinery producer, Komatsu Ltd. The origin of the city's textile industry goes back to the 17th century when a local lord promoted production of silk and tea. While Komatsu's textile industry declined drastically during the late 1970s and 1980s, its machinery industry prospered as the construction firm grew. Komatsu started its operation in 1912 and developed a network of suppliers and related industries in the city.

Nishiwaki (Hyogo)

Nishiwaki City specializes in cotton fabric woven with dyed yarns. Its products account for 60 percent of domestic market share in this specialty niche. The industry's roots are traced to 1793 when the city imported a weaving technology from Nishijin in Kyoto. It expanded greatly during the 1920s with the success in exports of cotton fabrics for shirt and bed linen in South East Asian markets. After WW II, the city's industry grew again with exports of specialty fabrics such as gingham. The organizational structure of the cluster is similar to those of Fukui and Ishikawa and built on a network of small firms with specific and complementary capabilities (dyeing, preparations, and weaving). The majority of such weaving firms again function as subcontractors working for trading companies and apparel firms and receive fees on consigned production.

Gifu (Gifu)

Gifu City is ranked among the largest three manufacturing locations of apparels. Its origin is relatively new and traced to the period right after WW II. The cluster arose from a peculiar historical circumstance that the people who returned from China after the war started selling used clothes in front of the train station of Gifu. Later, new entrants started to manufacture apparel with fabrics procured from the neighboring clusters specialized in fabrics (Hashima in Gifu and Ichinomiya in Aichi). More than 70 percent of Gifu's apparel makers specialize in women's clothes. Gifu has approximately 900 apparel firms with a total of 11,000 employees whose major activities are in product design, sales, and distribution, and a large number of small sewing firms with a total of 10,000 employees.[5] Apparel firms place orders for sewing firms, and sewing firms in turn consign part of the work to a pool of area households. A large portion of sewing operations are thus carried out mainly by female workers who work for sewing firms (approximately 23,000 workers in the entire Gifu prefecture) and those who work at home as part-timers (another 20,000–30,000 workers).

Seto (Aichi)

Seto City, located adjacent to Nagoya, is well known for its ceramics goods. The cluster's roots can be traced to the Heian period (the 1100s) when the city started producing ceramic wares. The location factor was crucial for the development of this cluster as the area was well endowed with deposits of a certain type of earth indispensable for high quality ceramics. While the area's major products were traditionally ceramic wares such as tea cups and pots (*setomono*), the industry diversified into new products called novelty goods such as ceramic toys, dolls, and ornaments during the WW I as the production of these goods declined in Germany and the U.K. Approximately 400 firms (160 vertically integrated firms and 250 subcontractors) existed in the cluster with a total of 4,000 employees through the 1980s. The small subcontracting firms possess specialized skills in the several stages of the production process (cast designs, casting, baking, and painting). Their primary target is the U.S. market of mid-quality products.[6]

Morodomi (Saga)
Morodomi in Saga prefecture is currently a part of the furniture cluster in the region. The cluster arose rather recently after 1955 when a toll bridge over Chikugo River was built connecting the cities of Ohkawa in Fukuoka and Morodomi. Ohkawa at that point had already developed as a major production location of furniture and was in search of new locations to expand its manufacturing base. The neighboring town, Morodomi, was located in the middle of typical agricultural area and was not linked conveniently with Ohkawa because of the Chikugo River. The new bridge significantly reduced transportation costs required to travel between these two cities and thus expanded the size of the market and viable economic area. With the new bridge built, furniture makers in Ohkawa moved into Morodomi and invested in new capacity. In 1966 the toll of the bridge was eliminated. The number of firms in Morodomi increased from six in 1956 to 41 in 1971.[7]

Ota (Gumma)
The roots of the automobile parts cluster in Ota City are traced back to the establishment of Nakajima Aircraft in 1918. While Nakajima as a manufacturer of military aircraft grew rapidly during the 1930s and through the early 1940s, the company was divested after WWII. A part of the divested company became Fuji Heavy Industries that manufacture automobiles (Subaru cars) and aircraft. Some of the old Nakajima employees started new business to supply parts and machinery to Fuji Heavy Industries. These spin-offs of Nakajima and other new entrants grew significantly during the 1950s and 1960s and formed an important network of auto parts suppliers in the city. The cluster is presently structured hierarchically with more than 70 firms operating as first-tier, second-tier, and third-tier suppliers for Fuji Heavy Industries. Average sizes in employment of these three classes of suppliers in the region are estimated 258 for the first tier, 24 for the second tier, and six for the third tier. While Fuji Heavy Industries is the cluster's core assembler, Ota's auto parts manufacturers also do business with other auto assemblers such as Nissan Diesel in Ota City, Daihatsu and Hino in Gumma prefecture, and Nissan, Honda, and Isuzu in the neighboring regions.[8]

Itabashi (Tokyo)
During the 1960s, approximately 95 percent of binoculars sold in the world market were produced in Itabashi in Tokyo. At the height of its growth in this period, the Itabashi area had around 220 assemblers and 600 related businesses in various stages in the preparation and production of components such as mirrors, lenses, and prisms. While the number of assemblers was reduced to 60 because of the emerging new competition from South Korea, Taiwan, and Hong Kong and the declining demand through the 1980s, the area remains the dominant production location in the world with a world market share of 75 percent.[9] The cluster's roots are traced to the early 1900s when Japan introduced the optical technology of Zeiss from Germany. A cluster of optical equipment manufacturers arose in Itabashi during this period. Later, binocular manufacturers moved into this area to use skills and capabilities accumulated in the existing network of supporting and related industries, exploiting their agglomeration economies.

Tsubame (Niigata)
Like the silk cluster in Kiryu described earlier, the silverware and kitchen utensils clusters in Tsubame City arose during the Edo period (1600–1865) as a major production site of traditional Japanese-style nails. The rise of Tsubame as a production site of nails is often explained by its location near copper mines.[10] The industry's modern history began in 1911 when Tsubame's businesses started manufacturing Western-style silverware to fill the gap in world demand caused by the sharp decline of silverware exports from Europe and the United States. At that point, Tsubame's firms had already accumulated technical skills and competencies in metal working

and processing that was required to produce silverware. After WW II, Tsubame's businesses leaped to the rank of major export industries in Japan as sales to the U.S. market grew rapidly. Floods of exports to the U.S. market, however, induced a U.S. sanction of imports of silverware in 1959. To circumvent the restriction of exports of silverware, some of the firms diversified into houseware and kitchen utensils, sparking new businesses in this new field.[11]

The structure of inter-firm relationships is best characterized by hierarchical subcontracting relationships among different types of firms with complementary skills. Manufacturers that take orders from trading companies and wholesalers subcontract out several stages in the production process to first-tier suppliers who have metal working and processing capabilities. First-tier suppliers in turn ask second-tier suppliers to polish final products before shipping to the manufacturers.[12]

Sanjyo (Niigata)

Sanjo City is a neighbor city of Tsubame City and a major manufacturing site of hand tools. The cluster arose after WW II and developed gradually during the 1970s and 1980s as exports grew significantly. The prior existence of supporting and related industries in Tsubame certainly played an important role to provide seed for this newer cluster. The cluster in Sanjyo is organized with a structure similar to the one in Tsubame. A large number of subcontractors (approximately 400 in 1985) exist with complementary skills in metal working and processing and work for a smaller number of manufacturers. Thus, it is characterized as a subcontracting system structured vertically along different stages of the production process.

Seki (Gifu)

Seki City, located in Gifu Prefecture, is an old town that prospered as early as in the Kamakura Period (1185–1333) because of its geographic location. The city was located at the intersection of two major corridors: the route connecting two ancient capital cities, Kyoto and Kamakura, and the route connecting two strategic regions at that time, Mino and Hida. Because of its strategic importance and heavy traffic of warriors, the city soon became well known for sword forging. It is believed that a cluster of approximately 300 sword masters worked in the city during the Muromachi period (1333–1568).[13] While the city remained prosperous through the Edo period (1600–1865), it faced a major threat when the new Meji government banned the making and carrying of swords. It was quite natural that Seki's sword manufacturers quickly repositioned to cutlery manufacturing and took advantage of its sword forging skills and the existing supporting and related industries. A cluster of cutlery manufacturers thus arose in the Seki city. Their market share in the Japanese market is particularly high (more than 50 percent) in knives, Japanese-style kitchen knives, and cutlery for barbers. Because the production process of cutlery involves several layers of different types of activities, cutlery makers (approximately 200 firms in 1991) subcontract out most of these activities to smaller subcontractors with different skills and capabilities. The large majority (70 percent) of these subcontractors operate as tiny establishments with fewer than three workers.

Sabae (Fukui)

Sabae City in Fukui prefecture specializes in the manufacturing of eyeglass frames. The cluster's roots are traced to the late 1900s and the early 1910s when the prefecture government helped transplant manufacturing skills of eyeglass frames with a goal to develop the region's weak economy. Highly skilled technicians from Tokyo and Osaka that had been the largest clusters of eyeglass frames were sent to Sabae and helped diffuse their skills and technology. By the 1930s, Sabae's frame production surpassed those of Tokyo and Osaka, making it as the largest cluster of eyeglass frames in Japan. The cluster continued to grow after WW II and became dominant in the Japanese market controlling approximately 90 percent of the market by the end of 1980s.[14] There are approximately 1,000 small- and medium-sized firms in this eyeglass frame cluster. The majority of these firms are very small, and their average size is 7.9 workers. The production process of an eyeglass frame is divided into approximately 150–250 stages and requires relatively labor-intensive skills. Several types of firms with different skills and competencies coexist and constitute a cluster of related industries in the city.

Key drivers of cluster formation

What is the key driving factor that underlies these 14 clusters in Japan? Several important drivers are likely to emerge from the descriptions of the clusters given above, which are listed in column 4 of Table I.

Historical conditions

The roots of some clusters go back to the Edo period in the 17th and 18th centuries (Kiryuu, Komatsu, Tsubame, and Nishiwaki), yet others can be traced to the periods as early as the 12th century (Seto and Seki). These clusters had already been known for their products by the time when they transformed their manufacturing systems to the modern systems. Through their long histories, these clusters accumulated the skills required to manufacture high-quality specialty products. One factor that made these cities important historical manufacturing locations may be the availability of raw materials and key ingredients nearby (Seto and Tsubame). Another factor may be historical circumstances such as the existence of an extensive network of routes connecting major cities (Seki). Clusters may also arise from historical accidents and discontinuities as observed

TABLE I
Characteristics of 14 manufacturing clusters in Japan

Location (Prefecture)	Products	Startup period	Key initial conditions	Key features in industrial organization
Kiryuu (Gunma)	Silk, man-made silk, and synthetic fabrics and weaves	1600s (Edo)	Historical cluster (silk); Foreign technology import (Jacquard Loom)	Extensive subcontracting; Coexistence of firms with complementary skills and capabilities
Ishikawa	Synthetic fabrics	mid-1960s	High demand growth for polyester after 1966; Regional government policy to promote the synthetic textile industry	Extensive subcontracting; Coexistence of firms with complementary skills and capabilities
Fukui	Synthetic fabric	early 1900s (Meiji)	Technology transfer from other cluster in Japan (Kiryuu); Prefecture government helped nurture the industry through its operation of technology center between 1910–30	Extensive subcontracting; Coexistence of firms with complementary skills and capabilities
Komatsu (Ishikawa)	Silk General machinery for construction machinery	1640 1921	Historical cluster (silk); Existence of a large assembler	Network of supporting and related industries; Vertically structured subcontracting system for a large assembler (Komatsu)
Nishiwaki (Hyogo)	Cotton fabric	1793	Historical cluster (cotton fabrics) Technology transfer from other cluster in Japan	Extensive subcontracting Coexistence of firms with complementary skills and capabilities
Gifu (Gifu)	Apparel	late 1940s	Historical circumstances; Prior existence of related industries nearby; Availability of large pools of female workers in the region	Extensive subcontracting; Extensive use of female part-time workers

TABLE I *(Continued)*

Location (Prefecture)	Products	Startup period	Key initial conditions	Key features in industrial organization
Seto (Aichi)	Ceramic novelty goods	1100s (Heian)	Historical cluster (ceramics); Access to high-quality raw materials	Extensive subcontracting Coexistence of firms with complementary skills and capabilities
Morodomi (Saga)	Furniture	1955	Construction of a new bridge connected two neighboring cities; Reduction in transportation costs Expansion of viable economic area	Subcontracting
Ota (Gunma)	Automobile parts	1918	Existence of large assemblers (Nakajima in pre-War period) and Fuji Heavy Industries (in the post-War period); Prior existence of supporting industries inherited by Fuji Heavy Industries	Hierarchically structured assembler-supplier relationship; A large cluster formed with other assemblers (Nissan Diesel in Ota; Daihatsu and Hino in Gunma; Nissan, Honda, and Isuzu in neighboring regions)
Itabashi (Tokyo)	Binoculars	early 1900s (Meiji)	Foreign technology import from Zeiss, Germany; Large military demand during the Korean war; Prior existence of related industries (optical equipment)	Existence of several integrated makers; Extensive subcontracting; Coexistence of firms with complementary skills and capabilities
Tsubame (Niigata)	Silverware, kitchenware, and metal household ware	1600s (Edo)	Historical cluster (Japanese-style nails); Import substitution during the WW I; Repositioned by diversifying into household wares during the 1960s to circumvent VERs in the U.S. market	Hierarchically structured subcontracting system; Coexistence of firms with compelementary skills and capabilities
Sanjo (Niigata)	Hand tools	late 1940s	Geographic proximity to other cluster (Tsubame); Prior existence of related and supporting industries in the neighboring cluster	Extensive subcontracting; Coexistence of firms with complementary skills and capabilities
Seki (Gifu)	Cutlery	1100s (Kamakura)	Historical cluster (sword forging); Importance of geographic location as a hub connecting major cities; Repositioned into cutlery production after the Meiji government banned the making of swords	Extensive subcontracting Coexistence of firms with complementary skills and competencies
Sabae (Fukui)	Eyeglass frames	1910s (Meiji)	Technology transfer from other clusters in Japan (Tokyo and Osaka); Regional government policy to develop the region's economy	Extensive subcontracting Coexistence of firms with complementary skills and capabilities

Source: People's Finance Corporation (1987, 1995), MITI (1996), SMEA (1997), and Ito and Urata (1997, 1998).

in the emergence of the silverware cluster in Tsubme during WW I and the apparel cluster in Gifu, which can be traced to the development of used-clothes market in front of the train station after WW II.

Existence of large assemblers

The second factor that is to some extent determined by historical circumstances is the existence of one or a few large firms that manufacture products based on assembly-type operations. Examples from Komatsu and Ota illustrate this point. The machinery cluster in Komatsu had its beginnings in the establishment of a construction machinery company, Komatsu. The automotive parts cluster is another classic example where Nakajima Aircraft and later Fuji Heavy Industries started their operations in Ota. The existence of these large assemblers stimulated the entry and growth of other firms that supply parts and related products to them.[15]

Prior existence of supporting and related industries in the region

The automotive parts cluster in Ota illustrates the importance of prior existence of supporting industries in the region. A network of supporting and related industries was nurtured by Nakajima Aircraft during the pre-war period, which was in turn inherited by Fuji Heavy Industries after the war. Nakajima's employees spun off after the war to create new parts firms to supply Fuji Heavy Industries. The cluster created a network of automotive parts industries with the skills accumulated through Nakajima's aircraft manufacturing history.

Another example is the case of binocular clusters of Itabashi in Tokyo. That cluster emerged building upon the existing network of optical equipment and precision instrument manufacturers in the region. A number of binoculars makers and suppliers for their parts were stimulated to enter the region because of the existence of related industries.

Prior existence of supporting and related industries in the neighboring region

As prior existence of supporting and related industries in the same region plays an important role to foster a new cluster in a different field, their prior existence in the neighboring regions also stimulates the growth of other clusters. The case of the hand tools cluster in Sanjo illustrates this point. Sanjo is located closely to Tsubame's silverware cluster that has its beginnings in a much earlier period. Tsubame's cluster had already created a network of small- and medium-sized subcontracting firms with the special skills in metal working, forging, processing, and polishing when the cluster in Sanjo emerged (Figure 1). Another example is the case of Gifu's apparel cluster. That cluster took advantage of its geographic proximity to the textile fabric clusters in neighboring regions. The cluster in Gifu primarily procured the requisite fabrics from the neighboring clusters.

Pooled labor market for part-time workers

Some of Japan's clusters gained advantages from the fact that they got access to pooled labor markets of part-time workers in their regions. The apparel cluster in Gifu resorted to a large pool of part-time female workers who offered the requisite skills while alleviating disadvantages caused by cyclical demand fluctuations. By the same token, the textile clusters in Ishikawa and Fukui also took advantage of the existence of large pools of part-time workers from the regions' agricultural sectors.

It is important to note, however, that these part-timers normally work as subcontractors for first-tier and/or second-tier suppliers in several stages of the production process that require the most labor-intensive work. Their skill levels are generally much lower than those of regular workers. It is not clear from the case analysis whether Japan's localized industries supported pooled labor markets for skilled workers and engineers. This issue of skill formation and labor market will be discussed later in Section 4 of this paper.

Reduction in transportation costs

A significant reduction of transportation costs expands economically viable geographic space and increases the size of relevant market. The expansion of an economically viable geographic space will in turn attract new businesses. The furniture

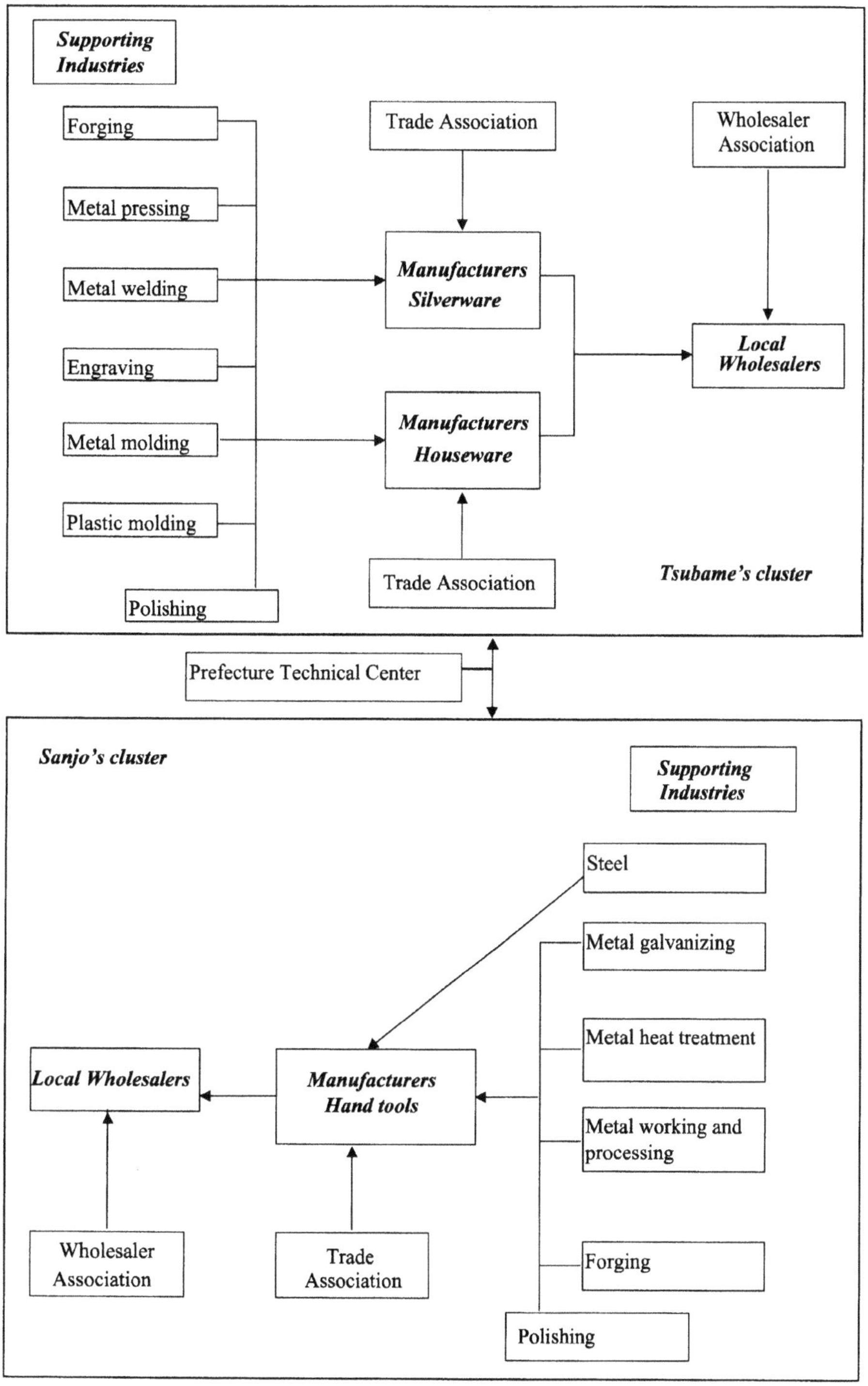

Figure 1. Structure of the Tsubame-Sanjo Cluster.

cluster in Morodomi illustrates this point. Morodomi's furniture cluster emerged only after a new bridge was constructed and linked two cities previously divided by a river. Furniture makers in the neighboring city invested in Morodomi, responding to a great reduction in transportation costs, which stimulated the growth of many new businesses in the newly created economic zone.

Regional government policy

The regional governments often played important roles in providing seed for new clusters. Typical examples of prefecture government policy are given by the cases of Ishikawa and Fukui prefectures that took initiatives to nurture and modernize their textile industries with the goal in developing the regions' ailing economies. Fukui's prefecture government also designed the startup of the eyeglass frames clusters in Sabae with the same goal in developing the regional economy.

One of the policy tools Japan's prefecture governments used was the establishment of public testing and research centers, and technology centers to guide and foster technological developments of particular products. The first technology center was established in 1894 in the Hyogo prefecture where textile spinning was the strategically important industry. During the period between 1894 and 1926, a total of 41 public testing and research centers and technology centers were established in different prefectures throughout Japan to promote technological developments in textiles, ceramics, agriculture, chemicals, and food. The public technology centers for textiles in Fukui and Ishikawa mentioned above were among these first technology centers in Japan.

A large number of public testing and research centers and technology centers were established in the subsequent periods, opening 46 centers during the 1927–45 period and another 57 centers during the 1946–64 period.[16] The major functions that these centers are expected to provide are (1) technological guidance and consulting, (2) testing and inspection, (3) R&D, (4) seminars, and (5) dissemination of information on latest technologies and products.

Technology transfer

A factor closely related to government policy is the import of technology from other locations. A technology can be imported from other domestic clusters in Japan and foreign countries. The textile clusters in Fukui and Nishiwaki imported technologies from other textile clusters in Japan. The same applies to Sabae's eyeglass frame cluster, which imported the requisite technologies and skills from other related clusters in Tokyo and Osaka. On the other hand, Kiryu's textile cluster procured the Jacquard technology from abroad, and the binoculars produced in Itabshi were built on the technology imported from Germany. Imports of new foreign technologies and their diffusions provided seed for the formation of clusters.

The eight factors given are not meant to substitute one for another. Instead, several of them are often present together and complement each other when a cluster emerges in a particular region. This list of key driving forces is by no means exhaustive, but it is considered important for the 14 major clusters in Japan studied in this paper. While these are derived from the experience specific to Japan, they are similar to and thus consistent with the previous lists of driving forces for industrial localization derived mainly from the U.S. and European experiences. Porter (1990, 1998), drawing on histories of U.S. and European clusters, identifies (1) historical circumstances; (2) unusual, sophisticated, or stringent demand; (3) prior existence of supplier industries, related industries, or entire related clusters; (4) existence of one or two innovative companies; and (5) chance events. The work of Krugman (1991) suggests key factors for the formation of an localized industry: (1) historical accidents, (2) labor market pooling, (3) supply of specialized inputs, and (4) technological spillovers. In addition, Krugman (1991) argues that industrial localization is promoted by the confluence of economies of scale, transportation costs, and demand.

Evolution of clusters

The initial conditions that shaped the emergence of a cluster may not remain unchanged in the long run. Rather, they may change because of historical events, technological innovations, and unexpected shifts in demand. Some of the clusters studied in this paper faced such discontinuities that these discontinuities forced the clusters to reconsider their business strategies. Through the process of repositioning, a cluster's original products are often phased out and replaced by new products. Some clusters decline eventually.

Historical event

Unexpected historical events may force firms in cluster to diversify into new fields. The houseware cluster in Tsubame emerged while some of the city's manufacturers repositioned from silverware to this new business to circumvent the VERs imposed on Japanese silverware exports in the U.S. market during the 1960s. The cutlery cluster in Seki emerged after the Meji government banned the making of swords. In both cases, the manufacturers adopted diversification strategies into new but related businesses that rely on the clusters' core competencies. The skills required in the new fields were already accumulated in the clusters through their histories of prior business fields.

Technological change

Development of new production processes and emergence of new products often change clusters' configurations of product lines. Our examples of textile clusters illustrate this point. All the silk clusters were forced to shift their products to man-made silk during the 1920s and to synthetic fabrics in the post-war years. Another example is a cluster specialized in traditional hand tools used for the construction of Japanese-style wooden houses (Miki in Hygo prefecture).[17] That cluster has been shrinking owing to the emergence of new construction methods that do not require much use of such traditional tools at house construction sites.

Demand condition

Unexpected demand growth and decline often change the growth path of a cluster. The unexpected increase in demand in the international market of silverware during WW I triggered the growth of Tsubame's cluster. The demand growth for polyester during the 1960s helped the repositioning of the textile clusters in Fukui and Ishikawa. The large military demand created during the Korean War for binoculars played an important role for the emergence of the cluster in Itabashi. And, the expansion of Japan's auto industry certainly helped the development of Ota's cluster of auto parts.

International competition

Clusters often lose their international competitiveness and decline over time. When a cluster that relies heavily on export markets declines, its cause is often traced to at least three main factors: (1) aggregate economic fluctuations, (2) emerging new industries abroad, (3) shifts in foreign demand. Fluctuations of Japanese yen against foreign currencies are the most significant of the aggregate conditions because they can dramatically affect clusters' cost conditions relative to their counterparts in foreign countries. The clusters that specialize in more labor-intensive production processes face major threats from newly industrialized countries because Japanese workers' relatively high wages offset clusters' advantages based on subcontracting and specialized skills. All the 14 clusters except Ota's automobile parts clusters have been facing major competitive threats from international rivals in recent years.

3. Structure of industrial clusters in Japan

Inter-firm linkage

Our examples of clusters indicate that there are at least three distinctive features in Japan's clusters in terms of inter-firm linkages (column 5 in Table I): (1) the extensive use of subcontracting between manufacturers and suppliers; (2) the hierarchically structured relationships between manufacturers, first-tier suppliers, and second-tier suppliers; and (3) the coexistence of a large number of firms with different but complementary skills in the cluster.

The first two characteristics are not necessarily the features specific to clusters, but they are the features specific to Japan's manufacturing system in general (e.g., Uekusa, 1987; Asanuma and Kikutani, 1992).

On the contrary, concentration of numerous firms with complementary skills in a business field within a certain geographic area is considered the distinctive feature of clusters. Figure 1 shows a schematic picture of this feature in Tsubame's silverware and houseware clusters and the nearby hand tools cluster in Sanjo. In both clusters, the firms in various supporting industries create a horizontal network among themselves based on their complementary capabilities.[18] These firms supply for manufacturers through vertical subcontracting relationships. In addition to manufacturers, suppliers, and wholesalers, there are several local institutions that coordinate member firms' activities, facilitate the communications between them, and disseminate technological and product information. They are local trade associations, wholesalers associations, local chambers of commerce, and prefecture technical centers.

While Tsubame's silverware and houseware clusters consist of 148 silverware manufacturers and 127 houseware manufacturers in 1991,[19] the numbers of manufacturers in some clusters are much smaller. Clusters in which one or few large manufacturers form hierarchically structured subcontracting relationships with smaller suppliers are often observed in the machinery and automobile industries. Our examples of the auto parts cluster in Ota and the machinery cluster in Komatsu illustrate this type of assembler-supplier cluster.[20]

Size

To see the general pattern of firm and cluster sizes in Japan, Table II shows several descriptive statistics for the 537 clusters in Japan surveyed by the Small and Medium Enterprise Agency in 1996. A cluster in this survey is defined as a group of firms in a business field in a geographic space. The survey includes clusters with values of production over Yen 500 million in 1996. The range of products in this survey varies widely from indigenous foods for purely domestic markets to machinery for export markets. Of the 537 clusters, 36 percent of them existed before the Meiji period (before 1868), 28 percent of the clusters emerged during the Meiji period (1868–1912), and 21 percent of the clusters started after 1945. Among the 537 clusters, 126 clusters are found in textiles and constitute the largest number of clusters in Japanese manufacturing, accounting for 23.5 percent of the total.

The number of firms per cluster varies across industries, ranging from 241 in textiles to 82 in food processing. Average size of cluster measured in terms of employment per cluster varies again widely among industries. An average cluster in textiles is likely to employ approximately 5,000 workers and likely to be the largest when compared with clusters in other industries. On the other hand, a typical cluster in wood products and furniture employs 823 workers and is likely to be the smallest. On average, in 1996, a cluster in Japan employs approximately 1,500 workers.

A typical firm in a clothing cluster in Japan employs 24 workers, while a typical firm in a

TABLE II
Number of clusters, average cluster size, and average firm size, by industry (1996)

Industry	Number of clusters	Number of firms/cluster	Employment/cluster	Employment/firm
Food processing	83 (15.5%)	82	1,260	15.37
Textiles	126 (23.5%)	241	1,518	6.30
Clothing	34 (6.3%)	208	4,986	23.97
Wood products and furniture	78 (14.5%)	102	823	8.07
Clay, stone, and glass products	62 (11.5%)	125	920	7.36
Machinery	56 (10.4%)	128	1,986	15.52
Miscellaneous	98 (18.2%)	111	1,175	10.59
Total	537 (100.0%)	145	1,496	10.32

Source: SMEA (1997).

textile cluster employs only six workers. Average firm size in food processing and machinery is in between these two polar cases, employing approximately15 workers. On average, again in 1996, a typical firm in a manufacturing cluster in Japan employs approximately 10 workers.[21]

Some clusters are highly fragmented with large numbers of small firms. A typical example of such a case is textile clusters. According to Table II, a typical textile cluster in Japan consists of 240 firms with fewer than seven employees. On average, 145 firms exist in a cluster in Japan, each employing approximately 10 workers.

Sources of advantage in Japan's clusters

Interpreting the seminal work of Marshall (1920), Krugman (1991) pointed out that the advantage of concentrated production is generated by three distinctive sources: labor market pooling, specialized inputs, and technological spillovers. In this section, we will first lay out these three causes with additional consideration and then examine which one of them is most important for the clusters in Japan by reviewing the SMEA survey result.

Labor market pooling

By concentrating a number of firms in an industry in the same location, a localized industry gains an advantage from offering a pooled market for workers with specialized skills. Both workers with specialized skills who seek employment and firms that seek such workers are better off if they get access to the pooled labor market in the same location (Marshall, 1920; Krugman, 1991).

Whether this factor is relevant and important for Japanese clusters depends presumably on the mobility of skilled workers between firms within a cluster and between geographic areas. Because Japanese workers tend to stay in the same firm until retirement, the benefit of agglomeration arising from labor market pooling for skilled workers may be relatively small in a Japanese cluster. On the other hand, this advantage may be more important in labor markets for part-time workers. As in the cases of apparel and textile clusters, part-time workers are often female workers who are local residents and work at home. Their wages are under normal circumstances much lower than regular employees.

Availability of firms with specialized skills and competencies

Agglomeration is created in a localized industry because it can support suppliers with specialized skills and capabilities. Capacity utilization of specialized machinery can be increased and maintained at a high level in a localized industry that produces the same kind of products. This in turn makes the localized industry more efficient (Marshall, 1920; Krugman, 1991).

If the minimum efficient scale of production varies across a range of products and through different stages of the production process, then manufacturers can choose an optimal combination of operations by working closely with a number of specialized suppliers. Manufacturers can benefit from the availability of such suppliers as they choose a right technology in response to the scale of production at each stage of the process through a subcontracting-based manufacturing system.

The availability of the number of firms with complementary skills also allows manufacturers to produce a large variety of product. If variety is produced through a wide range of materials and components that are handled efficiently by specialists as well as through stages of specialized operations, then manufacturers will benefit from working with suppliers with such capabilities.

While such division of labor can be contracted between firms in the different geographic spaces, it is more efficiently and easily organized between nearby firms. An example of the mechanical pencil industry in Japan shows that the manufacturer may suffer from working with suppliers scattered geographically in different stages of the production system (Mishina, 1993). The long travel distance of work in process impaired the timeliness of delivery and therefore reduced production efficiency in this case.

Technology spillovers

Because firms in a localized industry are proximate, information flows easily among them. Localization, therefore, generates knowledge spillovers between nearby firms (Marshall, 1920).

Whether such knowledge spillovers are confined within a particular geographic space or go beyond a geographic boundary has been disputed in the existing literature (Krugman, 1991; Audretsch, 1999). The empirical work that addresses these issues of knowledge spillovers seems to show that, at least in the United States, knowledge spillovers tend to be geographically bounded within the geographic area where the new knowledge was created (e.g., Jaffe et al., 1993; Audretsch and Feldman, 1996).

A variety of regional institutions work as vehicles that facilitate the transmission of knowledge across firms within the same cluster in Japan (Figure 1). Public technical centers managed by the prefecture governments offer technical consulting services and seminars and disseminate information on new technology and product. Local chambers of commerce, trade associations, and business organizations coordinate business activities within clusters and provide market and technical information. Local wholesalers and general trading companies disseminate information on emerging new markets, products, and technologies.

Table III summarizes the result of the questionnaire survey conducted by the SMEA in 1996, which was described in the previous section of this paper. Out of the 537 clusters studied in this survey, a total of 471 clusters responded to the questionnaire. Of the 471 respondents, 138 are classified in textiles and apparel; 73 are in wooden products and furniture; 54 are in stone, clay, and glass; and 50 are in machinery and metal products. Table III presents the number of respondents who consider a specific source of advantage important as a percentage of the total number of respondents in the industry in the survey. The respondents are not restricted to choose only one item among the advantages listed in the questionnaire.

Looking at column 2 in Table III, the largest number of clusters (42.6 percent of 471 clusters) found specialization and division of labor as an important advantage that clusters create. An equally important advantage is the ease of procurement within clusters (42.3 percent). This result suggests that agglomeration occurs in a cluster because it can support suppliers that possess specialized skills. Such capabilities are complementary to each other, which allow divisions of labor among them. Manufacturers benefit from the existence of specialized suppliers because they can choose optimal combinations of technologies for a wide range of products.

The second source of advantage for a localized industry that Japanese firms consider important is likely to arise from the fact that it facilitates diffusion of technology and technological coop-

TABLE III
Sources of advantage in Japan's clusters, by industry (response rate in percentage)

Advantages	All industries	Textile and clothing	Wood products and furniture	Stone, clay, and glass	Metal products and machinery
Ease of procurement	42.3	23.9	50.7	59.3	50.0
Access to labor market	6.8	5.1	5.5	3.7	8.0
Availability of skilled workers and engineers	10.0	9.4	13.7	5.6	8.0
Specialization/division of labor	42.6	53.6	47.9	31.5	64.0
Access to supplier/subcontractor	24.2	30.4	23.3	13.0	38.0
Access to customer base	10.8	11.6	12.3	13.0	6.0
Competitive environment	19.5	16.7	20.5	25.9	14.0
Diffusion of technology and technological cooperation	31.2	37.6	26.0	46.4	16.0
Opportunity for business alliance	11.9	8.0	13.7	14.8	10.0
Access to market information	24.8	29.0	16.4	16.7	24.0
Regional policy	27.4	26.8	23.3	20.4	28.0
No advantage	2.8	2.9	1.4	1.9	0.0
No. of clusters in sample	471	138	73	54	50

Source: SMEA (1997), Table 17.

eration. This result seems to suggest that new technological knowledge spills over easily among the firms within the same cluster. Of the 471 clusters, 31.2 percent of them choose diffusion of technology as an important advantage of clustering.

On the contrary, access to a labor market and availability of skilled workers are considered less important sources of advantage in Japan's clusters. Only 6.8 percent of the clusters in the sample choose the access to labor market as an important advantage, and 10 percent of them consider the availability of skilled workers important.

This result obtained from the full sample remains basically unchanged for different industries, although there are some industry-specific differences. Table III shows the survey results for four different industries. Among the industry-specific differences, the most notable is the importance of specialization and division of labor. This advantage is considered the most significant in metal products and machinery with the highest response rate of 64 percent. Ease of procurement (with 50 percent response rate) and access to suppliers/subcontractors (with 38 percent response rate) are other advantages that are important in this industry. This result is quite consistent with the underlying manufacturing process commonly used in this industry that consists of several stages of highly specialized components production.

4. Development of firm capabilities in Japanese clusters

Skill formation

The analysis in the previous section finds that the existence of suppliers with specialized, complementary skills is the most likely source of agglomeration in a Japanese cluster. On the other hand, the SMEA survey does not seem to provide evidence that supports the hypothesis that the creation of a pooled labor market for skilled workers in a localized industry offers an advantage to both local firms and workers.[22]

Why is a pooled labor market for skilled workers not important source of advantage in Japanese cluster? The way in which skills are created and developed in Japanese firms, and the way in which such human skills are allocated among firms may provide an answer. As is well known, on-the-job training is the most commonly used method to train workers in Japanese corporations (Koike, 1988). The prevalence of on-the-job-training in Japan is based on the premises that most skills are learned only by doing, and that some of these skills are specific to the firm or to the plant.

This firm-specific nature of human skills in turn tend to discourage the worker to move to another firm since the worker will lose some of the skills acquired in the firm if the worker moves to the another firm. The firm will not be able to replace the worker easily within a short period with a new recruit without impairing efficiency. This in turn motivates both workers and firms to use a mechanism that is internal to firms rather than a mechanism that use external markets to allocate human resources (Odagiri, 1992).

Table IV shows the SMEA survey result on skill formation and procurement of skilled workers. As is expected, it is quite evident from this table that more than 80 percent of Japan's industrial clusters use on-the-job-training as the method to train workers and develop their skills. This pattern holds consistently across different industries. While firms in Japan's industrial clusters are likely to use on-the-job-training as the most important method to develop human skills, they are less likely to procure them from other firms in the same cluster. Asked whether firms recruit skilled workers from other firms in the same cluster, approximately 20 percent of clusters responded positively to this question. This relatively low response rate for the use of external markets to source skilled workers by Japanese firms contrasts starkly with the high response rate for the use of on-the-job-training, which suggest their preference for an internal mechanism to allocate human resources.

In sum, the analysis in this section and the previous section suggests that the firms in an industrial cluster in Japan are more likely to benefit from supporting large numbers of suppliers with specialized skills. Some of the human skills in these firms are firm-specific and developed internally within the firms through on-the-job-training. Since such skills are only infrequently acquired from other firms in the same cluster, a localized industry in Japan is less likely to support a pooled labor market for skilled workers.

TABLE IV
Skill formation and procurement of skilled workers, by industry (response rate in percentage)

	Foods	Textile	Clothing	Wood products and furniture	Stone, clay, and glass	Machinery	Others	Total
On-the-job training	84.7	79.1	100	86.5	80.7	90.6	81.9	84.2
Inter-firm cooperation in skill formation	15.3	16.5	14.8	17.6	17.5	17.0	15.7	16.4
Recruit outside the cluster	9.7	5.2	14.8	6.8	8.8	11.3	9.6	8.5
Recruit from other firms in the cluster	16.7	27.0	25.9	17.6	12.3	22.6	18.1	20.2
Number of clusters in sample	72	115	27	74	57	53	83	481

Source: SMEA (1997), Table 23.

Development of technological assets

While the access to a pooled labor for skilled workers in an industrial cluster in Japan is unlikely to be an important source of agglomeration, technology spillovers are more likely to be an advantage of clustering. How does a cluster facilitate the diffusion of new technology and other knowledge? As was discussed earlier in this paper, knowledge spillovers among firms in the same cluster can occur through various institutions such as trade associations, public testing and research centers, public technical centers, wholesalers associations, and local chambers of commerce. In addition to such institutions, various forms of inter-firm cooperation and contacts within a cluster are also likely to facilitate knowledge spillovers.

Table V summarizes the SMEA survey result on the pattern of inter-firm cooperation in Japan's industrial clusters. Out of the 123 clusters that responded to the question of what types of inter-firm cooperation they participate in, 64 percent of them pointed out joint R&D as a vehicle for collaboration, and 26 percent of them saw their firms participate in technological alliance. This general pattern remains virtually unchanged for different industries except in wooden products and furniture where technological alliance is not important. It is also worth noting that the frequency with which Japanese firms in a cluster exchange business information and reference each other through informal channels is not trivial.

Another interesting pattern that emerges in Table V is that the types of partnership that include equity ownership and therefore ownership control

TABLE V
Inter-firm cooperation within cluster, by industry (response rate in percentage)

	Foods	Textile and clothing	Wood products and furniture	Stone, clay, and glass	Machinery	Others	Total
Joint R&D	80.0	65.6	66.7	57.1	61.1	57.9	64.2
Technology alliance	20.0	31.3	5.6	28.6	38.9	26.3	26.0
Joint production	6.7	3.1	16.7	14.3	5.6	10.5	8.9
Production contract	6.7	15.6	11.1	14.3	11.1	21.1	13.8
Marketing contract	6.7	6.3	0.0	4.8	11.1	5.3	5.7
Informal exchange of business information and reference	0.0	31.3	27.8	9.5	27.8	15.8	20.3
Capital participation	6.7	6.3	0.0	4.8	0.0	0.0	3.3
Joint Venture	6.7	0.0	0.0	0.0	0.0	5.3	2.4
Number of clusters in sample	15	32	18	21	18	19	123

Source: SMEA (1997), Table 54.

are not common in a Japanese cluster. Among the 123 clusters, only 3.3 percent of them report partnerships that involve capital participation, and a mere 2.4 percent of them report joint ventures as a common form of alliance.

Table VI summarizes the SMEA survey result on alliance partners. The questionnaire asked who are the most likely partners of alliance. Among the 127 clusters where their firms formed alliance, 60.6 percent of them formed alliances with public research and testing centers and technical centers. The response rate is the highest for machinery where more than 80 percent of clusters involve partnerships with such public institutions. On the contrary, forming a partnership with a university is relatively rare for the firm in a cluster. Only11 percent of the clusters are involved in partnerships with universities. When a firm in a cluster form alliances with other firms, its partners are likely to be small- and medium-sized firms rather than large firms. Indeed, in the majority of clusters are partnerships formed among SMEs, but only 5 percent of them involve large firms as partners.

In sum, the evidence suggests that public institutions such as prefecture testing and research centers and technical centers play an important role in facilitating inter-firm cooperation between firms in a localized industry. Joint R&D efforts and technological alliances serve as the most commonly used vehicles for access to new technology and other assets in Japan's clusters. Acquiring or augmenting technological assets and other assets through capital participation and joint venture is unlikely in Japanese cluster.

5. Cluster performance

The analysis has thus far focused on the structural features of Japan's clusters. This section attempts to shed some light on some issues of cluster performance.

Firm exit in cluster

Do all the firms in Japan's clusters perform equally well and survive in their markets? In other words, how frequently do firms in clusters exit? Entry into and exit from industry have been used extensively in the previous empirical literature of industrial organization to infer the extent of competitive performance of industry. Do firms in clusters face more volatile or more stable environment? While there is no published data available to answer this question for Japan, the SMEA survey provides some statistics that can be used to shed some preliminary light on this issue. The survey shows the number of exits of firms that belong to clusters during the three-year period of 1994–96 without making any reference on their entry dates. By using these data and an estimate of average number of firms in clusters presented in Table II of this paper, Table VII presents an estimate of exit rate for seven manufacturing industries in Japan.

The first column of Table VII shows the number of exits per cluster by industry. The most distinctive pattern that emerges from this is that the numbers of exits in textile (15.37) and clothing (8.22) are among the highest. The numbers of exits for other industries are more comparable ranging between 1.79 and 2.75.

TABLE VI
Alliance partner within cluster, by industry (response rate in percentage)

	Number of clusters in sample	Public research and testing institution	University	Small and medium firm	Large firm
Foods	16	75.0	18.8	31.3	0.0
Textile and clothing	35	60.0	5.7	60.0	5.7
Wooden product and furniture	18	44.4	11.1	55.6	0.0
Stone, clay, and glass	21	57.1	9.5	47.6	9.5
Machinery	18	83.3	16.7	44.4	11.1
Miscellaneous	19	47.4	10.5	52.6	0.0
Total	127	60.6	11.0	50.4	4.7

Source: SMEA (1997), Table 54.

TABLE VII
Number of exits and exit rate, by industry (1994–96)

Industry	Exits/cluster	Firms/cluster	Exits/firms in cluster
Food processing	1.79	82	0.022
Textile	15.37	241	0.064
Clothing	8.22	208	0.040
Wood product and furniture	2.48	102	0.024
Clay, stone, and glass product	2.75	125	0.022
Machinery	2.68	128	0.021
Miscellaneous	2.67	111	0.024
Total	7.00	145	0.048

Source: The author's estimate based on Table 12 in SMEA (1997).

Since the number of exits presented in the first column is not adjusted for the total number of firms in clusters, the third column shows the exit rate, defined as the number of exits divided by the number of firms in a typical cluster (column 2). The pattern of exit rate is virtually the same as that of the unadjusted number of exits in column 1. The exit rate for textile is the highest with 6.4 percent followed by that for clothing with 4.0 percent. The exit rates for the rest of the sample are again comparable ranging between 2.1 percent and 2.4 percent.

The relatively high exit rate for the textile and clothing industries is presumably explained by the recent increase in international competition in these markets. Significant recent increases in imports of textile and clothing in Japan from her neighboring Asian countries injected competitive pressure and restrained domestic prices for these goods (Yamawaki, 1992). Facing such competitive pressure, some of the Japanese firms in these markets were forced to exit from their markets.

Unfortunately, this paper is unable to answer the question of whether Japanese firms in clusters are more likely to survive than those outside clusters because of the unavailability of exit rates comparable between these two samples of firms. Comparison of performance between insiders and outsiders is needed in future research. In recent years, an increasing number of empirical studies in industrial organization have examined patters of *gross* entry and exit for many industrialized countries and their link to firm and industry performances. Similar empirical research for Japan is indeed needed urgently.

The finding in Table VII, however, implies that not all the firms in a cluster perform equally well and survive when faced with international competition. While clusters may provide firms that belong to them with common cluster-specific and region-specific advantages, such advantages may be offset by firm-specific disadvantages. As the estimate of exit rate for textile and clothing suggests, some inefficient firms in the cluster, albeit small, are forced to exit. Thus, clustering does not necessarily guarantee that all the firms benefit equally from it, but each firm's firm-specific resource and capability instead may play a more important role in shaping the firm's viability in the industry.

Agglomeration and regional economic growth

Does the presence of cluster in a region increase its economic growth? Does agglomeration of economic activities in a region create externalities and improve productivity? Despite the importance of these questions, empirical research that provides evidence to answer these questions is quite scarce at least in Japan. An exception is the statistical study by Morikawa (1997) that examined the relationships between various measures of regional economic performance and agglomeration during the period of 1975–91 in Japan. By using data sample at the level of prefecture, Morikawa estimated equations that explain regional economic growth by the extent of agglomeration of general economic activity, the presence of general machinery industry in the region, initial economic condition of the region, and policy variables.

His regression result shows that regional shipment growth is positively related to a proxy for agglomeration measured by manufacturing shipment per geographic area. On the contrary, he finds that real labor productivity growth in the region is not statistically related to the proxies for agglomeration measured by population density and regional GDP per geographic area. On the basis of this finding, he concludes that agglomeration of general economic activity is more likely to help expand the size of regional economy, but it is less likely to help increase labor productivity growth.

More interestingly, his work finds that the strong presence of general machinery industry in the region significantly increases the region's productivity growth. This finding is consistent with the hypothesis that the presence of machinery industry in the region creates externalities and helps augment productivity growth of other industries in the region. This result further provides statistical evidence that is consistent with the anecdotal evidence in Section 3 of this paper, confirming that the existence of supporting and related industries are likely to create cluster-specific advantage.

6. Conclusions

This paper has provided an overview of the evolution and structure of industrial clusters in Japan. The emergence of Japan's clusters is related to several factors: historical circumstances, prior existence of large manufacturers, prior existence of supporting industries, prior existence of related industries in neighboring geographic areas, reduction in transportation costs, regional government policy, and technology transfer. Japan's industrial clusters generate advantages by supporting large numbers of suppliers with specialized capabilities and by organizing market structures that encourage inter-firm linkages and facilitate the transmission of knowledge among firms.

This list of drivers and advantages of industry localization is quite consistent with lists derived from the experiences in the United States and Europe. Aside from the difference in historical circumstances, the distinctively Japanese element lies in the ways in which Japanese firms organize their business activities and the local governments promote local clusters. The extensive use of subcontracting; the hierarchical relationship between manufacturers and multiple layers of suppliers; the small size of suppliers; the importance of on-the-job-training; the low degree of labor mobility of skilled workers between firms; the preference for internal labor markets to external labor markets to allocate human resources; the establishment of various public testing, research, and technical centers by the local governments; the existence of various institutions such as trade associations, business associations, and wholesalers associations; and the roles such institutions play in facilitating the communication between firms in a cluster, are all important characteristics of Japan's industrial organization that distinguish Japan's industrial clusters from those in other countries such as in the United States.

Among the advantages identified in the paper, that created by the existence of specialized suppliers in a localized industry is considered the most important element in creating agglomeration economies. A supplier's skills and capabilities complement other suppliers' skills and capabilities, which in turn complement manufacturers' skills and capabilities. Through such a network, firms develop the skills specific to a cluster. The case analysis of this paper finds that firms develop and accumulate such skills over time, which in turn become important assets that often determine the cluster's evolution path.

Acknowledgements

For helpful comments and suggestions I am grateful to David Audretsch, Bee Yan Aw, Shujiro Urata and other participants of the project on The Role of Small and Medium Enterprises in Development, organized by the World Bank Institute.

Notes

[1] The number of SMEs in manufacturing is 816,881 in 1994, and total employment by SMEs is 8,878,531 in 1994. Total number of SMEs in the economy is 6,469,167, which accounts for 99 percent of all enterprises. Total economy-wide employment by SMEs is 41,415,237 in 1994.

[2] The description below draws heavily from People's Financial Corporation (1987, 1995), MITI (1996), and Ito and Urata (1997, 1998).
[3] People's Finance Corporation (1987, 1995).
[4] Ito and Urata, Table 10 (1997).
[5] People's Finance Corporation (1995).
[6] People's Finance Corporation (1987, 1995).
[7] People's Finance Corporation (1995).
[8] Ito and Urata (1997) and MITI (1996).
[9] People's Finance Corporation (1987).
[10] Ito and Urata (1997).
[11] People's Finance Corporation (1987, 1995).
[12] Ito and Urata (1997).
[13] People's Finance Corporation (1995).
[14] People's Finance Corporation (1995).
[15] Similar examples are the cases of Hitachi in the city of Hitachi and Yamaha in Hamamatsu (MITI, 1996).
[16] As of 1991, 171 public testing and research centers and technology centers exist in Japan (JICA, 1992).
[17] Not included in the sample of 14 clusters.
[18] Firms specialized in polishing often work as second-tier subcontractors. See Ito and Urata (1997, 1998).
[19] The numbers of subcontractors are 182 in silverware and 265 in houseware. In addition, there are more than 1,000 subcontractors specializing in polishing (Ito and Urata, 1997, Table 8).
[20] This tendency that Japanese automobile manufacturers form clusters with suppliers is observed for their U.S.-based companies as well. See Head, Ries, and Swenson (1995).
[21] The SMEA survey does not include in the sample the assembler-suppliertype cluster in which one or few large manufacturers operate as a core.
[22] This result complements the paper's earlier finding that some clusters in Japan benefited from the existence of pooled markets for part-time workers in labor-intensive industries, but not necessarily from pooled labor markets from skilled workers.

References

Asanuma, B. and T. Kikutani, 1992, 'Risk Absorption in Japanese Subcontracting: A Microeconometric Study of the Automobile Industry', *Journal of the Japanese and International Economies* **6** (March), 1–29.

Audretsch, D. B., 1999, 'The Economic Role of Small- and Medium-Sized Enterprises: The United States', paper prepared for the World Bank Workshop on Small and Medium Enterprises, August 13–14, 1999. World Bank, Washington, DC.

Audretsch, D. B. and M. P. Feldman, 1996, 'R&D Spillovers and the Geography of Innovation and Production', *American Economic Review* **86** (June), 630–640.

Head, K., J. Ries and D. Swenson, 1995, 'Agglomeration Benefits and Location Choice: Evidence from Japanese Manufacturing Investments in the United States', *Journal of International Economics* **38** (May), 223–247.

Ito, M. and S. Urata. 1997, 'Chushokigyo to hushokigyo enjoseisaku (1): 3 sanchi no hikaku chosa (Small and Medium Enterprises and Policy Toward Them)', *Keizaigaku Ronshu* **63**(10), 1–20.

Ito, M. and S. Urata, 1998, 'Chushokigyo to hushokigyo enjoseisaku (2): 3 sanchi no hikaku chosa (Small and Medium Enterprises and Policy Toward Them)', *Keizaigaku Ronshu* **64**(4), 49–73.

Jaffe, A., M. Trajtenberg and R. Henderson, 1993, 'Geographic Localization of Knowledge Spillovers as Evidence by Patent Citations', *Quarterly Journal of Economics* **63**, 577–598.

JICA, 1992, *Nihonno jibasangyo shinkoseisaku kenkyu (Research on Japan's Policy Toward Regional Clusters)*, Tokyo: Japan International Cooperation Agency.

Koike, K., 1988, *Understanding Industrial Relations in Modern Japan*, New York: Macmillan.

Krugman, P., 1991, *Geography and Trade*, Cambridge, MA: MIT Press.

Marshall, A., 1920, *Principles of Economics*, New York: Macmillan.

MITI, 1996, 'Sangyo shuseki fudoki (Industrial Localization)', An interim report. Ministry of International Trade and Industry, Tokyo.

Mishina, K., 1993, 'Tombow Pencil Co., Ltd.', Harvard Business School Case, 9-692-011. Harvard University, Cambridge, Mass.

Morikawa, M., 1997, 'Machinery Industry and Regional Economic Growth: Factors in the Economic Development of Japan's Prefectures', *Tsusankenkyu Review* **10** (December), 64–90. [In Japanese.]

Odagiri, H., 1992, *Growth Through Competition, Competition Through Growth: Strategic Management and the Economy in Japan*, New York: Oxford University Press.

People's Finance Corporation, 1987, *Endaka de yureru jibasangyo (Regional Clusters Under the Appreciation of Yen)*, Tokyo: Small and Medium Enterprise Research Center.

People's Finance Corporation, 1995, *Tenki wo mukaeta chiikikeizai: kawaru jibasangyo no yakuwari (Regional Economies Under Transition: Changing Roles of Regional Clusters)*, Tokyo: Small and Medium Enterprise Research Center.

Porter, M., 1998, 'Clusters and the New Economics of Competition', *Harvard Business Review* **76** (November-December), 77–90.

Porter, M., 1990, *The Competitive Advantage of Nations*, New York: Free Press.

SMEA, 1997, *Zenkoku no sanchi: heisei 8 nendo sanchi gaikyochosa kekka (Japan's Industrial Clusters: The 1996 Survey Result)*, Tokyo: Small and Medium Enterprise Agency.

Uekusa, M., 1987, 'Industrial Organization', in K. Yamamura and Y. Yasuba (eds.), *The Political Economy of Japan, Vol. 1: The Domestic Transformation*, Stanford, CA: Stanford University Press.

Yamawaki, H., 1992, 'International Competition and Japan's Domestic Adjustments', in K. Anderson (ed.), *New Silk Roads: East Asia and World Textile Markets*, Cambridge, U.K.: Cambridge University Press.

Firm and Group Dynamics in the Small and Medium Enterprise Sector in Indonesia

Albert Berry
Edgard Rodriguez
Henry Sandee

ABSTRACT. This paper discusses the role of clusters and subcontracting as factors in the evolution of small and medium firms in Indonesia during the last quarter century. It is argued that a number of such firms have become successful exporters of rattan furniture, wood furniture and garments on the strength of subcontracting relationships with foreign investors and buyers as well as agglomeration economies achieved by clustering in selected locations. Examples are provided to show that clustered enterprises are more likely to be in the exports business and to adopt product and process innovations as compared to more dispersed firms. Public policy support for fostering subcontracting links and cluster formation is also discussed.

1. Introduction

Developing countries value small and medium enterprises (SMEs) for several reasons. Viewed in static terms, the main argument is that SMEs, on average, achieve decent levels of productivity, especially of capital and all factors taken together (that is, total factor productivity), while also generating relatively large amounts of employment. It is thus better on the productivity front than micro-enterprise and better on the employment-generating front than large enterprise.

Albert Berry
Department of Economics
University of Toronto
150 St. George Street
Toronto, Ontario
M5S 1A1, Canada

Edgard Rodriguez
Department of Finance
Ottawa
Canada

Henry Sandee
The Free University
Amsterdam
The Netherlands

In dynamic terms, the sector is viewed as being populated by firms most of which have considerable growth potential. Though the great majority of micro-enterprises tend not to graduate from micro to a larger size category (Liedholm and Mead, 1999), many SMEs will grow significantly without exiting this broad size category. Other firms may eventually become large; this is the "seed-bed for large firms" function of SMEs.

Apart from the process of firm growth, it is important that SMEs achieve rising productivity over time through both investment and technological change. Large enterprises in developing countries achieve productivity increases to a great extent simply by borrowing from the shelf of technologies available in the world. For SMEs as a group it is not so evident that processes such as foreign direct investment, technology licensing, joint ventures, and access to engineering and other advances will provide the productivity increases needed. As capital becomes less scarce and the range of technologies available expands in the world, SMEs need productivity increases if they are to maintain or increase their contribution to overall development.

A third aspect of the dynamics of the SME sector that distinguishes it from larger enterprise is the high entry and exit rates. The process of rapid turnover raises a set of issues about possible impacts on the economic efficiency of the sector and about policies that may curtail such efficiency losses as are associated with it.

Finally, it is often argued that one advantage of SMEs is their flexibility, relative at least to larger firms. This is construed by some as a plus in industries and economies that, for whatever reason, face rapidly changing market conditions, including sharp macroeconomic downturns such

Small Business Economics **18**: 141–161, 2002.

as those that have bedevilled most of the countries of East Asia over the last few years.

This paper undertakes a selective review of evidence from Indonesia on the SME manufacturing sector, with emphasis on these issues of firm dynamics. Section 2 reviews the role and growth records of the SME sector in recent times, in the context of overall economic development. Section 3 looks at selected factors affecting the productivity, competitiveness, and survival of Indonesian SMEs, including their involvement in clusters and subcontracting activities. Section 4 takes a special look at Indonesian SMEs in the more open economy that has been evolving over the last couple of decades. Section 5 reviews Indonesian response to the economic crisis of the last couple of years. Section 6 provides a discussion of public policy support for subcontracting and cluster formation.

2. Trends in the SME sector of Indonesia

Indonesia has achieved a strong and widely applauded growth and development performance since the late 1960s, that is, until the crisis set in during 1997. Average GDP growth was 6.8 percent over 1970–1997, with per capita income rising at 4.7 percent. Industrialization proceeded apace, with manufacturing output growing at an average of 12.4 percent per year, first under an import substituting industrialization (ISI) policy and then, since 1986, an increasingly open economy strategy. Since 1970 manufacturing rose from 10.3 percent of GDP (current prices) to 25 percent in 1996, while the employment share of the sector rose from 7.8 percent in 1971 (World Bank, 1980, p. 122) to 12.6 percent in 1996.[1] While average labor productivity in the economy as a whole was rising at about 3.9 percent, that in manufacturing was increasing at 7.3 percent. The role of manufacturing products in total exports jumped dramatically, from 4 percent in 1984 to 48 percent in 1992, with the absolute level (current dollars) having risen by 8–9 fold from 1.8 billion to 16.1 billion dollars (Hill, 1997, p. 41). These included both labor intensive products whose competitiveness lay in the country's low wages and other products that relied on natural resources and special policy support.

Manufacturing in Indonesia remained dynamic in the 1990s up until the crisis, which began in 1997. Enabling macro and regional economic policies, including the development of financial, trade, and physical infrastructures, contributed to the growth of medium and large industry. In some industries this growth has been at the expense of small enterprise, as in the cases of bamboo weaving and palm sugar processing (Sandee and Rietveld, 2000). In other industries small firms have done well (Hill, 1996).

Structural change under growth

During the New Order period under Suharto, Indonesia experienced a rapid rise of large-scale manufacturing. Enormous factories have become prominent in Jakarta, Surabaya, Medan, Bandung, and Semarang, as well as along main trunk roads throughout Java. To an important extent, large-scale manufacturing in Indonesia is characterized by its concentration on labor-intensive assembly, and it is increasingly oriented toward export markets. In spite of the impressive growth of large-scale manufacturing, the relative importance of the small-scale sector has not declined greatly. According to Hill (1992, p. 249), the principal explanation of the latter's resilience is its "ability to exploit market niches, to concentrate on activities not characterized by economies of scale, to serve particular markets not of commercial interest to larger firms, and to produce goods not easily adapted to mass production technologies." Clustering is an additional factor that may explain the resilience of small-scale industries. A main feature of industrial organization in Indonesia, and in particular Java, is the tendency for small-scale industrial enterprises to group together by geography and by economic subsector. Clustering offers agglomeration economies that allow small-scale industries to participate profitably and competitively in wide trade networks. The resilience of the small-scale industry sector reflects the fact that small enterprises have not been static during Indonesia's long period of economic growth. There is ample evidence of their technological upgrading as a necessary condition to "stay on board" during the growth years (Sandee and others, 1994; Sandee, 1995; van Diermen, 1997).

The small firm's continuing role as the locus of most employment in Indonesia's manufacturing

TABLE I
Size composition of Indonesian manufacturing establishments, 1986 and 1996

Year	Size of establishment (number of workers)	Number of establishments	Employment (thousands of workers)	Percent of employment	Average size of establishment (number of workers)
1986	<5	1,422,593	2,700.1	52.4	1.95
	5–19	98,129	787.7	14.9	8.03
	20 and up	12,902	1,728.7	32.7	134.0
	20–99	10,008	(400.3)	(7.57)	[40.0]
	100 and up	2,894	(1,328.4)	(25.13)	(459.0)
	Total	1,533,624	5,286.5	100.0	3.45
1996	<5	2,501,585	4,878.1	48.6	1.95
	5–19	228,987	1,831.9	18.2	8.0
	20 and up	28,798	3,329.5	33.2	115.6
	20–99	22,283	(891.3) (779.9)	(8.88) (7.77)	[40.0] [35.0]
	100 and up	6,509	(2,438.2) (2,549.6)	(24.32) (25.43)	(374.6) (391.7)
	Total	2,759,370	10,039,549	100.0	3.45

[ ] Assumed.
( ) Deduced based on the assumed figures.
Note: Figures are available from the 1986 and 1996 sources for the whole category of establishments with 20 or more workers. For the category 20–99 it is possible to make an approximate estimate of average size, based on the size distribution usually observed. For 1986 our best estimate is 40 workers. When this estimate has been made it is then possible to deduce the average size of the category 100 and up, together with the rest of the figures shown in round parentheses in the 1986 panel. For 1996, the average size of establishments with 20 or more workers is less than in 1986; 40 would thus seem to be an upper limit estimate of the average size within the 20–99 category; if it is the true figure, then the leftward of the two estimates in round parentheses for the other categories where estimates are made is the implied figure. As a lower limit to likely average size within the 20–99 category we have chosen 35 workers; were it the true figure then the rightward set of figures in round parentheses would hold.
Source: The 1986 and 1996 industrial censuses.

structure is reflected in the fact that as of 1996 nearly half of all workers were found in units of under five workers and two-thirds in ones of under 20 (Table I). About a quarter were found in establishments of 100 or more workers and probably close to a fifth in those of over 500 workers.[2] Labor productivity, however, is much greater in larger plants with the result that though the very small ("household") sector has nearly half of the employment it probably generates only 9–10 percent of output[3] while plants of 100 (500) and up generate about 70 percent (46 percent) of that output.[4] The labor productivity gap thus appears to be one of the largest observed among developing countries (Berry and Mazumdar, 1991). As of 1974–1975 the striking aspect of these gaps in Indonesia was not so much that between small establishments (5–19 workers) and the medium/large range but that between household workers and everyone else.[5]

Other notable features of Indonesian manufacturing are its widespread dispersion in rural areas and the already noted prevalence of clusters, where about half of manufacturing employment was located according to Sandee (1995, p. 10). Clusters are important in absolute and relative terms in most major categories. There is not much variance in average firm size within most clusters; usually there are two to three workers, with the main reliance on family labor. Some more dynamic clusters do use considerable paid labor. Rural industry is characterized by its instability (Klapwijk, 1997) and the low incomes it generates. World Bank (1985) argues that the returns to labor (per man hour) are substantially lower (as much as 70 percent) in activities outside the rice labor market. On the basis of this somewhat unusual characteristic of the rural wage and income structure this source concluded that there was a labor surplus in many Javanese villages but that there did exist mechanisms that prevent such surplus from bidding down the agricultural wage rate. Whatever the labor market mechanisms involved, rural industry is frequently associated with low earnings. Low-income urban dwellers seem more typically to opt for trade and services.

Opinions have been divided on the likely impact of economic growth on these low-income jobs in rural industry. Rising rural incomes are likely to generate more than proportional increases in demand for goods and services of household enterprises, but beyond a certain income level people begin switching to the more standardized products of larger firms, which are less likely to be found in rural settings. Urbanization and the expectation that demand would shift from their low-quality products has led to the prediction that rural industry will tend to decline.

As noted, the last couple of decades have seen very rapid growth of manufacturing output: at about 11.3 percent per year (1975–1996), with both employment (6.1 percent) and labor productivity (4.9 percent) contributing strongly to this output growth.[6] Very significant changes have occurred in the composition of output by branch and in the share of output being exported. In the light of such growth and change, it is perhaps surprising that the size structure of the sector has shifted only marginally. The large labor productivity gaps by size appear to have remained (although the lack of clearly comparable output figures from the 1996 manufacturing census make this judgement somewhat speculative for the period since the mid-1980s)[7] but not widened, implying that significant investment and technological upgrading has occurred across the full size spectrum. Employment growth has been rapid in all the size categories, and industrial concentration has tended to decline somewhat. Evidence on firm-level growth is very limited, but considerable dynamism has clearly characterized certain groups of firms.

Over the intercensal period 1974/1975–1986, the broad size structure of employment remained virtually unchanged. Employment grew at 5.6 percent per year on average with establishments of under five workers retaining about 55 percent of the total labor force, based on the population census definition, which focuses on the main activity of the person. There seems also to have been little change within the medium-large (M/L) group, although the data presented by Hill (1998, p. 71) show some jumpiness. Over the next intercensal period (1986–1996), unadjusted figures indicate that manufacturing employment was growing even faster, at about 6.6 percent per year, and again only a modest change seems to have occurred in size structure. Table I suggests that establishments of over 100 workers retained their 25 percent share, those of under five dropped a bit from 52.4 to 48.6 percent, while the middle range from 5 to 99 workers gained from 22.5 percent to about 26–27 percent.[8]

The failure of the larger establishments to increase their share of total employment (assuming these figures are roughly accurate)[9] flies in the face of considerable belief that concentration has increased in many branches of industry and overall. It confirms Bird's (1999) conclusion, based on an analysis of 102 industries over 1975–1993, that there has been a long-run downward trend. The simple average four-firm concentration ratio declined from 64 percent to 54 percent and the percentage of industries characterized as highly concentrated fell from 39 percent to 28 percent.

Clearly comparable figures on labor productivity are not available to permit an accurate measure of trends since 1986. The average for all manufacturing seems to have been about 4.5 percent over this decade. Data on establishments referred to as "small business" and defined (for the manufacturing sector) as being without legal entity and/or employing fewer than 20 persons show this group to have labor productivity about one-thirteenth that of the other (medium and large) establishments in 1996 (Saleh et al., 1999, Table VI). If the same productivity gap held between plants of fewer than 20 workers and those with 20 and up, then labor productivity increase over 1986–1996 for those with fewer than 20 workers would have been about 2 percent per year. It seems likely, however, that the 1996 productivity gap between plants of fewer than 20 workers and those with more was a bit lower (than 13 to 1), in which case the labor productivity growth of the plants with fewer than 20 workers may have been as fast as 4 percent per year or even a bit more. In any case there appears little doubt that productivity growth in the smaller establishments was substantial. Whether it matched or even exceeded that in the M/L range cannot yet be ascertained.

It is accepted that total factor productivity

(TFP) better measures the relative efficiency of SME firms and their advances over time than does labor productivity. A number of studies in various countries have used this indicator to assess relative efficiency across size categories.[10] Unfortunately, TFP is harder to measure than is labor productivity, owing to imprecision in the figures on capital (and human capital as well). The questionable quality problems of the Indonesian data have steered some analysts away from its use. There have, nevertheless, been a few analyses of how TFP has changed over time in the M/L sector as a whole, the most recent and perhaps the most accurate of which is Timmer's (1999, p. 87). He reports that TFP fluctuated without trend over 1975–1983 and then rose by about 6 percent per year over 1983–1995, for a 20-year average increase of 2.8 percent per year. By 1995 TFP was at 176 percent of the 1975 level, with labor productivity at 220 percent of it. The figures indicate that capital input accounted for 60 percent of the output growth over this period, labor for just 18 percent, and TFP growth for 22 percent. No TFP estimates have to our knowledge been undertaken by size category of establishments. It seems likely, however, that the quite marked improvements that have characterized the M/L sector since the mid-1980s have been shared by the smaller establishments in that group and perhaps by small firms as well.

Growth of total employment results both from creation of new firms (minus the exit of existing ones) and from the employment growth of existing firms. Though no organized information is available to permit a disaggregation between these two sources, scattered evidence illustrates the fact that firm growth is important. Steel (1993, p. 15) notes that there was considerable graduation into the larger size categories over 1975–1990. Whereas, in 1990, 63.7 percent of all M/L employment was located in establishments with 500 or more workers, only 28.8 percent of the initial year employment of this set of establishments was found in that size range.[11] Hill (1998, p. 71) presents somewhat similar information for three size categories. In 1990, whereas the 500 and up category accounted for 65.7 percent of total value added, firms created in that size range accounted only for 41.7 percent of it (Table II). More directly related to our concerns here, establishments currently in the small and medium range (20–99 workers) produced only 7.0 percent of valued

TABLE II
Size distribution of manufacturing value added in Indonesia, by current establishment size and by initial year establishment size, 1977–1991

	Current year size group (by number of workers)			Initial year size group (by number of workers)		
Year	20–99	100–499	500+	20–99	100–499	500+
1977	9.0	24.2	66.8	15.9	35.8	48.2
1978	8.8	25.2	66.1	16.7	34.3	49.1
1979	8.1	25.7	66.3	18.9	36.1	45.0
1980	7.3	25.0	67.7	20.3	33.6	46.1
1981	6.6	23.8	69.6	20.9	31.9	47.2
1982	6.9	25.1	68.1	23.1	32.4	44.5
1983	6.4	23.3	70.3	23.7	30.0	46.3
1984	6.4	22.7	70.8	25.4	28.8	45.8
1985	12.0	30.3	57.6	27.3	28.6	44.2
1986	8.4	27.3	64.3	27.5	28.3	44.2
1987	7.4	27.0	65.7	25.7	29.3	45.0
1988	9.1	28.6	62.3	27.3	30.8	42.0
1989	7.6	27.4	65.0	26.0	30.7	42.3
1990	7.0	27.3	65.7	25.4	32.9	41.7
1991				25.4	36.4	38.3

"Initial year" refers to the shares of establishments based on their size distribution at the commencement of the data series (1975) or when the establishment commenced operations.
Source: Hill (1997, p. 71).

added, but those created in that range produced 25.4 percent. Hence, those who had graduated up from this size category accounted for a hefty 18.4 percent of output, more than twice what firms currently in the size range were producing. With the passage of time this ratio has risen (from under 2 in 1977 to 3.6 in 1990). More important, the share of all value added by establishments of 20 workers and up that comes from those starting in the 20–99 range rose from 15.9 percent in 1977 to 25.4 percent in 1990.

Further evidence on the growth trajectories of firms comes from the study of SME exporters by Berry and Levy (1999). These firms were doubtless atypically capable of growth because of their success in breaking into export markets and are thus better thought of as giving a feel for how fast growth can be under those circumstances. The 32 rattan firms interviewed began operations with an average of 136 workers and had 377 by date of sample in 1992, by which time their average age was about 10 years. The 34 garment firms started with an average of 218 workers and had 1,109 by date of sample.[12] Some of these firms had begun with very few workers; seven of the rattan firms began with an average of 5.7 workers and had expanded to an average of 270 by time of survey, and eight garment firms that started with an average of 4.6 wound up with 167. Still, a lower share of this Indonesian sample of exporting SMEs had started small (defined by number of workers) than in a comparable study of SME exporters from Colombia (Berry and Escandon, 1999, p. 173). This could be consistent with the two sets of firms having comparable initial levels of capital, however, since wages are higher in Colombia and the labor/capital ratio therefore lower.

3. Productivity growth and the role of clusters, subcontracting, and "strategic alliances"

Labor productivity at the firm level rises owing to increased capital per worker and to technological change. At the level of the industry or of manufacturing an additional factor usually tending to raise labor productivity is the reallocation of resources toward higher productivity groups of firms. TFP rises as a result of technological change and this reallocation of resources to more productive firms (i.e., to just two of the three factors that explain rising labor productivity).

Raising productivity by technological upgrading (in the broadest sense to include not just better machinery but also improvements in workplace organization, inventory handling, product design, etc.) is achieved through a variety of mechanisms. It is accepted that most small firms will be less able to handle this process successfully on their own than will larger ones. Accordingly, much attention has been given to the possible roles of subcontracting and clustering as arrangements that make such advances more easily accessible to small firms, and to collective support systems, including those of the public sector and of private associations. The Japanese experience is viewed as the paradigm for the importance of subcontracting in creating the conditions for a major SME role in a strong and internationally competitive manufacturing sector. Italy's export-oriented clusters have become a model for the role of clusters in competitive export activities. These two phenomena are of course not limited to export settings, though they may have their most impressive manifestations there.

Indonesia's clusters and exports

What are the sources of rising productivity in Indonesia's SMEs? As was discussed, the evidence suggests that although absolute levels of labor productivity in most SMEs remain quite low[13] levels have been rising significantly over the last couple of decades. Probably productivity has risen at rates not far from those of the larger firms for which the data referred to above clearly confirm substantial improvements.

There are no general data on the sources of productivity gains of SMEs or their relative importance in Indonesia. But some suggestions do emerge from the few studies available. In their analysis of sources of technological capability for exporting SMEs in rattan furniture, Jepara wood furniture, and garments (three important export industries in which SMEs play significant roles), Berry and Levy (1999, p. 50) highlight several points:

1. Private channels have been the dominant mechanisms for acquiring such capability in all three sectors.

2. Subcontracting is pervasive in all three industries and has been crucial to harnessing traditional skills for export production, especially in Jepara.
3. Employment of expatriates is an especially powerful mechanism for acquiring technological capability in the rattan and garment sectors, but this practice is concentrated disproportionately among *non-pribumi* entrepreneurs who have the advantage of being embedded in an extended (ethnic) community that transcends national boundaries.
4. Collective support mechanisms (public sector and private associations) have played only a limited role overall; they have been more important to the smaller *pribumi* firms but their overall value has been limited by pervasive institutional weaknesses.

These case studies illustrate the range of mechanisms at work in the process of technology upgrading. Much of it involves ideas coming from the outside, but on-the-job learning by both employees and the entrepreneur are rated very highly as well (Berry and Levy, 1999, pp. 51, 59).[14] A considerable shifting of relevant skills among firms also occurs when employees are hired from one to another.

Foreign buyers are the most important single source of outside technological support in all three industries (true also of marketing). This reflects both the importance of strong mutual interest in raising productivity for this process to be successful and the fact that the buyer's product preferences and specifications have implications for the technological capability that a firm needs. Expatriate employees were second most important in rattan and garments, two industries in which there had been dynamic activity in the East Asia region for some time before Indonesia's sudden emergence as a significant producer.[15] As was noted, however, their importance was much greater to *non-pribumi* entrepreneurs than to the *pribumis*. Equipment suppliers were moderately useful, especially to the (few) *pribumi* entrepreneurs in the garment sector. Similar firms provided considerable information in the garment industry, especially to the *pribumi* entrepreneurs, and the technical literature mattered to a fair number of firms.

On the other side of the ledger, private consultants were of limited importance, as were the public sector providers, the industry associations, and the "foster parents."[16] This said, however, the fact that none of these last sources is by itself widely cited as important to firms' technological advances does not mean that they are unimportant when taken together. Different sources matter to different firms, so each is cited by a few firms, and their total significance may be greater than might at first appear. Moreover, collective sources (public and private nonprofit) have clearly been more important to firms that started smaller and to those run by *pribumi* entrepreneurs. The latter suggests that rather than concluding that such sources are not necessary, ways should be found to make them better in the future than in the past.[17] Doing so requires recognition of what such collective sources can do best and how they can best do it. It is important that collective providers not try to do too much, nor to replace private mechanisms when these have real potential.

The authors point to the merits of "light touch" public support/intervention, which focuses on bringing private actors together, facilitating their contacts, and the like. One of the best examples of this, most directly relevant to the marketing needs of the surveyed rattan SMEs but also surprisingly relevant to technological learning, is support for fairs, both in-country and abroad (where it involves subsidizing trips to those fairs). Private consultants appear destined to play only a marginal role for the foreseeable future, although here too this is not grounds for writing them off, but simply for keeping their limited potential role in perspective.

Unfortunately, it is not possible to say to what degree the above findings on sources of technological advance in SMEs in three exporting industries can be generalized to the majority that have weaker or no links to exporting. The role of foreign buyers would of course be absent and the benefits and density of subcontracting very probably less. We suspect that technological improvement is on average slower in the domestic market-oriented SMEs[18] because these important sources of technology are weak and because the achievement of export capacity is likely to require a higher-than-average level of performance. But we believe that most of the same sources of gains are at work in the broader universe of firms as well, that their relative importance is probably rather similar, and that the policy conclusions reached on the basis of the study of exporting SMEs is also more generally applicable.

Subcontracting has played a central role in the successful integration of SMEs into dynamic manufacturing sectors in countries such as Japan and Korea, where it has been a major vehicle for the achievement of rising and eventually high levels of productivity in those firms. This role is clearly less in Indonesia at this time, but at the same time not inconsiderable. The issue is how its role will evolve in future. Its prevalence in the exporting SMEs studied by Berry and Levy (1999, pp. 53–55) is encouraging. Three quarters of rattan furniture exporters were subcontracting principals, with half of these subcontracting complete orders and 80 percent specific tasks. Quality maintenance involves technical assistance to the subcontractors. One function of in-house capacity among Jepara exporters is to demonstrate quality control and to spin off new capable subcontractors. Subcontracting is encouraged by large export orders, fluctuating orders, and the risks associated with a heavy investment by a single firm in such circumstances, as well as by the lower costs that subcontractors can often achieve. Kinship, friendship, or former business contacts also encourage subcontracting.

Meanwhile, the striking importance of clusters of small firms in Indonesia, in both rural and urban areas, suggests that membership in a cluster has a significant influence on a firm's productivity.[19] The general literature on clusters has focused on sources of static productivity gains, such as economies of scale in purchase of raw materials or machinery, sale of output, or spread of risk associated with demand fluctuations.[20] More recently, it has also taken account of the dynamic advantages of this structure, as with sharing in R&D expenditures, diffusion/sharing of information on new designs, processes, products, etc. (Sverisson, 1993; Schmitz, 1995). Klapwijk (1997, p. 167) argues that a conducive socio-cultural milieu sustaining trust and reciprocity, an active involvement of traders, and strong government initiative at the local level may be at work in central Java to render rural industrial clusters (RICs) a fertile seedbed for technological change and thus a positive factor in rural industrialization. Some clusters reflect collaboration among a number of extended families that have a long history of cooperation and coexistence.

The main difference between clustered and dispersed rural industry in Indonesia[21] is that the clustered industry is primarily oriented to markets outside its own community (Poot and others, 1990, p. 194). Products are on average less perishable or local-taste specific. Examples in Indonesia are batik; leather and products (including footwear); some food processing activities (e.g., coconut, sugar); wood working (e.g., carving), bamboo and rattan; bricks and tiles; pottery and some metal products, such as agricultural tools; and iron wares.

Technological change is more likely when the clusters are linked to urban or international markets. Klapwijk (1997) suggests that only those RICs that specialize in the production of discrete products in small batches to customers' orders are likely to survive in the long run. This limits the prospects to such sectors as clothing, footwear, mechanical engineering, and furniture, with a high need for flexibility at the shop floor and where economies of scope do not inhibit the division of tasks among several enterprises. Though many rural clusters will not survive as development moves along, there are interesting examples of successful upgrading, finding of new market niches, etc. Subcontracting arrangements often link such rural industries to nearby urban or even international markets (Weijland, 1994). Section 4 below provides some details on the cases of wooden furniture from Jepara and garments from Bali.

There is increasing empirical evidence that small firms that are parts of clusters are in a better position to adopt innovations when compared with their dispersed counterparts. Sandee's (1995) study of five roof tile clusters in central Java province (the heartland of small-scale cottage industry (SSCI) in the country) illustrates several of the elements at work. Through the 1980s the demand for roof tiles increasingly shifted toward urban areas, where customers pay more attention to quality. This meant that upgrading was important to retain or increase demand. As a result, some clusters have stagnated and others have grown through a process of technological change or adaptation that encompasses changes in processes of production, in patterns of interfirm cooperation, in employment conditions, and in the marketing of new output.

The range of experiences has been wide. In two cases (Mayong Lor and Klepu) the process was demand driven. The buyers, agents from urban building material shops, largely took care of the financial, technical, and marketing sides of the adoption and competed with each other to do so, a reflection of the expanding urban demand for press tiles. The pioneer adopters of the hand-press technology were young males who had used it elsewhere in rural Java. Since its introduction in the early 1970s, virtually all of the producers in these clusters have adopted the technology (Sandee, 1995, p. 170).[22] Female producers, however, had very little chance to do so. Their firms were usually taken over by men as the technological shift proceeded. Access to credit was a general constraint on adoption and was felt especially acutely by female producers. The fact that innovation adoption requires a more intensive involvement of both producers and workers may also militate against women, given their other (household) responsibilities (Sandee, 1995, p. 179).

In producer-driven clusters such as Karanggeneng, networks of producers are at the heart of the process of technology upgrading. Producers organize to finance new equipment, share indivisible capital, and gain access to new markets. In buyer-driven clusters, collaboration among producers and traders obviates the need to form such producer networks. Urban building material shops play a key role in assuring demand but also provide loans for purchase of presses and renting out mixers. In both cases, innovation trickles down among an increasing number of producers. Diffusion is stimulated by the growing involvement of suppliers, "while the government principally contributes by improving the environment" (Sandee, 1995, p. 170). In the producer-driven clusters, pioneer adopters remain the most important actors by stimulating innovation adoption by those producers whom they can trust and control, especially relatives. Urban building material shops get involved through establishing relationships with the pioneer adopters.

Sandee also studied two clusters where institutional support was the driving force behind adoption. The success of Karanggeneng motivated the government to intervene in these other clusters, and its involvement was more direct since the producers and buyers had not yet demonstrated the degree of interest shown in Kananggenerg. These institution-driven innovation processes suffered from too little involvement by other actors; and when government support dried up, the innovations came to a standstill. The process has been hampered by difficulties in gaining access to press-tile markets, so adopters have tended to stick with traditional tiles and much of their press-tile capacity is under-utilized (Sandee, 1995, p. 171). Sandee concludes that the government has focused too much on the supply side of the innovation adoption process while underestimating the need to link clusters to more dynamic markets prior to the introduction of such change.

In all the cases Sandee studied, the government has contributed to innovation by improving the environment for tile production. Government assistance programs tend to be oriented to the provision of technical and financial assistance to single enterprises. This may be cost effective in clusters where initial impacts trickle down but otherwise less so. Most rural tile producers only know about alternative technologies in general terms, but not in enough detail to have a good feel for the benefit/cost ratio of upgrading. Rural clusters would benefit from regular but simple training programs by the government in which the sharing of information on the more advanced technologies figures prominently. Perhaps assistance programs should operate through longer-run links with selected producers rather than as in the present one-shot system. More general policies, such as those in the credit area, also affect market conditions. The larger tile firms have favorable access to the KYUK program, and smaller rural firms would benefit from the abolition of such preferential treatment because these smaller firms typically lack the credit needed to establish or expand their business (Sandee, 1995, p. 180). And the central role of buyers and others in adoption raises seldom-considered policy options.

4. Export success of Indonesian SMEs

As economies turn outward it becomes more important for any group of firms to be able to gain export markets or to compete effectively with imports that no longer have to jump high protectionist fences. It has been widely accepted that for SMEs to succeed on the export front (how they do in competing with imports must be judged differently) SMEs must have some way to lower transactions costs, which tend to have an important fixed cost component. Subcontracting is one route, whether with larger scale manufacturers or with commercial intermediaries. Berry and Levy (1999) reported that it was common among medium-sized exporters in rattan, Jepara furniture, and garments.

The second recognized route is by reaping the advantages of clustering. All studies show that export-oriented small clusters operate in buyer-driven commodity chains requiring continuous upgrading and adaptability, which in turn requires a professional interaction on tailor-made product specifications between buyers and producers (Knorringa, 1998). The buyers provide an effective "assistance package."

Van Diermen (1997) and Cole (1998) show how small enterprises penetrate export markets via buyer-driven trade networks, in the cases of Jepara (carved wooden furniture, see Appendix 1) and Bali (garments, see Appendix 2). In both cases there are brokers, agents, and traders that function as intermediaries between international buyers and small-scale producers. Foreigners have played an important role in modernizing the Jepara furniture industry and linking it to global markets (Schiller and Martin-Schiller, 1997), as well as in the case of Bali garments.

Indonesia's small industry (establishments of 5–19 workers) seems to have shared nicely in the manufactured export boom of recent years. The absolute level of direct exports rose from US$137 million in 1983 to 2.1 billion in 1992 (Hill, 1998, p. 49), and its share of such exports increased from 10 to 13.2 percent, after reaching 17.3 percent in 1987. As with larger industry, the main items are garments, textiles, and footwear, together accounting for 60 percent. This growth has been achieved substantially by finding niche markets and adapting costs and quality to market demand (Thee, 1993). A significant and no doubt rapidly increasing share of SME output has been exported indirectly through subcontracting arrangements.

5. Response to crisis

Indonesia has suffered a severe economic setback over the last couple of years, with GDP falling by some 13–15 percent in 1998 alone. How has the SME sector responded? What does its response tell us about the sector and its potential? What policy instruments are pertinent to this situation?

It has often been argued that one of the advantages of many SMEs is their flexibility, and related capacity to, for instance, weather storms, shift from product to product, expand and contract easily. SMEs may therefore be expected to do relatively better under volatile macro conditions than large firms producing more standardized products, where reorganizations of the assembly line take time (Sandee et al., 1998, p. 3). Sunk costs are lower in smaller firms and labor-capital struggles are less frequent, another source of flexibility. At the same time it is often argued that SMEs are the first victims of macro-economic crises such as this one. The issue is important for several reasons. First, a flexible SME sector, able to adjust smoothly to severe shocks, is clearly a major plus as a country tries to mitigate the effects of those shocks and to avoid large increases in poverty. Also, even if many SMEs show impressive agility in general, certain types of shocks might destroy firms with good longer run potential, raising the question of what policy instruments might help to avoid that outcome. Finally, it is to be expected that any given macroeconomic crisis will affect different SMEs in different ways, and that appropriate policies to support SMEs will vary widely according to how those firms are placed in the economy.

When the recent crisis in Indonesia led to a major devaluation, it raised the potential profitability of exporting industries such as Jepara furniture, while many domestically oriented industries were under strain owing to weakening local demand. Best placed are industries that export a lot or compete with imports and at the same time do not rely heavily on raw material imports or imported machinery and equipment. Jepara is such a case. Worst off are those relying on domestic demand and not competing with imports (which the devaluation will help to cut out) but drawing heavily on imports of material or capital goods.

These various effects are apparent in Indonesia. van Diermen and others (1998, p. 32) report that some SME groups such as Jepara and the traditional barik cloth weaving industry in Central Java have been doing well. Nails, latches, and door bolts are now produced locally rather than imported as before, in spite of the quality disadvantage vis-à-vis the imports. In some export cases some of the potential benefits to the Indonesian firms are negotiated away by foreign buyers. While the currency devalued by 60 percent in real terms (80 percent in nominal terms) the textile and garment industries' international buyers have insisted on discounts of 20–40 percent, so the rupiah price increases are less than might be expected (van Diermen and others, 1998, p. 24). Also foreign banks' unwillingness to accept Indonesian banks' letters of credit has reduced the benefits to exporters (van Diermen and others, 1998, p. 40). At the negative end of the spectrum is the demise of *tahu* producers in West Java and small clove cigarette (*kretek*) producers in Central Java, in both cases caused by a steep rise in the price of inputs. Another example of small-scale enterprises in distress are those garment producers (often operating in subcontracting networks) who depend on a steady flow of imported cloth and other raw materials.

There is no doubt that SMEs have fared very differently according to the sector. Unfortunately, though considerable evidence has been built up on trends in selected industries, on the broader question of how well the SME sector as a whole has been able to defend itself and maintain its income levels against the effects of the crisis, one can only guess at this point. Susenas surveys provide useful data on employment trends, but the country's statistical apparatus is not up to the task of identifying short-run earnings trends in the cottage and small-scale sectors. Earnings levels can only be reasonably well gauged when an economic census (or sometimes a population census) is done. There is nonetheless a widespread impression that small-scale enterprises have been weathering the crisis better than larger companies (Cameron, 1999). Two distinct interpretations of the resilience of small-scale firms in the current period of economic distress have been highlighted. First, a recent paper by Jellinek and Rustanto (1999) argues that there has been an unprecedented upsurge of the small-scale sector, with new economic opportunities in blacksmith communities, for furniture makers, fishing, agricultural tools, brick and tile making, and small-scale vending activities. They report that cottage industries almost completely destroyed over the past 20 years are finding it hard to keep up with the new orders. They judge that the economic crisis offers renewed opportunities to a small-scale sector that was gradually losing ground during the New Order. In this view, a policy correction, mainly through the depreciation of the rupiah, has created growth prospects for "communal-capitalist systems currently being created by the people themselves." A second view is that many small-scale enterprises have been performing well in recent decades, even though they often faced considerable discrimination, especially relative to the opportunities enjoyed by the conglomerates (Poot, 1997). Being less reliant on formal markets and formal credit funds, small-scale enterprises are able to respond quicker and more flexibly to sudden shocks than can their larger counterparts.

We now turn to a brief review of available evidence on this issue. The second view of the pre-crisis period appears much more consistent with the statistics reviewed above. Nonetheless, both may offer insights into the events of the crisis period itself. Among recent studies of the impact of the crisis Hill (1999) reports that the manufacturing sector has contracted at about the economy-wide average (–15 percent) since its outbreak, though there are differences between export-oriented and local market activities. He concludes that every sector has shed labor, with the exception of agriculture, and that the biggest decline has occurred in manufacturing.[23] Both Hill and Cameron (1999) feel that small-scale enterprises are weathering the crisis better than larger companies, because they are less reliant on formal markets and less reliant on now far more costly borrowed funds.

Various surveys have attempted to measure the social and economic impact of the crisis, focusing especially on how it has affected poverty, education, and health (Wetterberg et al., 1999; Poppele et al., 1999; Cameron, 1999). They generally report that urban areas have been hit harder than rural ones. They also report that both the urban and rural areas of Java have been hit hard relative to other regions, the impact on rural areas being related to the relatively high density of urban-rural linkages on Java as a consequence of which urban economic distress trickles down to rural areas. The surveys estimate also that unemployment rates for 1998 were up to some 6 percent, substantially below earlier forecasts of massive unemployment flowing from such a major economic downturn. This suggests that workers who have lost their jobs in the formal sector have been able to find alternative (possibly part-time) employment in the informal sector.

The most general statistical evidence on trends in the labor market comes from the large annual Susenas survey (corresponding to the month of January, in the middle of the rainy season when agricultural activity is likely to be most prominent). Comparison of the figures for 1995, 1997, and 1998 shows little change in the structure of employment by job position.[24] The "paid workers" category continued to dominate manufacturing employment (of persons 10 and up) with about two-thirds of the total, including both the so-called formal and informal branches of manufacturing. This category gained a couple of points at the expense of the unpaid worker category.[25] Self-employment of people who run their own business, with or without workers, has remained virtually constant at a quarter of the total. However, between 1997 and 1998, those with their own business but no workers moved up a couple of points while those with temporary or unpaid workers dropped the same amount, possibly reflecting the effects of shrinking businesses. This latter shift was apparent both in urban and in rural areas, and has characterized the economy as a whole, not just manufacturing. Since some self-employment trade and service activities have a "last resort" character, it is likely that the adjustment process has involved a shift into these.

A few surveys have focused more specifically on the impacts of the crisis on SMEs. The Akatiga Foundation of Bandung monitored the performance of 800 small-scale entrepreneurs in four provinces during 1997–1998, reporting that 28 percent of the producers showed improved performance while the remainder lost or saw no significant change. Export-oriented small firms did better than domestic counterparts. Moreover, small-scale enterprises in Java suffered more than on other islands of the archipelago and those in urban areas more than their rural counterparts. The survey identified various coping strategies by small-scale entrepreneurs to deal with economic adversity, including working at lower profit margins and lowering labor costs (Akatiga Foundation, 1999). The study reports also that the social safety net programs of the Indonesian government have given rise to an upsurge of microenterprises, especially in sectors characterized by low entry barriers.

Musa's (Musa and Priatna, 1998) survey on access to credit for small and medium enterprises during the crisis, based on a sample of some 300 firms in eight provinces and various sectors, reports that self-finance has remained the main source of funds for investment and working capital. More than 75 percent of small firms were fully reliant on their own funds to finance business activities and fewer than 13 percent had access to formal finance, with the number declining slightly since the outbreak of the crisis.[26] The limited exposure of small-scale business activities to borrowed funds from the formal sector is presumably one of the factors explaining the resilience of these activities during the current period of economic distress. The main coping mechanisms of the sampled firms include the use of cheaper inputs to replace expensive (imported) materials and the downsizing of the labor force. Of respondents, 80 percent have seen their business shrink (though only 21 percent report laying off workers); in 12 percent of cases it stayed constant and 8 percent have achieved an increase, the latter occurring mainly in those activities that export and have limited need for imported materials.

Timberg (1999, p. 12) also concludes that the overall immediate effect of the monetary crisis on SMEs and the financial institutions that serve them has been relatively mild. However, he feels that some of the ensuing changes in financial institutions might have stronger negative effects, in particular the increased conservatism of lenders and the enhanced role of the foreign bank owners who have less feel for Indonesian SMEs. Accordingly, he recommends consideration of some measures to counter those changes.

Scattered evidence from surveys undertaken by the Ministry of Cooperatives and Small and Medium Enterprise Development[27] taken together with the cited Susenas data and with basic economic logic leave little doubt that the SME sector has on balance felt some negative impact from the crisis. The crisis creates pressure for firms to adopt adjustment strategies to cut costs and to redirect output to new market opportunities whenever possible. The Susenas evidence to the effect that there have been no major changes in the structure of manufacturing employment suggest only modest job loss in small-scale firms. Either most firms have been able to cope without major reductions in their workforce or the creation of new firms has offset such reduction. Of course, the picture may become different if economic recovery does not come soon, and more drastic adjustment strategies may be needed.

A look at specific industries helps to identify the range of effects from the crisis. There is evidence of rapid growth and employment generation in the small-scale furniture industry, especially in Jepara but also in North Sulawesi (Sandee et al., 1998; Jellinek and Rustanto, 1999; Akatiga Foundation, 1999). This industry exemplifies an economic activity that uses domestic inputs and has plenty of export potential. Large and small firms in the furniture industry are developing long-term linkages to overcome the present insecure environment. Foreign actors play an important role as intermediary between domestic production networks and international buyers and also contribute to easing the credit constraint caused by the collapse of the Indonesian banking system. Policy has contributed positively to the transition through the development of the provincial harbor to accommodate container transport, the simplified procedures for foreign investors, and the improved facilities for clearing exports. As for the impact of the recent events on the smaller enterprises, some of those already engaged in exporting (usually indirectly) are being pressured by contractors and large firms to sign long-term contracts; some may become disguised wage labor. The fast growth has produced greater standardization and a stricter division of labor and tasks among firms. Prior to the crisis the small firms had access to various trade networks. Sandee wonders whether these changes will diminish the overall flexibility of the industry and have a negative effect on regular quality upgrading, which has been the norm in the past and will remain very needed in future.

The experience in the construction materials sector contrasts considerably with that of furniture, as befits its nontradable character. Wiradi (1998) reports that brick making in certain villages in West Java has collapsed as a consequence of the substantial decline in urban building activities. Sandee (1998), however, found that tile and brick makers in specific villages of Central Java maintained pre-crisis production levels through a gradual replacement of urban markets by rural ones. This replacement was fuelled by the relatively good condition of farmers in the area and the channeling of funds from the social safety net programs into rural building activities (Sandee, 1999).

Another small-scale manufacturing activity that has suffered much from the crisis is copper handicrafts (Sandee, 1998). Producers in a mountain village in Central Java were known for their modern designs that were popular throughout Java, especially in the urban areas. They occasionally export, but their trade networks remain embryonic. The industry is partially dependent on imported inputs and has suffered much from the substantial price increases. The shrinkage of urban demand has forced many firms to downsize. However, recently production has recovered slightly owing to increased rural demand, leading to a production shift back to traditional products such as those kitchen utensils that are popular in rural areas. These products have a much higher local content than do the modern designs. The outbreak of the crisis has not thus far enabled producers to develop export networks.

Evidence on the resilience and successful adjustment of some types of small-scale enterprises suggests the importance of clusters. For instance, the furniture, roof tile, cloth weaving, and metal casting industries are all examples of agglomerations of firms that operate in the same subsector. In all these cases, clusters consist of both small and large firms that compete and collaborate. Joint action and external economies appear to be key factors that explain the successful adjustments of the small-scale firms in such clusters.

6. Public policy support for subcontracting and clusters

The main agent for SME promotion is the Ministry of Industry. Up to early 1994 most programs were formulated, monitored, and executed by the Directorate General of Small Industries. The directorate in Jakarta handles policy formation, administration, and training of the provincial and regency offices of the ministry. These officers, attached to all *Kabupaten* (regencies) in the country, are responsible for the execution and monitoring of the programs. Many extension workers are experts in the field of small business development and are well aware of the specific constraints and prospects for local small enterprise, though frequently without the resources to deliver assistance in accord with their ideas. The combination of its being free to the client and the enormous size of the nationwide target group[28] means that this technical (nonfinancial) assistance must be provided at relatively low average cost. Some extension workers have also played a successful intermediate role in linking small firms to larger businesses or to the banking sector.

The size of the target group has resulted in a pattern of "one-shot services" to small firms, with little possibility of providing follow-up, given the many firms that have not received any assistance at all. The typical assistance package consists of a one or two day training course on such topics as entrepreneurship, bookkeeping, marketing, and management. Most of the programs do not have a clear budget and are dependent for their resources on the creativeness of the staff at the various levels in raising funds from the private sector, banks or other sources (including foreign nongovernmental organizations (NGO)) (Sandee, 1995, p. 153). This situation implies the absence of a clear budget by which plans can be translated into concrete projects. Over the years, most departments have been able to secure some foreign funding for specific programs and projects that made it possible to formulate assistance packages encompassing more than one-shot interventions and brief training courses. Such foreign donor sponsored interventions have been the exception. Foreign donors concentrate their efforts on the training programs of the Ministry, so the scope of its activities varies over time.

The two main foci of the Ministry's efforts are the linking of small industries to larger private and state firms and the provision of support to clusters. One of the main aims of the first type of programs is to ease the marketing constraints faced by small industries (e.g., by inducing large firms to set up subcontracting linkages under which the small firms supply inputs through putting-out systems). It also involves the use of some profits of state enterprises to provide financial assistance to develop linkages between small and large firms. These programs aimed at networking assume that the principal growth constraint for small-scale industries is their limited access to markets. The ministry also supports the participation of small firms in national and international trade fairs with trips being financed by large firms.

The second main activity of the ministry is a specific project (BIPIK) designed for clustered small industry (*sentra industri*), set up with foreign sponsorship in the late 1970s and taken over fully by the government in the 1980s. Cluster formation is an explicit aim of the BIKIP program (Klapwijk, 1997, p. 65). Enterprises in the *sentra* are encouraged to form cooperatives. The Indonesian government has long recognized the importance of agglomerations of small-scale industrial enterprises operating in the same subsector, and there is awareness that such clusters may be highly effective entry points for the provision of assistance, reaching a large number of producers at low costs through targeted interventions. The cluster development program gives high priority to stimulating innovation. It is believed that, without process and product innovations, the majority of small industry clusters will not be able to adjust to structural changes in the dynamic Indonesian economic environment. The program consists of courses provided by extension workers and the introduction of new equipment to demonstrate to the producers the advantages of technological change. Occasionally, new equipment is donated to certain producers at the end of the course in the hope that they will learn to use it and that there will be others who purchase it themselves. The program's budget is limited; typically, approximately US$1000 per cluster is available for training and donation of equipment. Similar to the other forms of assistance, it is nonrecurring, given the fact that so many clusters have not yet received any assistance. Sandee and others (1994) estimated that in 1993 some 28 percent of the 4,250 clusters in the province of Central Java had received assistance so far. Like all such programs, this one has suffered in its implementation from a lack of finance and of qualified personnel. Klapwijk (1997, p. 65) reports that the extension officers generally have little technical or business experience, and training or other technical facilities have been largely provided according to the direction of central planners, rather than having been adapted to local needs (Sandee and others, 1994). Where it can collaborate with other entities the BIPIK can achieve more.

There is surprisingly little insight into the effectiveness of the different programs, but a general impression that they have not matched the overall challenge. Participation rates of small enterprises in those government programs present in Central Java are low: 6.6 percent for the subcontracting program, which links small firms to large government and private firms, and 3.8 percent for the cited BIPIK training program, which focuses on clusters (Sandee, 1995, p. 155). Most programs target a certain number of small producers to receive assistance. Thus the share of clusters reached is much higher than that of firms. As of 1991, BIPIK's participation in support of the clusters in various industries ranged from under 20 percent for food processing and handicrafts to 80 percent for metal-working, whose clusters are often linked to large firms through subcontracting (Sandee, 1995, p. 160). Textiles/leather are also high at 50 percent, reflecting the fact that they feature prominently in the country's export diversification strategy. BIPIK gives priority to clusters with real business opportunities, and, since it does not do separate business opportunities assessments for each cluster, it tends to repeat successes where possible. This strategy is implicit in its targets for coverage of clusters each year and its modest budget. Given the objective of wide coverage there is virtually no opportunity to return to previously attended clusters. Training within a cluster is directed at dynamic male producers (correlated with size), who are presumably expected to diffuse what they learn. Projects are aimed at producers and not at the other actors in the production or marketing chain.

The success and effectiveness of the assistance programs is typically measured by whether the annual outreach targets have been achieved, though the growth of the small enterprise sector in terms of number of units and of employment is viewed as an indicator that service provision is bearing fruit. Quality is often deficient, and many sessions seem to involve a lot of theory and not much on the actual running of the business. On the other hand, programs sponsored by foreign NGOs are usually well enough funded, are tailored to the needs of the target groups and better monitored, and generally include attention to marketing issues and a credit component. Though these programs are presumably more successful in terms of benefits per client firm, they are relatively expensive. There is need for nationwide programs, which means the key is to strengthen the existing ones.

On the basis of his visits to and time spent with extension officers Klapwijk (1997, p. 68) concludes that, though problems of funds and competence remain, the local extension offices of the ministry have become the prime nodes of the implementation of the package of programs aimed at small industry promotion and that the ministry does act as an intermediary among the other numerous parties involved. Formal enterprises are dealt with individually and cottage clusters through the *sentra*, while dispersed cottage enterprise is left out. Officers mediate with banks and with large enterprises, engage in marketing, etc. For banks trying to meet their obligations, the local extension office is the natural starting point. The same is true for the cottage group looking for any particular service. In some *sentra* the officers have been directly responsible for the cluster by introducing new industries as alternatives to the earlier more marginal activities. In all of the *sentra* visited, attempts had been made to form cooperatives or at least entrepreneur's associations. The effort has been successful in only a few cases, as where a cooperative started to alleviate poverty developed into a putting-out system. More generally the BIPAK programs probably do have the effect of raising awareness of the benefits of collaboration. In many cases the co-ops are dormant, usually because they do not fulfil clear needs of the group (Klapwijk, 1997, p. 71).

Some degree of interfirm cooperation between entrepreneurs occurred in most of the *sentra* visited. Sometimes the cooperation was dense, often involving order sharing and subcontracting and sometimes a degree of specialization among firms. BIPIK has sometimes used "motivators," dynamic producers from certain clusters. In the roof tile case these motivators were invited to Jakarta to learn about new production techniques and marketing strategies. Often an expert from the private sector is hired as tutor. Occasionally BIPIK has established a technical service center in a cluster, where producers can get access to expensive and heavy machinery (Sandee, 1995, p. 160). (Appendix 3 provides additional information on the Cluster Development Program in Indonesia.)

Appendix 1: The case of Jepara: An example of a large cluster

Jepara is a very large cluster, employing over 40,000 permanent workers in more than 2,000 small enterprises and 100 large and medium ones scattered across 80 villages (Sandee and others, 1998, p. 3). About 30 percent of the value added is directed toward the domestic market, mainly supplied by small and medium producers where the technology is relatively basic. This is a craft industry little changed over the years and occupies 70 percent of the cluster's workforce. Domestic demand has risen rapidly since the mid-1980s. Producers can now more often produce for stock without bearing the risk of changing consumer tastes (Sandee and others, 1998, p. 4). The export industry benefited from the improvement of the provincial harbor in Semarang, which facilitated door-to-door container transports, from improved credit facilities, and from greater participation of foreign traders and producers in the industry. A major breakthrough was participation in a trade fair in Bali in 1989.

Jakarta-based furniture producers used to buy Jepara's furniture. They have gradually been replaced by professional intermediaries who place large orders for sale in the west. A few foreign companies have taken up production in the cluster to better control quality. Most foreigners are active as partners of Indonesians, and this partnership permits a legal way to get around tax problems that frustrate foreign firms. The top 10 firms control 50 percent of exports, so this segment is much more concentrated than the domestic one. Foreigners may account for as much as 25 percent of exports. The industry is known for its rapid and successful imitation of product lines that are popular in the west. Jepara's exports are aimed at the low-income segment of the markets in the countries to which they go, and competition is rising from China, Vietnam, and Cambodia.

Small firms are mainly subcontractors. They get advance payments to finance production. There are now multi-layered subcontracting relationships in the cluster, and it has large numbers of mobile skilled craftsmen who offer services to the highest bidder and have in recent years been overwhelmingly employed by joint ventures or foreign firms that offer the highest wages. Over 1989–1996, when the number of enterprises went up by 3.5 times or so, average size jumped from 12.4 to 15 workers. Registered foreigners rose from 20 to 154, and others are unregistered. Value per cubic meter almost doubled, indicating an increase in average quality.

Regional and local government agencies have created an increasingly enabling environment through various infrastructure projects, harbor improvements, and one-stop facilities to curtail bureaucratic delays. The regional government has promoted participation of producers in trade fairs, especially helpful to exports. A specific academy has been created where technical and management training is provided. Basic technical skills and general lessons on the regional furniture industry have been introduced into the primary curriculum.[29] Government agencies and NGOs have played a limited role in providing technical assistance to the industry, and most of the technical assistance has come from private channels.

Appendix 2. The case of Bali's exports

Bali has several export industries based on strategic business alliances, including garments, silver jewelery, wood carving, quilting, leather products, bamboo furniture, ceramics, stone carving, and textiles (Cole, 1998, p. 257). All of the export industries compete internationally on the basis of highly flexible small-batch production, quick turnaround times, and a capacity for rapid adjustment to new designs. The ability to develop new designs and methods that have no roots in traditional Balinese culture shows in every case.

A number of positive social characteristics are of special interest. (1) Most production is based on thousands of rural village work groups and small/micro enterprises networked through small and medium scale assembly/finishing firms. (2) There has been a rapid growth of indigenous entrepreneurship, especially in the assembly/finishing firms. (3) Capital for expansion is largely self-financed through retained earnings, while until the 1990s working capital was largely covered by down-payments from foreign buyers. (4) There have been no specific government subsidies or protection; that is, the successes were neither planned nor anticipated by government. With the provincial government focusing on agriculture and tourism, the initial stages of this development went all but unnoticed by the state (Cole, 1998, p. 258).[30]

Garments are a typical case, including the fact that there are no roots in local indigenous craft production. Production activity started around 1975 and hit a peak at around US$160–185 million around 1994. The success was built on simple foot-treadle sewing machines and part-time seasonal rural village labor.

It was necessary to compete for quotas with larger Indonesian producers with advanced technologies and based in the main centers. There was a sharp rise in unit values from $1 around 1982 to $3 per kilogram around 1986, reflecting rapid quality and design improvements. Achieving this in a context where there were many new entrants each year constituted an impressive performance.

Initial conditions appeared far from propitious. Labor was cheap, but the Balinese were averse to factory work (they still are) and had no garment-making skills. Labor laws made it difficult to employ more than 40–50 workers on one site (Cole, 1998, p. 262). There was no modern management, no experience in international markets, capital was scarce, and there were few paved roads and little running water or electricity. One important plus was the new international airport.

Nearly all the experts were convinced that not only did Bali have no future in manufacturing, but also that encouragement of anything other than traditional crafts would destroy the island's cultural heritage and thus undermine the sustainability of tourism. It did have a handful of "Balinized Chinese" with experience in the tourist retail trade, a group of low-budget tourists living for extended periods in Bali, the nearby airport, and an untapped market for cheap beach wear in Australia. The situation had a fair amount in common with the Jepara case, though of course the latter was built on skills.

Old Javanese sarongs and embroidered *kebaya* (traditional blouses) were popular with tourists. Some retailers started collecting these used items and then began producing low quality facsimiles in small traditional tailor shops. Foreign buyers induced an expansion of output by down payments, gifts of machines, etc. Then the Australian entrepreneurs and their local counterparts copied new-wave designs. Quality control was still minimal. The mushrooming demand led to a putting-out system, which evolved into a set of full-scale subcontracting networks. Skilled tailors were in short supply, and many of the new recruits were young women who would return to their villages after a stint. Producers enticed these women to continue to work in their villages and provided machines. Clusters of workers grew up around these trained women. The local representative of the ministry of trade played an important role in streamlining the processing of small-batch exports. What took 5–7 days in Surabaya took just 24 hours here. And the governor of Bali decided, on the advice of this representative, not to close down the Australian entrepreneurs after getting complaints that they were illegally engaging in business. This gave a degree of freedom to operate, unheard of at that time elsewhere in Indonesia.

Over time the foreigners moved out of day-to-day involvement and into more purely managerial roles. Returns for the dozen or so mainly foreign entrepreneurs who innovated were enormous, but they took much risk and suffered severely in the 1980 recession (they were unaware of business cycles) while trying to shield their local producers from its effects. The rather shocked local producers were still heavily dependent on individual alliances with foreigners for production assistance and access to foreign markets. But they were ready for a new set of foreign buyers with a more sophisticated set of business, production, and design skills. Many of these were American tourists looking for entrepreneurial opportunities.

Higher value designs required much precisely targeted consultation tailored to a firm's needs. These new "buyer-consultants" were willing to work for months with the producer firms, attracted by high returns and the pleasant setting of Bali, though there were high risks because before any sales could be closed the full up-front costs had to be borne. Few foreigners had more than a couple of good years in a row before a bad one or a collapse, while the producers could steadily improve their scale and production efficiencies with minimal risks.

Despite the heavy involvement of the buyers, rejection rates at the last stage were still in the 20–30 percent range, tolerable because the rejects could be dumped on the local market.[31] When a firm's skills outgrew the first buyer-consultant it often moved up to a higher value one. Many innovative designs and techniques were pioneered during this period. New buyer-consultants with higher valued designs poured in as the reputation improved.

"Knocking off" the design innovations of competitors became a serious problem. Among the various responses to this problem was the use of distant work groups to help keep the new design a secret. By the mid-1980s the ability to handle dispersed production made it possible to move into East Java with its virtually unlimited labor supply. This dispersion improved the income distribution implications of the industry. As the Chinese entrepreneurs relied more on the putting-out system, they had to depend on go-betweens, middle managers who were almost always *pribumis*. When orders exceeded demand, rather than go to a competitor the firm would typically pass orders to these intermediaries, and sometimes the buyer-consultant would offer to help them to set up their own manufacturing operations. As a result the share of value-added generated by *pribumi* entrepreneurs rose from almost nothing in 1977 to nearly 50 percent in 1987.

A group of linked industries eventually took off as well, with the foreign buyers again involved in advising (Cole, 1998, p. 267). The packer-shippers were one such important industry. They were expert at cutting through the Indonesian bureaucracy and eventually the thorny problem of U.S. and European import restrictions.

Around the mid-1980s the first expansion phase petered out, and a different growth process took its place. The returns to buyer consultants, which had apparently been quite high, were squeezed at this time (Cole, 1998, p. 270). The immediate cause of the exit of many American buyer-consultants in 1985 was the new set of immigration officials and the bribes they sought. Though these officials were transferred the next year, considerable damage had been done. Possibly material quality problems also started to limit this growth process. The large textile producers in Bandung and Jakarta responded poorly to the needs of the Bali exporting sector. Their greater attention to the needs of the large Java garment exporters led to some spill-over benefits in the form of a greater variety and better quality of textiles. The Bali industry had some access to imports, though this was limited by tariffs and the nonoperability of the duty-drawback system for small firms: high bureaucratic costs, delayed and short-changed refunds, and lack of public knowledge about it.

With no more exciting new designs paving the way, the retail prices of Bali items in importing countries began to fall, but order volumes were increasing and discount retailers were in the act (Cole, 1998, p. 272). Quality control now eroded, and the Bali garments acquired a reputation for poor quality. Large buyers began to insist on release of letters of credit payments on arrival and inspection in the importing country rather than at point of shipment as before. Several Bali-based producers tried to shift to large factory production to control quality decline and address bigger orders. But this did not lead to a new cycle of rising unit values, probably because of the increase in unit costs related to more expensive machinery, capital investment in construction, and a permanent labor force that could not be laid off seasonally. The shift toward a larger batch low information limited service industry was reflected in the fact that by the early 1990s Bali was increasingly in competition with other low wage countries (China, Vietnam, and the Philippines) and large factory producers in Indonesia. Whether the dispersed production system would allow another wave of innovation as the base for a new growth phase is unclear. The experience of Italy seems to demonstrate that it is not a total obstacle.

Another dynamic cluster has been the coppersmiths in Desa Tumang, where firms with more than 50 workers co-exist with numerous household enterprises (Sandee and Rietveld, 2000). The firms with more than 50 workers use faxes to communicate with national and international customers and call on the household enterprises when orders exceed their capacity. The household enterprises produce basic utensils for sale at local markets (i.e., a different market segment from the large ones). Though operating in different market segments, their simultaneous presence leads to efficiency gains. But the majority of clusters here are dormant or embryonic, located in rural areas, producing items for poor rural consumers. There is virtually no paid labor and few synergies because most operate independently. Sometimes firms cluster for proximity to a resource or to cut transaction costs of buyers, though most of these items are not of much interest to urban traders.[32]

Appendix 3. Cluster development program in Indonesia

A survey undertaken by Sandee and others (1994) to assess the effectiveness of the cluster development program found that assistance is relevant and helpful in the case of dynamic clusters. Such clusters evince a demand for technical and also financial assistance to accommodate growth processes that have been put on track by producers and buyers. Thus traders frequently requested that producers in a woven cloth cluster shift to new designs in high demand. Such sales prospects stimulated producers to participate in training courses organized by the cluster development program of the ministry.

Such successes notwithstanding, the reviews by Sandee and others (1994) and Sandee (1998) found that the cluster development program was not effective in bringing about technological change in the majority of clusters in Indonesia. This majority can be labeled "dormant" or "embryonic" and are located in rural areas and produce basic products for poor local consumers but of little interest to urban traders. These clusters consist of so-called cottage enterprises, where the average number of workers per enterprise does not exceed five, and paid workers are virtually absent. The clusters are "pockets of poverty" with limited collaboration among firms. Current assistance programs, which consist of supply-side measures, are not effective in promoting small enterprise development in embryonic clusters. Interestingly, these clusters are presently very much the focal point of broadened assistance programs in Indonesia that aim at poverty alleviation. Poor rural industry clusters are considered effective entry points for new programs.

Available evidence suggests, however, that broadening supply-side measures have not been very effective in fostering small enterprise development. There is a need to develop strategies that aim at linking producers in dormant or embryonic clusters to markets. Visits to buyers, retailers and wholesalers, and markets and fairs may be useful to establish new trade networks that are outlets for new products.

The experience in Indonesia of one of the authors (Sandee) points to the importance of increasing the mobility of producers in dormant clusters. Purchasing a car with limited funds allows producers from several clusters to become aware of new business opportunities elsewhere. Such insights may significantly increase the impact of technical and financial assistance to be provided after producers are aware of the existence and convinced of the accessibility of more rewarding trade networks.

A major challenge for advocates of the introduction of business development services in Indonesia will be the design and provision of sustainable services to these dormant clusters. The clusters are the centre of the state's pembinaan strategy and the core of the people's economy. Government assistance will be there for years to come, and it is highly relevant to assess whether it is possible to render it more effective.

Notes

1 Based on adjusted population census figures for 1971 (World Bank, 1980, p. 122) and data from ILO (1997, p. 126) for 1996.

2 Judging from the distribution of employment in the medium and large establishments as reported for example by Steel (1993).

3 Berry and Mazumdar (1991, p. 49) report a household share of 11 percent for 1986 and 6.8 percent for the small category (5–19 workers).

4 Based on an estimate of a bit over 80 percent from plants of 20 workers and up and the 1985 breakdown by size among plants in that range provided by Hill (1997, p. 71).

5 The labor productivity per man day gap of nearly 5:1, according to some estimates, between workers in plants of five to nine workers and household workers must be interpreted with care, however. Possibly days worked are misleading for this group. But the data leave little doubt that the gap is big.

6 Employment growth estimates are approximations, given the problems involved in measuring employment in the cottage sector. Here we use the 5.6 percent per year estimate reported by Hill (1997, p. 48) for the intercensal period 1975–1986 and the census numbers themselves to estimate the growth over 1986–1996 (Table I).

7 Nothing can yet be said about productivity on the basis of the 1996 census since no value added figures have been published at time of writing.

8 The average number of workers per establishment increased only very marginally from 3.4 to 3.6 workers. Unless the average number of workers fell in one or both of the household and the small categories, it must have fallen in the large/medium category, from 134 in 1986 to just 111 in 1996. There are some arguments to suggest that average size would have fallen in each category rather than only in the large/medium one, since employment was growing very fast

so there must have been a great number of new firms. By using the census figures on firms without legal entity, we can see that the average for those with less than five workers was 1.95. We would expect that the inclusion of the few very small firms with legal entity would increase this figure very marginally, perhaps to as much as 2. Thus a very low number here does not seem possible and 2 seems in the appropriate range. The 1986 figure was also 1.95 (Table I). By using also the same average for the 5–19 establishments leaves us with the conclusion that the average size of those with 20 workers and up fell considerably over this decade, from about 134 to about 116. Assuming the same average of 40 for the 20–99 category (a guess in both years) the average of the 100 and up category would fall from 459 in 1986 to just 375 in 1996. If the average of the 20–99 category had fallen to 35 by 1996 (which seems extreme), then the top category would still have fallen to 392. Note that this contrasts with what one would have expected on the basis of Steel's (1993) estimates for the first part of this period, more precisely for 1985–1990, during which period he believed that this category (5–99 workers) was the slowest growing. Possibly the early 1990s were very different from the late 1980s, or possibly his estimates were off base for the latter period. He interprets his high estimate of growth in household sector employment as related in part to a structural shift from rural self-employment to urban wage employment, which drives the increasing share of manufacturing employment which is paid, noting that the substantial growth of household employment is contrary to speculation that it is in decline.

[9] Note that Hill's estimate of total employment in 1986 was 6.11 million, contrasted with the census figure of 5.29 million. If the upward adjustment based on the population census figures for 1996 is smaller than in 1986, then the growth rate will have been less than the 6.6 percent just cited.

[10] Given the high turnover and the pattern of change at the firm level among SMEs, any static comparisons among such firms or between them and other groups such as micro-enterprise and large enterprise must be interpreted with caution. It is to be expected that there will be a wide range of productivity and efficiency levels among SMEs in most industries at most points of time. Some are recently created and are still operating at modest efficiency levels. Some will never succeed and will soon exit. Others are very efficient and may be growing fast as a result. In industries where most firms are either small or medium at creation, comparisons of average efficiency between the SME sector and the large enterprise sector must be interpreted with great care.

[11] Steel (1993, p. 18) also provides upward and downward graduation rates of firms over 10 years by size at creation. These reveal significant movement in both directions. For most size categories the likelihood of graduating upward is not too different from that of moving to a lower category, except for the top one, which by definition has only downward movement. These figures alone do not permit any assessment of whether the "representative" establishment shrinks or grows. They probably tend to understate the net upward movement.

[12] Unpublished data from the surveys.

[13] Whether this is also true for TFP is much harder to say.

[14] All statistical results from this study are based on firms' responses to a questionnaire designed to elicit their views on the relative importance of various sources of technological capability.

[15] In both cases the rapid growth of output and exports from Indonesia has been the result of market interventions. Prior to the mid-1980s raw rattan was exported to Taiwan and the Philippines, the main rattan furniture producers. The take-off in Indonesia followed the banning of such exports. In the case of garments the fact that neighboring countries had fulfilled their quotas under the Multifibre Agreement and were suffering rising wages made Indonesia an interesting supply platform.

[16] An Indonesian plan referred to in Section 6.

[17] Collective sources of technological advance are more important in other countries that have dealt successfully with the institutional challenges to making them effective.

[18] This view is consistent with the results reported by Sjoholm (1999), though his results are not by themselves persuasive given the methodological limitations of the study.

[19] Note that subcontracting and clustering are not mutually exclusive; a good deal of the former can go on in the context of the latter. We separate them in the discussion here partly because they are different phenomena and partly because the literature tends to focus on one or the other.

[20] There appears to be a considerable gap in gross output between cottage enterprises in clusters and those not so located (70 percent overall), especially in textiles. However, the differential varies widely by industry (it is negative in a couple of cases) and could be due to differences in average number of workers or in the products produced as well as to productivity gains associated with clustering (Klapwijk, 1997, pp. 61–62). The data are not comparable between rural industrial clusters (RICs) and all cottage industry, since RICs sometimes include large enterprises in the cluster. Still, the low average establishment sizes suggest that the bulk of workers are in quite small establishments.

[21] Klapwijk (1997) defines RIC as having at least five industrial enterprises, producing similar goods and located in a rural area or small town, with the enterprise average size under five workers. This contrasts with the use of the term to refer to the shift of large and medium industry from urban to rural settings, based in part on the thinking of the International Labor Office about rural industrialization in developed countries.

[22] As several authors have pointed out, traders may be so dominant that individual producers do not have much to say about the process (Cawthorne, 1995; Knorringa, 1996).

[23] Susenas data report a smaller decline in manufacturing employment but we are not in a position to assess the comparability of the figures used.

[24] At time of writing we did not have data on structure of employment by sector. Total manufacturing employment was recorded at 377,959 (1995), 376,048 (1997), and 373,158 (1998) persons, respectively. As the number of observed households went up slightly throughout the period 1995–1998, this may indicate that manufacturing employment in Indonesia has actually declined since the outbreak of the crisis.

[25] It may be that these survey findings covering 1997–1998 are still too early and that more substantial shifts will be visible only in later years.

[26] As expected, financing has become more difficult than before, with a sharp decrease in loans from outside parties. Suppliers have stopped giving a grace period. The average loans outstanding for these firms have fallen from Rp. 65M before the crisis to 26.5M as of March 1998, as previous loans are repaid and no new ones are available; 36 percent of respondents have been late with an instalment. Before the crisis the ratio of collateral to loan averaged 100–200 percent; now it is over 200 percent.

[27] See Tambunan (1999).

[28] The Ministry of Industry's definition of small enterprise, which includes about 95 percent of all enterprises, involves ownership by an Indonesian and a total asset value not exceeding Rp 600M, excluding land and buildings. This contrasts with the Central Statistical Office's definition of 5–19 workers for small and under five workers for cottage. Many firms with up to 100 workers and some with more do not exceed the Ministry's capital limit (Sandee and Rietveld 2000).

[29] Hill (personal communication), however, questions whether the state monopoly on wood supply has been favorable for a sustainable exploitation of forests; rather, he suspects that serious problems of input supply may be just around the corner. The constant harassment of foreigners in the cluster by the authorities may also redound negatively even to the welfare of Indonesians.

[30] When, in the mid-1980s, the Ministry of Industry provided some sporadic assistance in the form of worker training, the impact was negligible because the total effort was small relative to the size of the industry by that time. In any case, it did not address the real challenge, which was new flows of high quality information.

[31] Whereas the lower quality Jepra furniture is sold in the domestic market, the Bali garment rejects tend to go to the tourist market.

[32] On the limited efficiency gains, see Nadvi and Schmitz (1994) and Weijland (1994).

References

Akatiga Foundation, 1999, 'Crisis Impact Monitoring Study on Small-Scale Enterprises'. Report to the Asia Foundation, Jakarta.

Berry, Albert and José Escandón, 1999, 'Colombia's Small and Medium Exporters and their Support System', in Brian Levy, Albert Berry and Jeffrey B. Nugent (eds.), *Fulfilling the Export Potential of Small and Medium Firms*, Boston: Kluwer.

Berry, Albert and Brian Levy, 1999, 'Technical, Financial and Marketing Support for Indonesia's Small and Medium Industrial Exporters', in Brian Levy, Albert Berry and Jeffrey B. Nugent (eds.), *Fulfilling the Export Potential of Small and Medium Firms*, Boston: Kluwer.

Berry, Albert and D. Mazumder, 1991, 'Small-Scale Industry in East and Southeast Asia: A review of the Literature and Issues', *Asian-Pacific Economic Literature* **5**(2), 35–67.

Bird, Kelly, 1999, 'Concentration in Indonesian Manufacturing, 1975–1993', *Bulletin of Indonesian Economic Studies* **35**(1), 43–74.

BPS, 1986, *Statistik Industri 1986*, Jakarta: Biro Pusat Statistik.

Bruch, M. and U. Hiemenz, 1984, *Small and Medium Scale Industries in the ASEAN Countries: Agents or Victims of Economic Development?* Boulder, Colo.: Westview Press.

Cameron, L., 1999, 'Survey of Recent Developments', *Bulletin of Indonesian Economic Studies* **35**(1), 3–40.

Cawthorne, P. M., 1995, 'Of Networks and Markets: The Rise and Rise of a South Indian Town, The Example of Tiruppur's Cotton Knitwear Industry', *World Development* **23**(1), 43–56.

Cole, William, 1998, 'Bali's Garment Export Industry', in Hal Hill and Thee Kian Wie (eds.), *Indonesia's Technological Challenge*, Singapore: Institute of Southeast Asian Studies.

Dwipayana, A. A., 1998, 'Usaha Kecil dan Birokrasi. Studi tentant Pelayanan Perijinan bagi Usaha Kecil di Gianyar'. Report for The Asia Foundation, Jakarta.

Godfrey, M., 1993, *Labour Market Monitoring and Employment Policy in a Developing Economy: A Case Study of Indonesia*, New Delhi: International Labour Office.

Hill, H., 1992, 'Manufacturing Industry', in A. Booth (ed.), *The Oil Boom and After: Indonesian Economic Policy and Performance in the Suharto Era*, New York: Oxford University Press.

Hill, Hal, 1996, 'Industrial Policy and Performance: 'Orthodoxy' Vindicated', *Economic Development and Cultural Change* **45**(1), 147–174.

Hill, Hal, 1998, *Indonesia's Industrial Transformation*, St. Leonards, New South Wales: Allen and Unwin.

Hill, H., 1999, 'Indonesia in Crisis', Unpublished draft postscript for the second edition of *The Indonesian Economy since 1966*, Cambridge: Cambridge University Press.

ILO, 1997, *Yearbook of Labor Statistics 1997*, Geneva: International Labor Office.

Jellinek, L. and B. Rustanto, 1999, 'Survival Strategies of the Javanese During the Economic Crisis', Consultancy Report to the World Bank, Jakarta.

Klapwijk, Martin, 1997, *Rural Industry Clusters in Central Java, Indonesia: An Empirical Assessment of their Role in Rural Industrialization*, Amsterdam: Vrije Universiteit.

Knorringa, P., 1996, *Economics of Collaboration: Indian Shoemakers Bewteen Market and Heirarchy*, London: Sage.

Knorringa, P., 1998, 'Cluster Trajectories in Developing Countries: Towards a Typology', Preliminary draft, Institute of Social Studies, The Hague.

Liedholm, Carl and Donald Mead, 1999, *Small Enterprises and Economic Development: The Dynamic Role of Micro and Small Enterprises*, New York: Routledge.

Musa, Agustina and Ple Priatna, 1998, 'The Policy Reform for Capital of SME (Small-Medium Enterprises) in Indonesia: Impact Analysis of Financial Crisis: Study Report', Report to the Asia Foundation, Jakarta.

Nadvi, K. and H. Schmitz, 1994, 'Industrial Clusters in Less Developed Countries: Review of Experiences and Research Agenda', Discussion paper 39. Institute of Development Studies, Sussex.

O'Connell, C., 1993, 'Stability, Jobs and Income Generation in Indonesia', Report to the International Labor Organization, Jakarta.

Patten, Richard H., Jay K. Rosengard and Don E. Johnston Jr., 1998, 'Improving Microfinance and Small and Medium Enterprise (SME) Finance in Indonesia', Mimeo. Harvard Institute for International Development, Cambridge, Mass.

Poot, H., 1997, *Indonesia, SMEs, Finance and BPDs*, Rotterdam: Netherlands Economic Institute.

Poot, H., A. Kuyvenhoven and J. Jansen, 1990, *Industrialization and Trade in Indonesia*, Yogyakarta: Gadjah Meda University Press.

Poppele, J., S. Sumarto and L. Pritchett, 1999, 'Social Impacts of the Indonesian Crisis: New Data and Policy Implications', Mimeo, A SMERU report. Social Monitoring and Response Unit, Jakarta.

Saleh, Kusmadi, Rusman Heriawan and Mohamad Rum Ali. 1999, 'Indonesian Small Business Statistics', Paper presented at the Conference on the Economic Issues Facing the New Government, Jakarta, August 18–20.

Sandee, H. 1995. *Innovation Adoption in Rural Industry: Technological Change in Roof Tile Clusters in Central Java, Indonesia*, Amsterdam: Vrije University.

Sandee, H., 1998, 'The Impact of the Crisis on Small-Scale Industries in Indonesia: Some Preliminary Findings From Central Java', Discussion paper. Vrije University, Amsterdam.

Sandee, H., 1999, 'The Impact of the Crisis on Village Development in Java', Workshop Report. *Bulletin of Indonesian Economic Studies* **35**(1), 141–143.

Sandee, H., P. Rietveld, H. Supratikon and P. Yuwono, 1994, 'Promoting Small-Scale and Cottage Industries in Indonesia: An Impact Analysis for Central Java', *Bulletin of Indonesian Economic Studies* **30**(3), 115–142.

Sandee, H., R. K. Andadari and I. Hunga, 1998, 'Pugutan and Sumbangan in a Central Java Case Study', Report to the Asia Foundation, Jakarta.

Sandee, H., R. K. Andadari and S. Sulandjari, 1998, 'The Impact of Indonesia's Financial Crisis on Clustered Enterprise: A Case Study on the Jepara Furniture Cluster', Discussion paper. Vrije University, Amsterdam.

Sandee, H., and P. Rietveld, 2000, 'Innovation Adoption in Rural Industry Clusters: A Comparison of a Roof Tile and Copper Handicraft Cluster in Indonesia', in Arni Sverrson and Meine Pieter van Dijk (eds.), *Local Economies in Turmoil: The Effects of Deregulation on Small and Medium Sized Enterprises in Transitional Economies*, New York: Macmillan.

Schiller, J. and B. Martin-Schiller, 1997, 'Market Culture and State in the Emergence of an Indonesian Export Furniture Industry', *Journal of Asian Business* **13**(1), 1–23.

Schmitz, H., 1995, 'Small Shoemakers and Fordist Giants: Tale of a Supercluster', *World Development* **23**(1), 9–28.

Steel, William F., 1993, 'Small Enterprises in Indonesia: Role, Growth and Strategic Issues', Development of Studies Project 194. BIDE-DAI, Jakarta.

Sjoholm, F., 1999, 'Exports, Imports and Productivity: Results From Indonesian Establishment Data', *World Development* **27**(4), 705–716.

Sverisson, A., 1993, 'Innovation as a Collective Enterprise: Case Studies of Carpenters in Nakjura, Kenya', Discussion paper 189. Research Policy Institute, University of Lund, Lund, Sweden.

Tambunan, T., 1999, 'The Performance of Small Enterprises During the Economic Crisis: Evidence from Indonesia', Paper prepared for Conference on The Economic Issues Facing the New Government, Jakarta, August 18–20.

Thee, Kian Wie, 1993, 'Industrial Structure and Small and Medium Enterprise Development in Indonesia', Working paper. World Bank Economic Development Institute, World Bank, Washington, D.C.

Timberg, Thomas, 1999, 'What We Know About Small and Medium Enterprise (SME) Finance in Indonesia', Paper prepared for the Conference on The Road to Indonesian Economic Recovery, Jakarta, August 19.

Timmer, Marcel P., 1999, 'Indonesia's Ascent on the Technology Ladder: Capital Stock and Total Factor Productivity in Indonesian Manufacturing, 1975–1995', *Bulletin of Indonesian Economic Studies* **35**(1), 75–98.

Van Diermen, Peter, Thee Kian Wie, Mangara Tambunan and Tulus Tambunan, 1998, 'The IMF 50-Point Program: Evaluation the Likely Impact on SMEs', Report to the Asia Foundation, Jakarta.

Weijland, H., 1994, 'Trade Networks for Flexible Rural Industry', in P. O. Pederson, A. Sverrisson and M. P. van Dijt (eds.), *Flexible Specialization: The Dynamics of Small Scale Industries in the South*, London: Intermediate Technology Publications.

Wetterberg, A., S. Sumarto and L. Pritchett, 1999, 'A National Snapshot of the Social Impact of Indonesia's Crisis', *Bulletin of Indonesian Economic Studies* **35**(3), 145–152.

Wiradi, G., 1998, 'Rural Java in a Time of Crisis: With Special Reference to Curug Village, Cirebon, West Java', Paper for workshop on The Economic Crisis and Social Security in Indonesia, Berg-en-Dal, The Netherlands.

World Bank, 1980, *Indonesia: Employment and Income Distribution in Indonesia*, Washington, D.C.: World Bank.

World Bank, 1985, *Indonesia: Wages and Employment*, Washington, D.C.: World Bank.

World Bank, 1987, *World Table 1987*, Washington: D.C.: World Bank.

World Bank, 1989, 'Indonesia: Small and Medium Industrial Enterprise Project', Staff Appraisal Report. World Bank, Washington, D.C.

Subcontracting and the Performance of Small and Medium Firms in Japan

Fukunari Kimura

ABSTRACT. This paper provides an empirical analysis of the choices made by Japanese firms with respect to subcontracting status, that is, whether to take in work as subcontractor, to outsource work to subcontractors, to do both or to do neither. It shows that the probability of working as a subcontractor, a choice made by many small firms in Japan, is negatively related to size, foreign sales and technological capability. Furthermore, profits do not appear to be higher for subcontracting firms; indeed, they are highest for the group that does not get involved in any type of subcontracting, whether as a supplier or as an outsourcer.

1. Introduction

In the Japanese economy, subcontracting has been regarded as an important source of efficiency and competitiveness for industries such as textiles, general machinery, electric machinery, and automobiles. Other countries such as Taiwan and Korea also have subcontracting though the historical background and the detailed structure are somewhat different owing to different initial conditions. In Japan the pattern of subcontracting has a close link with the pattern of firm size distribution.

Subcontracting has been a major research topic in the literature on the Japanese economy. However, the focus of research has been the mechanism of individual subcontracting arrangements, rather than the sectoral or macroeconomic implications. Quantitative analysis on the basis of official statistics has not yet been conducted extensively. In considering the applicability of subcontracting arrangements to other countries, it is important to specify when subcontracting emerges and becomes effective. This paper briefly reviews the past literature on subcontracting in Japan and analyzes its main characteristics by using manufacturing censuses. Owing to data availability, the focus is placed on subcontracting in the manufacturing sector.

The next section clarifies the concept of subcontracting. Section 3 reviews the historical and theoretical background of the subcontracting system. Section 4 presents Japanese industry-level data of subcontracting from the 1960s to the 1980s. The relationship among firm size, internalization pattern, and subcontracting is explored in particular. Section 5 utilizes micro data of Japanese manufacturing firms in FY1994 to analyze the relationship between subcontracting and other characteristics of firms.

2. What is subcontracting?

Subcontracting (*shitauke*) is not always specified in an explicit manner. Surprisingly, it is not clearly defined even in official statistics. Nevertheless, this word is used quite often because Japanese share a loose consensus on the meaning of this word. In its broadest meaning, subcontracting refers to the purchase of a part of a product or process from a different company. Some researchers stress the asymmetric relationship between a large downstream firm and a small upstream firm. Kawasaki (1998, p. 38) defines a subcontracting relationship as "a contractual relationship in which a large firm asks a small firm to conduct a commissioned work (producing parts, components, or finished products) under a dominant position."

Faculty of Economics
Keio University
2-15-45 Mita, Minato-ku
Tokyo 108-8345
Japan
E-mail: fkimura@econ.keio.ac.jp

Small Business Economics **18**: 163–175, 2002.

There also seems to be a general consensus that subcontracting is a long-term arrangement. A one-shot transaction cannot be called a subcontracting arrangement. In addition, the relationship is sometimes expected to include risk-sharing arrangements, technology diffusion mechanism, and distinctive subcontractor control, such as "*kanban* system" (see Uekusa 1987, p. 500). However, the arrangement is not necessarily an exclusive one; a subcontractor may have multiple clients. In addition, financial links are sometimes observed.

Statistically, the Ministry of International Trade and Industry (MITI), Government of Japan (GOJ), defines subcontracting as follows:[1] "A contractual arrangement between a firm and a 'parent' firm with larger capital or larger number of employees. The former firm is commissioned to produce products, parts, attachments, materials, or components used as inputs in the parent firm's production, or to produce or repair facilities, equipment, tools, and others which the parent firm uses in production. When a firm purchases non-customized parts, components, and others through a usual marketing channel, it is not regarded as subcontracting. In subcontracting, a parent firm orders the work directly to a subcontractor with assigning a plan, quality, spec, form, design, or others."[2]

Although this definition is still fuzzy, the questionnaire for the statistics includes questions on subcontracting, which seem to be filled out without much difficulty.

3. Historical and theoretical foundation of subcontracting

The public view on subcontracting in Japan has drastically changed over time. Traditionally, partially under the influence of Marxian economics that dominated the academic literature in Japan, researchers emphasized the asymmetry between large and small firms in the subcontracting relationship. It was thought that large firms had monopsonic power in determining prices, imposing conditions on product quality and delivery, and using smaller firms as a buffer for business fluctuations. The dualistic structure in labor and capital markets was also emphasized as a background of the subcontracting system.

In the 1970s and 1980s, as Japanese gained confidence on their economic system, the view swung toward the opposite end. Researchers in managerial science and the "neoclassical" school of economics highlighted the efficiency-enhancing nature of subcontracting system.[3] In particular, a number of detailed case studies on the automobile industry revealed that the stratified subcontracting system enhanced static and dynamic efficiency. Since then, subcontracting has been regarded as one of the important components of the Japanese economic system,[4] with presumed benefits in (1) saving costs to search and select new suppliers, (2) having successful quality enhancement and cost reduction in cooperation with subcontractors, (3) successfully providing incentives for subcontractors' investment in relation-specific assets, (4) having efficient risk-sharing mechanism, and (5) sometimes maintaining a good relationship by a certain amount of share holding (but not necessarily restricting suppliers' counterparts).

What conditions are necessary for the emergence of subcontracting? We need to approach this issue from both an historical and a theoretical perspective.

The historical perspective is essential to specifying the condition for the emergence, existence, and evolution of subcontracting system. There is an ongoing academic discussion on whether the Japanese economic system was "continuous" across the period of WW II or was rather "disrupted" by the war. However, it is at least true that the Japanese economy inherited from the pre-war economic system a portion of the economic conditions that consisted of initial conditions guaranteeing the emergence of post-war subcontracting system. What follows is a list of hypothesized initial conditions.

First, in the latter half of the 1940s and 1950s, there existed a distinctive dualistic structure between large and small enterprises, but the gap was not too large in terms of, for instance, technology and entrepreneurship to prohibit them from constructing efficient subcontracting arrangements. Second, Japan then had an international comparative advantage in labor-intensive manufactured goods, and abundant supply of labor was available for SMEs. At the same time, SMEs did not have direct access to foreign technology and an export marketing channel, which left room for large firms to utilize SMEs. Third, the government conducted a series of SME promotion policies. For example, the policies had multiple channels helping financial arrangements, managerial practice and technology, cooperative organizations, modernization scheme through advice, and tax concessions. Financial support to compensate for liquidity constraints was particularly important.[5] In addition, some policies were implemented to protect weak SMEs from the viewpoint of social policy as well as competition policy.[6]

Subcontracting is a long-term relationship and thus has a strong path-dependent nature. With the comfort of long-term commitments, large enterprises provided technological assistance to SMEs. The long-term relationship stabilized the financial condition of SMEs. Such a system seemed to work well in the high-growth period of 1955–73. The changes in the economic environment after 1973, however, forced firms to make some modification of the subcontracting system. The Japanese economy faced slower growth rates and became labor-scarce at the same time. SMEs were acquiring more human capital, higher technological level, and more vigorous entrepreneurship. The development of the financial sector gradually removed liquidity constraints of SMEs. From the latter half of the 1980s, the globalization of Japanese firms accelerated. In the changing economic environment, path-dependent and an interlocking nature of subcontracting sometimes slowed down necessary restructuring of industrial organization. Many SMEs faced difficulties in finding new customers when a production plant of the client moved out to foreign countries. On the other hand, there are a number of SMEs that successfully made foreign direct investment and got out of old rigid subcontracting connection.

As for the theoretical perspective, the issue is how to theoretically formalize the endogenous emergence of industrial organization structure and linkages. One of the important issues of discussion is a firm's choice of how to obtain parts and components from upstream: choices over (1) vertical integration (internalization), (2) subcontracting, and (3) competitive spot bidding. We need to specify the conditions for firms to choose 2 instead of 1 or 3. Subcontracting must be efficient in both the static and dynamic senses in some conditions.

Following Maruyama (1996), we summarize the theoretical foundation of subcontracting in four approaches. The first is the transaction cost approach.[7] On the basis of the assumptions on bounded rationality and opportunism in human behavior, the transaction cost approach characterizes transactional environment by introducing uncertainty, frequency in transactions, and relation-specific assets. Taking these characteristics into consideration, a firm decides whether to internalize certain transactions or not. Subcontracting arrangements can be interpreted as one of the devices to save transaction costs. Along this line, Asanuma (1989) conducts a detailed case study and finds the reshuffling of subcontractors in the process of model changes in the automobile industry. He provides the detailed classification of supplier arrangements and proposes the concept of relation-specific skill. Barney (1999) explicitly discusses a firm's boundary decisions with the capabilities of its potential partners by using the concept of transaction cost, though he uses the word "outsourcing" rather than "subcontracting."[8]

The second is the game theory approach. This approach emphasizes a long-term cooperative relationship between upstream and downstream firms based on repeated game, reputation, and coordination. The formulation of coordinating relationship is explained by using the game theoretic concepts.

The third is the economics of information approach. This approach is based on the contract theory, particularly the principal-agent model in which long-term relationship works for fostering efficient risk-sharing arrangements under incomplete information.[9]

The fourth is the network approach. This approach advocates that the Japanese interfirm relationship is interpreted as an "intermediate" organization (*chuukan soshiki*) in which the market principle and the organizational principle coexist. It emphasizes that under a certain economic environment, interfirm relationship with an efficient synergy of competition and coordination is constructed.[10, 11]

From these four approaches we can extract theoretical predictions on industrial characteristics suited for subcontracting. The transaction cost approach and the network approach suggest that subcontracting, rather than vertical integration, is chosen when the upstream production requires specialized technology or uses particular productive factors such as specialized machines or unskilled labor in the secondary labor market. Instead of purchasing parts and components in the spot market, subcontracting may be chosen when parts and components are customized and had better be supplied from upstream firms with long-term relationship. The game approach presents the stability and path-dependent nature of subcontracting arrangements. The information approach describes the logic of saving monitoring costs, which partially explains why subcontracting is chosen instead of purchasing in the spot market. Overall, theoretical foundation of subcontracting suggests that technological characteristics are the key for an industry to develop subcontracting system.

4. Sectoral pattern of subcontracting

Data on subcontracting in Japan are from *Chuushou Kigyou Sougou Kihon Chousa (Basic Survey of SMEs)* (1966) and *Kougyou Jittai Kihon Chousa (Basic Survey of the Industrial Sector)* (1971, 1976, 1981, 1987) conducted by the Small and Medium Enterprise Agency (SMEA) and MITI.[12] These are based on a carefully designed sampling survey with 176 industries and 11 employment sizes. They include the data of by-industry shares of firms working as subcontractors.

Table I presents the percentage of firms working as subcontractors by industry from 1966 to 1987. The table includes firms with less than 300 workers only. The figures indicate that the importance of subcontracting arrangements widely varies across industries. Industries such as food products and petroleum and coal products do not use subcontracting system much. On the other hand, industries extensively using subcontracting include the ones that have labor-intensive production process such as textiles and clothing and

TABLE I
The percentage of firms working as subcontractors

	1966	1971	1976	1981	1987
Manufacturing total	53.3	58.7	60.7	65.5	55.8
Food products	16.5	30.2	14.5	17.5	8.2
Textiles	79.8	75.9	84.5	84.9	79.6
Clothing	73.6	71.4	83.9	86.5	79.0
Wood and wood products	35.0	43.8	42.9	48.0	21.7
Furniture and fixtures	45.6	49.4	41.2	51.6	38.5
Pulp, paper, and paper products	51.1	43.9	44.8	51.6	41.1
Publishing and printing	46.3	51.0	50.8	59.0	21.7
Chemicals	40.2	38.7	37.1	38.5	–
Petroleum and coal products	30.0	30.7	27.0	38.9	18.1
Plastic products	–	–	–	–	68.5
Rubber products	62.3	54.3	61.1	71.8	65.3
Leather and skin products	60.0	64.5	62.5	68.8	64.6
Ceramics, soil and stone products	33.8	34.0	29.4	36.6	35.4
Iron and steel	66.0	66.0	70.4	72.0	52.3
Nonferrous metal	67.0	69.7	68.7	73.6	61.7
Metal products	66.3	71.7	74.8	48.6	70.9
General machinery	70.7	75.8	82.7	84.2	74.5
Electrical machinery	81.4	78.9	82.3	85.3	79.4
Transport equipment	67.1	77.9	86.2	87.7	79.6
Precision machinery	72.4	70.7	72.4	80.9	70.1
Other manufacturing	50.9	58.7	56.5	62.2	43.4

The figures are only for firms with less than 300 workers.
Data sources: SMEA and MITI (1969, 1974, 1979, 1984, 1990).

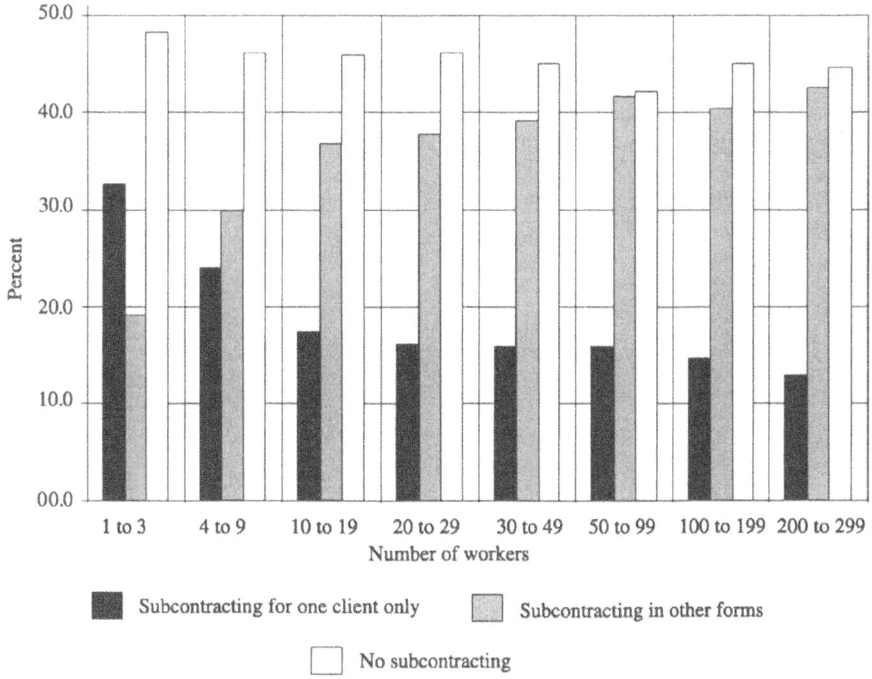

Figure 1. Pattern of subcontracting, 1971.

the ones that have multi-layered vertical production flows such as machinery industries. The nature of production technology certainly affects the effectiveness of subcontracting system. It must also be noted that each industry's figures are largely stable over time.

Subcontracting is a long-term arrangement but is not necessarily a rigid, exclusive contract. Figure 1 shows subcontracting patterns in 1971 with firms classified into three modes: (1) working as a subcontractor for one client only, (2) working as a subcontractor not for one client only, and (3) not working as a subcontractor.[13] The figure indicates that it is rather common for an SME to work as a subcontractor for multiple clients, and for this to happen more frequently as firm-size increases.

Figure 2 presents the by-size pattern of subcontracting for selected industries in 1987. The firm size and the percentage of working as subcontractors are negatively correlated in most of the industries. Such a pattern was not very obvious in earlier years possibly owing to vigorous reshuffling in the high growth era but became clearer through the 1970s and 1980s. Transport equipment industry is an exception in that the subcontracting system has three or four layers and some subcontractors are actually quite large in size.

5. Subcontracting and the characteristics of individual firms

So far we reviewed the historical data of the Japanese subcontracting system and investigated the pattern of subcontracting across industries as well as its relationship with the size distribution of firms. Unfortunately, the data used in the last section are available only at the aggregated level, and thus it is difficult to further analyze subcontracting with connecting various characteristics of individual firms. To supplement the analysis, we use the questionnaire-level micro data of *Kigyou Katsudou Kihon Chousa (Basic Survey of Business Structure and Activity), 1994 F/Y* compiled by MITI (hereinafter we call it BS94) in this section.

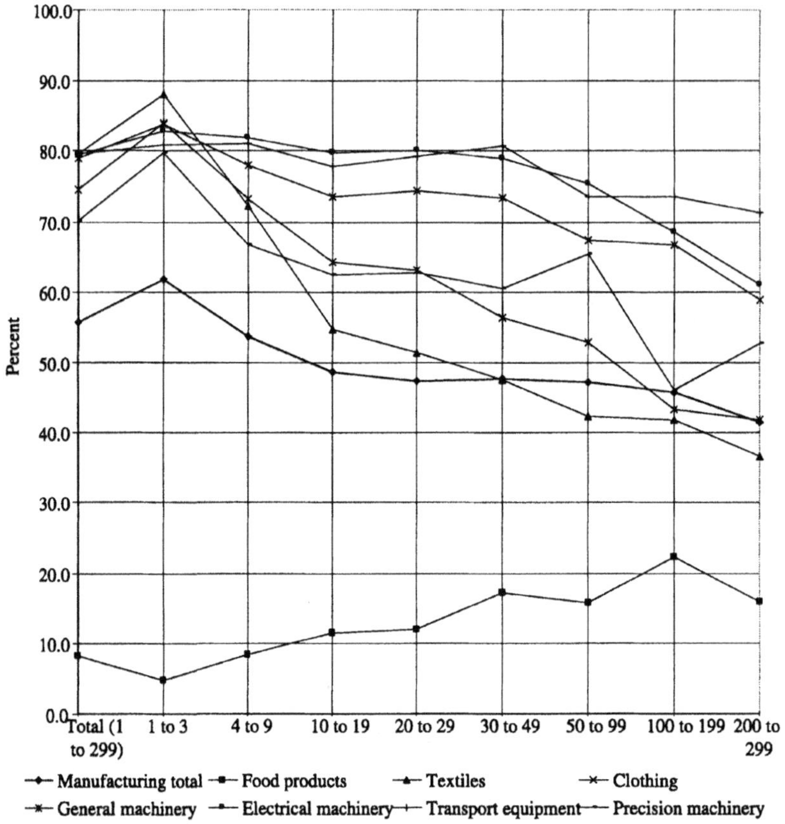

Figure 2. The percentage of firms working as subcontractors by firm size, 1987.

We must note that the experience of Japan in the 1990s may not be directly relevant to the current LDCs because Japan faced various types of structural adjustment issues as a developed country, not issues for developing countries. The subcontracting system was probably an efficient device for enhancing resource allocation in the past but was rather critically reviewed in the 1990s.

This survey was first conducted in FY1991, then in FY1994, and annually afterward. The main purpose of the survey is to capture the overall structure of Japanese corporate firms in light of their diversification, internationalization, interfirm linkages, and strategy on R&D and information technology. The strength of the survey is its complete census coverage and the reliability of figures. We must, however, be careful that the survey only covers large domestic firms and large foreign affiliates in specific industries. The domestic firms to be covered have more than 50 workers, capital of more than 30 million yen, and be in mining, manufacturing, wholesale and retail trade, or restaurants. The foreign affiliates are defined as being 50 percent Japanese owned percent. The survey includes questions on commissioning production (*itaku seisan*) or not, using subcontractor(s) (using *shitauke*) or not, and working as a subcontractor (doing *shitauke*) or not.

We concentrate on the Japanese machinery industry (general machinery, electric machinery, transport equipment, and precision machinery), for which subcontracting arrangements are particularly important. Table II summarizes the major characteristics of Japanese firms in machinery industries in FY1994. The statistics covers 3,723 firms located in Japan. In the table, firms located in Japan are classified as firms with 50–300 workers, firms with 301–1,000 workers, and firms

TABLE II
Characteristics of firms in Japanese machinery industry, 1994

	(a) With 50–300 workers	(b) With 301–1,000 workers	(c) With 1,001 or more workers
Firm size:			
Number of regular workers (L)	137	534	4,178
[number of persons]	(67)	(188)	(8,706)
Total sales (SALES)	3,304	16,332	209,231
[millions of yen]	(3,295)	(12,896)	(631,186)
Economic performance:			
Ratio of tangible assets to	6.44	7.14	9.89
regular workers (KLRATIO) [millions of yen per person]	(6.69)	(6.64)	(7.09)
Ratio of operating surplus to	0.0549	0.0416	0.0383
total sales (PAIRATIO)	(0.1636)	(0.0442)	(0.0331)
Ratio of gross value added to	0.5527	0.4625	0.4233
total sales (VARATIO)	(0.2318)	(0.2089)	(0.1972)
Foreign sales (1) (PROBEXP):	0.2588	0.4259	0.6883
1 positive; 0 zero	(0.4381)	(0.4948)	(0.4639)
Foreign sales (2) (REXP):	0.0319	0.0529	0.1400
ratio to total sales	(0.095)	(0.1274)	(0.1847)
Product differentiation:			
R&D expenditure (1) (PROBRD):	0.4596	0.6926	0.8827
1 positive; 0 zero	(0.4985)	(0.4617)	(0.3223)
R&D expenditure (2) (RRD):	0.0090	0.0141	0.0299
ratio to total sales	(0.0236)	(0.0231)	(0.0302)
Ratio of advertisement	0.0024	0.0031	0.0034
expenditure to total sales (RADV)	(0.0059)	(0.0177)	(0.0050)
Linkage:			
Commissioning production (PROBCOM):	0.8872	0.9086	0.9136
1 yes; 0 no	(0.3164)	(0.2883)	(0.2814)
Using subcontractor(s) (PROBUSUB):	0.7350	0.8012	0.8519
1 yes; 0 no	(0.4414)	(0.3993)	(0.3558)
Working as a subcontractor (PROBWSUB):	0.4550	0.3383	0.1636
1 yes; 0 no	(0.4981)	(0.4734)	(0.3705)
Ratio of foreign stock	0.0101	0.0210	0.0692
ownership (FRATIO)	(0.0877)	(0.1187)	(0.2031)
Number of establishments (ALLEST)	2.70	5.68	19.63
	(2.72)	(7.23)	(32.90)
Number of domestic affiliates (DAFFI)	0.40	1.23	11.36
	(1.14)	(2.29)	(24.53)
Number of foreign affiliates (FAFFI)	0.05	0.36	4.73
	(0.53)	(1.49)	(9.50)
Number of firms in the sample:	2,589	810	324

Notes:
Machinery industry includes general machinery, electrical machinery, transportation equipment, and precision machinery.
Figures are unweighted averages. Standard deviation is in parenthesis.
Data source: The MITI database.

with 1,001 or more workers. Figures stand for the mean and standard deviation of each indicator. These figures include activities of all the establishments the firms have but do not include those of domestic and foreign affiliates. Because the micro data have fat tails and some of the variables cannot be normally distributed, the means and standard deviations must be interpreted with caution.

Table II shows that larger firms tend to have

higher capital-labor ratios (KLRATIO), larger foreign sales (PROBEXP and REXP), larger R&D expenditure ratios (PROBRD and RRD), and larger advertisement expenditure ratios (RADV). The figures lucidly reveal the pattern of internalization. The ratio of gross value added to total sales (VARATIO) gets smaller as the firm size becomes larger.[14] Although VARATIO can be influenced by various factors such as the type of activities and profitability, one possible interpretation is that small firms tend to be in the upstream of value chain and concentrates on production activities while large firms are likely to be in the downstream.[15] The number of establishments and domestic/foreign affiliates (ALLEST, DAFFI, and FAFFI) gets larger with the firm size. The ratio of foreign stock ownership (FRATIO) also increases with the firm size. The probability of using subcontractor(s) (PROBUSUB) increases from (a) 74 percent to (b) 80 percent and (c) 85 percent. The probability of working as a subcontractor (PROBWSUB) drastically declines from (a) 46 percent to (b) 34 percent and (c) 16 percent.

An interesting fact is that the mean of the ratios of operating surplus to total sales (PAIRATIO) is the highest at 5.5 percent for (a), and then (b) 4.2 percent and (c) 3.8 percent. This of course may not simply mean that that larger, more capital intensive, more R&D and advertisement intensive, and more foreign-exposed firms perform poorly. PAIRATIO may not be a proper measure to compare the performance of firms in different size. We need to take into consideration that larger firms tend to locate in the downstream of value chain, and large firms may earn profit in their affiliates. In addition, we only check a single year's data. After all, the standard deviations, particularly the one for (a), are very large relative to the magnitude of means. Nevertheless, we can at least say that the Japanese SMEs in the machinery industry perform relatively well. This means that interfirm linkages make the de-internalization strategy of small firms effective in Japan. Small firms tend to keep themselves slim by giving up foreign operation, R&D, and advertisement and concentrate on production activities with subcontracting arrangements. In contrast, Doms and Jensen (1998) advocate that in case of the U.S. manufacturing sector, MNEs owned by Americans have superior performances when compared with both U.S. affiliates of foreign firms and local indigenous establishments without foreign affiliates.

To see the relationship between the subcontracting pattern and the characteristics of firms, Table III classifies firms into four groups as follows: Group 1, a firm not using subcontractor(s), and not working as a subcontractor; group 2, a firm not using subcontractor(s), but working as a subcontractor; group 3, a firm using subcontractor(s), and working as a subcontractor; and group 4, a firm using subcontractor(s), but not working as a subcontractor.

Groups 2, 3, and 4 present a clear size pattern: As a firm gets larger, it is less likely to work as a subcontractor and more likely to use subcontractors. There are many firms belonging to Group 3, which implies that the subcontracting system in the Japanese machinery industry is multi-layered. Group 2 includes only 178 firms, but there probably exist a large number of firms of this type with less than 50 workers. VARATIO is the largest for Group 2 while the smallest for Group 4, confirming the upstream-downstream pattern. PAIRATIO is the highest for Group 1, though the standard deviation is quite high. This suggests that there exists a group of small high-performance firms independent of the subcontracting system.

Table IV tabulates simple correlations between pairs of variables. Except the correlation between the number of regular workers (L) and total sales (SALES), correlations are overall small so that we do not worry about a multicollinearity problem in regressions.

We do not claim any simple causal relationship among variables. A firm is supposed to decide how to utilize subcontracting arrangements, jointly with the decisions on its size, R&D, foreign sales, and others. However, some regression analysis is conducted just to see the controlled associations among variables. Table V reports the results of logit estimation in which the dependent variables are PROBUSUB and PROBWSUB.[16] These are the major findings: First, the coefficients for L and KLRATIO are significantly negative in the regression for PROBWSUB, while those are positive but not significantly different from zero for PROBUSUB. This means that small firms tend to work as subcontractors while firms regardless of size may use subcontractors. The subcontracting system is multi-layered, which is shown in positive coefficients for PROBWSUB in the PROBUSUB regression and PROBUSUB in the PROBWSUB regression.

Second, the coefficient for VARATIO is negative in the PROBUSUB regression while it is positive in the PROBWSUB regression. Our interpretation is that firms using subcontractor(s) de-internalize a part of the production activities, and firms working as a subcontractor concentrate on production activities. On the other hand, the coefficients for REX and RRD are positive in the PROBUSUB regression and negative in the PROBWSUB regression. Firms using subcon-

TABLE III
Characteristics of firms in Japanese machinery industry, 1994, by subcontracting pattern

	Group 1	Group 2	Group 3	Group 4
Using subcontractor(s)	No	No	Yes	Yes
Working as a subcontractor	No	Yes	Yes	No
Firm size				
Number of regular workers (L)	477	212	282	925
[number of persons]	(2,992)	(272)	(560)	(3,835)
Total sales (SALES)	17,790	4,063	8,253	43,401
[millions of yen]	(142,895)	(5,645)	(24,497)	(288,333)
Economic performance				
Ratio of tangible assets to	7.21	5.71	5.89	7.77
regular workers (KLRATIO)	(7.87)	(6.19)	(5.02)	(7.47)
[millions of yen per person]				
Ratio of operating surplus to	0.0561	0.0441	0.0481	0.0501
total sales (PAIRATIO)	(0.0802)	(0.0529)	(0.2126)	(0.0648)
Ratio of gross value added to	0.5418	0.5728	0.5368	0.4929
total sales (VARATIO)	(0.2311)	(0.2574)	(0.2397)	(0.2112)
Foreign sales (1) (PROBEX)	0.3236	0.1461	0.1944	0.4810
1 positive; 0 zero	(0.4682)	(0.3542)	(0.3959)	(0.4998)
Foreign sales (2) (REX)	0.0460	0.0156	0.0174	0.0745
ratio to total sales	(0.1207)	(0.0660)	(0.0682)	(0.1440)
Product differentiation				
R&D expenditure (1) (PROBRD)	0.4979	0.2809	0.4356	0.7009
1 positive; 0 zero	(0.5003)	(0.4507)	(0.4960)	(0.4580)
R&D expenditure (2) (RRD)	0.0117	0.0057	0.0068	0.0173
ratio to total sales	(0.0261)	(0.0197)	(0.0208)	(0.0268)
Ratio of advertisement	0.0032	0.0010	0.0015	0.0035
expenditure to total sales (RADV)	(0.0120)	(0.0024)	(0.0118)	(0.0064)
Linkage				
Commissioning production (PROBCOM)	0.8006	0.7921	0.9427	0.9081
1 yes; 0 no	(0.3999)	(0.4069)	(0.2324)	(0.2890)
Ratio of foreign stock	0.0146	0.0033	0.0027	0.0340
ownership (FRATIO)	(0.1067)	(0.0412)	(0.0412)	(0.1510)
Number of establishments (ALLEST)	3.88	2.49	2.94	7.22
	(5.77)	(3.25)	(4.13)	(16.95)
Number of domestic affiliates (DAFFI)	1.04	0.36	0.65	2.68
	(6.26)	(1.05)	(2.56)	(11.44)
Number of foreign affiliates (FAFFI)	0.32	0.03	0.14	1.03
	(1.90)	(0.21)	(1.46)	(4.61)
Number of firms in the sample	717	178	1,327	1,501

Notes:
Machinery industry includes general machinery, electrical machinery, transportation equipment, and precision machinery. Figures are unweighted averages. Standard deviation is in parenthesis.
Data source: Same as Table II.

TABLE IV
Simple correlations between variables

	L	SALES	KLRATIO	PAIRATIO	VARATIO	REX	RRD	RADV	PROBCOM	PROBUSUB	PROBWSUB	FRATIO
L	1.0000											
SALES	0.9123	1.0000										
KLRATIO	0.0925	0.0974	1.0000									
PAIRATIO	–0.0191	–0.0157	0.0654	1.0000								
VARATIO	–0.0783	–0.0759	–0.0349	0.1045	1.0000							
REX	0.1887	0.1622	0.1914	0.0271	–0.0646	1.0000						
RRD	0.1793	0.1357	0.0538	0.0450	–0.0055	0.2529	1.0000					
RADV	0.0414	0.0365	0.0543	0.0372	0.0245	0.0938	0.1449	1.0000				
PROBCOM	–0.0047	0.0018	–0.0248	–0.0160	–0.0337	0.0210	0.0157	0.0084	1.0000			
PROBUSUB	0.0303	0.0260	–0.0017	–0.0130	–0.0643	0.0284	0.0321	–0.0104	0.1743	1.0000		
PROBWSUB	–0.0887	–0.0690	–0.1249	–0.0174	0.0693	–0.2017	–0.1741	–0.1031	0.0823	0.2354	1.0000	
FRATIO	0.1841	0.1552	0.0642	0.0176	–0.0031	0.1568	0.0910	0.0427	–0.0443	0.0269	–0.1104	1.0000

Number of observations = 3723.

TABLE V
Determinants of subcontracting status

	Dependent variables	
	PROBUSUB Using subcontractor(s) = 1 Otherwise = 0	PROBWSUB Working as a subcontractor = 1 Otherwise = 0
Constant	0.0558169 (0.360)	–1.461543** (–8.446)
L	0.0000338 (1.163)	–0.0004064** (–4.693)
KLRATIO	0.0052952 (0.885)	–0.297447** (–4.448)
PAIRATIO	–0.0849547 (–0.301)	–0.0292907 (–0.118)
VARATIO	–0.8176049** (–4.521)	0.6379953** (3.927)
REX	0.8841049* (2.251)	–3.853797** (–7.127)
RRD	6.386876** (3.167)	–13.00605** (–5.688)
RADV	0.2509413 (0.054)	–56.75889** (–5.461)
PROBCOM	1.023187** (8.882)	0.37993** (2.962)
PROBUSUB	– –	1.450414** (14.993)
PROBWSUB	1.41165** (14.609)	– –
FRATIO	0.0010676* (2.510)	–0.0026925** (–3.652)
Log likelihood	–1868.9965	–2155.592

Number of firms in the sample = 3723.
Note: t-statistics are in parentheses.
** Significant at the 1% level.
* Significant at the 5% level.

tractor(s) tend to internalize exporting activities and R&D while firms working as a subcontractor are likely to de-internalize these activities. The internalization pattern and subcontracting thus seem to be closely related.

Third, the coefficient for FRATIO is positive in the PROBUSUB regression and negative in the PROBWSUB regression. This suggests that affiliates of foreign firms and/or firms with a high proportion of foreign shares may actively use subcontractors in Japan while they are less likely to work as subcontractors. It may thus be unfair to criticize that subcontracting system is a closed club only for pure Japanese participants, excluding foreigners' participation. Rather, foreign investors may simply purchase stocks of good Japanese machinery firms that use subcontractors in an effective manner.

Fourth, PAIRATIO has negative signs for both regressions though not significantly different from zero. We must at least admit that belonging to subcontracting system does not seem to be a clear strength anymore in the 1990s.

Acknowledgements

The author would like to thank Cristina Boari and other participants in the World Bank Institute's project on The Role of Small and Medium Enterprises in Development for a number of constructive comments and for encouragement. The research assistance provided by Takamune Fujii and Hiromichi Nakagawa is gratefully acknowledged.

The MITI database used in Section 5 was prepared and analyzed in the cooperation with the Research and Statistics Department, Minister's Secretariat, Ministry of International Trade and Industry, Government of Japan. However, opinions expressed in this paper are those of the author.

Notes

1 The definition is based on SMEA and MITI (1979).

2 The author made the translation into English. The MITI statistics also uses the concept of "outsourcing (gaichu)." The difference between outsourcing and subcontracting is again unclear, but it seems that subcontracting is specifically a long-term commitment between large and small firms. Watanabe (1997, pp. 101–104) obviously defines outsourcing differently though. Another concept, "commissioning production (itaku seisan)," includes outsourcing and other types of commissioned production such as OEM.

3 On the drastic change in views on SMEs, see for example Sato (1989), Tsuchiya and Miwa (1989), Miwa (1990), and Watanabe (1997).

4 See Asanuma (1989) and Fujimoto (1997) for example.

5 Nugent and Nabli (1992) claim that the access to financial resources is important for the development of SMEs.

6 "Unfair" trade practices of large parent companies (clients) were strongly criticized by media, and in response, the government enacted a specific law to prevent from undue delays of payments of subcontracting fees and other improper trade practices in 1956 (Shitauke Daikin Hou).

7 Williamson (1979, 1985) provides the theoretical foundation of transaction costs and governance structure. Macneil (1983) presents the concept of relational contract. Monteverde and Teece (1982) conduct an empirical study on a transaction cost theory of vertical integration.

8 The author would like to thank Christina Boari for the reference.

9 Kawasaki and McMillan (1987), Asanuma and Kikutani (1992), Lyons (1996), and Taylor and Wiggins (1997) are in the references.

10 Along this line, Kooij (1991) is one of the references.

11 As for subcontracting system, there are a number of other research papers from different angles. For example, Suzuki (1993) and Montalvo and Yafeh (1994) investigate the nature of technology transfer relating to subcontracting. Fujimoto (1997) conducts a detailed empirical study on the product development function of subcontracting in case of Japanese automobile industry.

12 If available, the data for older years would provide an analysis more relevant to the current LDCs. Although the Survey was initiated in 1957, questions on subcontracting were not included until 1967, unfortunately.

13 The question for subcontracting modes unfortunately disappeared in the 1976 survey and after.

14 Gross value added is calculated simply by subtracting the value of purchases from the value of sales.

15 This interpretation is possible because the material cost for subcontracting work is counted for the subcontractor, not for the client, in the Japanese statistics. This may not be the case for statistics in Korea, Taiwan, and other countries.

16 The probit estimation provides similar results.

References

Asanuma, Banri, 1989, 'Manufacturer-Supplier Relationships in Japan and the Concept of Relation-Specific Skill', *Journal of the Japanese and International Economies* **3**(1), 1–30.

Asanuma, Banri and Tatsuya Kikutani, 1992, 'Risk Absorption in Japanese Subcontracting: A Microeconometric Study of the Automobile Industry, *Journal of the Japanese and International Economies* **6**(1), 1–29.

Barney, Jay B., 1999, 'How a Firm's Capabilities Affect Boundary Decisions', *Sloan Management Review* **40**(3), 137–145.

Doms, Mark E. and J. Bradford Jensen, 1998, 'Comparing Wages, Skills, and Productivity between Domestically and Foreign-Owned Manufacturing Establishments in the United States', in Robert E. Baldwin, Robert E. Lipsey and J. David Richardson (eds.), *Geography and Ownership as Bases for Economic Accounting*, Chicago: University of Chicago Press.

Fujimoto, Takahiro, 1997, *Seisan Shisutemu no Shinkaron: Toyota Jidousha ni Miru Soshiki Nouryoku to Souhatsu Purosesu (Evolutionary Theory of Production System: Organization Capability and Product Development Process of Toyota Automobile Company)*, Tokyo: Yuhikaku. [In Japanese.]

Kawasaki, Asuo, 1998, 'Kokumin Keizai to Chuushou Kigyou (The National Economy and SMEs)', in Keizou Fujita and Masami Takeuchi (eds.), *Chuushou Kigyou Ron (The Economics of SMEs)*, Fourth Edition, Tokyo: Yuhikaku. [In Japanese.]

Kawasaki, Seiichi and John McMillan, 1987, 'The Design of Contracts: Evidence from Japanese Subcontracting', *Journal of the Japanese and International Economies* **1**(3), 327–349.

Kooij, Eric van, 1991, 'Japanese Subcontracting at a Crossroads', *Small Business Economics* **3**(3), 145–154.

Lyons, Bruce R., 1996, 'Empirical Relevance of Efficient Contract Theory: Inter-Firm Contracts', *Oxford Review of Economic Policy* **12**(4), 27–52.

Macneil, Ian R., 1983, 'Values in Contract: Internal and External', Northwestern University Law Review **78**(2), 340–418.

Maruyama, M., 1996, 'Kigyou-kan Kankei (Inter-Firm Relationship)', in *Nihon Keizai Jiten (Encyclopedia of the Japanese Economy)*, Tokyo: Nihon Keizai Shinbun-sha. [In Japanese.]

Miwa, Yoshirou, 1990, *Nihon no Kigyou to Sangyou Soshiki (Japanese Firms and Industrial Organization)*, Tokyo: The University of Tokyo Press. [In Japanese.]

Montalvo, Jose G. and Yishay Yafeh, 1994, 'A Microeconometric Analysis of Technology Transfer: The Case of Licensing Agreements of Japanese Firms', *International Journal of Industrial Organization* **12**(2), 227–244.

Monteverde, Kirk and David J. Teece, 1982, 'Supplier Switching Costs and Vertical Integration in the Automobile Industry', *Bell Journal of Economics* **13**(1), 206–213.

Nugent, Jeffrey B. and Mustapha K. Nabli, 1992, 'Development of Financial Markets and the Size Distribution of Manufacturing Establishments: International Comparisons', *World Development* **20**(10), 1489–1499.

Sato, Yoshio, 1989, 'Small Business in Japan: A Historical Perspective, *Small Business Economics* **1**(3), 121–128.

SMEA and MITI, 1969, *Dai 3 Kai Chuushou Kigyou Sougou Kihon Chousa Houkokusho, 1966 (The 3rd Basic Survey of SMEs, 1966)*, Tokyo: Zaidan Houji. [In Japanese.]

SMEA and MITI, 1974, *Dai 4 Kai Kougyou Jittai Kihon Chousa Houkokusho, 1971 (The 4th Basic Survey of the Industrial Sector, 1971)*, Tokyo: Zaidan Houji. [In Japanese.]

SMEA and MITI, 1979, *Dai 5 Kai Kougyou Jittai Kihon Chousa Houkokusho, 1976 (The 5th Basic Survey of the Industrial Sector, 1976)*, Tokyo: Zaidan Houji. [In Japanese.]

SMEA and MITI, 1984, *Dai 6 Kai Kougyou Jittai Kihon Chousa Houkokusho, 1981 (The 6th Basic Survey of the Industrial Sector, 1981)*, Tokyo: Shadan Houji. [In Japanese.]

SMEA and MITI, 1990, *Dai 7 Kai Kougyou Jittai Kihon Chousa Houkokusho, 1987 (The 7th Basic Survey of the Industrial Sector, 1987)*, Tokyo: Shadan Houji. [In Japanese.]

Suzuki, Kazuyuki, 1993, 'R&D Spillovers and Technology Transfer Among and Within Vertical Keiretsu Groups: Evidence from the Japanese Electrical Machinery Industry', *International Journal of Industrial Organization* **11**(4), 573–591.

Taylor, Curtis R. and Steven N. Wiggins, 1997, 'Competition or Compensation: Supplier Incentives under the American and Japanese Subcontracting Systems', *American Economic Review* **87**(4), 598–618.

Tsuchiya, Moriaki and Yoshirou Miwa (eds.), 1989, *Nihon no Chuushou Kigyou (SMEs in Japan)*, Tokyo: University of Tokyo Press. [In Japanese.]

Uekusa, M., 1987, 'Industrial Organization: The 1970s to the Present', in K. Yamamura and Y. Yasuba (eds.), *The Political Economy of Japan*, Stanford: Stanford University Press.

Watanabe, Yukio, 1997, *Nihon Kikai Kougyou no Shakaiteki Bungyou Kouzou: Kaisou Kouzou, Sangyou Shuuseki kara no Shitaukesei Haaku (The Structure of Social Division of Labor in the Japanese Machinery Industry: Understanding Subcontracting System from the Viewpoint of Stratified Structure and Industry Agglomeration)*, Tokyo: Yuhikaku. [In Japanese.]

Williamson, Oliver E., 1979, 'Transaction-Cost Economics: The Governance of Contractual Relations', *Journal of Law and Economics* **22**(2), 233–261.

Williamson, Oliver E., 1985, *The Economic Institutions of Capitalism: Firms, Markets, Relational Contracting*, New York: Macmillan.

Government-Business Coordination and Small Enterprise Performance in the Machine Tools Sector in Malaysia

Rajah Rasiah

ABSTRACT. This paper compares the performance of small and medium size subcontractors in the machine tools industry in two different states of Malaysia, Penang and Kelang Valley. It is shown that while Penang has developed a fairly successful small and medium subcontracting industry, Kelang Valley has not. The difference in performance (measured by value-added) is due in part to differences in the extent and quality of government-business coordination. In contrast to Kelang Valley, the relatively autonomous state government of Penang took a pro-active approach to business development and provided support to its small and medium enterprises (mainly Chinese-owned) in the form of public training and market-information exchange.

1. Introduction

Small and medium industries (SMIs) continue to draw considerable attention in economic debates. In addition to the scope and flexibility offered by smallness, SMIs have also been considered by a number of analysts in Malaysia as better allocators of resources (see Chee, Lee and Foo, 1981; Chee, 1986). However, the performance of SMIs in the manufacturing sector has been overshadowed by a general decline in establishments and employment over the period 1978–95 (see Figures 1 and 2). While a lack of support by the government dominated their operations in the 1970s and early 1980s, the late 1980s have seen strong support both through subsidies (e.g., preferential loans, tax exemptions, and promotion campaigns). Yet, the majority of SMIs have performed relatively poorly when compared to large foreign firms.

INTECH
United Nations University
Maastricht
The Netherlands
E-mail: Rasiah@intech.unu.edu

The relatively smaller role played by SMIs in Malaysian manufacturing can be partly attributed to the structure of manufacturing as well as politics in the country. First, large export-oriented manufacturing firms in Malaysia are dominated by foreign ownership competing at the technology frontier globally, while local ownership has dominated SMIs. Second, the allocation of state support to alleviate poverty and inequality in the country took on ethnic dimensions with state subsidies being directed largely at indigenous startups with little entrepreneurial experience and weak business networks.

However, the success of firms in particular settings cannot just be explained by size. *Inter alia*, industry differences and the coordination networks firms embed also explain why firms succeed in some places and fail in others. The latter has become increasingly important following the growing knowledge disparity (creation and appropriation) between sites, which is particularly significant in the electronics and related industries where the miniaturization process and product cycles have been developing exponentially. The competitiveness of firms is not just determined by the actions of the individual firms, but also the whole network (relationships) they are tied to.

The significance of business networks and outsourcing have stimulated the demand for proximate sourcing when involving requirements that need quick and reliable supplies. Given the imperfections associated with markets, firms have also relied on trust and loyalty to augment outsourcing relationships. Government support has also become important to support the creation and maintenance of institutions and other supplier support instruments such as subsidies to establish supplier firms. However, given the potential for

Small Business Economics **18**: 177–195, 2002.

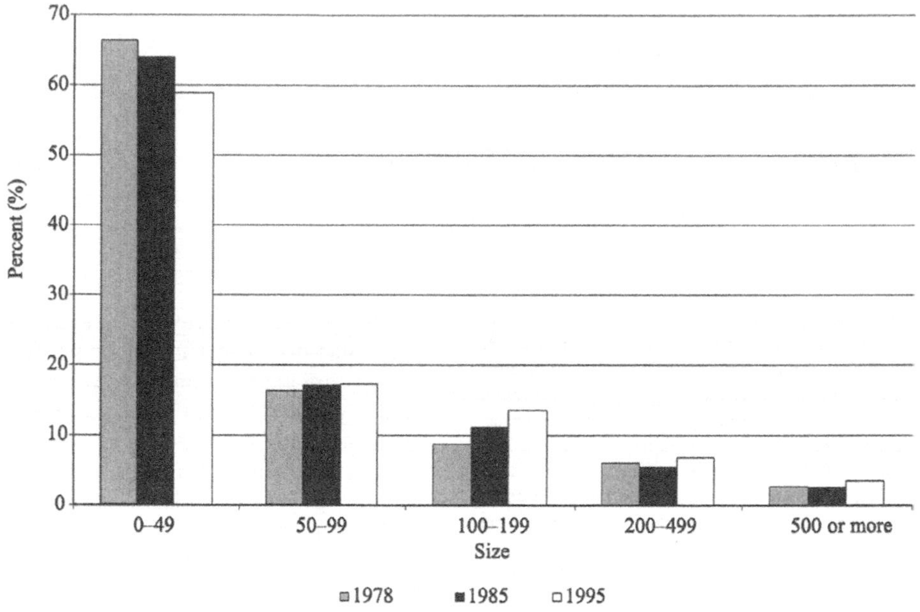

Source: Compiled from data supplied by the Statistics Department, Malaysia.

Figure 1. Distribution by establishments, manufacturing, Malaysia, 1978–95.

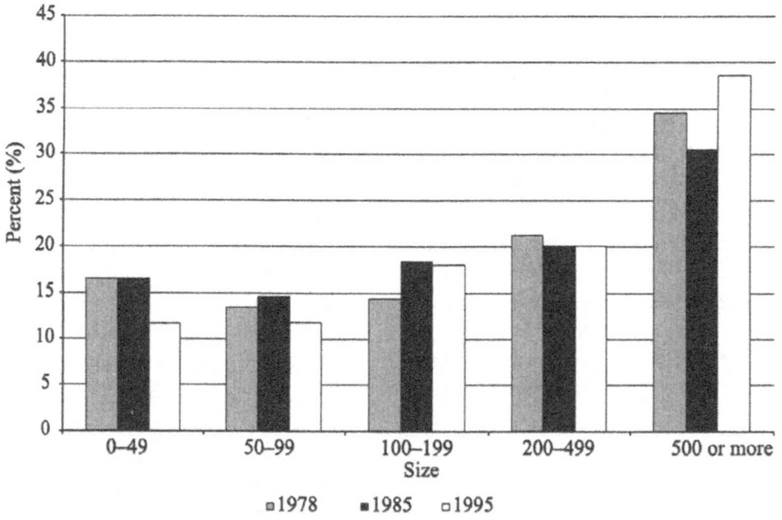

Source: Compiled from data supplied by the Statistics Department, Malaysia.

Figure 2. Distribution of Manufacturing Firms by Employment, 1978–95.

government failure, firms have also often resorted to systemic relationships that require business coordination of government support. The Silicon Valley (Saxenian, 1997), Keihin District (Best, 1990), and Emilia Romagna (Brusco, 1982) are examples of relatively successful examples of effective industrial networks.

This paper examines the role of government-business coordination in the differential performance of machine tool supplier firms linked to foreign microelectronics multinationals in Malaysia. Section 2 provides an overview of the regulatory environment in Malaysia within which SMIs have operated. Section 3 discusses local-level socio-political factors which have affected SMI development in Malaysia and provides an empirical analysis for the case of the machine tools industry in two states, Penang and Kelang Valley. Section 4 takes a detailed look at the performance of selected machine tool industries in these states in terms of growth and technological deepening. Section 5 concludes.

2. SMIs and the overall regulatory environment

The development of SMIs in Malaysia's manufacturing sector was initially constrained by weak government support. During colonialism, the British introduced financial support for small and craft industries under the Rural Industrial Development Authority (RIDA), largely to reduce discontent among the Malays (see Rasiah, 1995, chapter 3). Such lukewarm initiatives were continued with greater financial support after independence under the Rural Development Ministry. It was not until the late 1970s that official policy attempted to earmark SMIs for support, albeit its development remained uncoordinated and cumbersome until SMI activities were given direct prominence by the Ministry of Industrial development following the launching of the Industrial Master Plan in 1986. The umbrella concept of marketing, originally introduced in 1983, was augmented with the Subcontract Exchange Program (SEP) in 1986 and the Vendor Development (VDP) Program in 1992. In addition to the extension of export-oriented double tax deductions to SMIs from 1986, the government introduced the Industrial Technical Assistance Fund (ITAF) and complementing credit guarantee supports as well as matching efforts in the late 1980s. A separate Small and Medium Industries Development Corporation (SMIDEC) was incorporated in the 1990s to govern their activities.

Being generally small and medium in size and dominated by Chinese ownership, local machine tool firms did not have a promising future. Much of the initial federal support for the evolution of machine tool firms came indirectly, and in some sense fortuitously. There was no clear effort to attract microelectronics firms with the purpose of spawning local machine tool firms when the government first launched its export-oriented industrialization policy following the Investment Incentives Act in 1958. Microelectronics multinationals only began relocating in Malaysia after the Free Trade Zone Act was enacted in 1971 and the subsequent opening of the zones in 1972. National Semiconductor, the first semiconductor firm to commence operations in Malaysia, built its factory in Bayan Lepas in 1971 and started production in 1972.

Government efforts to woo export-oriented manufacturing firms have been critical at least in four important ways: (1) The federal government's free trade zone (FTZ) legislation offered financial benefits in the form of pioneer status, which gave tariff exemptions on imports and exports and tax holidays over a period of 5–10 years (firms were thus exempted from corporate income tax of 35 percent and development tax of 5 percent); on expiry of the pioneer status, where firms have often been granted investment tax credit[1] that has given further tax exemptions for 5–10 years (the exemptions have been equivalent to approved investment, and losses during the allowance period can be replaced after the period); and in the form of licensed manufacturing warehouses (LMWs) where FTZs could not be established (LMWs share similar privileges as firms located in FTZs). (2) Amendments to the Employment Act of 1955 in the late 1960s and the Industrial Relations Act of 1967 imposed tighter controls on labor organization. The government did not allow unions in the semiconductor industry until 1989. (3) Government leaders offered unofficial guarantees to safeguard multinational corporate interests to ensure effective production coordination (e.g., for power supplies and customs regulation). (4) The local state government offered subsidized land, water, electricity, and other physical infrastructure.

Though the potential for the development of local machine tool firms emerged through the redeployment of multinationals, the regulatory environment generally disadvantaged their development until the late 1980s. Because the local machine tools firms were primarily ethnic Chinese controlled, official policy towards them was generally discriminatory. Firms with an employment size of 25 and above and a paid up capital exceeding 250,000 were required to obtain licensing that often necessitated compliance with national ethnic restructuring conditions.

More importantly, regulations seriously restricted local enterprises from supplying multinationals located in FTZs and LMWs. Until the 1990s government legislation defined sales and purchases to and from FTZs and LMWs as exports and imports, respectively, and therefore subjected such transactions to the normal customs duties (see Rasiah, 1992). Multinationals preferred imports to service their inputs rather than acquiring those inputs from firms located in the principal customs area to avoid cumbersome customs procedures. Also, machine tool firms operating in the principal customs area have generally relied on imports of metals and machinery, which have generally been subjected to tariffs. Multinationals, thus, had the option of purchasing machine tool supplies from local manufacturers relying on tariff-imposed imports against tariff-free imports from abroad. Under such circumstances, ceteris paribus, multinationals for long preferred sourcing their supplies from abroad than from local suppliers. Hence, official government policy generally erected enormous obstacles to the development of local machine tool firms.

Machine tool firms generally enjoyed little state support because they were Chinese owned. In fact, the machine tool industry received strong impetus only following its classification among the promoted industries in the Industrial Master Plan of 1986. Being complementary to the operations of the strategic industries such as electronics, the industry enjoyed similar incentives, though, the extent of foreign direct investment was extremely small. The Promotion of Investment Act of 1986 offered the industry equal duty exemptions if located in FTZs or LMWs and export incentives such as the double tax deduction on exports and export credit refinancing. The extent of take up was, however, small owing to information asymmetry involving the tooling industry, which is largely characterized by small and medium firms, and the lack of multinational deployment of machine tool production owing to the smallness of the Malaysian market.

Under such circumstances the machine tool industry did not develop as fast as the industries it was expected to service, especially the electronics and automobile industries. Imports have consistently exceeded output over the years 1984–94.[2] The widening gap between sharply rising demand from user industries and slow growth in domestic production capabilities has continued to aggravate the trade deficits involving the industry. Demand slowed in 1985 owing to a fall in GDP, but imports still grew. Unlike Taiwan where domestic production capabilities rose to reverse imports so that the trade balance began improving strongly since the 1970s (see Fransman, 1985), it has consistently shown high deficits in Malaysia (see Table I). The share of imports in machine tool domestic demand gradually rose between 1984–90 before falling slightly in 1994.

3. SMI and Local Level Government-Business Coordination

Institutions play important roles to solve collective action problems and enhance coordination between firms and between firms and the government. In Malaysia, ethnic-based political economy conditions have underpinned the nature of institutional development. Small- and medium-sized non-*Bumiputera* ethnic businessmen have often faced difficulties accessing benefits offered by the federal government. Favorable ethnic and class similarities supported state–firm networking in Penang. Local Chinese management in microelectronics firms, machine tool firms, most leaders of the Gerakan Party, and state parastatals with past schooling and other peer group relationships helped greater networking in Penang. The lack of federal support and the pressure from two alternative ethnic parties, one largely led by bourgeois Chinese within the ruling government (i.e., the Malaysian Chinese Association) and the other by a populist opposition party (i.e., the Democratic

TABLE I
Machine tool industry in Malaysia, selected statistics 1984–94

	1984	1985	1990	1994
Gross output ('RM million)[a]	358.0	226.1	566.5	1,337.3
Import ('RM million)[a]	256.8	267.3	1,191.2	2,537.3
Export ('RM million)[a]	10.3	20.6	54.8	172.7
Imports in domestic demand[b]	59.2	56.5	70.0	68.5
Export share in output[c]	4.0	9.1	9.7	12.9
Trade balance[d]	–94.4	–85.7	–91.2	–87.3
Mean employment[e]	24.9	25.8	36.5	43.0

[a] Figures in current prices.
[b] Percentage of imports in domestic demand measured as output plus imports minus exports.
[c] Percentage of exports in output.
[d] Percentage of net exports in total machine tool trade measured as exports plus imports.
[e] Employment per establishment.
Source: Malaysia, External Trade Statistics, various issues; Malaysia, Industrial Surveys, various issues.

Action Party) encouraged greater networking and offered the checks and balances to reduce unproductive collusion efforts. While the Chinese face cultural differences, the differences cannot be considered significant enough given the integration through their intra-ethnic networking since 1970. Similarly, the cultural differences among Malays in Penang and the Kelang Valley cannot be considered significant. Also, both microelectronics firm locations show strong concentrations of Chinese population.

The structural differences between Penang and Kelang Valley produced two distinct sets of local machine tool development experiences in Malaysia. Machine tool firms located in Penang have experienced rapid growth from the early 1980s, while firms in the Kelang Valley have generally performed poorly. The official regulatory environment that faced Penang firms can be said to have emerged only indirectly and has largely been similar to that faced by Kelang Valley firms. Government policy stimulated the redeployment of microelectronics multinationals to Malaysia. Microelectronics multinationals have become the prime technology suppliers and output purchasers of machine tool firms in Penang. These firms emerged as a direct response to the federal and local state governments' efforts to encourage foreign direct investment. The intermediary role by the local state government and its development corporation were critical in the establishment of initial links with foreign multinationals and subsequently effective supply of infrastructure and other facilities, including federally coordinated incentives from 1989. Like Kelang Valley firms, Penang's machine tool firms' production technology and markets were simple and small until microelectronic multinationals fostered their expansion. The initial period of emergence and expansion of output was also characterized by little federal government support, including antilinkage biases generated by cumbersome customs regulations associated with FTZ coordination. The local state, embodied by a strong ethno-political relationship with the management of both the microelectronics firms and machine tool firms, played a critical role in the establishment of buyer-supplier ties in Penang. The lack of similar conditions and relationships restricted such developments in the Kelang Valley.

Socio-political factors restricted effective coordination in the Kelang Valley while enhancing it in Penang. There has been greater collaboration between the small- and medium-scale Chinese businesses and the Gerakan-led Penang state government than between the Chinese businesses and the United Malays National Organization (UMNO) led Selangor state government. Chinese middle class leadership of the Gerakan party helped the poorer and lower middle class Chinese owners of machine tool SMIs access local state support for their activities. Support for the historically dominating ethnic Chinese in medium- and small-scale businesses has helped greater institutional coordination in the former than in the latter. Unlike large businesses where the politically connected ethnic *Bumiputeras* have often been important partners with ethnic Chinese, interethnic business collaboration among small- and medium-scale enterprises has generally been very thin. The Penang government, thus, has played a more important role in the development of the absorptive capacity of the entrepreneurially better-equipped Chinese in Penang than their counterparts in the Kelang Valley. Better coordination in Penang led to the formation of the Penang Skills Development Centre (PSDC) in 1989 to resolve the growing shortage of industry-specific skills training. The center enjoyed substantial support from the state government, including rental of only RM1 annually for its huge building.

In addition, the operations of Micro Machining (later re-incorporated as Micro Components Technology), owned by National Semiconductor but sold in the 1990s to Towam, helped generate some amount of human capital in Penang. Five firms reported either being owned by Micro Machining's former employees or absorbing staff from that firm. While the contribution of Micro Components Technology in the success of BG, BI, BJ, and CB was reported important in the interviews we conducted, it was not statistically significant in our regressions for the whole sample (see Appendices 1 and 2). Only the founders of the first three firms had engineering qualifications. Hence, the results were discarded. Similarly, investigations on wage differences to examine if better conditions in Penang attracted more skilled workers to Penang firms also proved largely insignificant. The average starting wage of manufacturing firms in Penang, and in Ulu Kelang and Sungai Way (in the Kelang Valley), in 1998 was RM400 monthly.

To test statistically the significance of government-business coordination in the performance levels of machine tool firms in Penang over Kelang Valley holding other variables constant, a control dummy was introduced in the normal Cobb Douglas function (see Appendices 1 and 2). Since it is effective government-business coordination that is being examined, two regressions were run, one with a location dummy (Penang = 1; Kelang Valley = 0) and the other with the former as a dummy (effective government-business coordination = 1; otherwise = 0). While the location dummy is easily defined, firms responses were coded for government business coordination. By using a Likert scale of 1–7, firms were asked to rank their order of preference on five aspects of government business coordination. Because it is extremely difficult to distinguish levels of better government-business coordination, the statistical findings should be secondary to the qualitative analysis in the paper. Firms were considered to enjoy strong government-business relationships if those firms reported effective coordination efforts from between them and state development corporations, federal institutions such as the Ministry of International Trade and Industry (MITI), Industrial Coordination Councils, or other related organizations (see Appendix 2). To improve the significance of the estimates, additional data, albeit all from Penang, were included so that $N = 32$. Efforts to obtain more supplier firm information from the four multinationals in the sample in the Kelang Valley did not materialize. The role of SMIDEC was not statistically tested because it was not formed by then. Followup interviews in 1998 showed that none of the firms in the sample, whether in Penang or in the Kelang Valley, considered SMIDEC as useful in their operations. In the Likert scale of 1–7 (1 being excellent; 2, very strong; 3, strong; 4, undecided; 5, weak; 6, very weak; 7, nonexistent or negative), two firms reported as weak, three as very weak, two as neither weak nor strong, and 25 as non-existent. Nevertheless, SMI support from the government was examined through the role of MITI. The following basic regression models were used:

$$Y = \alpha + \beta_1 X_1 + \beta_2 X_2 + \beta_3 X_3 + \mu \qquad (1)$$

$$Y = \alpha + \beta_1 X_1 + \beta_2 X_2 + \beta_4 X_4 + \mu \qquad (2)$$

Where Y is ln (value added); X_1 is ln(employment); X_2 is ln(fixed assets); X_3 is the dummy, location; X_4 is the dummy, government-business coordination; the coefficients β_1 and β_2 value added elasticities of employment and fixed assets, respectively; β_3 the coefficient of the dummy, location; β_4 is coefficient of the dummy, government business coordination; and μ is error term.

While both produced significant results, regression (2) by using government business coordination over location generated stronger results (see Table II): $\beta_4 > \beta_3$.[3] Hence, while the synergies involving a common location has been attractive, it appears that firms enjoying better government-business links have done even better.

The local state government and its Penang Development Corporation (PDC) worked closely with multinationals to stimulate export-oriented processing, assembly, and testing activities. The state got involved actively to reduce information imperfection linking multinationals with potentially capable local machine tool firms. The multinationals also identified potential local suppliers to meet their self-expansion plans. With multinationals managed by local employees, the room for seeking local supplies tended to be larger. Local private employees working for multinationals enjoyed greater ability to identify potential suppliers than state officials. Local firms without participation in high precision machine tool niches were not initially involved in multinationals quantitative and qualitative plans. The multinationals obtained state support to attract participation from potentially capable local suppliers reluctant to venture into risky and uncertain businesses such as precision engineering. The initial networks were formed around past suppliers in low-order sourcing, business associations, old boys associations, and past employment contacts, which expanded information on potentially capable local machine tool firms. To expand local businesses in the economy, the state leadership began to encourage strongly the formation of consultation committees to assist their development. Hence, when developments in microelectronics multinationals stimulated proximate machine tool sourcing, the channels for matching local SMIs with them began to develop.

Institutions were created or strengthened in Penang. The Chinese Chamber of Commerce worked closely with the state leadership and the PDC. The chief minister also actively promoted spinoffs between local businessmen and multinationals, including increasingly advising the PDC to promote local sourcing of components by multinationals.[4] Especially in the 1980s, systemic relations within intra-ethnic networks became fairly strong. Multinationals' reliance on the PDC to coordinate effectively security, infrastructural support, and to quell labor unrest helped strengthen the relationship between the local state and the multinationals. All eight microelectronics multinationals in Penang, irrespective of ownership, considered the state government as proactive in stimulating machine tool spinoffs (Rasiah, 1993). The PDC compiled a list of local suppliers in metal, plastics, and packaging industries from 1985 and has been upgraded annually since showing detailed information on their productive capacities. The PDC has also actively organized meetings, visits, and promotions to match and strengthen links between foreign multinationals and local firms. Given serious information asymmetry problems associated with backward small and medium firms, PDC's role here has been critical in effecting linkage coordination. Business council meetings between state officials and local managements of microelectronics multinationals have also been important in the promotion of local machine tool sourcing. Intel's strong support for local machine tool sourcing owes much to its former managing director's, Lai Pin Yong, active

TABLE II
Statistical results of regression Equations (1) and (2)

	α	β_1	β_2	β_3	β_4	
Equation (1)						$N = 32$
Coefficient	–0.382	0.988	0.601	1.054		Adj $R^2 = 0.861$
t-statistics	–0.278	6.419[a]	5.308[a]	3.478[a]		F-stats = 64.83[a]
Equation (2)						$N = 32$
Coefficient	–0.206	0.713	0.670		1.189	Adj $R^2 = 0.926$
t-statistics	–0.206	5.781[a]	8.081[a]		6.866[a]	F-stats = 129.40[a]

[a] Significant at 1 percent level.
Source: Computed from Appendices 1 and 2.

promotion of local vendors. The ethnic Chinese background of the state leadership that feared increased federal efforts to raise *Bumiputera* participation in the economy, local suppliers, and purchasing officers in multinational firms helped strengthen intra-ethnic networking (Khong, 1991).

Also, the development of local machine tool firms in Penang received a strong fillip following the opening of Micro Machining in the 1970s by National Semiconductor, a U.S. microelectronics subsidiary located in Penang. Micro Machining later changed its name to Micro Components Technology (MCT) before it was sold to Japanese controlled Towam in the 1990s. This machine tool firm acted as the prime training ground for cutting edge hardware machine tool activities and developed the founders of BG, BI, and BJ. CB reported having a skilled machinist who had worked previously at MCT.

Socio-political complementarity in Penang, particularly the small- and medium-scale business community aligned with the Gerakan party, enabled relatively strong political support and direct matching efforts linking microelectronics multinationals with local machine tool firms. This along with the state leadership's relative autonomy from the federal government allowed strong efforts to stimulate local machine tool sourcing by microelectronics multinationals. The smooth coordination role played by the Penang state government and the PDC has created strong cooperative relations between the state government and the PDC, local firms, and the multinationals. Hence, despite starting with backward capacities, proactive support for the local firms helped tap the spinoff potential that has emerged from growing flexibilization of production in electronics multinationals. Local machine tool sourcing received a boost when the federal government introduced incentives for firms meeting a 30 percent local sourcing condition in 1991. A further stimulus came when big *Bumiputera* enterprises began to capitalize successful Chinese firms involved in supplying electronics multinationals, and support of the state government helped three of Penang's local machine tool firms to attain tax benefits in the period 1989–98.

Like Penang, Kelang Valley had been a major center for colonial economic activities. Unlike Penang, however, its importance rose following independence. Kuala Lumpur remained the administrative and commercial capital of Malaysia. Port Klang replaced Penang as its chief port, and Subang became the site of its biggest international airport. In addition, like the ministries, Malaysia's prime industrial promotion agency, the Malaysian Industrial Development Auhority (MIDA) and other industrial parastatals, are also mainly located in the Kelang Valley. The synergies associated with good infrastructure and administrative and commercial centers obviously attracted many multinationals. Unlike Penang, however, Kelang Valley's socio-political structure offered little active support to start and strengthen machine tool subcontracting with microelectronics multinationals. The state not only did little to increase information about local suppliers engaged in machine tool activities, they also did little to attract the trust of local machine tool firms. The microelectronics multinationals often linked well with federal institutions to maintain customs and administrative coordination. Two managing directors of U.S. firms located in Ulu Kelang and Sungai Way in Kelang Valley reported meeting MIDA and MITI officials to help identify and coordinate the development of effective suppliers, but the meeting was not a success. Hence, weak network bonds in the Kelang Valley blocked the emergence of effective coordination mechanisms to solve collective action problems.

Politically, federal ethnic power relations has been reproduced at the level of the local state. *Bumiputera*-dominated UMNO has ruled Selangor since Malaysia's independence. The ethnic Chinese-dominated DAP has dominated only in Chinese-dominated urban constituencies. Given the proximity of federal institutions, multinationals generally coordinated their security, infrastructure support, and labor relations operations with federal institutions. The local state institutions have generally been bypassed by the microelectronics multinationals as a consequence. Dominated by *Bumiputera* employees, the SEDC has hardly enjoyed ethnic-based networking potential with multinationals as the purchasing officers in the latter have generally been ethnic Chinese. The Selangor State Economic Development Corporation's (SEDC) role has been limited to infrastructure development and the leasing of industrial land. In fact, its function stops once the land is leased to the firms. The SEDC has played no formal role in the promotion of local sourcing. Given the political and economic congruence of ethnic interests both at the national and state levels, there has been no political pressure on the local state to assume a direct role in promoting local sourcing involving non-*Bumiputera* firms.

Under such circumstances, the small- and medium-scale firms that have had a long entrepreneurial experience and show potential linkage development effects – dominated by ethnic Chinese ownership – have enjoyed little state support. The lack of state support has left these firms facing severe market failure problems, though ethnic congruence with the generally ethnic Chinese purchasing officers in the multinationals have encouraged some amount of local sourcing. Not only are microelectronics multinationals badly positioned to identify small- and medium-scale firms' potential capabilities, requiring detailed scrutiny and monitoring, they themselves have received little encouragement to participate in such risky and uncertain developments. Hence, both the microelectronics multinationals and have been reluctant to engage actively in upgrading the technological capabilities of the local machine tool firms. Local machine tool firms not only face finance problems, including accessing subsidized loans and technical assistance from the credit guarantee schemes and the industrial technical assistance fund (ITAF), but are also hardly prominent to attract the attention of potential multinational clients. Indeed, interviews show that the list of small- and medium-scale firms promoted by the government include relatively few machine tool firms operating in the Kelang Valley. Where it has involved active state promotion, such as those by the *Bumiputera* venture trust, Permodalan Usahawan Nasional Berhad (PUNB) stringent ethnic-based conditions apply.

The lack of political support has restricted the establishment and strengthening of sourcing relationships between microelectronics multinationals and local machine tool firms in the Kelang Valley. The intermediary coordination role played by the PDC in Penang has been missing in the Kelang Valley. Lacking state efforts through institutionalization of risks and other support services, microelectronics multinationals in the Kelang Valley reported lacking motivation to develop local machine tool capabilities. Unlike in Penang, where a proactive state leadership has played a critical role in stimulating links between local firms and microelectronics multinationals, state leadership in the Kelang Valley has generally avoided such a role (see Rasiah, 1996b). Since the federal state, *de facto*, has generally been the active governance agent in the Kelang Valley, national considerations embedded in the NEP and its successor, the New Development Plan (NDP), have dictated the promotion of local sourcing. *Inter alia*, ethno-class differences has restricted the effectiveness of the nationally coordinated SEP. Its success in stimulating subcontract relations between ethnic Chinese firms and microelectronics multinationals have been modest even after the enactment of the 30 percent local sourcing condition in 1991 for firms applying to enjoy financial incentives. Yet, 2,763 firms had registered under the SEP by 1993 (Ministry of International Trade and Industry, 1994, p. 260).

The federal state has only been slightly more successful than SEP in its promotion of the VDP involving the electric/electronics industry. Anchor companies began to support small and medium firms with an equity of not less than RM100 thousand that show *Bumiputera* participation in equity and employment of 70 percent and 55 percent, respectively. Participation in this program within the electronics industry has so far largely involved consumer and industrial electronics firms. Few of them, however, have established links with microelectronics firms. Sapura and Sharp were the initial anchor firms. This program has helped create *Bumiputera*-controlled suppliers from scratch within a short time in the electronics industry. The government planned to create 80 new vendors over the sixth and seventh Malaysia plans (Letchumy, 1993, p. 14). Subsidized loans and technical assistance offered through ITAF and venture companies such as PUNB have been critical in their development. Information asymmetry and other imperfections have combined to hamper local machine tool suppliers access to such productive rents in the Kelang Valley.

Socio-political divergence in the Kelang Valley – between the small and medium business community and UMNO-dominated political leadership both at the state and federal levels – stifled the development of complementary institutions to support the growth of ethnic Chinese-controlled small- and medium-scale businesses. With weak interethnic relations at the small- and medium-scale level, the Chinese business community involved in metal, tooling, foundry, rubber, and plastic works enjoyed little support to access microelectronics multinationals. Federal financial incentives associated with local sourcing also failed to generate local sourcing levels comparable to Penang. Hence, much of the domestic machine tool sourcing in the Kelang Valley has been met by foreign subsidiaries attracted to Malaysia. Kelang Valley microelectronics multinationals have also established supply links with Penang's machine tool firms. In addition, three Penang firms dropped plans to extend subsidiary operations in the Kelang Valley owing to a lack of complementary support from local state officials. These firms reportedly had considered opening subsidiaries in the Kelang Valley following encouragement from two U.S. multinationals located there.

4. SMI performance: growth and technological deepening

For the purpose of a more detailed study, we use 17 machine tool firms from Penang (13) and the Kelang Valley (four) to examine their growth and subcontracting experience with microelectronics multinationals. Data limitations prevented a detailed study of more firms. Given their small size and lack of information, these firms were selected from information provided by microelectronics multinationals operating in the two locations. Eight microelectronics multinationals were chosen for that purpose (see Table III). All firms in the sample have introduced flexible production techniques in production. The tracing procedure yielded 25 machine tool firms in Penang and nine machine tool firms in Kelang Valley. The interview response rate was 72.0 percent for Penang and 44.[4] percent for Kelang Valley.[5] Although the Japanese firm in the sample had begun using just-in-time (JIT) principles through its minimum stock turnaround technique from 1975, JIT did not lead to the development of local suppliers. The opaque control structures in Japanese firms precluded the potential for proactive participation in the development of local machine tool firms. Also, Japanese firms' extensive vertical integration and product diversification, including in machinery development, reduced the need for sourcing them locally, especially when local capacities had to be newly developed.

Much of production involving microelectronics multinationals in the 1970s in Malaysia expanded truncatedly. Located in free trade zones, multinational firms were neither required to nor enjoyed supporting capabilities to source locally. Both external and internal developments did not offer the stimulus for the development of local supply capacity. Not only were local firms little developed to participate in machine tool subcontracting relationships, microelectronics multinationals' offshore strategies emphasized little links domestically. These firms accessed primarily tax benefits (that stimulated transfer price potential), market

TABLE III
Microelectronics multinationals

Firms	Inception year	Equity (%)	Location	Flexibilization efforts	Substantial flexibilization
AA	1972	U.S. (100)	Kelang Valley	1983	1988
AB	1973	U.S. (100)	Kelang Valley	1982	1989
AC	1980	U.S. (100)	Kelang Valley	1984	1990
AD	1972	U.S. (100)	Penang	1982	1989
AE	1973	U.S. (100)	Penang	1980	1984
AF	1973	U.S. (100)	Penang	1983	1989
AG	1973	U.S. (100)	Penang	1984	1989
AH	1973	Japan (90); Malaysia (10)	Penang	1975	1978

Source: Author interviews (1993–98).

access to third countries (especially the generalized system of preferences), and cheap unorganized labor that allowed easy hiring and firing (see Lim, 1978; Rasiah, 1993). Production merely comprised the assembly of imported inputs for export. All exports went back to parent firms before being sold to wholesalers and retailers. Work organization typified neo-Taylorism, referred to as casualization by Sabel (1986) or low road to industrial restructuring by Sengenberger and Pyke (1991) and Hirst and Zeitlin (1991). Under such circumstances, microelectronics multinationals were not only little interested in deepening skills and training facilities in Malaysia (see Rasiah, 1996b), but also hardly saw a need to broaden proximate machine tool supply capacities. Malaysia is essentially a primary economy and hardly offered internally generated productive capacities. The country lacked a dynamic industrial policy to facilitate the creation and management of institutions to support industrial deepening and widening (see Rasiah, 1997). Manpower development institutions were relatively weak. The labor force was composed primarily of those who left school at an early age, though the relatively high literacy rates and fluency in English made those people easily trainable.

The general work organization began to change strongly from the 1980s as a consequence of competition and the volatility of demand. Especially in semiconductor production, where product cycles have become increasingly shorter and prices have fallen sharply, firms began to introduce rapid changes in work organization. Most high technology firms began to introduce flexible production systems, superimposing cellular manufacturing onto state-of-the-art human resource techniques such as total quality management (TQM) (Rasiah, 1993, 1994). Although the single Japanese microelectronics firm in the sample had began introducing JIT in 1975, Japanese style control structures had restricted the participation of local personnel in decision making. Japanese employees have continued to retain key technical and managerial positions in the firm. Indeed, the firm that used minimum stock turnaround (MST) techniques and small group activities used both flexible and Taylorist work organizations in the 1970s and early 1980s. From the 1980s, all firms irrespective of ownership began introducing flexible production techniques, integrating innovative capacity with execution throughout the division of labor and thereby reducing hierarchies and making job opportunities interlock in the process. The Japanese multinational, however, despite leading in technical expertise in flexible production systems, offered less stimulus for local machine tool sourcing. Key managerial positions were still controlled by Japanese employees and their own interfirm and intra-holding company sourcing links. The sharp fall in labor reserves from the late 1980s left even industrial and consumer electronics firms – particularly those located in the major industrial centers of West Peninsular Malaysia – introducing flexible production strategies (Rasiah, 1995, 1996a).

Offshore production involving microelectronic multinationals in Malaysia had transformed from a mobile activity (Lim, 1978; Rasiah, 1988) to a deep-rooted regional operation (Rasiah 1988, 1993). The growth of product and process customization within the rapidly growing Asia Pacific market enhanced such a development further. These developments, particularly to enable productive flexible specialization, has encouraged a strong impetus for proximate local machine tool sourcing and the intensification of employee training in-house and externally. Currency fluctuations too were important, but as Rasiah (1994) has argued, they accompanied rather than initiated such developments. Some elements of research and development in the redesigning of mature products such as the 80386 and 80486 microprocessors and EPROM chips has also emerged to tap the direct externalities generated out of the development of local labor's innovative faculties and changes in financial incentives (Rasiah, 1996a). Interestingly the appreciation of the ringgit after 1992 reversed the exchange rate advantage. The currency crash of 1997 did not help the firms ameliorate the problem until 1999 owing to a credit squeeze that has harmed access to loans. Interests rates have from early 1999 began to fall sharply, thereby reversing credit flows in the Malaysian economy.

Direct and indirect (cutting edge process techniques) proxies, such as quality control circles (QCCs), small group activities, JIT, quick changeovers and multi-product lines, TQM, total preventive maintenance (TPM), and statistical process control (SPC), were used to trace the timing of application of flexibilization of production in the firms. A detailed longitudinal presentation of the absorption of flexible production techniques is undertaken in Rasiah (1994, Figure 2). As shown in Table III, the only Japanese microelectronic multinational in the sample began introducing flexible production techniques in 1975, achieving substantial application by 1978. The majority of firms, owned by U.S. capital, began absorbing flexible production techniques in 1980–84, achieving substantial application in 1984–90. Although company AE enjoyed substantial use of flexible production techniques by 1984, the remaining U.S. firms only achieved significant levels during 1988–90. Between the remaining firms, the absorption period has been similar.

The absorption of flexible production techniques from the 1980s and shortening product cycles has intensified layout reorganizations and machinery modifications. While the lone Japanese firm in enjoyed a flexible production organization from the 1970s, the seven U.S. firms, irrespective of location, have experienced substantial process reorganization and machinery modification since the 1980s. Modifications have often required improvements without complete machinery replacement. All microelectronics multinationals have as a consequence started a machinery support division to coordinate such service activities. Given higher transaction costs involved with enlarging hierarchies into dissimilar activities, the potential for out-sourcing of a significant share of these services began to grow in Malaysia. While latent demand grew strongly in all locations of microelectronics multinationals, the share of machinery out-sourcing and related services locally has tended to show a distinct variance between Penang and Kelang Valley. Local machine tool suppliers in the two regions also demonstrate substantial differences in productive capability.

Interviews with the eight firms show that all of them have experienced rapid reorganization, especially in layouts, machinery, and manpower. As shown in Table IV, Penang's machine tool firms are not only greater in number, they show a wider and more sophisticated range of products. The technological depth of Penang's machine tool suppliers, as measured by precision and human capital indices is clearly superior to Kelang Valley's suppliers (see Tables IV and V). Of the 17 firms studied in detail, 14 Penang firms performed high precision engineering and three assembled automated machinery compared to none in the Kelang Valley (see Table IV). Six Penang firms had engineers in their employment compared to none in the Kelang Valley firms (see Table V). The share of technicians and machinists in total employment among Penang firms exceeded 26.7 percent. Only one firm in the Kelang Valley managed to fall among Penang firms. The precision production machinery and precision testing machinery indices of Penang firms were generally far higher than that of Kelang Valley firms. It should be noted that Penang firms showed similar productive capacity as Kelang Valley firms in the late 1970s, none engaging in high precision engineering, working without scientific process control techniques, and none producing automated machinery. Also, all of Penang's suppliers interviewed regarded microelectronics multinationals as key to their development. Substantial inflow of technology involving U.S. microelectronics multinationals, and gradual two-way interfacing with software and hardware has helped upgrade local firms technological capabilities. Only BO among the four Kelang Valley supplier firms considered microelectronics multinationals as an important agent for its growth.

The technology trajectory of local machine tool firms in Malaysia has involved five stages of development. Stage one has typically characterized production of simple crude parts that have been fabricated into final components by more developed suppliers or the microelectronics multinationals themselves in-house.

The second stage has involved the manufacture of jigs, fixtures, moulds, and dies with low precision levels. Stage three is characterized by high precision engineering of small batch components. Stage four either involves the production of small batches with high precision requirements or the manufacture of semi-automated machinery, or both. The former has involved a range of products using similar horizontal technologies, while the latter has generally involved the microelectonics industry. Although microelectronics multinationals have been the main initiators, consumer electronics and disk drive firms have started acquiring

TABLE IV
Local machine tool firms, Penang and the Kelang Valley, 1993

Firm	Ownership (equity %)	Location	Inception year	Process techniques	Employment	Sales (RM million)	Products
BA	L_C(100)	Penang	1979	TMS, JIT, QCC	45	2.5	Precision components
BB	L_C(100)	Penang	1983	TMS, JIT, TQM QCC, SPC	22	1.4	Precision parts, automated machinery
BC	L_B(60) L_C(40)	Penang	1988	TMS, Codified instructions	15	0.3	Precision fabrication
BD	L_C(100)	Penang	1987	QCC and SPC	34	1.5	Precision parts, automated machinery
BE	L_C(100)	Penang	1991	TMS, Codified instructions	17	0.3	Precision parts
BF	L_C(100)	Penang	1976	JIT, TQM, TMS, TPM, QCC, SPC	200	20.0	Precision components, automated machinery
BG	L_I(100)	Penang	1978	Codified instructions	22	2.6	Precision parts, moulds, and dies
BH	L_C(100)	Penang	1984	JIT, SPC, QCC	85	10.0	Precision components
BI	L_C(100)	Penang	1980	JIT, TPM, QCC, TMS	68	15.0	Precision parts, automated machinery
BJ	L_C(100)	Penang	1984	JIT, TPM, QCC, TMS	40	2.5	Precision parts
BK	L_C(100)	Penang	1950	JIT, TQM, TPM, QCC, TMS	120	10.0	Precision parts, automated machinery
BL	L_C(100)	Penang	1980	JIT, TQM, TPM, QCC, SPC	40	1.7	Automated machinery
BM	L_C(100)	Penang	1982	JIT, TQM, TPM, QCC, SPC	128	12.0	Simple parts fabrication, jigs, fixtures, moulds, and dies
BN	L_C(100)	Kelang Valley	1988	Codified instructions	18	0.15	Moulds, dies, jigs, and fixtures
BO	L_C(100)	Kelang Valley	1988	Codified instructions	14	0.36	Jigs, fixtures, moulds, and dies
BP	L_C(100)	Kelang Valley	1984	Codified instructions, QCCs	32	0.56	Simple parts fabrication, moulds, dies, jigs, and fixtures
BQ	L_C(100)	Kelang Valley	1975	TQM, QCC	69	2.5	Parts fabrication, jigs, fixtures, moulds, and dies

Notes: L_C – Local Chinese; L_B – Local *Bumiputera*; L_I – Local Indian; T – Taiwanese.
Source: Author interviews (1993).

high precision parts from machine tool firms. In stage five, firms either undertake large volume precision engineering of components or small batch fully automated machinery, or both. Disk drive multinationals have become major purchasers of large batch parts from selected machine tool firms. Firms in stage five generally enjoy original equipment manufacturing (OEM) capability (i.e., they enjoy the capacity to supply orders by using their own production capabilities). Given the cumulative and complementary nature of these stages, firms specializing in the higher stages in the technology trajectory also often perform the lower operations. It is only when firms pass through stage five that original design manufacturing (ODM) and original brand manufacturing (OBM) stages emerge. The transition through these stages is not discrete as firms that have OBM

TABLE V
Capital deepening indices, local machine tool suppliers, Penang and the Kelang Valley, 1993

Firm	Engineer index[a]	Technician/ machinist index[b]	Precision production machinery index[c]	Precision testing machinery index[d]	Precision tolerance level (± inches)		
					Grinding	Milling	Stamping
BA	0.0	26.7	27.6	33.3	0.00005	0.00005	0.001
BB	0.0	68.2	21.1	23.1	0.0001	0.0005	n.a.
BC	0.0	40.0	15.0	30.0	0.0002	0.0005	n.a.
BD	0.0	60.0	11.8	40.0	0.0002	0.0002	n.a.
BE	0.0	45.2	45.2	26.5	0.0001	0.0002	n.a.
BF	2.0	47.0	34.3	78.9	0.00005	0.00005	0.001
BG	0.0	40.9	38.9	33.3	0.0002	0.0002	n.a.
BH	0.0	42.4	47.2	29.4	0.0001	0.0005	n.a.
BI	1.5	44.1	55.1	71.4	0.0001	0.0001	0.002
BJ	2.5	50.0	25.0	60.0	0.0001	0.0002	n.a.
BK	1.7	41.7	38.9	33.3	0.0001	0.0005	0.002
BL	2.5	52.5	33.3	60.0	0.0001	0.0001	n.a.
BM	1.7	49.2	29.2	73.3	0.00005	0.00005	0.001
BN	0.0	22.3	5.6	6.7	0.001	0.001	n.a.
BO	0.0	20.6	6.8	10.8	0.0002	0.0005	n.a.
BP	0.0	27.6	12.2	11.7	0.001	0.001	n.a.
BQ	0.0	35.4	6.2	21.5	0.001	0.001	0.02

[a] Refers to percentage shares in total employment.
[b] Refers to percentage shares in total employment.
[c] Refers to their intensity in total production machinery.
[d] Refer to their intensity in testing machinery, respectively.
Source: Author interviews (1993).

facilities that also manufacture the lower production stages.

None of the local machine tool firms studied here has participated in ODM and OBM activities, though six firms in Penang reported having designing capabilities. The prime cutting edge machinery used in production is still imported by the microelectronics firms in the sample, because none of the local supplier firms has managed to move up to ODM and OBM activities. Nevertheless, within the limited range of machinery and component markets entered by local firms, suppliers in Penang tend to have production capabilities superior to supplier firms in the Kelang Valley. Penang firms using the proxies – share of precision production and testing machinery indices, engineer and technician/machinist indices, and level of precision tolerance – tend to show higher productive capabilities. Also, BF from Penang has started plans to locate a machine tool plant in China to service microelectronics and disk drive firms.

Penang and Kelang Valley machine tool firms also demonstrate considerable differences in their technological relationships involving microelectronics multinationals. Machine tool firms in both Penang and the Kelang Valley were backward in the 1970s. From simple fabrication, several of Penang's local machine tool firms have gradually moved up the technology trajectory while those of Kelang Valley have generally remained entrenched in stages one and two activities. Technological deepening in Penang has involved substantial technology transfer from microelectronics multinationals. In addition to upfront capital and guaranteed markets, microelectronics firms have also developed prototypes and subcontracted them out to local machine tool firms. Process and product knowledge was transferred, and the development of local firms was monitored by the principal buyers. As the local firms participated actively in the quantitative and qualitative needs of the microelectronics multinationals, the multinationals' own self-expansion efforts saw swift technological deepening in the local machine tool firms in Penang (Rasiah, 1994). As the local firms passed through the learning cycle, the relationships changed to involve increasing in-house participation in technology development. BF, BI, BK, and BM subsequently managed to gain sufficient synergies to participate actively in the development of their own capabilities. Increased in-house development capabilities enabled BF and BK to attain relative freedom from their foster multinationals in the 1990s. Local machine tool firms hardly had similar technology transfer from microelectronics multinationals in the Kelang Valley despite the dominance of U.S. ownership. Relying strongly on in-house technology development both in the 1970s and the 1980s, local machine tool firms in the Kelang Valley failed to achieve similar levels of technological deepening.

The lack of consequent development in supplier networks has resulted in increased in-house workshop machine tool production in Kelang Valley microelectronics multinationals. Some microelectronics multinationals in addition have also began purchasing machinery from Penang's machine tool firms. For example, AC bought four automated wire bonders from BF. AA acquired six wire bonders from BK in Penang in 1990, while its subsidiary in Seremban acquired eight wire bonders from BK in 1992. The growing reputation of Penang firms led to microelectronics firms in the Kelang Valley to encourage them to start subsidiary operations in the Kelang Valley. As a result, BF, BI, and BK considered starting subsidiary plants in the Kelang Valley in 1996.[6] Such plans were, however, abandoned after a careful study owing to a lack of state support, rising costs of production resulting from rising wages from the late 1980s, intermediate inputs, utilities, and an appreciating exchange rate until the financial crash of 1997.

Overall, backward sourcing by microelectronics multinationals in Malaysia has been very small owing largely to the overwhelming composition of imported wafers. The share of local production inputs in microelectronics multinationals in 1993 ranged from 0.5 percent in AC to 7.5 percent in AE.[7] Although the pecuniary share of machine tool inputs sourced by most microelectronics firms has been relatively small, ranging from 2.5 percent by AC to 33.7 percent by AE in 1993, it has risen steadily in Penang firms. The average share over the period 1988–93 ranged from 1.2 percent in AC to 18.5 percent in AE.[8] When AE is excluded, the next best figures come from AG, which sourced 8.3 percent of its machine tools from local firms on average over the same period. As was noted earlier, local machine tool firms have yet to break into ODM and OBM activities. Total sales of local machine tool firms linked to microelectronics multinationals have, however, expanded considerably. From virtually scratch operations at inception, local machine tool sales rose to millions of ringgits in 1993. BF recorded gross sales of RM20 million in 1993 (see Table III). Here again, Penang firms show a superior performance record over Kelang Valley firms. All five firms that achieved gross sales figures of at least RM10 million in 1993 are located in Penang.

Whatever the classifications used, it can be seen that Penang's local machine tool suppliers generally show higher growth and technological deepening than their counterparts in the Kelang Valley. Yet local firms in both regions had similar productive capabilities in the 1970s. Both sets of microelectronics firms have been dominated by U.S. ownership, and local firms have been dominated by ethnic Chinese ownership. Given their similar initial capabilities and the latent demand generated by the microelectronics firms, this contrasting experience within the same national polity distinguishes the influence of local structural specificities on the development of institutional coordination.

5. Conclusion

This paper has looked at the nature of government-business coordination as a factor in the development of SMEs in Malaysia. It has shown that the better performance of small machine tool firms in Penang compared to those in Kelang Valley can be attributed to differences in the quality of government-business coordination. The different ethno-class specificities in Penang and the Kelang Valley have set structural constraints in the development of government-business coordination in the two locations.

Relatively complementary local socio-political structure helped enhance effective coordination between markets, institutions, and firms to enhance the development of small- and medium-scale machine tool firms in Penang. The specific nature of local politics in Penang, and the local political leadership's relative autonomy over the federal government, helped the local state to support ethnic Chinese small- and medium-scale businesses more actively. The special intermediary role of the Penang Development Corporation has been instrumental in forging strong state-business-multinational coordination. Thus, markets, trust, and in-house command worked complementarily to coordinate the expansion and deepening of machine tool subcontracting firms in Penang.

Although similar machine tool demand also emerged in the Kelang Valley, constraints imposed by a stifling local socio-political structure restricted the expansion of similar machine tool relationships between microelectronics multinationals and local small- and medium-scale firms. The local state offered little proactive support to forge links between microelectronics multinationals and local small- and medium-scale machine tool firms in the Kelang Valley. Unlike its counterpart in Penang, the Selangor Economic Development Corporation has hardly played any coordinating role to link microelectronics multinationals with local firms in the Kelang Valley. The official vendor development programs promoted by the federal government have remained underutilized.

The relatively open nature of managerial control in U.S. firms has facilitated greater participation by local personnel in holding strategic positions to establish and strengthen links with local machine tool firms. In Penang, the common ethno-political background of owners of local machine tool firms, state leadership, important purchasing officers, and managing directors of microelectronics multinationals helped overcome problems of networking, thereby stimulating greater support for the development of local machine tool subcontracting. U.S. firms also dominate microelectronics manufacturing in the Kelang Valley, but the lack of similar state participation has restricted the development of complementary state-business links. The lone Japanese firm in the sample located in Penang did not initiate the development of local machine tool capabilities because of their restrictive managerial control structures. These findings have also been supported strongly by the statistical analysis reported in the paper.

Acknowledgements

Comments from Shujiro Urata, Hiroki Kawai, Farrukh Iqbal, Migara De Silva, Jeffrey Nugent, Paitoon Wiboonchutikula, Carl Liedholm and other participants of the World Bank Institute project on the Role of Small and Medium Enterprises in Development are gratefully acknowledged.

Notes

1 This allowance was renamed the Investment Tax Allowance following the Promotion of Investment Act of 1986.

2 A longer time series was not possible owing to the aggregation of the industry with other industries in the preceding years. The available industrial production index is that of all machinery industries, including electronics, which significantly distorts the actual growth of the industry.

3 See Appendix 1 for the data used in the regressions.

4 Interviews with PDC officials conducted by the author in 1986.

5 The firms that did not respond claimed not to have information records or was too busy to meet datelines required.

6 Interviews conducted in 1993 and 1998.

7 These figures exclude building and service expenses.

8 Among other things, the average figure takes into account large machinery purchases during major upgrading exercises.

Appendix 1. Machine tool suppliers reporting links with semiconductor multinationals, 1993

Firms	Sales RM mn	Value added RM mn	Employment	Fixed assets RM mn	Location dummy	Staff with experience working in micro component technology	Government-business coordination dummy
BA	2.5	0.55	45	2.8	1	0	1
BB	1.4	0.322	22	1.1	1	0	1
BC	0.3	0.045	15	0.8	1	0	0
BD	1.5	0.285	34	1.2	1	0	1
BE	0.3	0.042	17	1.5	1	0	0
BF	20	5	200	10	1	0	1
BG	2.6	0.6344	22	2.7	1	1	1
BH	10	2	85	6.8	1	0	1
BI	15	3.9	68	8.6	1	1	1
BJ	2.5	0.475	40	2.8	1	1	0
BK	10	2.12	120	6.3	1	0	1
BL	1.7	0.289	40	2.6	1	0	0
BM	12	2.64	128	8.8	1	0	1
BN	0.15	0.018	18	0.3	0	0	0
BO	0.36	0.0396	14	0.68	0	0	0
BP	0.56	0.0784	32	0.71	0	0	0
BQ	2.5	0.3375	69	3.6	0	0	0
BR	5.2	0.988	145	1	1	0	1
BS	8	1.44	290	1.5	1	0	1
BS	1.5	0.3315	45	0.4	1	0	1
BT	3.2	0.6144	25	1.3	1	0	1
BU	0.8	0.12	39	0.2	1	0	1
BV	2.3	0.4347	48	0.8	1	0	1
BW	0.6	0.1092	26	0.4	1	0	1
BX	0.9	0.1611	35	0.5	1	0	0
BY	2.4	0.5352	34	1.8	1	0	1
BZ	8	1.944	92	1.9	1	0	1
CA	1.9	0.4009	42	1.5	1	0	1
CB	10	2.33	135	2.2	1	1	1
CC	0.3	0.048	22	0.6	1	0	0
CD	0.9	0.1656	25	0.4	1	0	1
CE	1.2	0.2112	44	0.5	1	0	1

Source: Compiled by author (1993–98).

Appendix 2.
Likert scale results of firms responses to government business coordination (1–3 = 1; 4–7 = 0)

	Chamber of commerce with government support	Ministry of International Trade and Industry (located in Kelang Valley)	State officials (including development corporations) directly assisting	Support from private-public coordination councils (e.g., Penang industrial coordination council)	Overall government-business dummy
BA	1	0	0	0	1
BB	1	0	0	0	1
BC	0	0	0	0	0
BD	1	0	0	1	1
BE	0	0	0	0	0
BF	1	1	1	1	1
BG	1	0	1	0	1
BH	1	0	1	0	1

APPENDIX 2 *(Continued).*

	Chamber of commerce with government support	Ministry of International Trade and Industry (located in Kelang Valley)	State officials (including development corporations) directly assisting	Support from private-public coordination councils (e.g., Penang industrial coordination council)	Overall government-business dummy
BI	1	0	1	1	1
BJ	0	0	0	0	0
BK	1	1	1	1	1
BL	0	0	0	0	0
BM	1	0	1	1	1
BN	0	0	0	0	0
BO	0	0	0	0	0
BP	0	0	0	0	0
BQ	0	0	0	0	0
BR	1	0	1	0	1
BS	1	0	0	0	1
BT	1	0	1	0	1
BU	1	0	0	0	1
BV	1	0	0	0	1
BW	1	0	1	0	1
BX	0	0	0	0	0
BY	1	0	0	0	1
BZ	1	0	0	0	1
CA	1	0	0	0	1
CB	0	0	1	0	1
CC	0	0	0	0	0
CD	1	0	0	0	1
CE	0	0	1	0	1
CF	0	0	1	0	1

Note: Firms responding as extremely strong (1), very strong (2), strong (3), undecided (4), weak (5), very weak (6), nonexistent or negative (7).

References

Best, M., 1990, *The New Competition*, Cambridge, MA: Harvard University Press.

Chee, P. L., 1986, *Small and Medium Industries in Malaysia*, Kuala Lumpur: Forum Press.

Brusco, S., 1982, 'The Emilian Model: Productive Decentralization and Social Integration', *Cambridge Journal of Economics* **6**(2), 167–184.

Chee, P. L., D. Lee and R. T. Foo, 1981, 'The Case of Labour Intensive Industry in Malaysia', in R. Amjad (ed.), *The Development of Labour Intensive Industry in ASEAN Countries*, Bangkok: International Labour Organisation.

Hirst, P. and J. Zeitlin, 1991, *Reversing Industrial Decline? Industrial Structure and Policy in Britain and Her Competitors*, Oxford: Berg Publishers.

Khong, S. M., 1991, 'The Service Sector in Malaysia: Structure and Change', Unpublished Ph.D. thesis, Cambridge University, Cambridge.

Lim, L. Y. C., 1978, 'Multinational Firms and Manufacturing for Export in Less Developed Countries: The Case of the Electronics Industry in Malaysia and Singapore', Unpublished Ph.D. thesis, Michigan University, Ann Arbor.

Nathan, R. et al., 1969, 'The Penang Master Plan', paper submitted to Penang Government. Penang.

PDC, 1971, *Annual Report*, Penang: Penang Development Corporation.

Rasiah, R., 1988, 'The Semiconductor Industry in Penang: Implications for NIDL Theories', *Journal of Contemporary Asia* **18**(2), 24–46.

Rasiah R., 1992, 'Foreign Manufacturing Investment in Malaysia', *Economic Bulletin for Asia Pacific* **63**(1), 63–77.

Rasiah, R., 1993, *Pembahagian Kerja Antarabangsa: Industri Semikonduktor di Pulau Pinang*, Kuala Lumpur: Malaysian Social Science Association Press.

Rasiah, R., 1994, 'Flexible Production Systems and Local Machine Tool Subcontracting: Electronics Component Multinationals in Malaysia', *Cambridge Journal of Economics* **18**(3), 279–298.

Rasiah, R., 1995, *Foreign Capital and Industrialization in Malaysia*, New York: St. Martin's.

Rasiah, R., 1996a, 'Industrialization as Engine of Growth and Industrial Policy in Malaysia', *Managerial Finance* **9**(2), 79–102.

Rasiah, R., 1996b, 'Changing Organisation of Work in the

Electronics Industry in Malaysia', *Asia Pacific Viewpoint* **37**(1), 21–38.

Rasiah, R., 1997, 'Class, Ethnicity and Economic Development in Malaysia', in G. Rodan, K. Hewisen and R. Robison (eds.), *Political Economy of South-East Asia*, New York: Oxford University Press.

Rasiah, R., 1999, 'From a Backyard Workshop to a Modern Machine Tool Factory: Eng Hardware', in K. S. Jomo, G. Felker and R. Rasiah (eds.), *Industrial Technology Development in Malaysia: Firm and Industry Studies*, London: Routledge.

Sabel, C., 1986, 'Changing Models of Economic Efficiency and their Implications for Industrialization in the Third World', in C. F. D. Alejandro et al. (eds.), *Development, Democracy and the Art of Trespassing*, Notre Dame, IN.: Notre Dame University Press.

Saxenian, A. L., 1997, *The Regional Advantage*, Cambridge, MA: Harvard University Press.

Sengenberger, W. and F. Pyke, 1991, 'Small Firm Industrial Districts and Local Economic Regeneration: Research and Policy Issues', *Labour and Society* **16**(1).

Market Reforms, Technological Capabilities and the Performance of Small Enterprises in China

Yueping Wang
Yang Yao

ABSTRACT. This paper shows that the domestic and foreign trade liberalization of the Chinese economy since the late 1970s has led to much dynamism among small and medium firms. Such firms have grown at a rapid pace and have increased their share of value added in the Chinese economy. At the same time, they have recorded gains in total factor productivity. However, after two decades of decontrol, the potential for further growth among small and medium industries is limited unless further liberalization is undertaken and government policies pertaining to the allocation of credit, levy of taxes, and grants of research and other subsidies are applied in a more even-handed fashion.

Introduction

During the past 20 years, China has maintained a high economic growth rate that has attracted worldwide attention. Small enterprises have contributed the lion's share to this achievement. In 1995, small enterprises accounted for 62.5 percent of China's total industrial output and 73.6 percent of its industrial employment. While most large- and medium-size enterprises are still owned by the state, China's small enterprises are overwhelmingly private. In 1995, 78.5 percent of all the small enterprises were private, and their share of the national industrial output amounted to 36.1 percent. This feature has made small enterprises the most vibrant element in the national economy.

The causes for the success of China's small enterprises are several. First, the success has been made possible by general economic reforms that have released China's economic energy and are gradually accelerating it to its full throttle. Second, the success has been stimulated by the huge market for basic consumer goods that was not targeted by the planned economy before the reforms took place. Third, the newly established small enterprises are agile in responding to market signals, emerging and vanishing constantly, avoiding the fate of the state firms that are plagued by redundant employees and nonperforming capital. Last, rural communities and local governments have played a significant role in helping the development of small enterprises at the township and village level.

However, China's small enterprises have also raised incomes. While it is widely acknowledged that small enterprises, especially those in the countryside, the so-called township and village enterprises (TVEs) have played an important role in creating employment, fulfilling market needs, and increasing competition, some scholars and government agencies have noted that they are wasting precious resources because of their technical incompetence. For example, a report issued by the State Council in 1990 stated: "Compared with large and medium enterprises, their (small enterprises') technology is backward, their consumption of materials and energy is high, and their product quality is low. . . . They compete with large and medium enterprises for materials, energy, capital, and markets, making large and medium enterprises not able to fully utilize their production and technical potentials. From a social point of view, this trend of "smallization" and diversification will inevitably aggravate the inefficiency in industrial production." (Industrial

Yueping Wang
Institute of Industrial Development
State Development Planning Commission
Peoples Republic of China
E-mail: wangyuep@btamail.net.cn

Yang Yao
China Center for Economic Research
Beijing University
Peoples Republic of China

Small Business Economics **18**: 197–211, 2002.

Census Office of the State Council and Institute of Economic State Planning Commission, 1990). Other people blame small enterprises for the sluggish growth of large enterprises and the technology intensive sectors, and call the flow of capital to small enterprises the "adverse allocation" of resources (Yin, 1997). While these criticisms are warranted to the extent that small enterprises are technically less efficient than larger enterprises, they fail to reconcile the obvious conflict between small enterprises' fast growth and their technical incompetence. While an in-depth analysis is beyond the scope of this paper, we do contend that these criticisms miss the point by overlooking small enterprises' superior allocation efficiency that is made possible by their nimble responses to market signals. Their success suggests that gains from their allocative efficiency may outweigh their losses from technical inefficiency. Nevertheless, the problem raised by these criticisms constitutes a good starting point for our analysis.

In this paper we first present measures of the technical efficiency gap between small and larger enterprises in industry and study its historical trend. Then, based on several recent studies, we discuss the abilities, patterns, and unique characteristics of China's small enterprises in industry in acquiring technical capacities.

The paper is organized as follows. In Section 1 we review the development of small enterprises in China. In Section 2 we present measures of the gap between small and larger enterprises. In Sections 3 and 4 we study the pattern and sources of technology acquisition by small firms and discuss the factors that have impeded their technical advancement. Section 5 reviews business challenges facing China's small enterprises in the future.

1. Recent evolution

China's industrial scale classification convention is different from international standards. International criteria for scale classification are mainly based on a firm's number of employees, capital, and sales volume. For example, in Canada, "small business" is defined as a firm with fewer than 50 employees (fewer than 100 employees in the manufacturing sector), or less than \$5 million of sales volume. "Medium-sized business" is a firm with an employment size between 50 (100 for manufacturing sector) and 500 employees, or sales volume between \$5 million and \$20 million. In China, however, a rather complicated classification system is adopted. Roughly speaking, there are two kinds of classification methods.

The first method is based on output capacity and is applied to industries with a limited number of products. For example, in the iron and steel industry, a "small enterprise" is defined as an enterprise with annual production capacity of fewer than 100,000 tons, "medium enterprise" is between 100,000 and 600,000 tons, and "large enterprise" is over 600,000 tons. In the electricity sector, "small" is defined as an annual production capability of fewer than 50,000 kilowatts, "medium" is between 50,000 and 300,000 kilowatts, and "large" is over 300,000 kilowatts. The second method is based on the original value of fixed capital and is applied to firms with diversified products. Still, it differs in different sectors. In general machinery manufacturing sectors, for instance, an enterprise with fewer than 15 million Yuan of original value of fixed capital is a "small enterprise," 15–50 million Yuan is "medium," and 50 million and more is "large." In instrument-making industries, however, those with fewer than 10 million Yuan of original value of fixed assets is defined as "small enterprise," 10 million to 30 million Yuan is "medium," and 30 million Yuan and over is "large." According to the Third National Industrial Census conducted in 1995, the average numbers of employees in large, medium, and small enterprises were 3,755, 893, and 15, respectively. Therefore, compared with other countries, China's large and medium enterprises employ far more employees.

Contribution of small enterprises to China's national industrial economy

Small enterprises have been playing an important role in China's national industrial economy and have achieved rapid growth since the introduction of broad market-oriented economic reforms in the late 1970s. Small enterprises have been the major engine behind China's industrial economic growth. The total number of small enterprises in industry had increased from 344,000 in 1978 to 7,963,000 in 1996. In terms of comparable statistics, in the period from 1985 to 1995, the number of small enterprises in industry increased by 2.164 million, accounting for 99.33 percent of all the newly established enterprises in that period. The output value of small enterprises increased by 4,429.5 billion Yuan, accounting for 62.31 percent of the total new output created; employees in small enterprises increased by 32.87 million, consisting of 66.12 percent of all the new jobs created in that period. In 1995, the number of small firms was 7.32 million, accounting for 99.7 percent of the national total; the number of employees of small firms was 108 million, making up 73.6 percent of the whole industrial labor force. In terms of output, 5,139 billion Yuan were created by small enterprises, accounting for 62.5 percent of the gross national industrial output (Table I and Table II).

Small enterprises are the backbone of China's economic growth and the major contributor to newly created employment. Meanwhile, they are the major source for the revenues of county and smaller administration units. Before the mid-1980s, they were invested and managed by administrative units at various levels. For instance, state-owned small enterprises were basically set up by municipal or county governments; collective enterprises were mostly held by TVEs, usually with vaguely defined property rights, a property to which many authors have attributed the success of the TVEs (e.g., Weitzman and Xu, 1997; Chang and Wang, 1997). Public ownership still takes a rather important role, with the number of state or collectively owned small firms being about one-fifth of the total, and their output being near two-thirds of the total. However, other types of ownership have flourished in the last 10 years. Table III presents breakdown statistics for different kinds of ownership in 1995. Specifically, the number of firms in the private sector accounted for 78.5 percent of the total number, and their output accounted for 36.1 percent of total output. The disproportion of the number of output of the firms in the private sector shows that their average size was much smaller than that of the public firms. After the Fifteenth Congress of the Chinese Communist Party held in late 1997, many small public firms have been sold to private owners or transformed into joint shareholding. Although no statistics have come out, it is likely that the share of public small firms has dropped dramatically in the last year.

TABLE I
The share of small enterprises in China's industrial economy: 1980–96 (in percent)

Year	Number of firms	Output value	Employment
1980	98.93	56.82	n.a.
1985	99.85	57.70	76.51
1995	99.69	62.45	73.59
1996	99.70	65.59	n.a.

Sources: China Industrial Statistical Yearbook, various years.

Causes of the growth of China's small enterprises in industry

The success of China's small enterprises, especially the TVEs, has attracted the attention of the international academic community. Several factors

TABLE II
Scale distribution of China's industry: 1995

Categories	Number of firms		Output value		Employment	
	Amount (thousand)	Share (%)	Amount (billion yuan)	Share (%)	Amount (million persons)	Share (%)
Total	7,341.5	100	8,229.7	100	147.4	100
Large firms	6.4	0.09	2,182.8	26.52	24.1	16.35
Medium firms	16.6	0.23	907.8	11.03	14.8	10.06
Small firms	7,318.5	99.69	5,139.1	62.45	108.5	73.59

Sources: State Bureau of Statistics, 1996.

TABLE III
Ownership structure of China's small firms in industry: 1995

Ownership	Number of firms		Output value	
	Amount (thousand)	Share (%)	Amount (billion Yuan)	Share (%)
Total	7,318.5	100	5,139.1	100
State	102.3	1.4	675.1	13.1
Collective	1,470.9	20.1	2,377.7	46.3
Individual[a]	5,403.6	73.8	963.3	18.7
Private[b]	287.5	3.9	233.9	4.6
Foreign and joint venture[c]	43.2	0.6	674.7	13.1
Other	10.9	0.2	214.4	4.2

[a] Individual firm is defined as a privately owned firm with no more than eight hired employees.
[b] Private firm is defined as a privately owned firm with more than eight hired employees.
[c] Include firms solely owned by foreign, Hong Kong, Taiwan, or Macao capital, and their joint venture with Chinese partners.
Sources: Author calculation based on the Third National Industrial Census.

have been identified as having contributed to their fast growth.

First, the fast growth of the small firms in China was made possible by the reforms carried out in both rural and urban areas. The rural reforms have re-established the family farming system and raised the prices of agricultural products. The enhanced productivity provided critical initial capital for the establishment of numerous small firms in the rural areas. The urban and industrial reforms have gradually released resources to the market, so small firms that were not covered by plans could get access to needed materials (Lin and Yao, 1998).

Second, a large market for labor-intensive consumer goods was left un-addressed prior to the 1980s as a result of the heavy industry-oriented development strategy pursued by China (Lin, Cai and Li, 1994). This gave small enterprises a perfect opportunity to fill the gap. In the 1980s, small firms produced 80–90 percent of the output in textile, garment, leather, furniture, and plastic products. Those industries led the growth in the country in that period. At the end of the 1980s, demand for durable consumer goods picked up. Although China's industrial structure has continued to become lighter, the growth has mainly happened in durable consumer goods such as television sets and refrigerators. Some small firms have successfully taken this opportunity and developed into large firms that produce national brand products.

Third, small firms grew outside the planning economy and have developed a strong ability to respond to market signals. One of their sources of advantage is their link with labor intensive industries (Lin and Yao, 1998). China is a country with low capital endowment and abundant labor. This is especially true for its rural areas. Therefore, engaging in labor intensive industries is cost effective. This is why a heavy presence of small enterprises in labor-intensive industries such as textiles and garments has been observed. In addition, small enterprises' share in China's export is also remarkable. By 1996, the export share of township and village firms reached 48 percent of the total export. Among the remaining 53 percent, small enterprises in the cities also accounted for a large share. The nimbleness of Chinese small firms is also shown by their response to the changes of relative factor prices. As labor became more expensive, small firms began to increase their capital stocks relative to their workforce. For example, per worker capital stock of small enterprises (at or above township level) increased by 5.44 times from 1980 to 1995.

Fourth, small enterprises at the township and village level received much needed assistance from local governments and communities in their early stage of development. Coming out of the planning era, it was difficult for individuals to set up private firms in the 1980s. In addition, China is still a society beholden to administrative hierarchy. In this social and economic setting, local governments possess advantages over individuals in accessing critical resources such as land, bank loans, and raw materials. Therefore, the support of local governments is found by some studies to be a key factor in TVE development (e.g., Jin and Qian, 1998).

2. Technical efficiency considerations

There are several ways to measure a firm's technical efficiency. Among them, total factor productivity (TFP) is a comprehensive and popular measurement. Tidrick (1986) studied the TFP of China's state enterprises in the period of 1953–83. Jefferson, Rawski, and Zheng (1992) compared the growth and efficiency of state and collective firms. Several Chinese scholars have also done similar work (e.g., Shi, Qin, and Chen, 1985; Shi and Qin, 1987; Li, Zheng and Gong, 1993). Several studies have directly compared the TFP of different types of firms. Jefferson, Rawski, and Zheng (1990) compared the TFP of state, collective, and private enterprises based on an estimation of a production function with three inputs, that is, labor, capital, and middle inputs (Table IVa). According to their study, the TFP of Chinese firms kept increasing in the 1980s. Before 1984, the growth rate of state firms was larger than that of collective firms, but the trend was reversed after 1984. Wu (1992) studied the TFP gap between state firms and rural enterprises (mostly small ones) in the 1980s. He showed that the TFP of rural firms was only 39.1 percent of that of state firms in 1980, but picked up through the 1980s and reached 58.8 percent of the TFP of the state firms. Guo (1998) did similar work by estimating a production function with only labor and capital as input but extended the comparison into the 1990s. While finding similar trends in the 1980s, they also found that collective and other types of firms maintained a higher TFP growth rate than state firms did in the 1990s (Table IVb). Bao (1992) and Shen (1996) studied the TFP of the TVEs in Jiangsu province. Bao (1992), by estimating a growth function, showed that TFP growth contributed 44.5 percent to the output growth of the TVEs in the province when the elasticity's of capital and labor were set to 0.4 and 0.6. Shen (1996), on the other hand, obtained the elasticity's by estimating a translog production function and found that technical progress contributed 43 percent to the output growth of the TVEs in the province in 1979–93. The results of these studies, however, are sensitive to the deflators used in the calculation, especially that for output (Zhang, 1993).

By using a sample of 14,760 firms surveyed by the Third National Industrial Census, Yao (1998) estimated the TFP gaps between different firm sizes and different types of ownership. He adopted the stochastic frontier model to estimate the production functions of 12 major industries. The production function was of Cobb-Douglas type and had only labor and capital as inputs. A TFP index was obtained based on the estimation of the production function, and a multivariate regression analysis was carried out to determine the TFP gaps. His results showed that when compared with large firms, medium and small firms were 20 percent and 49 percent less technically efficient, respectively. However, collective and private firms were 22 percent and 57 percent more efficient than state firms, respectively. These results are robust to the changes of variables included in the regression analysis. It is interesting to find that the state firms, most of which are large, were far less efficient than collective and private firms, most of which are small. This finding indicated that the efficiency gap between state firms and collective and private firms was very significant and that the size advantage of state firms was overridden by the lack of a proper incentive structure.

To show the historical change, we estimate the TFP growth of Chinese firms by scale during 1981–95. It is impossible to get firm level data for this long period. Therefore, we use aggregate data for our calculation. The output we use is the total amount of value-added created by each category of firms. This enables us to exclude from our analysis intermediate inputs whose data are hard to obtain, and only include labor and fixed capital. Labor is the total number of employees at the end of each year, and capital is the net value of fixed capital. All financial data are deflated to the 1980 constant prices. Output is deflated by the overall industrial price index; fixed capital is deflated by the heavy industrial price index. In the calculation, constant return to scale is imposed to the technology. The shares of capital and labor are set to 0.4 and 0.6. These are actual figures calculated

TABLE IVa
TFP growth by ownership in industry (in percent)

	Annual growth rate					Contribution to output growth			
	Output	Capital	Labor	Intermediate use	TFP	Capital	Labor	Intermediate use	TFP
State owned enterprises									
1980–87	8.44	6.74	3.27	6.62	2.14	18.2	3.9	52.5	25.4
1980–84	7	4.5	2.97	5.77	1.81	14.7	4.3	55.1	25.9
1984–87	10.38	9.8	3.68	7.7	2.57	21.4	3.7	50.1	24.8
Collective enterprises									
1980–87	17.68	13.58	5.36	14.51	4.62	11.8	4.1	57.9	26.2
1980–84	15.06	10.09	5.68	12.49	3.88	12	5.1	57.1	25.8
1984–87	21.11	18.39	4.94	16.67	5.83	11.8	3.3	57.3	27.6

Source: Jefferson, Rawski and Zheng (1990).

TABLE IVb
TFP growth by ownership in industry (in percent)

	Annual growth rate				Contribution to output growth		
	Output	Capital	Labor	TFP	Capital	Labor	TFP
1981–85							
State-owned	8.1	7.7	3.5	2.9	38	25.9	36.1
Collective	17.5	17.5	9	5.1	40	30.9	29.1
Others	26.6	29.3	12.9	7.1	44.1	29.1	26.8
Total	10.3	9.2	5.6	3.3	35.7	32.6	31.7
1986–1990							
State-owned	5.1	10.3	2.6	–0.6	80.8	30.6	–11.4
Collective	9	13.3	2.8	2	59.1	18.7	22.2
Others	35.9	39.9	25.9	4.4	44.5	43.3	12.2
Total	6.9	11.3	3	0.6	65.5	26.1	8.1
1991–95							
State-owned	4.4	10.7	0.2	0	97.3	27.7	0
Collective	13.4	11.1	–0.2	9.1	33.1	–0.9	67.8
Others	55	57.2	41	7.5	41.6	44.7	13.7
Total	12.2	14.9	2.1	5	48.9	10.3	40.8

Source: Guo (1998).

based on the 1995 input-output table. Other figures such as the one with the above weights reversed and those in between have also been tried, but the relative order of firms with different sizes is not changed substantially.

We have conducted two sets of calculation. One is the TFP growth and contribution of TFP to value-added growth in the periods of 1981–85 and of 1986–95, the other is the level of TFP index in 1985 and 1995. The first set is based on the standard growth equation, and the second set creates an output-input index by the formula TFP $= Y/L^{0.6}K^{0.4}$. The results are presented in Tables Va and Vb, respectively. The estimates of the contribution of TFP to the output growth are close to but lower than what reported in the World Bank (1997) report, *China 2020*, that puts TFP's contribution to GDP at 43 percent. The TFP gaps between small and large firms are smaller than what obtained by Yao (1998). As the differences

TABLE Va
TFP growth rate by scale in industry: 1981–95

	Value-added	Annual growth rate			Contribution (percent)		
		Capital	Labor	TFP	Capital	Labor	TFP
1981–85							
All firms	9.73	7.92	5.60	3.40	31.90	33.87	34.23
Large and medium	7.61	6.39	3.00	3.25	33.59	23.65	42.76
Small	13.39	10.97	7.07	4.76	32.77	31.68	35.55
1986–95							
All firms	9.43	11.90	2.56	3.13	50.50	16.27	33.23
Large	12.54	14.20	6.91	2.71	45.31	33.07	21.62
Medium	6.66	9.28	4.20	0.43	55.74	37.87	6.39
Small	7.48	10.17	0.52	3.10	54.41	4.14	41.45

Note: Include only firms at levels of village and above.
Sources: Author calculation based on the data from the Second and Third National Industrial Census and China Industrial Statistical Yearbook (1992).

TABLE Vb
TFP level index by scale in industry: 1985 and 1995

	1985	1995
All	0.53	0.72
Large	0.74	0.95
Medium	0.59	0.62
Small	0.46	0.62
Large	1.00	1.00
Medium	0.80	0.65
Small	0.62	0.65

Note: Include only firms at levels of village and above.
Sources: Same as in Table Va.

between our calculation and Yao's approach are substantial, it is hard to assess the comparability between the two results.

As shown in Table Va, the contribution of TFP to value-added growth was smaller in small firms than in larger firms in the period of 1981–85. In the period of 1986–95, however, TFP contribution was much higher in small firms than in larger firms. In addition, small firms' TFP had a higher growth rate than larger firms' in both the periods of 1981–85 and of 1986–95 although the gap was quite narrow in the latter period. As a result, the TFP gap between small and large firms, as shown by small firms' TFP as percentage of large firms', had not been narrowed dramatically from 1985 to 1995 (Table Vb).

Another interesting result revealed by our calculation is that the contribution of labor to output growth decreased considerably from 1981 to 1995. This was especially true for small firms. In fact, in the period of 1986–95, their employment growth rate was merely 0.52 percent annually. This shows that the capacity of small firms, TVEs in particular, to absorb employment decreased dramatically in the last decade. In other words, small enterprises became much more capital-intensive than they were 20 years ago. As an example, the net value of fixed capital per-employment in small firms was increased by 36 percent in the five years (during 1981–85), while the same indicator was 92 percent during 1986–90 and 146 percent during 1991–96.

To summarize, both our calculation and calculations done by others have shown a considerable gap between smaller and larger firms' technical efficiency. Nevertheless, this fact does not warrant the criticism accusing small firms for wasting resources and hurting China's overall industrial development. As we will see in the next section, small firms are more efficient in using the technology they currently possess. This means that their inferior technical efficiency is brought about mainly by the lack of adequate technology and not by the lack of efficient use of technology. Therefore, attention should be paid to finding the impediments to their obtaining necessary technologies.

3. Factors affecting technology acquisition

In the last section we showed that China's small enterprises have been catching up to larger enterprises quickly in their technical capacities, although a gap still remains. In this section, based on several existing studies, we will analyze the factors that affect small enterprises' incentives to acquire production and management technology.

In 1989 and 1990, the Ministry of Sciences and Technologies conducted a survey of 105 enterprises with more than one million output per year in Yichang, Hubei province, to study the factors affecting the firms' technical advances and innovations (MST study). During 1991–93, a group of researchers in Tsinghua University conducted six rounds of surveys on 1,051 firms to study their technical innovations (Tsinghua study). In 1994–95, the Development Research Center and the State Statistical Bureau, both under the State Council, studied technical innovations at the enterprise level in Fujian and Gansu provinces (DRC and SSB study). In 1995, the Development Research Center conduct a comprehensive study on the functions of research institutions and governments in promoting technical progresses in six major industries (DRC study). The analysis below draws heavily on these studies.

Resources and incentives for technical innovations

In China, human and financial resources for technical innovations are concentrated in large and medium state enterprises. However, the incentive structure in these state firms hinders efficient innovations and their dissemination. In contrast, small firms lack the resources for adopting new technology although they are flexible in responding to market signals and thus could be more efficient in the application of technologies. Therefore, there is a mismatch between innovation resources and the capacities to use them efficiently.

Several studies verified the existence of this mismatch. The MST study (Jia, 1994) showed that in the 1980s when plans still maintained a dominant role in the economy, an enterprise's access to plans on supplies and sales was clearly correlated with its size, ownership, and administrative affiliation (Table VI). Large firms, state firms, and firms with higher administrative affiliation were more closely tied to the plan, so they were more likely to get planned resources. Many large and medium firms did not use up the funds allocated for technical innovations, indicating that they lacked the incentives to engaging in such activities. In contrast, small enterprises were more willing to adopt new technology because they faced pressures from two sides: From inside, their equipment were out of date; from outside, the market competition was intense. The surveys conducted by the Tsinghua study showed that 84.7 percent of the TVEs surveyed expressed willingness to adopt pertinent new technology if they had enough funds (Fu and Deng, 1994).

There are several reasons why small firms are more efficient in using the technology they possess. First, most of the small firms grew

TABLE VI
Access to planned resources by type of firm in industry in the 1980s

	By scale			By ownership		By affiliation			
	Large	Medium	Small	State	Collective	Central	Municipal	County	Township
Planned production	26.3	21.9	17.2	24.2	10.6	14.8	21.6	0	0
Planned material supply	58.5	19.6	21.4	21.0	24.5	54.0	21.0	17.9	0
Investment:									
Allocated by plan	22.2	5.6	3.7	6.9	2.1	31.5	3.1	6.7	7.5
Bank loans	46.2	48.3	50.6	51.5	47.9	24.6	53.0	27.7	45.0
By firm itself	31.5	46.2	42.2	41.6	43.6	43.9	41.6	65.7	47.5
Sales through the plan	18.6	3.6	12.8	9.0	11.2	8.3	10.5	0	0

Sources: Jia, Ma and Tang (1994).

outside the plan, having very limited access to financial capital, materials, and technicians provided by the plan, so they are more sensitive to market discipline. Second, most of the small firms are TVEs that are owned by local townships and villages, so they can use community resources (such as land and buildings) to save costs. In addition, they have more autonomy to act according to market signals. Last, because their ownership is shared by a small group living locally, small enterprises are more closely monitored and have a harder budget constraint than state firms (Hong and Yuan, 1997).

Entering the 1990s, the situation has changed tremendously. The DRC and SSB study showed, that thanks to the reforms carried out in the 1980s, market demands and competition became the major impetuses for all kinds of firms to engage in technical innovations. Government planning played a limited role in promoting technical innovations at the enterprise level. However, state-owned large and medium firms still relied more on government to provide key information and technology than small firms did. In addition, since the extent of the reforms was unevenly distributed among different regions, the role of the government was also different. For example, the function of the government in Gansu province, a province that is slow in catching up with the average of the country in adopting reform initiatives, was much more important than in Guangdong province and Shanghai that lead the country in reforms (Fan, 1997).

Patterns of technical progress

The patterns of technical progress are quite different among firms with different sizes. These differences arise as a consequence of different incentive structures, market competition, and financial constraints faced by different firms. First, large firms generally spend more on technical innovations than small firms do because they have more financial resources and skilled manpower to do that (see our description in Section 1). For example, the Tsinghua study showed that on average innovation expenditures of firms in China's manufacturing sector were 0.5 percent of their total sales; the ratios for large, medium, and small firms, however, were quite different, being 0.78 percent, 0.34 percent and 0.37 percent, respectively. The MST study also revealed a similar pattern, with the ratios for the three groups of firms being 2.08 percent 1.30 percent, and 1.15 percent, respectively.

Second, although small firms spend less on innovations, they tend to spend more on acquiring existing new technologies and concentrate on using those technologies more efficiently. In addition, new technology is usually bought in the form of new and advanced equipment. For instance, the DRC and SSB study showed that among the objects of expenditures on technical progress, new equipment accounted for 68 percent; the rest, in descending order, were R&D, buying external techniques, new product testing, and advertisement of new products. The MST study divided technological expenditures into two categories: R&D and other expenditures. The latter was in turn broken into four subcategories: purchases of external technology, application of new technology, acquirement of new production capacities, and innovative sales. A surprising result was that small firms spent a larger portion of technological expenditures on R&D than large firms. Among other expenditures, smaller firms spent a smaller proportion of money in acquiring new production capacities than larger firms, although acquiring new production capacities accounted for the largest chunk for all the firms with different scales. For the other three subcategories, small firms spent a higher proportion than large firms (Table VII). This shows two things. First, most of the spending by large firms was used to increase their production capacities. Second, small firms were more concerned than large firms about how to absorb new technology and transform the technology into marketable products. The DRC and SSB study also supported this conclusion.

Third, small firms put more emphasis on obtaining suitable technology while large firms are more concerned about how advanced the technology is. In terms of ownership type, the percentage of new equipment decreased in the order of foreign and joint ventures, state and collective joint ventures, collective firms, and state firms. However, the new equipment in small firms were mostly domestically made and less advanced. In contrast, large firms had much more internationally advanced equipment.

TABLE VII
Distribution of technical spending by firm size (in percent)

Size of firm	Acquiring technology	Application of technology	New production capacity	Sales of new products
All firms	18.4	12.9	56.4	12.3
Large	10.0	3.4	76.6	10.0
Medium	13.6	15.2	66.8	4.4
Small	23.4	8.8	53.2	14.6

Note: Spending includes only the category of "Other" as defined in Jia et al. (1994).
Sources: Jia et al. (1994).

Fourth, small firms have a higher success rate than large firms in transforming new technology into new products. Table VIII, adopted from Jefferson et al. (1993), shows that the percentage of the value of new products in total output value was highest for TVEs and lowest for state firms. The MST study showed similar trend for firms in Yichang city (Table IX). Small firms introduced more new products and had higher commercial success rates than large firms, collective firms performed better than state firms, and firms belonging to low administrative units performed better than those belonging to higher administrative units.

Complementary to the above two studies, the Tsinghua study showed that small firms tended to use technology to improve their overall profitability while large firms tended to use technology to improve the efficiency of productive inputs such as labor and materials. When asked which aspects had been improved by adopting new technology, large firms' answers were concentrated in savings of labor and materials and improvement of product quality whereas small firms' answers were concentrated in improvements of labor productivity, variety of products, and profitability. These differences are consistent with the observation that

TABLE VIII
Share of new product value in total output by ownership (in percent)

Year	All firms	State-owned		Urban	
		Large and medium	Small	Collective	TVE
1985	10.2	9.2		9.4	15.5
1989	26.9	19.8	37.3	26.4	38.8
1985–89	14.0	10.0		15.0	22.0

Sources: Jefferson et al. (1993).

TABLE IX
New products of firms in Yichang: 1985–89 (in percent)

	By scale			By ownership		By affiliation			
	Large	Medium	Small	State	Collective	Central	Municipal	County	Township
New products[a]	58	64	59	62	60	61	60	63	83
Success rate[b]	74	80	83	81	82	78	81	97	75
New product value in total in 1989	37	26	29	25	35	35	25	25	65

[a] The percentage of the number of new products in total number of products.
[b] The percentage of new products that were commercially successful.
Sources: Jia et al. (1994).

large firms have made more technical innovations but do not have better performance than small firms.

4. Sources of new technology

China's small enterprises obtain new technology from several sources. Because they do not have adequate capacities to conduct their own innovations, they are more likely to buy technologies from outside sources than large firms are. For instance, the DRC and SSB study showed that the proportion of purchased technologies increased as firm size was reduced. In addition, the MST study showed that smaller firms tended to more rely on domestic technology than larger firms did. Table X shows the percentages of firms in Yichang city buying domestic and foreign technology by size, ownership, and affiliation. Obviously, larger firms, state firms, and firms belonging to city and central governments were much more likely to buy technologies from abroad than their respective peers. In particular, firms at the county and township level hardly bought any technologies from abroad.

The most important channel for small enterprises to obtain technology is to cooperate with an outside source. This can take several forms: acting as a supplier for a large firm, cooperating with a research institute or a university, forming a joint venture with a foreign firm, and cooperating with other small firms. Cooperation with large firms secures the market for a small firm's products and enables it to specialize. Cooperation with research institutes and universities enables small firms to quickly get access to new technology, new products, and necessary training. Cooperation with a foreign firm not only provides a small firm with much needed capital, but also brings new production and management technologies and enlarges its market. Last, cooperation with other small firms also enables a small firm to specialize, making it much easier to improve its core products. In addition, specialization among local small enterprises improves the local industrial structure and reduces excessive local competition. Yan and Zhang (1995) and He et al. (1996) showed that when compared with firms of the same size, firms engaged in outside cooperation had more standardized products, higher labor productivity, more qualified labor force, and more investment in technical innovations than those not engaged in outside cooperation (Table XI). In addition, these firms are keener to use "appropriate" technologies. For example, the percentage of equipment made in the 1980s in these firms was 69 percent, 2 percent lower than in firms without outside cooperation; but their percentage of equipment made in the 1970s was 27 percent, 8 percent higher than the other group of firms. However, there was less old equipment in these firms, too. Their percentage of equipment made in the 1950s was 4 percent, 6 percent lower than in the other group of firms.

Human capital is the most important factor that determines a firm's technical efficiency. The majority of small firms, TVEs in particular, rely on hiring or contracting with urban technicians and experienced workers to improve their human capital. In the 1970s when TVEs just started, these firms relied on young urban technicians who were previously sent out to the countryside to be "re-educated" by peasants. Entering the 1980s, these young technicians returned to the cities, and TVEs began to turn to contracting with retired urban technicians and experienced workers, or hiring experts from research institutes and universities as consultants. Almost every TVE in the Yangtze

TABLE X
Percentage of firms buying domestic or foreign technologies in Yichang: 1985–89 (in percent)

	By scale			By ownership		By affiliation			
	Large	Medium	Small	State	Collective	Central	Municipal	County	Township
Domestic technologies	40.0	45	43.3	44.3	42.4	57.1	44.1	16.7	50.0
Foreign technologies	40.0	22.5	3.3	15.7	3.0	14.3	13.3	0	0

Sources: Jia, Ma and Tang (1994).

TABLE XI
Comparison between firms with and without outside cooperation: 1990

	Cooperating firms (A)	Other Firms (B)	A/B
Number of Workers	228	211	1.08
With high school or above education (percent)	25.9	24.5	1.06
Technicians (percent)	4.6	3.1	1.48
Trained workers	8.0	4.5	1.77
Contracted outside technical and management personnel	4.9	2.2	2.25
Innovation spending (thou. Yuan)	127.5	16.2	7.87
Standardized products (percent)	50.5	31.3	1.61
Equipment made in 1980s (percent)	69.0	71.0	0.97
Pre-tax profit per worker (thou. Yuan)	2.83	2.6	1.06

Sources: Yan and Zhang (1995).

River delta hired retired workers from Shanghai in their early stage of development. These workers brought information and expertise to the firms and have contributed tremendously to the early development of the TVEs in that area.

The Chinese government is keen in improving the technical capacities of small firms, especially the TVEs. Although the coastal areas are flourishing with numerous small firms, the inland areas are falling behind. On the other hand, many research institutes and universities have redundant researchers who do not have enough funding to conduct research. Because of this, the central government initiated the "Star Plan" in the mid-1980s. The Star Plan aims at improving the technical capacities of small firms, especially those of the TVEs. As a result, 80 percent of the technical developments covered by the plan are designated for TVEs. Every Star Plan project is assigned a research institute to provide technical support. The government provides favorable treatment to Star Plan projects in the areas of technology imports, equipment purchases, and human resource training. Financial institutions also have preferential terms toward Star Plan projects.

The major accomplishments designated for the Star Plan are to (1) establish a group of model TVEs with adequate technology, (2) develop production equipment that is suitable for TVEs, and (3) train key technicians and management personnel for TVEs. Because of the good coordination between various levels of the government, TVEs, research institutes, and banks, Star Plan projects have been quite successful. For instance, in the Seventh Five-Year Plan period (1986–1990), 88.6 percent of the Star Plan projects supported by the central and provincial governments were completed in two years and recovered their investments also in two years (He et al., 1996). In 1997, the Ministry of Sciences and Technologies conducted a survey on the 108 Star Plan projects financed by the World Bank in the period of 1991–97. It showed that among all the surveyed projects 18.03 percent developed new manufacturing methods for existing products, 62.3 percent developed new products that did not exist countrywide or province-wide, and 80.64 percent reached the level of advanced technology (Cao and Zhao, 1998). However, as the Star Plan is managed by the government and requires intensive resource input, its coverage is still quite low. Take Jiangsu province as an example. During 1986–90, Jiangsu implemented an average of 230 Star Plan projects each year. Excluding the projects implemented in agriculture and the county-and-above level enterprises, the remaining projects only covered 0.1 percent of the total number of enterprises at the township and village level, and only accounted for 1.18 percent of the total number of new projects in each year (He et al., 1996).

Last, FDI has become a major source for small enterprises to obtain foreign technologies. During 1986–95, the share of FDI (including capital from Hong Kong, Macao, and Taiwan) in China's industrial growth was 18.26 percent. Entering the 1990s, FDI has become the most important source of technological imports in monetary terms (Wang, 1997). FDI not only brings new production and management technology to the joint ventures, but also provides spill-over benefits to other firms. Yao (1998) estimated that a 1 percent increase of the number of foreign (not including Hong Kong, Macao, and Taiwan) solely owned or joint venture firms in an industry, the technical efficiency of each firm in that industry will increase by 1.1 percent. In terms of scale, most FDI goes to establish small firms, and small FDI (including Hong Kong, Macao, and Taiwan) firms accounted for 95.95 percent of the total number of FDI firms. However, the presence of FDI in China's industry is still limited. For instance, small FDI firms only accounted for 6.5 percent of the total number of small firms, 9.76 percent of the total number of firms at the township and village level, 13.14 percent of the total output of all small firms, and 28.08 percent of the output of firms at the township and village level.

5. Business challenges facing small firms

Although China's small firms have made remarkable technical progress, the efficiency gap of nearly 50 percent indicates that small firms still have a long way to go to catch up with the large firms. In this section, we will analyze the major impediments that have hindered small firms' technical advance.

Several studies show that the lack of financial resources is an important impediment. The Tsinghua study showed that the lack of funds, qualified personnel, and information were the three most important impediments among its sample firms (Gao, 1997). The MST study also showed that the lack of financial resources was a serious obstacle to technical innovations at the firm level.

Lack access to the formal financial market is a problem for small firms in many countries. The problem is even worse in China. For example, the output of TVEs now accounts for half of the national total industry, but they get less than 10 percent of formal loans each year. Except for some projects with limited coverage (e.g., the Star Plan), China does not have any specific policies geared toward small firms. Under this circumstance, small firms have to resort to informal and in many cases underground financial institutions to get loans. High interest rates and questionable activities of these informal institutions have caused serious problems in some parts of the country, and prompted the central government to launch a nationwide campaign to curb illegal financial activities. However, the campaign has gone beyond just eliminating underground financial organizations and has closed numerous semi-formal credit associations in the rural areas and several regional stock exchanges that were managed by local governments and designated for small firms to issue stocks. The recent reforms have also created new pressures on small firms. Because banks are now required to bear their own risks in their lending activities, they have become more cautious in issuing loans. This hurts small firms more than large firms because small firms are perceived to be more risky. The recent privatization programs also hurt small firms to some extent. Local governments are no longer allowed to guarantee bank loans for any enterprises, so TVEs no longer have the convenience they had before. In addition, banks regard a default by a private firm as more serious than a default by a state firm (Wang, 1998). Therefore, getting formal bank loans is becoming harder for small firms. The Chinese government has realized the problems. Recently, the central bank asked each commercial bank to set up a department specialized in issuing loans to small firms.

Another impediment to small firms is the lack of information intermediaries, or marketing and research firms. In a survey of 207 foreign firms that had business in China, Wang and Shi (1997) found that information intermediaries played an insignificant role in providing these businesses with information. The most important channels for these firms to obtain information in China were business visits, personal and business contacts, exhibitions, and contacts with other foreign firms. The intermediaries such as market research and forecasting firms that are widely consulted in developed countries were not mentioned in their answers. Right now, there are only several market research firms whose services are confined to large cities such as Beijing and Shanghai. Most of other cities do not even have such firms, not to mention the vast countryside where most of the small firms are. There are national and local semi-official industrial associations whose function is supposed to offer information to their members. However, this function is not carried out seriously. Even if it is, the high membership fees charged by the associations put off the willingness of small firms to join. In this aspect, large firms have certain advantages over small firms because they can conduct their own R&D while the latter do not have that capacity.

In addition, small enterprises themselves do not have adequate personnel to conduct technical innovation, or even to implement existing technology. Because of this shortcoming, the technology small firms adopt is simple and easily imitated by others. A common observation is that TVEs in one locality all produce the same product, indicating there is strong externality with a technical innovation. On the one hand, this externality is conducive to economic development at the local level; on the other hand, it discourages firms from introducing new products or new production practices. This has much to do with China's imperfect legal system. Although there are laws providing protection for patents and intellectual property rights, the implementation of these laws is weak.

Acknowledgements

Comments from Shujiro Urata, Farrukh Iqbal, Fukunari Kimura, Migara De Silva, Albert Berry, Jeffrey Nugent, Rajah Rasiah, Edgard Rodriguez, and other participants of the World Bank Institute project on The Rpole of Small and Medium Enterprises in Development are gratefully acknowledged.

References

Bao, Z., 1992, 'Factors Contributing to the Growth of Jiangsu's TVEs in the 1980s', *Jiangsu Jingji Tansuo (Research on Jiangsu Economy)* **3**, 3–6. [In Chinese.]

Cao, H. and J. Zhao, 1998, 'World Bank Financed Star Projects', *Zhongguo Keji Luntan (The China Forum of Sciences and Technologies)* **3**, 23–26. [In Chinese.]

Chang, C. and Y. Wang, 1997, 'The Nature of the Township-Village Enterprises', in W. Hai (ed.), *Chinese Township Village Enterprises: Nature, Experience, and Reforms*, Beijing: United Press.

China Industrial Statistical Yearbook, 1991, 1992, Beijing: China Statistical Press.

China Industrial Statistical Yearbook, 1997, Beijing: China Statistical Press.

Fan, X., 1997, 'A Survey of Technical Innovations at the Firm Level', *Qiye Guanli (Firm Management)* **3**, 22–24. [In Chinese.]

Fu, J., and X. Deng, 1994, 'An Analysis of TVEs' Adoption of Technologies', *Qiye Jishu Jinbu (Enterprise Technical Advances)* **11**, 21–23. [In Chinese.]

Guo, J., 1997, *An Analysis of Enterprises Technological Innovation in China*, Beijing: Tsinghua University Press. [In Chinese.]

Guo, K., 1998, *A Study of the Quality of Growth*, Beijing: Jingji Guanli Press. [In Chinese.]

He, B., J. Gu and Y. Yan, 1996, *Technological Transfer and Technical Advancement in China*, Beijing: Jingji Guanli Press.

Hong, Y. and G. Yuan, 1997, 'A Property Rights Explanation to the Efficiency of the TVEs', *Guanli Shijie (Management World)* **4**, 98–106. [In Chinese.]

Industrial Census Office of State Council and Institute of Economic of State Planning Commission, 1990, *The Current Status of Chinese Industries*, Beijing: Renmin Publishing House. [In Chinese.]

Jefferson, G., T. Rawski and Y. Zheng, 1990, 'Comparison of the Productivity Growth Between State and Collective Firms in China', *Shuliang Jingji Jishu Jingji Yanjiu (Study of Quantitative and Technical Economics)* **8**, 22–31. [In Chinese.]

Jefferson, G., T. Rawski and Y. Zheng, 1992, 'Growth, Efficiency, and Convergence in China's State and Collective Industry', *Economic Development and Cultural Change* **40**(2), 239–266.

Jefferson, G., T. Rawski and Y. Zheng, 1993, 'Comparison of Technical Innovations Among Different Types of Firms', *Shuliang Jingji Jishu Jingji Yanjiu (Study of Quantitative and Technical Economics)* **9**(4), 35–47. [In Chinese.]

Jia, W., C. Ma and S. Tang, 1994, *Technical Innovations*, Beijing: Zhongguo Jingji Press.

Jin, H. and Y. Qian, 1998, 'Public vs. Private Ownership of Firms: Evidence from Rural China', *Quarterly Journal of Economics* **113**(3), 773–808.

Li, J., Y. Zheng and F. Gong, 1993, *Trends of the Chinese Productivity*, Beijing: Shehui Kexue Wenxian Press. [In Chinese.]

Lin, J. Y. and Y. Yao, 1998, 'China's Rural Industrialization in the Context of Rethinking the East Asian Miracle', CCER, Working Paper Series. Beijing University.

Lin, J. Y., F. Cai and Z. Li, 1994, *The China Miracle: Development Strategy and Economic Reform*, Shanghai: Sanlian Press. [In Chinese.]

Lu, C., L. Liu and W. Zhang, 1993, 'The Statistical Problems in the Study of China's Industrial Productivity', in J. Li, Y. Zheng and F. Gong (eds.), *Trends of the Chinese Productivity*, Beijing: Shehui Kexue Wenxian Press. [In Chinese.]

Schaeffner, J., 1996, 'Premiums to Employment in Larger Establishments: Evidence from Peru', Mimeo, Department of Economics, Stanford University, Palo Alto, CA.

Shen, K., 1996, 'An Empirical Study of the TVE Growth in Jiangsu', *Zhongguo Gongye Jingji (Chinese Industrial Economy)* **2**, 5–8. [In Chinese.]

Shi, Q. and B. Qin, 1987, 'TP-DEA Model for Estimating Technical Progress', *Jishu Jingji Yanjiu (Study of Technology and Economics)* **2**, 1–14. [In Chinese.]

Shi, Q., B. Qin and J. Chen, 1985, *Technological Progress*

and Economic Growth, Beijing: Kexue Jishu Wenxian Press.
State Bureau of Statistics, 1996, *Abstracts of the Third National Industrial Census*, Beijing: China Statistics Press.
Tidrick, G., 1986, 'Productivity Growth and Technological Change in Chinese Industry', Staff Working Paper 761. World Bank, Washington, DC.
United Nations, 1992, *World Investment Report: 1992*, Beijing: The Chinese University of Foreign Trade Press.
Wang, Y., 1997, 'FDI and Industrial Development in China', Working Paper Series 1997013. China Center for Economic Research, Beijing University.
Wang, Y., 1998, 'New Issues in the Development of Small Enterprises', *Zhongguo Zhongxiao Qiye (Chinese Small and Medium Firms)* **9**, 12–13. [In Chinese.]
Wang, X. and L. Shi, 1997, 'Improving China's Environment for Technological Imports: Views from Foreign Companies', *Shuliang Jingji Jishu Jingji Yanjiu (Study of Quantitative and Technical Economics)* **14**(10), 83–87. [In Chinese.]
Weitzman, M. and C. Xu, 1997, 'Chinese Township-Village Enterprises as Vaguely Defined Cooperatives', in W. Hai (ed.), *Chinese Township Village Enterprises: Nature, Experience, and Reforms*, Beijing: United Press.
World Bank, 1997, *China 2020: Development Challenges in the New Century*, Washington, DC.: World Bank.
Wu, Yanrui, 1992, 'Productivity Performance of Chinese Rural Enterprises: A Comparative Study', Working paper series. Chinese Economic Research Unit, The University of Adelaide, Adelaide, Australia.
Yan Y. and S. Zhang, 1995, *Technical Advancement of Chinese TVEs*, Beijing: Nongye Keji Press.
Yao, Y., 1998, 'Non-State Factors and the Technical Efficiency in China's Industrial Sector', *Jingji Yanjiu (Economic Research)* **12**, 29–35 [In Chinese.]
Yin, X., 1997, 'An Analysis of the Trend of China's Industrial Scale Structure', *Guanli Shijie (Management World)* **3**, 136–146. [In Chinese.]
Zhang, X., 1993, 'A Study on China's Industrial Productivity', *Shuliang Jingji Jishu Jingji Yanjiu (Study of Quantitative and Technical Economics)* **10**, 36–41. [In Chinese.]

Small and Medium Enterprises in Thailand: Recent Trends

Paitoon Wiboonchutikula

ABSTRACT. This paper reviews the evolution of small and medium firms in Thailand in recent years. It shows that such firms did not preserve their share of total employment during the period 1987-96; indeed, their share fell from 60% to 52% over this period. Much of this decline was felt in the category of very small firms (with less than 10 workers). This aspect is explored further by looking at small firm employment shares in three sub-periods of varying overall economic growth rates. It is found that when overall economic growth is high, the share of small firms tends to contract possibly because many small firms become medium in size and others disband because their owners can find more remunerative employment in larger firms. In slower growth periods, the employment share of small firms appears to rise probably because larger firms may be taking in less new workers or even laying off workers. The paper also calculates productivity measures (technical efficiency and total factor productivity) and shows that different measures give different rankings by size of firm.

Introduction

Despite much local discussion of the important role of small and medium enterprises (SMEs) in economic development, there are not many studies available for the case of Thailand. This paper uses data made available recently to study the experience of SMEs in Thailand in the ten or so years before the major economic crisis of 1997. The data come from three main sources namely, the Ministry of Industry (MOI), the Ministry of Labor and Social Welfare (MOL), and the National Statistical Office of Thailand (NSO). The MOI and MOL provide time series data on number of industrial firms and employment classified by firm size. The NSO's industrial census provides data on output, inputs, and many characteristics of Thailand's disaggregated industries for 1997. The data set classified by firm size is available upon request from the NSO.

This paper is divided into three sections. The first section reviews the evolution of SMEs in Thailand in terms of their number, employment, export capability and subcontracting activity. The second section examines their productivity using such measures as technical efficiency and total factor productivity (TFP). The third section provides information on constraints faced by SMEs as ascertained from surveys.

1. Recent evolution and characteristics of Thai SMEs

Growth

The data used for this study was obtained from the Ministry of Industry (MOI) and the Ministry of Labor (MOL). The data are available for firms of all sizes (including those with fewer than 10 workers) and they are available annually. Unfortunately, the data are reliable for only two variables: number of establishments and number of workers. Data on value and other factors of production are not available from these sources. Nevertheless, time series data from the above sources are able to provide useful information on the growth of firms by size and other contributions of SMEs to economic development.

The MOI data cover statistics of establishments which register with the Ministry of Industry as required by law. Some micro or cottage industries are exempt from registration. Thus, the number of establishments and employment of these industries from the MOI data could be underestimated. On the other hand, the MOL statistics are estimated from two sources of information. First is an annual survey conducted by the Department of Labor Protection and Welfare, and the survey

Faculty of Economics
Chulalongkorn University
Phaya Thai Road
Bangkok 10330
Thailand

Small Business Economics **18**: 213–226, 2002.

covers establishments with 10 or more workers. The second is data from monthly inspections of firms of all sizes (including those micro industries with fewer than 10 workers) in all provinces of the Department of Labor Protection and the Department of Labor Safety. The following discussions will be based mainly on the MOL data set because the data cover a longer time series (from 1987 to 1996) than the MOI data. However, the MOI data set will be compared with the MOL[1] and the NSO data[2] to detect and explain possible discrepancies among the different data sources.

Tables Ia and Ib show that most industrial firms in Thailand were small and medium size. About 60 percent of the 92,100 industrial firms reported by the MOL in 1996 were micro industries employing fewer than 10 workers;[3] 28 percent were small-sized firms; 10 percent were medium-sized firms; and only 2 percent were large firms.

From 1987 to 1996, the number of firms in the

TABLE Ia
Number of firms by size, 1987–96

Size of employment (persons)	Region, Whole Kingdom							
	1987	1989	1990	1992	1993	1994	1995	1996
1–9	31,990	36,189	34,991	41,924	43,510	47,051	49,527	54,991
10–49	9,641	12,853	12,694	17,391	18,330	20,601	23,573	25,912
50–299	2,576	3,726	3,900	5,752	6,367	7,385	8,599	9,094
> 300	537	854	1,027	1,499	1,649	1,844	2,007	2,098
Total	44,744	53,622	52,612	66,566	69,856	76,881	83,706	92,095

Source: Ministry of Labor and Social Welfare, Yearbook of Labor Statistics, various issues.

TABLE Ib
Share of firms by size, 1987–96 (percent)

Size of employment (persons)	Region, Whole Kingdom							
	1987	1989	1990	1992	1993	1994	1995	1996
1–9	71.50	67.49	66.51	62.98	62.29	61.20	59.17	59.71
10–49	21.55	23.97	24.13	26.13	26.24	26.80	28.16	28.14
50–299	5.76	6.95	7.41	8.64	9.11	9.61	10.27	9.87
> 300	1.20	1.59	1.95	2.25	2.36	2.40	2.40	2.28
Total	100.00	100.00	100.00	100.00	100.00	100.00	100.00	100.00

Source: Computed from Table Ia.

TABLE Ic
Growth rates of firms by size, 1987–96 (percent)

Size of employment (persons)	Region, Whole Kingdom			
	1987–96	1987–90	1990–95	1995–96
1–9	6.02	2.99	6.95	10.47
10-49	10.99	9.17	12.38	9.46
50-299	14.02	13.82	15.81	5.60
> 300	15.14	21.61	13.40	4.43
Total	8.02	5.40	9.29	9.55

Source: Computed from Table Ia.

micro industry group declined whereas firms in other size groups increased.[4] In fact, Table 1c shows that the growth rate of the number of firms was the highest for large-sized firms (growing at 15 percent a year) followed by medium-sized firms (14 percent), small firms (11 percent), and firms in micro industries (6 percent).[5]

If we break the 1987–96 period into three subperiods, namely, the high industrial growth period of 1987–90, the moderate growth period of 1990–95, and the slow growth period of 1995–96,[6] Table Ic shows more useful detailed information about the growth rates of firms of different sizes. During the high growth period, the total number of firms grew at 5.4 percent with large firms growing the fastest at 22 percent, followed by medium firms (14 percent), small firms (9 percent), and firms in micro industries (3 percent). During the moderate growth period, the total number of firms grew at a rate faster than the previous period at 9.3 percent with medium firms growing the fastest at 16 percent, followed by large firms (13 percent), small firms (12 percent), and cottage firms (7 percent). During the slow growth period, before Thailand's financial crisis began in 1997, the total number of firms grew at 9.6 percent, about the same rate as in the previous period. However, in sharp contrast to the previous period, firms in the micro industries had the highest growth rate of 11 percent, followed by small firms (9 percent), medium firms (6 percent), and large firms (4 percent).

Therefore, during the high industrial growth period, the number of large firms grew the fastest, followed by firms of all other sizes in descending size order. The reason is probably that new firms that started up during the boom period were mostly medium or large size. Moreover, firms of all sizes expanded their production and employment, and they moved up in classification from a small-sized firm to a large-sized one. Specifically, a number of micro industries graduated into SMEs, and a number of SMEs in turn succeeded in growing to large-sized firms. During the moderate growth period, production and employment generated by either existing or new large firms slowed down. If new firms entered the industrial sector in this period, then they were mostly medium-sized ones. In the period of exceptionally slow industrial growth in 1995–96, prior to the financial crisis, it turned out that the size cohort that grew the most rapidly was the group of micro and small industries. The number of medium and large firms starting their operations during this period could be very limited. If there were new firms, then they would be micro or small industries that were started up by retrenched former employees who become self-employed entrepreneurs for survival in difficult times.[7]

Employment generation

During 1987–96, SMEs employed about 45 percent of total industrial workers whereas large firms employed about 47 percent and micro industries employed about 8 percent. Over time, employment in micro industries and small-sized firms grew slower than employment in medium and large firms. As a result, we see from Tables IIa and IIb that in 1987 large firms employed about 40 percent of the total industrial labor force, medium-sized industries 29 percent, small-sized industries 20 percent, and micro industries employed 12 percent. In 1996, employment in the large firms increased to 48 percent of total industrial employment, and micro industries employed only 6 percent of total industrial employment. These tables thus show that the share of employment in micro and small industries declined whereas the share of employment in medium and large firms increased during 1987–96.

The growth of employment in the industrial sector also varied with industrial output growth. If we break the period 1987–96 into three subperiods of varying industrial growth rates, we find from Table IIc that during 1987–90 when industrial growth rate was the highest, employment in the industrial sector grew rapidly at an annual rate of 16.8 percent. During 1990–95, when industrial production growth slowed down, the employment growth also slowed down to 13.7 percent. Finally, during the period just before Thailand's economic crisis in 1997, as industrial growth dipped further, the growth of employment in the sector decelerated to only 5.9 percent.[8]

The next question is how did SMEs perform relative to large firms in terms of employment growth during the above three periods of varying industrial output growth and employment growth.

Table IIc shows that during the high growth

TABLE IIa
Employment by firm size, 1987–96 (number of workers)

Size of employment (persons)	Region, Whole Kingdom							
	1987	1989	1990	1992	1993	1994	1995	1996
1-9	114,799	132,112	131,793	164,393	172,423	189,456	201,325	218,435
10-49	195,016	265,546	252,756	347,875	369,090	420,801	486,031	534,120
50-299	283,510	417,217	437,502	661,708	735,886	846,231	986,099	1,050,336
> 300	395,430	688,424	813,244	1,198,816	1,299,378	1,428,251	1,568,274	1,634,765
Total	988,755	1,503,299	1,635,295	2,372,792	2,576,777	2,884,739	3,241,729	3,437,656

Source: Ministry of Labor and Social Welfare, Yearbook of Labor Statistics, various issues.

TABLE IIb
Share of employment by firm size, 1987–96 (percent)

Size of employment (persons)	Region, Whole Kingdom							
	1987	1989	1990	1992	1993	1994	1995	1996
1-9	11.61	8.79	8.06	6.93	6.69	6.57	6.21	6.35
10–49	19.72	17.66	15.46	14.66	14.32	14.59	14.99	15.54
50–299	28.67	27.75	26.75	27.89	28.56	29.33	30.42	30.55
> 300	39.99	45.79	49.73	50.52	50.43	49.51	48.38	47.55
Total	100.00	100.00	100.00	100.00	100.00	100.00	100.00	100.00

Source: Computed from Table IIa.

TABLE IIc
Growth rates of employment by firm size, 1987–96 (percent)

Size of employment (persons)	Region, Whole Kingdom			
	1987–96	1987–90	1990–95	1995–96
1-9	7.15	4.60	8.47	8.16
10-49	11.19	8.64	13.08	9.43
50-299	14.55	14.46	16.25	6.31
> 300	15.77	24.04	13.13	4.15
Total	13.85	16.77	13.69	5.87

Source: Computed from Table IIa.

period of 1987–90, employment in large firms grew the fastest at 24.0 percent a year, followed by the growth of employment in the medium-sized firms (14 percent), small-sized firms (9 percent), and micro industries (5 percent). During the slower growth period of 1990–95, employment in the medium-sized firms grew the fastest at 16 percent, followed by the employment growth of the large firms (13 percent), small firms (13 percent), and micro industries (8 percent). Finally, during the stagnation period of 1995–96, employment grew at the fastest rate of 9 percent in the small industries, followed by the growth rate of micro industries at 8 percent. Employment in medium and large firms grew at rates of only 6 and 4 percent, respectively.

Therefore, the contribution of SMEs to employment growth seems to exhibit some relationship with industrial growth rates. During the high growth period, large and medium firms seem to contribute more in terms of employment growth because many small firms graduated to become larger firms. The employment generation of a previously small firm became the contribution of a medium or a large firm. During the period of slowest growth or stagnation, not only did employment of large firms grow the slowest, but many firms also laid off workers and some even ceased operations altogether. In this situation, it is possible that we simultaneously observed the growth of many small firms and, in particular, firms of micro industries whose owners were former employees of a medium or a large firm. Many of these new business creators were formerly unemployed and possessed entrepreneurial ability or spirit to set up their own production for survival in their home towns during this difficult time. In this sense, we may view SMEs, particularly the small ones, as crisis shock absorbers that not only help provide employment during difficult times, but also prepare new entrepreneurs for graduating to run a larger firm when the economy recovers. It is interesting to note that during 1995–96 the growth rates of employment growth of micro and small industries were the highest in the northeast region and the provinces surrounding Bangkok, two areas that are the sources of most of Thailand's workers.

Despite the fact that as more new small firms started up and they became sources of employment during the stagnation period, the capacity of SMEs to generate employment during normal times needs further investigation. This is because for the whole period of 1987–96, the proportion of SME employment out of total employment was much lower than the proportion of the number of SME firms out of total industrial firms, suggesting that large firms absorb more employees than SMEs. However, although SMEs generate less employment per firm by definition, they may be considered to created greater employment if it can be shown that they are more labor-intensive and thus employ a greater number of workers per unit of capital input or investment.

Export capability

Table III shows the percentage distribution of the number of firms of 3-digit ISIC industries by export-output ratio and by size group in 1997. The data are obtained from the National Statistical Office's (NSO) unpublished database, and in the questionnaire exports are defined as both direct and indirect exports. On average over all industries, about 22 percent of firms exported some of their production while 78 percent produced only for the domestic market. Large firms exported proportionately more than small- and medium-sized firms. About 70 percent of large firms had some exports whereas only 40 and 10 percent of medium and small firms, respectively, exported some of their production.

Of all exporting firms, 52 percent exported less than 50 percent of their production; 42 percent exported more than 50 percent; and about 6 percent produced solely for the export market. This distribution of export-output ratios did not vary much across firm size groups. This means that although large firms were more likely to export than small- and medium-sized firms, exporting firms of any size were equally likely to have any export-output ratio.

Exporting industries where small- and medium-sized firms account for a high proportion of industry employment were textiles and textile products, garments, leather and leather products, furniture, chemical products, rubber and rubber products, plastic products, special purpose

TABLE III
Percentage distribution of firms by export percentage and by firm size group

Size	100%	> 50%	50%	< 50%	With export	Without export
S	1.92	2.22	0.69	4.33	9.16	90.84
M	10.28	11.81	1.86	15.47	39.42	60.58
L	17.90	26.08	1.57	24.63	70.18	29.82
Total	5.38	6.78	1.03	8.84	22.03	77.97

Source: Computed from NSO (1999).

machinery and equipment, insulated wire and cable, electrical equipment and components, precision instruments, watches and clocks, and miscellaneous products. They are mostly labor-intensive, traditional exporting industries.

Exporting industries where large firms dominate the industries' employment were office machinery and equipment, electronic parts and components, radio and television, electrical machinery, and transport equipment. Most of these industries are new exports in the last decade with production techniques more capital-intensive than the traditional ones.

Subcontracting and commission work

Small-and medium-sized firms generally have more subcontracting work than large firms. Data for 1999 show that on average across all industries, receipts from subcontracting work in small, medium, and large firms were 3.3, 2.8, and 1.4 of sales volume, respectively.[9] Subcontracting work was concentrated in the following industries: textile products, clothing, leather products, wood products, furniture, paper products, publishing, printing, plastic products, nonmetallic mineral products, metal products, electrical machinery, and automobile parts.

Among industries, subcontracting work was most concentrated in clothing, wood products, plastic products, nonmetallic mineral products, and nonelectrical machinery and equipment. They were mostly labor-intensive and low-technology small- and medium-sized industries that produced either products that did not compete with imports or products for export.

There were some products in the groups of textile products, publishing and printing, electronic and electrical machinery and equipment, and transport equipment industries with subcontracting work available for small- and medium-sized firms. Larger-sized firms often performed commission work. Many of these products were in the so-called supporting industries where small- and medium-sized firms had linkages with large firms, but firms in the supporting industries were not necessarily small or medium sizes.

Examples of these supporting industries are found in automobile parts and electronic parts and components industries that produce intermediate goods for further processing in large assembly plants of the automobile s and electronics industries. For example, large firms, instead of producing parts and components in-house, will order them from a subcontracting firm so as to gain from the subcontractor's specialization and from the division of labor in the industry. These subcontracting firms are generally smaller than the parent firms that offer the production orders. In Thailand, a study by UNICO International Corporation (1995) found that just over 50 percent of these firms in Thailand were small- and medium-sized firms employing fewer than 200 workers. However, the other half were larger firms size. Before the crisis, firms in these supporting industries obtained much government promotion because high linkages between large and small- and medium-sized firms existed in these industries.

2. Capital intensity, technical efficiency, and TFP

The analysis of production techniques, technical efficiency, and total factor productivity (TFP) of small- and medium-sized firms is based on the NSO's 1997 census data. Output is denoted by either value of production or value-added. Material inputs include value of raw materials, purchased parts and components, and procurement of intermediate inputs. Labor input is represented by number of workers, and capital input is net book value of fixed assets. Fixed assets include buildings, machinery and equipment, vehicles, and office appliances. Wages include wages and salaries, benefits, and other payments to employees.

Table IV shows capital intensity, wage rate, labor productivity, and capital productivity by size category. On average across all industries, capital intensity, wage rate, and labor productivity (either output or value-added per worker) increased with size monotonically. But, as firm size increased, capital productivity (either output or value-added per unit of capital input) declined. In almost all industries, wage rate rose less than labor productivity as firm size increased.

In a majority of industries, small firms had the lowest capital intensity, lowest wage rate, lowest labor productivity, and highest capital productivity. Large firms had the opposite characteristics.

TABLE IV
Factor intensity, factor prices, and partial factor productivities by firm size group

Size	K/L	O/K	W/L	O/L	VA/L	VA/K
S	142,296.60	4.42	62,393.03	628,598.90	201,987.97	1.42
M	274,153.94	3.66	85,695.66	1,004,405.09	282,522.28	1.03
L	481,504.21	3.18	107,302.68	1,530,169.90	425,434.95	0.88
Total	394,333.28	3.31	96,928.71	1,303,541.25	366,749.90	0.93

Source: Computed from NSO (1999).
Note: O, for output; VA, value-added; M, material inputs; L, labor; K, capital; W, wage rate.

However, although medium-sized firms had higher capital intensity, wage rate, and labor productivity, but lower capital productivity than small-sized firms, the differences were smaller than the differences between the medium-size firms and the large firms.

In industries that are the most highly capital intensive, the capital intensity and the wage rates of small- and medium-sized firms were much lower than those of large firms. These industries were tobacco, beverages, paper and paper products, petroleum products, basic chemicals, glass and glass products, metal casting, fabricated metal products, and motor vehicles and most likely need scale economies to be efficient. In fact, the output of these industries was dominated by the production of large firms. In these industries, small- and medium-sized firms were able to coexist with large firms probably because the smaller size firms produced products of different characteristics or quality. In these industries, a study at a more disaggregated level of industrial classification will provide a better comparison of the characteristics of firms of different sizes.

There is another group of industries where capital–labor ratios did not vary much across size groups: textile products, clothing, footwear, leather products, wood and wood products, rubber products, plastic products, and furniture. Most of these industries were the least capital intensive and had above average export–output ratios. Because their capital intensity was not drastically different for firms of different sizes, large firms simply had large scale production and employment without significantly altering the production technique.

We examine how efficient Thailand's small- and medium-sized firms used their resources in the production of their outputs by measuring both technical efficiency and total factor productivity of firms of different size groups by using the 1997 industrial census data disaggregated at the 3-digit ISIC level. Technical efficiency indices are estimated by using frontier translog production functions. Total factor productivity indices are in turn computed directly from the definition.

Our estimation of technical efficiency is based on the concept and the estimation of the production frontier: maximum possible output for a given set of inputs. A firm in an industry can produce on or below the production possibility frontier. An efficient firm produces on the frontier whereas a technically inefficient firm produces below the maximum output on the production frontier.

The production function is specified in the following form:

$$\begin{aligned}\ln Y = {} & \ln A + \alpha_K \ln K + \alpha_L \ln L + \\ & \alpha_M \ln M + \frac{1}{2}\beta_{KK} (\ln K)^2 + \\ & \frac{1}{2}\beta_{LL} (\ln L)^2 + \frac{1}{2}\beta_{MM} (\ln M)^2 + \\ & \gamma_{KL} (\ln K)(\ln L) + \gamma_{KM} (\ln K)(\ln M) + \\ & \gamma_{LM} (\ln L)(\ln M) + \ln u\end{aligned}$$

where Y denotes real output, and K, L, and M represent capital, labor, and intermediate inputs, respectively. A is a constant term, and u is the error term. The error term is assumed to have the Gamma distribution with mean and variance equal to n. Richmond (1974) has shown that firm-specific efficiency measurement can be estimated by $\hat{Y}/Y$ and the average efficiency of the industrial sector level is equal to 2^{-n}.

In estimating the above frontier production

functions, we use cross-sectional data of 59 industries where the data of each industry are separated into three groups by size: small, medium, and large. Therefore, we are able to estimate the frontier production functions of industries separately for each size category. In other words, for all industry there is a single frontier for each size category and in the case of all industries, for all size categories.[10]

Our estimation results show that technical efficiency level of Thailand's industries in 1997 was approximately equal to 87.7 percent. Firms of different sizes had different efficiency levels. The efficiency indices of small, medium, and large firms were 87.9, 87.3, and 86.1, respectively. Although it is not possible to compare the indices across size groups, we can infer the room for improving the efficiency level of each group of firms. The room for improvement for firms of each group was not much different. In other words, both small- and medium-sized firms did not seem to operate less closer to their best observed performance (or the production possibility frontier) than larger firms did. Therefore, no evidence that small- and medium-sized firms are technically inefficient is found in our study. The fact that small- and medium-sized firms had an average efficiency greater than 87 percent indicated that their observed output constituted more than 87 percent of their maximum potential output given by the best observed performance of the industries. However, there remains room for further improvement in the performance of these firms. All can increase their output up to 13 percent through more efficient use of their given inputs and, therefore, provide a greater contribution to industrial growth.

Another method for assessing industrial performance of firms of different size groups is by computing TFP indices. The following measurement is modified from Ho (1980).

$$\frac{TFP_{ij}}{TFP_i} = \prod_{k=1}^{3} \left[\frac{PFP_{ijk}}{PFP_{ik}}\right]^{\alpha_{ijk}}, \quad \sum_{k=1}^{3} \alpha_{ijk} = 1$$

where

TFP_{ij} is the total factor productivity of j-th size group in the i-th industry;

$j = S, M, L$, and $i = 1, 2, \ldots, 59$;

TFP_i is the total factor productivity of firms of all sizes in the i-th industry;

PFP_{ijk} is the partial factor productivity of the k-th factor input of products of firm of the j-th size group in the i-th industry;

k is raw materials, labor, and capital inputs;

PFP_{ik} is the partial factor productivity of the k-th factor input of firms of all size groups in the i-th industry

and α_{ijk} is the factor share of the k-th factor of production of firms of the j-th size group in the i-industry

When the relative TFP measure equals one, it means that the total factor productivity of firms in the i-th size group equals the average total factor productivity for all firms in the industry. If the ratio is greater than one, then it means that the relative TFP of firms of the relevant size is larger than the average TFP of the whole industry.

For the entire industrial sector, small firms had a relative TFP greater than one whereas both medium and large firms both had relative TFP measures just about equal to one. Table V shows that small firms' relative TFP index was the highest at 1.03, followed by the TFP of medium-sized firms equal to 1.0, and the TFP of large firms equal to 0.99.

Out of 59 industries, in 25 industries small firms had the highest TFP indices, followed by 19 and 15 for medium and large firms, respectively. This shows that both small- and medium-sized firms did not perform worse than large firms. However, a qualification needs to be made that the differences in TFP between small- and medium-sized firms and large firms comes from the fact that the capital productivity of small- and medium-sized firms was much greater than that of large firms. Note that the capital input is represented by the net book value of fixed assets that includes

TABLE V
Total factor productivity indices by firm size group

Size	O/M	O/L	O/K	TFP
S	1.47	628.6	4.42	1.03
M	1.39	1,004.4	3.66	1.00
L	1.39	1,530.2	3.18	0.99

Source: Computed from NSO (1999).

tangible fixed assets but excludes rented assets. As it is likely that there were more small firms with rented fixed assets for production than large firms, the estimated capital input used in the small firms could be underestimated and, hence, the TFP overestimated. Furthermore, if smaller firms had older assets than large firms, their low book value of fixed assets would underestimate capital inputs, and therefore overestimate TFP of small when compared with large firms.[11]

If we divide industries into three groups (i.e., those predominated by small, medium, and large firms), and compute the relative TFP index of each group, then we obtain the results shown in Tables VI and VII. In the group of industries dominated by small firms, small firms had the highest TFP index. In the group of medium-sized industries, both small- and medium-sized firms performed better than larger firms. Finally, in the group of large industries it was the large firms that performed the best. This follows very well with the expectation that in the various groups of industries, firms with the same size as the predominant size in the group should be more productive than others to explain why that size was found most often in that group.

Another interesting finding (see Table VIII) is that although in most industries TFP of small- and medium-sized firms were not lower than TFP of large firms, small-scale industries (industries dominated by small firms) had lower TFP than medium and large-scale industries. The medium-

TABLE VI
Total factor productivity indices by firm size group (three inputs)

Firm size	Small-scale industry				Medium-scale industry				Large-scale industry			
	O/M	O/L	O/K	TFP	O/M	O/L	O/K	TFP	O/M	O/L	O/K	TFP
S	1.52	689.5	4.31	1.08	1.44	556.3	5.19	1.01	1.43	640.6	3.69	0.97
M	1.38	1,120.2	4.05	1.04	1.39	903.9	4.28	1.01	1.41	1,078.2	2.8	0.95
L	1.33	1,920.2	3.04	0.99	1.36	1,229.8	3.75	1.00	1.42	1,596.2	3.01	1.01

Source: Computed from NSO (1999).

TABLE VII
Total factor productivity indices by firm size group (two inputs)

Firm size	Small-scale industry			Medium-scale industry			Large-scale industry		
	VA/L	VA/K	TFP	VA/L	VA/K	TFP	VA/L	VA/K	TFP
S	235.9	1.48	1.30	170.0	1.59	1.05	193.2	1.11	0.91
M	310.9	1.12	1.14	252.1	1.19	1.04	311.1	0.81	0.85
L	474.4	0.75	0.95	322.8	0.98	0.99	473.3	0.89	1.02

Source: Computed from NSO (1999).

TABLE VIII
Total factor productivity indices of small, medium, and large-scale industries

Industry	Three Inputs				Two Inputs		
	O/M	O/L	O/K	TFP	VA/L	VA/K	TFP
Small scale	1.36	1,403.3	3.32	0.99	372.2	0.88	0.96
Medium scale	1.37	1,046.7	3.94	1.00	282.1	1.06	1.00
Large scale	1.42	1,470.2	3.01	1.00	435.1	0.89	1.00

Source: Computed from NSO (1999).

scale industries had about the same level of TFP as the large industries.

If we further group the industries by trade category (export oriented, import substitution, and nonimport-substitution[12])and compute the relative TFP index of each group, we find the results shown in Tables IX and X. In the group of export-oriented industries, small firms had the highest TFP index (1.09), followed by medium (1.02) and large firms (0.99), respectively. In both the groups of import-substitution and nonimport substitution industries, it was the large firms that had the highest relative TFP index, followed by the medium and small firms, respectively.

It should be noted that most nonexport-oriented industries are capital intensive, and firms in these industries probably need to expand their capacity to a certain size to become efficient. Meanwhile, export-oriented industries are very labor intensive, and the issue of firm size does not matter much. The export capabilities of these industries depend on their choice of production techniques rather than firm size.

3. Problems and needs of SMEs

Table XI shows a list of problems faced by firms of different sizes. About 65 percent of firms of all sizes admitted having problems in the areas of availability or prices of raw materials, labor, capital, demand, and government policies. The most frequent complaints were insufficient capital (high interest rates) and labor shortage (increased real wage rate), followed by marketing problems, uncertain government policies, and raw material shortages.

Small firms complained the most about the problem of insufficient capital. Their next most important problems were labor shortages and marketing. Medium-sized firms ranked insufficient capital and labor shortages as their first and second most important problems just as small firms did. However, they chose uncertain government policies as the third most important problem. Large firms mentioned labor shortages (high wages) as the most important problem, followed by uncertain government policies, and raw material shortages. The problems of insufficient capital and marketing were found to be less important when compared with small- and medium-sized firms.

TABLE IX
Total factor productivity indices of industries by trade category by and firm size group (three inputs)

Firm size	Export-oriented industry				Import-substitution industry				Non-import substitution industry			
	O/M	O/L	O/K	TFP	O/M	O/L	O/K	TFP	O/M	O/L	O/K	TFP
S	1.47	619.0	5.22	1.09	1.42	761.0	4.07	0.97	1.60	502.7	3.07	0.91
M	1.39	813.1	4.14	1.02	1.37	1,473.3	3.35	0.99	1.48	955.1	3.01	0.94
L	1.35	1,120.3	3.51	0.99	1.36	2,780.0	3.02	1.00	1.64	1,810.7	2.58	1.02

Source: Computed from NSO (1999).

TABLE X
Total factor productivity indices of industries by trade category and by firm size group (two inputs)

Firm size	Export-oriented industry			Import-substitution industry			Non-import substitution industry		
	VA/L	VA/K	TFP	VA/L	VA/K	TFP	VA/L	VA/K	TFP
S	198.3	1.67	1.34	223.4	1.19	0.90	189.0	1.15	0.77
M	228.8	1.17	1.06	398.3	0.91	0.96	308.2	0.97	0.84
L	291.4	0.91	0.97	736.3	0.80	1.02	706.8	1.01	1.06

Source: Computed from NSO (1999).

TABLE XI
Percentage distribution of number of firms by economic problem and by firm size group

Size	Labor shortage	Raw material shortage	Insufficient capital	Marketing	Uncertain government policies	Others
S	37.27	15.94	38.48	22.76	17.34	7.71
M	29.07	19.11	29.51	21.08	14.60	9.87
L	28.64	21.79	22.31	14.28	26.59	11.33

Source: Computed from NSO (1999).

In other words, problems of insufficient capital and marketing decreased with size. Problems of raw material shortages and adverse effects of government policies increased with size. However, the problem of labor shortages seemed to be considered as the first or the second most important by firms of all sizes.

This means that before Thailand's financial crisis, the problem of increased real wages (labor shortages) seemed to be a concern for firms of all industries and all sizes. The problems of unavailability of capital and marketing were more serious in small- and medium-sized firms than in large firms. Large firms were able to raise funds from commercial banks, financial institutions, and other sources more easily than small- and medium-sized firms. However, large firms faced problems of raw material prices (likely due to tariffs on intermediate products) and government policies and measures.

Although on average across all industries, the problem of government policies increased with size, there were only 31 out of 59 industries where the problem of government policies increased with size. For the rest of the industries, small- and medium-sized industries had problems with government policies just as large firms did.

Table XII shows the results of firm interviews by NSO in 1996 regarding the various kinds of support industrial firms needed from the government. Most firms gave reduced interest rate or increased supply of cheaper loans the highest priority, followed by reduced import tariffs, marketing and export promotion, and provision of training courses. However, the order of importance is different for firms of different size groups. For small firms, the order of importance went from reduced interest rate (greater supply of loans) to reduced tariffs and then to marketing promotion. For medium-sized firms, it went from reduced tariffs to reduced interest rate (greater supply of loans) and then to marketing promotion. The government support measures that large firms needed the most were reduced tariffs, followed by reduced interest rates and the availability of training courses.

The order of the needs for government support of firms by size group seems to be consistent with their complaints about problems they faced during operations. That is, most small firms complained about the problems of high interest rates, and, therefore, what they needed the most from the government was to make plenty of loans available for them. As firm size increased, the problem of financing fell to second place in importance, but the problems of high tariffs (particularly on raw

TABLE XII
Percentage distribution of number of firms by need of support and by firm size group

Size	Training	National resource development	Import tax reduction	Interest rate reduction	Marketing promotion	Others
S	22.07	12.18	29.94	44.11	24.14	5.27
M	26.48	16.81	46.16	42.74	29.05	5.12
L	31.16	18.45	55.86	42.45	30.53	6.29

Source: Computed from NSO (1999).

materials) and labor training increased. Government support for marketing and export promotion seemed to be more urgently needed in small- and medium-sized firms than in large firms.

The need for training facilities was the most prominent in textiles, clothing, non-electrical machinery and equipment, electronic parts and components, electrical goods, motor vehicles, and other capital-intensive heavy industries. In addition this need was equally important in firms of all sizes in these industries. In other words, this need is industry-specific, and it is applicable to all firms of all sizes in the same industries.

At the other end, the need for lower interest rates or increased supply of loans seemed to be shared by all industries, but more urgently needed by small firms than by large firms. Finally, the need for tariff reduction was listed as important in all industries and all firm sizes.

4. Concluding remarks

Small- and medium-sized companies form the majority of the country's industrial firms. They are labor intensive, have low import content of raw material inputs, and can link with large firms by subcontracting work for them. Not all small- and medium-sized firms are less technically efficient or less productive than large firms. The number of small-sized firms is also found to grow the fastest during the slow real income growth period. In this sense, one might view SMEs, particularly the especially small ones, as a cushion against low employment during difficult times. SMEs could create employment for former employees of failed firms, and at the same time prepare new entrepreneurs who might graduate to run large firms in better times.

However, in normal times not all small- and medium-sized firms are capable of generating more employment than large firms. Rather, it depends on the production techniques firms use. For labor-intensive export-oriented industries, firms will be able to generate high employment regardless of size. For capital-intensive industries, most small firms are less productive than large firms, and their expansion will not be able to generate high employment despite the large number of small firms.

Acknowledgements

I am indebted to Shujiro Urata, Farrukh Iqbal, and Migara De Silva who were helpful in their comments and managing this research project. I am particularly grateful to Albert Berry who made detailed comments and suggestions on an earlier draft. I also benefited from the comments of Carl Liedholm, Jeffrey Nugent, Rajah Rasiah, and other participants in the project on The Role of Small and Medium Enterprises in Development organized by World Bank Institute.

Notes

[1] It should be noted that different data sources from the MOI, the MOL, and the NSO define firm size differently. The MOL classifies firms into four groups: 1–9, 10–49, 50–299, and more than 300 workers and defines them as micro, small, medium, and large firms, respectively. The MOI classifies the firms into three groups: 1–49, 50–199, and more than 200 workers. Finally, the NSO classifies the firms into three groups: 10–49, 50–199, and more than 200 workers. The figures from these sources also show many variations. The number of firms in the group of 1-49 workers from the MOL dataset is about 80 percent of the number of firms of the same size group from the MOI data source, but the numbers of workers of firms from the two sources are about equal. Strangely, both the number of firms and the number of workers of firms in the size group of more than 300 workers from the MOL are greater than the number of firms and the number of workers in the size group of more than 200 workers from the MOI data source. This alerts us to be cautious with the use of data from different sources. Moreover, we may interpret the discrepancies to mean that the number of firms and employment of the micro- and small-sized firms from the MOL data source could be understated. Meanwhile, the number of firms and employment of large firms could be overstated. Fortunately, in our study we are interested in growth rates of the number of firms and employment rather than the exact values. Therefore, these possible biases should not affect much of our discussion as long as they are systematic over time.

[2] The comparison of data from the MOL, the MOI, and the NSO shows that while the numbers of firms and employment of firms with more than 200 workers from the NSO are about the same as the number from the MOI, the number in the small and medium-sized groups from the NSO are only about 70 percent of the number from the MOI. This means that if the MOI dataset were used as the benchmark for all comparisons, the NSO data could be understated in the groups of small- and medium-sized firms. We need to be cautious with the use of these data in the measurement of levels.

[3] We have mentioned earlier that while the employment figures of firms with size 1–50 workers for 1991–96 from the MOL dataset are close to the MOI figures, the number of establishments of firms of this size group from the MOL are

only about 80 percent as large as the number from the MOI data source. Therefore, it is possible to suspect that the number of firms of this size group from the MOL data source is underestimated. However, since the MOL dataset does not disaggregate the figures of firms with size 1-50 workers into micro industries (1–10 workers) and small-sized industries (10–50 workers), we are unable to know whether the underestimation of the MOL data comes from the group of micro industries or small-sized industries. Nevertheless, as Albert Berry commented as a discussant of this paper, the number of firms in the micro-industry category reported by the MOL seems rather low. We might postulate that the underestimation comes from figures in the micro-industry group.

[4] See Cortes, Berry and Ishaq (1987) for a discussion on why factors such as economic growth, existence of scale economies, and infrastructural improvement might explain the decline of firms in this micro-industry group over time.

[5] Owing to data limitations, we are, unfortunately, not able to decompose the growth of numbers of firms and employment of each size group into different sources of growth; that is, net creation of new firms (new firm entry minus the exit of existing firms) and number of firms graduating from a smaller size into a larger size group.

[6] During 1987–90, industrial production grew the fastest of the overall period of 1987–96 at 16.6 percent a year. During 1990–95, industrial production grew at a slower rate than the previous subperiod, and the growth rate was 11.2 percent a year. Finally, during 1996–97, the period before Thailand's financial crisis, the growth rate declined to 7.3 percent. These growth rates are computed from the National Economic and Social Development Board real value-added figures obtained from Bank of Thailand (various issues).

[7] According to Mead and Liedholm (1998), in times of recession firm exits increase and existing firms retrench workers. Usually the unemployed are forced to start new small businesses for survival despite the low rate of investment returns.

[8] Notice that employment growth rates computed from the MOL dataset are relatively high when compared with the National Economic and Social Development Board's industrial production growth rates. However, we do not need to combine these growth rates in our present analysis. Here we are only concerned with the relationship between the fluctuations of output growth and the growth of number of firms and employment.

[9] These figures of subcontracting work in total sales are lower than the figures in the Tambunlertchai and others (1986) study. However, while it is possible that the NSO figures could be underestimated, figures from this study could also be overestimated because their survey deliberately selected firms with subcontracting arrangements located in Bangkok and the neighboring provinces. The NSO figures are the average for all firms of all locations. It should also be noted here that Tambunlertchai and others (1986) find that subcontracting arrangements in Thailand started in the late 1970s, and there was little increase in the arrangements in the early 1980s. During the high output and export growth period in the decade before 1997, other studies suggest increases in subcontracting of small- and medium-sized firms from large export-oriented firms producing labor-intensive products such as garments, wood products, and jewelry. However, major industries such as automobile and electrical machinery and electronics industries did not seem to be able to subcontract out a large fraction of their parts and components input to local suppliers. Wiboonchutikula (1993) finds that they continued to rely on imported materials because local firms had not solved the problems of quality, reliability, and timely delivery. A small fraction of inputs that they subcontracted out were mostly non-specialized products in the paper products, metal products, and plastic products industries.

[10] A better study could be done if firm level data of each industry were available. Unfortunately, the NSO is reluctant to release these unpublished data for our study.

[11] I am indebted to Tom Connelly of Chulalongkorn University for suggesting an additional source of possible biases of TFP estimates of the small-sized firms.

[12] Import-substitution industries are defined as industries that import more than 10 percent of domestic utilization. Those that export more than 10 percent of their production are categorized as exportables. The rest of the traded goods are called nonimport-substitution industries.

References

Acs, Z. J., 1996, 'Small Firms and Economic Growth', in P. H. Admiraal (ed.), *Small Business in the Modern Economy*, Cambridge, MA: Blackwell.

Advanced Group Research, 1997, 'Small-and Medium-Sized Industries in Thailand', Report. Ministry of Industry, Bangkok [in Thai].

Akrasanee, N., V. Avilasakul and T. Chudasring, 1986, 'Financial Factors Relating to Small-and Medium Business Improvement in Thailand', in K. James and N. Akrasanee (eds.), *Small-and Medium Business Improvement in the ASEAN Region: Financial Factors*, Singapore: Institute of Southeast Asian Studies.

Bank of Thailand, *Monthly Bulletin*, various issues.

Berry, A. and D. Mazumdar, 1991, 'Small-Scale Industry in the Asian-Pacific Region', *Asian Pacific Economic Literature* **5**(2), 35–67.

Chiemprapha, C., 1993, 'The Development of TCC and Regional Chambers in Thailand with Particular Reference to the SMEs Supporting Activities', paper prepared for ZDH-Technonet Asia Project Review Conference, Singapore.

Cortes, M., A. Berry and A. Ishag, 1987, *Success In Small-and Medium-Scale Enterprises*, New York: Oxford University Press.

De Silva, Migara, 1998, 'SME Experience in East Asia: Cases of Japan, Republic of Korea and Taiwan', paper presented at the First Workshop on the Role of SMEs in Economic Development, San Francisco, CA.

Ho, S., 1980, 'Small-Scale Enterprises in Korea and Taiwan', Staff Working Paper 384. World Bank, Washington DC.

ILO, 1993, 'Development of Provincial Small- and Medium-Sized Enterprises: Thailand', Report, International Labor Office, Bangkok.

Kittiprapas, S. and P. McCann, 1999, 'Industrial Location Behavior and Regional Restructuring Within the Fifth

Tiger Economy: Evidence from the Thai Electronics Industry', *Applied Economics* **31**(1), 35–49.

Levy, B., 1994, 'Technical and Marketing Support Systems for Successful Small-and Medium-Sized Enterprises in four Countries', Policy Research Working Paper 1400. World Bank, Washington, DC.

Liedholm, C. and D. C. Mead, 1987, 'Small Scale Industries in Developing Countries: Empirical Evidence and Policy Implications', MSU International Development Paper 9. Michigan State University, East Lansing.

Little, I. M. D., D. Mazumdar and J. M. Page, 1987, *Small Manufacturing Enterprises: A Comparative Analysis of India and Other Economies*, New York: Oxford University Press.

Mead D. C. and C. Liedholm, 1998, 'The Dynamics of Micro and Small Enterprises in Developing Countries', *World Development.* **26**(1), 61–74.

Ministry of Labor and Social Welfare, *Yearbook of Labor Statistics*, various issues.

Muller, E., 1993, 'The Development of FTI and Regional FTI Clubs in Thailand with Particular Reference to SMEs', Paper presented at ZDH-Technonet Asia Project Review Conference, Singapore.

NSO, 1999, *Report of the 1997 Industrial Census, Whole Kingdom*, Bangkok, National Statistical Office.

Richmond, J., 1974, 'Estimating the Efficiency of Production', *International Economic Review* **15**(2), 515–521.

Sanguanruang S., S. Tambunlertchai and N. Sammapan, 1977, *Study of Small-and Medium Scale Industries in Thailand*, Bangkok: National Institute of Development Administration and Thammasat University [in Thai].

Tambunlertchai, S., W. Charmonman, S. Thitasajja and S. Thammavitikul, 1986, *Small- and Medium-Scale Industries in Thailand and Subcontracting Arrangements*, Tokyo: Institute of Developing Economies.

TDRI, 1990, *Rural Industry and Employment Project*, Bangkok: Thailand Development Research Institute.

UNICO International Corporation, 1995, 'Supporting Industries in Thailand', Report submitted to Japan International Cooperation Agency (JICA) and Ministry of Industry, Bangkok.

Wiboonchutikula, P., 1989, 'Technology Transfer in Small- and Medium-Scale Industries', paper prepared for ESCAP, Bangkok.

Wiboonchutikula, P., 1990, *Household Demand for Goods Produced by Rural Industry*, Bangkok: Thailand Development Research Institute.

Wiboonchutikula, P., 1993, 'Developing a Technology-Intensive Industry in Thailand: Computers and Their Peripherals', *Chulalongkorn Journal of Economics* **5**(2), 183–217.

Wiboonchutikula, P., R. Chintayarangsan and N. Thongpakde, 1989, 'Trade in Manufactured Goods and Mineral Products', Background Paper 4. The 1989 TDRI Year-End Conference, Thailand Development Research Institute, Bangkok.

Small Firm Dynamics: Evidence from Africa and Latin America

Carl Liedholm

ABSTRACT. This paper investigates the determinants of survival and growth among small and very small enterprises in Africa and Latin America. Location is found to be an important factor. Firms located in urban and commercial areas are more likely to survive during a given year than those located in rural areas or those being operated out of home. Urban and commercial location is also associated with faster growth, as measured by the number of employees hired in a given year. Studies are also cited to show that human capital matters, especially when it is in the form of vocational training or prior business experience.

1. Introduction

This paper examines the recent evidence from Africa and Latin America on the dynamic role of micro and small enterprises (MSEs). The contribution of MSEs in generating employment and income has become increasingly recognized around the world. To some observers, this is an encouraging sign: markets are working, and people are finding opportunities to participate in ways that empower and nourish many, particularly including those who are otherwise most disadvantaged. To other observers, however, this increase in the number of people engaged in micro and small enterprises is a sign of a failure of the economy to provide productive jobs; that is, people are forced to take refuge in activities that provide only minimal, subsistence support. Sorting out these differences is of great importance to those who wish to address the problems of poverty and growth.

Until recently, however, relatively little has been known about the dynamic contributions of MSEs. Such enterprises typically are hidden from view and easily elude the standard statistical nets. Although baseline surveys of MSEs have enabled static portraits of these enterprises to be drawn for many years, the surveys have shed little light on MSE's dynamic properties.

There is a growing interest in micro-level studies of firm dynamics. A recent review of the subject (Caves, 1998) highlights the outpouring of dynamic studies in the past decade, but notes that "the bulk of the research pertains to the United States and Canada" (p. 1948). Yet, a sizeable number of studies using new survey techniques have been conducted outside of the United States and Canada that can now provide new illumination concerning the patterns of enterprise births, survival or closure, and growth, along with the determinants of these change components. This paper will report on the findings of those dynamic studies that have been undertaken in Africa and Latin America.[1]

Among the data collection innovations that have enabled such studies to be undertaken in these areas have been the introduction of "closed" MSE surveys, continuous panel surveys, "tracer" surveys of MSEs that existed in the past, and modified baseline surveys that provide information concerning the growth of enterprises since its startup. Modified baseline surveys along with closed enterprise surveys were conducted in the Dominican Republic and in five countries in eastern and southern Africa: Botswana, Kenya, Malawi, Swaziland, and Zimbabwe. These surveys were all national in coverage and were based on a complete enumeration of all enterprises those areas (or clusters) chosen by stratified random sampling techniques. Modified baseline surveys, but without the closed enterprise surveys, were undertaken in Lesotho, Jamaica, and South Africa (two townships only). Panel surveys were con-

Department of Economics
Michigan State University
101 Marshall Hall
East Lansing
MI 48824
U.S.A.

Small Business Economics **18**: 227–242, 2002.

ducted in Jamaica, the Dominican Republic, Kenya, and Zimbabwe, and tracer surveys were executed in Nigeria, Kenya, and Sierra Leone.[2]

The universe of enterprises covered in these surveys includes all enterprises engaged in non-primary activities (i.e., excluding agriculture, forestry, hunting and fishing, and mining and quarrying, but including the transformation, transport, and marketing of primary products), where at least 50 percent of the output is sold (i.e., excluding products made primarily for home consumption), and engaging up to 50 workers (including unpaid family members, working proprietors, apprentices, and part-time workers). This means that this definition of micro and small enterprises (MSEs) encompasses establishments consisting of one person weaving baskets for sale in the market, and also includes factories with 40 or 50 workers using complex machinery. Microenterprises cover the smaller end of the MSE range; that is, enterprises with 10 or fewer workers.

The outline of this paper is as follows. A brief static picture of MSEs in Africa and Latin America that emerge from these surveys will be presented first. A dynamic overview of MSEs in these areas follows next, highlighting the new evidence on the turbulent process of MSE creation and closure as well as MSE expansion. The interrelationships between MSEs and the macroeconomy will then be explored. An examination of the policy implications will conclude the paper.

2. Static profile

The existing structure of MSEs provides a useful context for examining dynamic issues. Since much of this information is somewhat familiar by now, only the major features need be highlighted.

Magnitude

A key finding from the house-to-house baseline surveys is that the micro and small enterprise sector is far larger than is reported in most official statistics, which often cover only registered firms. In nation-wide surveys, the share of households reporting that some member of the household operated a micro or small enterprise ranged from about 20 percent in Botswana to over 40 percent in Malawi and Kenya. Survey results reveal that 17–27 percent of the working age population are employed in MSEs (see Table I for all aspects of this static overview). Employment densities – the number of people engaged in MSE activities per 1,000 persons in the population – ranged from 70 to 90 in Botswana, Kenya, Lesotho, and Malawi to well over 100 in Zimbabwe, Swaziland, the Dominican Republic, and Swaziland. The estimated MSE employment in the surveyed African countries is nearly twice the level of total employment in registered large-scale enterprises and the public sector.[3] Clearly, micro and small enterprises are a major source of livelihood for a significant proportion of the population in these areas.

Size distribution of MSEs

Most MSEs are very small. Typically, the majority of MSEs consist of one person working alone (see Table I). Self-employment is thus a central element in these economies. If one defines the MSE universe as those firms with 1–50 workers, the upper end of the tail – those with 10–50 workers – constitute less than 2 percent of the businesses in virtually all the surveyed countries in Africa. The Dominican Republic, however, does not fit this pattern, with a substantially smaller number of sole proprietorships and with a larger number at the upper portion of the small enterprise spectrum.

Labor force characteristics

The MSE labor force in the region is made up primarily of working proprietors and unpaid family members. With the majority of enterprises operating as one-person undertakings, it is not surprising that the largest employment category is working proprietors, a group that comprises more than half the MSE work force in most countries. When unpaid family members are added, the numbers reach three-fourths of the workers in most places. Only in a few countries do hired workers comprise as much as 20 percent of the MSE labor force. The two Latin American countries and Botswana stand out in this regard, and in in those countries a third or more of the labor force is made up of hired workers. Trainees and apprentices add a significant share of workers in some locations, particularly in West Africa; in

TABLE I
Characteristics of microenterprises

	Botswana	Kenya	Lesotho	Malawi	Swaziland	Zimbabwe	South Africa	Jamaica	Dominican Republic
MSE									
Employment/population age 15–64 (%)	17	18	17	23	26	27	na	na	19
MSE employment per 1,000 persons in the population	71	83	84	92	118	127	81	na	109
Share of all MSEs that are one-person enterprises (%)	65	47	79	61	69	69	47	62	22
Share of all MSEs with 10–50 workers (%)	3	2	1	1	2	2	1	2	18
Share of hired workers (%)	39	24	10	18	15	16	19	33	36
Locational breakdown of MSE employment (%)									
Urban areas	24	15	18	12	25	30	na	26	46
Rural towns	28	7	10	4	10	6	na	13	18
Rural areas	48	78	72	84	65	64	na	36	36
Sectoral breakdown of enterprises: Urban areas only (%)									
Manufacturing	15	18	35	29	33	64	17	39	21
Commerce	71	74	41	62	56	30	70	61	63
Sectoral breakdown of enterprises: Rural areas only (%)									
Manufacturing	34	27	62	36	70	75	na	35	15
Commerce	64	66	27	60	24	16	na	65	75
Share of enterprises owned by females (%)	75	46	73	46	84	66	62	49	46
Share of all workers that are females (%)	67	40	76	40	78	57	78	52	38

Source: Liedholm and Mead (1999).

southern Africa, as in Latin America, apprentices constitute under 10 percent of the MSE labor force.

Location

Most MSEs in the region operate in rural areas. The share of all enterprises in urban locations, cities and towns with at least 20,000 inhabitants, reaches as high as 46 percent in the Dominican Republic, but was 30 percent or less in the other countries (see Table I). Even adding enterprises in rural towns – generally, concentrations with 2,000–20,000 persons – still generally leaves well over half the enterprises in strictly rural areas of most countries. It is important to keep these facts in mind since many programs focus on enterprises in urban areas, where they are often more obvious and easier to reach.

Composition of activities

While many MSEs in Africa and Latin America are engaged in trading, a significant number are involved in manufacturing activities. It is a common perception that micro and small enterprises are overwhelmingly made up of vendors and other small traders. There is some truth to this perception, since in the two Latin American countries and in several southern African countries the majority of enterprises are engaged in commerce. It is important to recognize, however, that in all countries small manufacturing activities are also an important component of the MSE sector. Manufacturing activities are particularly significant in rural areas. In fact, in each of the African countries manufacturing enterprises constitute a higher share of MSEs in rural than in urban areas. By contrast, manufacturing was more prevalent among urban enterprises in the two Latin American countries.

Three activities have consistently been identified as the most important categories among micro and small manufacturing enterprises: textiles and wearing apparel, food and beverages, and wood and forest products. Survey results suggest that these three categories comprise about 75 percent of manufacturing enterprises in urban areas of many developing countries and nearly 90 percent of the enterprises in rural areas. Yet these apparent regularities hide wide variations from country to country and between urban and rural areas as to which activity is most important, as well as the nature of the most prevalent activities within each of these three broadly defined sectoral groupings.

Gender

Large numbers of MSEs in Africa and Latin America are owned and operated by women. Indeed, it is a striking fact that in five of the nine countries women outnumber men as owners and operators of micro and small enterprises (see Table I). Furthermore, since working proprietors are the single largest category of the labor force, the great majority of workers in such enterprises are also women. MSEs headed by women tend to be concentrated in a relatively narrow band of sectors or activities, such as beer brewing, knitting, dressmaking, crocheting, cane work, and retail trading. Finally, MSE's headed by women are more likely than their male counterparts to operate from the home (Liedholm and Mead, 1997). Since it is the home-based MSEs that tend to be hidden and overlooked, women owners of MSEs are more likely to be "invisible entrepreneurs."

Market linkages

The market linkages between firms in Africa and Latin America are rather limited. The vast majority of MSEs in these areas sell directly to final consumers rather than to other firms. Results from the surveys in Malawi, Swaziland, and Zimbabwe, for example, reveal that over 96 percent of the MSEs sell primarily to individuals, while in Jamaica 87 percent of MSE output is sold directly to final consumers (Liedholm and Mead, 1999). These same studies have indicated that MSEs in these areas that sell to traders and manufacturing firms are more likely to grow than those that sell directly to final consumers.

Subcontracting and clustering are two institutional arrangements that can enable MSEs to move beyond a direct sale of their output to final consuming. Subcontracting has been much less prevalent in Africa and Latin America than in Asia. This may be due to the somewhat smaller markets as well as to the propensity of the larger firms to import a large share of their needed inputs (Liedholm and Mead, 1987). Examples of successful subcontracting efforts, however, have begun to surface in several African countries where commercial, market-based linkages have been forged between independent enterprises (Grierson et al., 1997). Many types of enterprise competence can be purchased in the market, and this should be encouraged and not stifled and undercut through subsidized provision of the same services by governments or NGOs.

There has also been a growing worldwide interest in clusters. A number of analysts have argued that these geographical concentrations of enterprises in related activities have provided significant benefits to those who participate in them (Van Dijk and Rabellotti, 1997). While the great advantages that some enterprises have derived from such networks have been acknowledged in other parts of the world, virtually no evidence of the advantages of such networks have emerged from the African and Latin American survey results to date (Liedholm and Mead, 1999). When the limited examples of clustering in Africa are described, they tend to involve independent firms in the same industry selling directly to final consumers. Parker (1994) contends that linkages between firms in these clusters tend to be minimal owing primarily to the low levels of trust that exist these areas.

Efficiency

Substantial differences in economic efficiency by enterprise size have been detected in earlier studies that have analyzed detailed sales and production costs of MSEs in several developing countries (Liedholm and Mead, 1987). In particular, the data indicate that returns per hour of family labor are significantly higher for enterprises with two to five workers when compared with enterprises with only one person working alone. This increase in economic returns continues for the next higher size group, those with six to nine workers. Thereafter, the number of observations is small and the results more ambiguous. Similar results were found in a recent survey of MSEs in Kenya (Daniels and Mead, 1998). In all of these studies, the data suggest that one-person enterprises generate the lowest returns to the enterprise; even a small increase in size is associated with a substantial increase in economic efficiency, which for these very small enterprises is closely associated with the level of income generated for those who work in the enterprise.

3. Dynamics of MSEs

Micro and small enterprises are constantly churning. Most of these changes are missed, however, if one focuses just on the aggregate changes in the level of MSE activity over time. It is only when the individual components of these changes are scrutinized that the magnitude of this churning becomes apparent. Not only are new firms being created (new starts or births) while others are closing, but existing (surviving) firms are expanding and contracting in size. These components of change are sometimes summarized in two concepts: net firm creation, which is new starts (births) minus closures (deaths), and "mobility" or net firm expansion, which is firm expansion less firm contraction. Since the individual components move in opposite directions, however, these aggregate or net measures of change mask the magnitude of the flux that is taking place among MSEs.

New MSE starts

The evidence on new business starts (firm creation) in Latin America and Africa has been virtually nonexistent until recently. New findings, which are summarized in Table II, on new business starts in six countries reveal that the rate of new MSE starts is substantial. The annual rate of MSE new starts in these survey countries averages over 20 percent, ranging in a narrow band from 19.3 percent in Zimbabwe to 25.2 percent in Botswana.[4] Although the figures are still somewhat crude in most cases, they are broadly indicative and, given the techniques used, provide *lower-bound* estimates of the orders of magnitude involved.[5] These surprisingly high figures are substantially above the 10 percent rate typically reported for small enterprises in industrialized countries.[6] The majority of the churning is taking place among the smallest firms.

Most of the new firms being created are one-person establishments. Not only is the new start rate higher for one-person firms than for larger

TABLE II
Annual MSE new starts rate by initial size, Africa and Latin America

Country	Year	Enterprise size (number of workers), %			
		1	2–9	10+	Overall average
Botswana	91	32.9	11.5	4.2	25.2
Kenya	92	33.7	10.3	1.6	21.2
Malawi	91	26.9	14.1	13.1	21.7
Swaziland	90	26.3	10.8	2.4	21.7
Zimbabwe	90	22.8	10.6	18.7	19.3
Dominican Republic	93	na	na	na	20.6
Average		28.5	11.5	8.0	21.6

Source: Computed from individual country survey data. Averages are unweighted across the six countries.

ones as revealed in Table II, but there are also typically more self-employed firms in existence. Not much is known about the central forces driving the MSE new start rate. A recent study by Daniels (1995) for MSE in Zimbabwe indicates that the determinants of new starts differ between high and low return (profit) activities. For high return activities, initial capital requirements, experience of entrepreneurs already in the industry, and level of regulation – all of which are barriers to entry – are found to be all inversely related to the new start rate. For low return activities, the rate of new starts is related (*inversely*) only to the aggregate level of economic activity; for these firms, the lower the level of aggregate economic activity, the higher the rate of new starts, reflecting the importance of the push-factor in firm creation.

An important implication of these findings is that there is no overall scarcity of entrepreneurs in the Schumpeterian sense of individuals willing to incur the risk of establishing a new venture. Most of these new starts are one-person firms, which are typically the least efficient and remunerative of the MSEs. These firms tend to enter in greater numbers when the overall economy is weak.

MSE closures

The information on business closure rates in Africa and Latin America is somewhat limited. The most accurate figures come from the Dominican Republic, where researchers returned to the same locations over time to record business closures. By using this approach, researchers found that closure rates exceeded 20 percent per year in the early 1990s.[7] The Dominican Republic findings, which are probably not atypical, highlight the extreme volatility of MSE activity, where simultaneously one large segment is starting just as another large segment is closing. Why do MSEs close? A somewhat surprising survey finding is that only a portion, frequently a minority, of the closures can be attributed to the traditional "business failure," where the firm is not financially or economically viable. Somewhat less than one-half of the MSE closures in the region were due to such "business failures." Lack of demand and shortage of working capital were the two most frequently mentioned underlying causes of these business failures.[8] Why then did economically viable enterprises close? Approximately one-quarter of the MSEs closed for "personal reasons," such as illness or retirement, while the remainder closed because of even "better options" or because the "government forced them to close."

When are MSEs most likely to close? Most closures occur in the early years of a firm's existence. In Botswana, Kenya, Swaziland, and Zimbabwe, over 50 percent of the MSE closures had occurred within three years of startup.[9] MSE closures peaked before the end of the first year in Botswana and Swaziland, and between years one and two in Kenya and Zimbabwe. Clearly, MSEs are particularly vulnerable during the fragile initial years when they are learning how to operate the business.

What are the characteristics of the MSEs that close and how, if at all, do these differ from the characteristics of the survivors? The results of systematic analyses of closure patterns of MSEs in Botswana, Malawi, Swaziland, Zimbabwe (McPherson, 1995), and the Dominican Republic (Cabal, 1995) make it possible to paint an initial portrait of the type of enterprise that is most likely to survive. These studies employ "hazard analysis" to ascertain the key factors that determine the closure and survival patterns of such enterprises. The dependent variable in this analysis is the "hazard rate," which is the probability that a firm will close during the given year. The independent variables used to explain this rate are such variables as the age, sector, and location of the firm. Econometric techniques are used to estimate the relationships.[10]

What are the key characteristics of MSEs that are most likely to survive? In addition to age, the past growth patterns, initial size, sector, location, and gender of the owner might be expected to play a role.

An important finding from these studies is the recognition that growing MSEs are more likely to survive than those that remained the same size. The results from Zimbabwe, for example, indicate that for every 1 percent increase in employment, the MSE reduced its likelihood of closing during the year by approximately 5 percent (McPherson, 1995). Such findings are consistent with the notion that expanding MSEs have become more efficient – or perhaps, were more efficient to start with – and are thus more able to survive.

Somewhat surprisingly, however, the expected direct relationship between the MSE's initial size and its survival chances that is predicted by Jovanovic's learning model of firm growth (Jovanovic, 1982) is not supported by the data. In the Dominican Republic (Cabal, 1995), Malawi, Swaziland, and Botswana (McPherson, 1995) enterprise size has no significant influence on firm survival. In Zimbabwe, however, a statistically significant inverse relationship exists; that is, firms that started the smallest, other factors being held constant, are more likely to survive than their counterparts that started larger. These findings indicate that smallness, by itself, is no impediment to survival in these countries.

Another key result is that MSE survival rates varies significantly by sector. Retail trading MSEs in all three countries faced the highest closure risks. Such firms were almost 30 percent more likely to close during the year, for example, than their counterparts in woodworking. Real estate, wood processing, wholesale traders, and non-metallic metal enterprises were the least likely to close, while trading, transport, and chemical MSEs were the most likely to do so.[11]

Location also plays a central role in determining MSE survival. Urban MSEs, for example, had an almost 25 percent greater chance of surviving the year, holding all other factors constant, than their counterparts in rural areas.[12] Moreover, MSEs located in commercial districts were more likely to survive than those operated out of the home. Proximity to growing markets would thus seem to be an important factor in enterprise survival.

Does the gender of the entrepreneur affect the survival chances of MSEs? Overall, female-headed MSEs were less likely to survive the year, all other factors constant, than their male-headed counterparts. Relatively high percentages of the closings of female-headed MSEs in these countries, however, were due to personal and other nonbusiness failure reasons. When only closings caused by pure business failures were analyzed separately, the gender of the entrepreneur was no longer found to be significant determinant. Thus, in terms of closings caused by business failures only, female-headed and male-headed MSEs were equally likely to survive.

MSE expansion

To these changes resulting from the establishment of new firms and the closure of others must be added the growth from the net expansion of existing enterprises over time. The net expansion depicts the expansion less the contraction of those MSEs that survive and summarizes two opposing dynamic forces at work.

The change in the number of workers since startup is the indicator typically used to measure the magnitude of the net expansion of MSEs. This measure tends to be favored because it is most easily and accurately remembered by the entrepreneur and does not need to be deflated.

Recent studies have begun to shed light on the types of biases that might arise from the use of employment as a measure of expansion rather than alternative indicators such as changes in sales, output, or assets. Parker's (1994) analysis of the growth in Kenyan MSEs, for example, indicated that net increases in real sales were almost double the growth in employment. A similar pattern was detected in the Jamaican Quarterly Panel Survey of MSEs (Gustafson and Liedholm, 1995), where the change in real sales was twice the change in employment. Such findings highlight the lumpy nature of employment, which appears to increase with a lag after a sizeable growth in real sales, and indicate that the employment growth measures provide a lower-bound estimate of net firm expansion.

The high overall growth rates exhibited by the existing (surviving) MSEs is one of the most striking findings to emerge from the various surveys. Table III reveals that the average annual compound employment growth rate since startup across these six countries was 13.6 percent per year.[13] The country variations around this average are large, however, ranging from 4 percent in Swaziland to 24 percent in Kenya. These high growth rates are all the more impressive when it is recognized that, except for Botswana, they are at least double the overall growth in GDP in these countries during the 1980s. Moreover, even in absolute terms, the annual number of jobs created per firm is impressive (see Table III, column 4).

These rapid growth rates are even more impressive, however, when it is realized that the majority of the MSEs in the survey countries did not grow

TABLE III
Annual employment growth among small enterprises, alternative measures

	Average annual growth rate (simple averages, i.e., noncompound), %	Average annual growth rate (compound), %	Percent that grew	Average number of workers added per enterprise per year (all enterprises)
Botswana	8.4	6.3	20.1	0.12
Kenya	29.0	24.0	34.8	0.26
Malawi	10.5	9.0	22.8	0.12
Swaziland	6.6	4.1	19.9	0.08
Zimbabwe	7.4	5.6	19.3	0.08
Dominican Republic	15.1	12.6	29.1	0.08
Overall average	16.7	13.7	26.7	0.14

Source: Mead and Liedholm (1998).
Notes: Simple average growth rates are calculated as follows: [(current employment – initial employment)/initial employment]/enterprise age.
Compound growth rates are calculated as follows: $[(\text{current employment/initial employment})^{(1/\text{firm age})}] - 1$.
Overall averages in each case are weighted averages, based on the number of enterprises in the category and country.

at all since startup. Slightly more than one-quarter of the MSEs added workers, while over two-thirds remained the same size (see Table III).[14] MSE employment expansion was the exception rather than the rule, and this expansion was thus being propelled by a minority of the MSEs.

Of those MSEs that grew, over 90 percent added fewer than four workers. About 5 percent of the expanding MSEs "graduated" from the microenterprise seedbed and ended up with more than 10 workers. Thus, most of the employment expansion was due to the a relatively small share of all MSEs that grew. But of those that grew, most expanded by adding only a few workers.

Analysis of the determinants of enterprise growth

What are the determinants of the growth of existing small enterprises? Economic theory in this area is surprisingly sparse and is of only limited assistance.[15] By combining the theoretical insights with those that can be gleaned from the examination of the available empirical evidence, it is possible to identify the key variables that should be incorporated into the analysis.

Two key determinants small enterprise growth would be the age and initial size of the enterprise. "Learning models" of enterprise growth along with empirical evidence from the United States and the developing world support an *inverse* relationship between these two variables and enterprise growth.[16]

Sector would be another important determinant of enterprise growth. From the theoretical perspective, it is likely that firms in different sectors would face different product demands and encounter different cost structures on the supply side. The empirical evidence of sectoral differences in growth rates is quite extensive (Liedholm and Mead, 1999).

Another variable likely to affect the growth of existing enterprises would be location. Complementary enterprises grouped close together or enterprises located close to the final demand sources might be expected to grow more rapidly than their more isolated counterparts.[17] Enterprises of this type would more likely to be found in urban areas, particularly in commercial districts away from the home. Initial empirical evidence from Africa has indicated that urban enterprises typically grow more rapidly than their rural-based counterparts (Liedholm and Mead, 1999).

Various socioeconomic variables relating to the entrepreneur might also be expected to influence enterprise growth. Economic theory suggests, for example, that increases in "human capital," such as through increases in the experience or education of the entrepreneur, should lead to increases in enterprise growth.[18] The empirical evidence of this relationship, however, has been mixed

(Liedholm and Mead, 1991). In addition to "human capital," proprietor gender might also be thought to be an important determinant of enterprise growth. Downing and Daniels (1992), for example, posit that female entrepreneurs in Africa are more risk averse and thus less like to grow in comparison with their male counterparts. Initial empirical evidence would tend to support this view.

Finally, country should be a key determinant of the growth of small enterprises. In addition to marked differences in their political, cultural, and historical context, countries differ widely in their overall economic conditions, particularly in their aggregate levels and changes in per-capita output. Empirical evidence on the wide differences in country growth rates has already been presented.

The relationship between these key variables and enterprise growth has been analyzed recently by several scholars. McPherson (1992) examined this relationship by applying formal statistical methods to the baseline enterprise data generated from several African countries.[19] Parker (1994) used similar techniques to examine this relationship in Kenya, while Cabal (1995) extended the analysis to the Dominican Republic baseline data.[20] In these studies the individual contribution of each of the key variables thought to influence growth can be specifically determined while holding the effects of the other variables constant.

To provide an added perspective on these studies, similar statistical techniques were used to examine the determinants of enterprise growth in the six African countries with countrywide baselines: Botswana, Kenya, Lesotho, Malawi, Swaziland, and Zimbabwe. The data from these countries were analyzed by estimating an ordinary linear ordinary least squares regression of growth.[21] The growth measure used as the dependent variable was an absolute one: the annual jobs generated since startup per enterprise. Except for age and initial size, all the independent variables to explain growth were entered as dummy variables.[22] Because data from only the "surviving firms" were examined, the possibility of sample selection bias was investigated by using the Heckit model. Fortunately, the bias turned out to be insignificant in this case.[23]

The results of this particular analysis are summarized in Table IV. The following variables are found to be important determinants of enterprise growth:

TABLE IV

Determinants of enterprise growth: Growth tegression tesults from Botswana, Kenya, Lesotho, Malawi, Swaziland, and Zimbabwe

Variable	Coefficient	*t*-statistic
Firm Age	–0.009427*	–15.112
Initial Size	–0.015904*	–6.337
Sector Dummies (Base: trading)		
Manufacturing	+0.076250*	5.373
Services	+0.11285*	5.124
Strata Dummies (Base: urban)		
Rural towns	–0.10046*	–6.962
Rural villages	–0.05121*	–2.731
Locational Dummies (Base: home)		
Traditional market	–0.00857	–0.458
Commercial district	+0.29822*	15.401
Roadside	+0.12190*	5.052
Mobile	–0.00658	–0.283
Country Dummies (Base: Zimbabwe)		
Botswana	+0.14149*	4.904
Kenya	–0.06780*	–3.001
Lesotho	+0.03987	1.160
Malawi	+0.02504	1.462
Swaziland	+0.01613	0.764
Proprietor Gender (Base: female)		
Male	+0.12688*	9.461
Constant term	+0.12222*	6.983

Regression statistics: n = 20544; F = 51.59: Adjusted R^2 = 0.24.
* = significant at 1% level.

1. Enterprise age: The variable is statistically significant and negative, indicating a strong *inverse* relationship between enterprise age and growth. Thus, it is the younger firms that are more likely generate more expansion jobs per firm. Similar findings are reported from Parker's (1994) Kenyan study, Cabal's (1995) Dominican Republic study, as well as McPherson's (1992) study.
2. Initial size: This variable is also statistically significant and negative, revealing a strong *inverse* relationship between initial size and

growth. The smaller enterprises at startup thus add more expansion jobs per firm than their larger scale counterparts, a powerful finding for those concerned with employment creation. Again, parallel findings have been reported by other researchers (Parker, 1994) and McPherson (1992), although a positive relationship between initial size and growth was found in the Dominican Republic (Cabal, 1995).

3. Sector: The sector in which an enterprise operates helps explain growth as well. At the most aggregate level, it would appear from Table IV that enterprises in the manufacturing and service sectors are more likely to experience higher rates of growth than those in the reference category "trading." Yet, at a more disaggregated level, the specific sectors that were likely to generate more MSE expansion varied from country to country. In Swaziland, for example, enterprises in nonmetallic mineral grew less rapidly and enterprises in transportation grew more rapidly than retail trade. Parker (1994) found that sectoral differences were significant in Kenya, with all sectors except repairs growing more rapidly than trading. Cabal (1995) also reports that differences between sectors were significant in the Dominican Republic; that is, services were growing less rapidly and manufacturing growing more rapidly than trading. What these findings suggest is that sectoral differences are significant at the country level in explaining growth, reflecting perhaps each country's comparative advantage. At the same time, no universal sectoral growth patterns seem to emerge.
4. Location: Several of the locational variables also prove to significantly influence enterprise growth. Firms located in rural towns and villages grow less rapidly than their urban-based counterparts. Moreover, enterprises operating in commercial districts or along roadsides show markedly stronger growth than those based within the home. The findings from the other studies are generally similar, but with a few exceptions. McPherson (1992), for example, finds that firms in traditional markets also grow more rapidly than home-based enterprises. Parker (1994) reports that in Kenya firms operating in rural towns grow less rapidly than those in rural villages, and Cabal finds that size of location has no statistically significant affect on enterprise growth. In general, location has a strong influence on enterprise growth, although the specific effects sometimes vary at the country level.
5. Country: This variable is also found to be important in explaining enterprise growth. A glance at Table IV, for example, reveals that enterprises in Botswana grow *more* rapidly and those in Kenya grow *less* rapidly than their counterparts in Zimbabwe, the base country. Thus, even after controlling for enterprise age, size, sector, locational, and other factors, country effects still proved to be statistically significant. The positive coefficient for Botswana may be due, at least in part, to its high level of per-capita income as well as its exceptional growth in per-capita income.
6. Gender of entrepreneur: This socioeconomic variable proves to a significant determinant of enterprise growth. As indicated in Table IV, male-run enterprises grow more rapidly than those run by females, even after controlling for the effects of all the other variables. Similar results are reported by McPherson (1992) and Parker (1994). While these results provide support for the Downing and Daniels (1992) hypothesis that females are more risk averse than their male counterparts, they also could reflect the existence of some form of discrimination against female entrepreneurs.
7. Human capital: Although data limitations precluded the inclusion of "human capital" variables in the six country growth analysis, other recent growth studies provide some evidence that human capital does significantly affect enterprise growth. McPherson (1992) found, for example, that proprietors with vocational training had firms that grew 9 percent faster than firms run by proprietors without such training. For Kenya, Parker (1994) reports that entrepreneurs who had previously worked in another business showed markedly higher growth than those who had previously been unemployed.[24] She also found that business with workers trained formally at vocational schools show statistically significantly higher growth than those businesses with untrained workers once all other variables are controlled.

Perhaps proprietors are able to overcome their own technical shortcomings by hiring such workers. With respect to the effect of formal schooling on enterprise growth, however, the results are somewhat mixed. Cabal (1995) finds in the Dominican Republic that entrepreneurs who had completed secondary school grew more rapidly than those who did not. A similar result is reported in Parker's (1994) study of Kenyan entrepreneurs. McPherson (1992) also reports a similar finding for Zimbabwe, but discovers the relationship is not significant in Botswana or Swaziland. Whether or not the entrepreneur completed primary education did not prove to have a statistically significant effect on enterprise growth in any of the survey countries.

In summary, these analyses have revealed that several key variables are important determinants of the expansion of existing small enterprises. Controlling for the influence of other variables, enterprise growth in most cases is inversely related to initial size and age of the enterprise. In addition, variables such as the sector, location, country, and the human capital characteristics of the enterprise are shown to significantly influence its ability to add workers. Armed with this information on the many common characteristics of expanding firms, policymakers can now begin to identify from the large and heterogeneous population of small enterprises the important segment that is generating the expansion jobs.

4. MSE jobs and the macroeconomy

New jobs, as was noted earlier, come into being in micro and small enterprises in two different ways: through the creation of new businesses and through the expansion of existing enterprises. It can be hypothesized that the balance between these two sources of new jobs is strongly influenced by the state of the macroeconomy. When the economy itself is strong, MSEs are also thriving, expanding by engaging additional workers for their work force. At the same time, significant numbers of people close existing MSEs, since they are able to move on to other, more rewarding activities. Consequently, when the overall economy is strong, one might hypothesize that relatively more jobs will be created from net firm expansion than from net firm creation.

By contrast, when the economy is languishing, MSEs also face hard times; that is, few are expanding their employment levels, and in fact many may be laying off workers. But new people are still entering the labor force. This means that there is increased pressures on people to start new businesses, even if these yield only marginal returns. With fewer options available, more existing enterprises continue to persist in business, no matter how low the incomes they generate. Thus, when the economy is languishing, one might hypothesize that relatively more jobs will be created from net firm creation than from net firm expansion.

Findings from recent surveys in several countries provide support for this view of the impact of the macroeconomy on the patterns of MSE expansion. Table V presents the results from analyses derived from panel surveys conducted in the Dominican Republic and Zimbabwe over periods when the overall economy was both strong and weak.

The impact of the macroeconomy on pattern of employment growth is quite striking. During periods of rapid growth, expanding employment from existing enterprises made a major contribution to overall employment growth in both countries, while the contribution to overall employment from net firm creation was actually negative. By contrast, when the macroeconomy was languishing, the contribution of existing enterprises to overall employment growth declined substantially. Employment growth from net firm creation, however, switched from negative to positive and contributed more to overall employment than did the expansion of existing firms. Further support for the hypothesized relationship between the macroeconomy and net firm creation is provided by Daniels (1995), who found by means of regression analysis on Zimbabwe data over the 1988–1993 period that a 1 percent increase in GDP growth was associated with a 0.37 percent reduction in the rate of net firm creation.

A recent Kenya study reports a similar pattern (see Daniels and Mead, 1998). In 1994, a year in which real GDP per capita declined by almost 1 percent, about 70% of the net new jobs came into existence as a result of net firm creation, with only

TABLE V
Patterns of employment growth: The Dominican Republic and Zimbabwe

	Growth rate, GDP/cap (% per year)	Percent change per annum in employment in MSEs		
		From net firm creation	From expansion of existing enterprises	Total: net overall change in MSE employment
Periods of rapid growth				
Dominican Republic, March 1993	+5.5%	−1.7%	**+12.4%**	+10.8%
Zimbabwe, October 1993 to March 1998	+3.8%	−6.0%	**+12.5%**	+6.0%
Periods of slow or negative growth				
Dominican Republic, March 1993 to March 1994	+0.5%	**+1.7%**	−3.2%	−1.5%
Zimbabwe, September 1991 to October 1993	−3.0%	**+5.5%**	+1.5%	+7.0%

Source: Computed from data generated by Cabal (1995) for the Dominican Republic and by Daniels (1994) and McPherson (1998) for Zimbabwe.

30% coming from expansions. In 1995, a year in which the real GDP per capita increased by approximately 1 percent, these figures were reversed; that is, only about 30% came from net firm creation, and close to 70% came from an expansion of new enterprises.

The Kenyan study also provides some important insights into the net returns generated by these firms. The enterprises that expanded their employment in 1994 or 1995, the study reports, generated incomes that were more than twice the returns earned in those that were newly established during these two years.

This result is consistent with the previously described findings on firm dynamics and efficiency. The vast majority of new starts are one-person enterprises, which earlier studies have indicated is the least efficient size category. MSEs that are able to survive until the overall economy improves and are able to expand, adding even one or two workers, will be moving into a size category where their economic efficiency and net income is significantly higher. Moreover, the jobs created should be more permanent and possibly generate a higher wage.[25]

In sum, these data suggest that, when the economy is more buoyant, a significant number of new employment openings in MSEs come from an expansion of existing enterprises, resulting in jobs that produce better incomes for those working in the enterprises. Closure rates may go up as well, as people are able to move out of marginal activities into other jobs that yield higher returns. In times of national stagnation, by contrast, large firms as well as existing MSEs tend to cut back on their employment; fewer enterprises close, and a larger percentage of new jobs result from inefficient one-person enterprises being started. MSEs, however, act as a "shock absorber" when the economy is languishing, because overall employment in MSEs continues to expand.

5. Policy implications

An array of policy and project implications flow from these survey findings of MSE dynamics. At the general policy level, broad-based macro policy reform aimed at creating a more dynamic economy can be an effective vehicle for fostering the productive expansion of existing MSEs. Conversely, when the overall economy is distorted or stagnant, relatively little of this kind of expansion takes place.

The influence of specific government rules and regulations on the MSE growth is the subject of some debate. Snodgrass and Biggs (1996), for example, argue that most governmental regulations fail to reach the smallest firms; that is, as these firms increase in size, however, they become more visible and more subject to government regulation and taxation, thus introducing a disincentive to expand beyond a certain threshold. DeSoto (1989) has described the high transactions costs associated with registration in Peru. Yet, MSEs enumerated in our African or Latin American surveys rarely mention direct governmental controls or taxation as problems of central concern and were rarely cited as a binding constraint for these enterprises (Liedholm and Mead, 1999). Indeed, recent evidence from Africa indicates that taxes, when measured in terms of taxes actually paid by firms, were regressive by enterprise size and that registration and other governmental regulations did not inhibit the growth of MSEs in the countries studied (McPherson and Liedholm, 1996).

There is evidence, however, that governmental policies often discriminate against MSEs relative to their larger scale counterparts in the areas of access to and the prices of inputs. Numerous examples of overall policy distortions that are not neutral by enterprise size have been cited in the literature (see, e.g., Haggblade et al., 1986; Liedholm and Mead, 1987). The differential effects of the import duty structure provides a useful illustration. Large enterprises can typically import their capital equipment at low or zero import duty rates through investment promotion schemes. Small firms typically do not qualify for such schemes and also find that their capital equipment, such as sewing machines and outboard motors, is classified in the tariff code as a luxury consumer good and is taxed accordingly. Eliminating such distortions "with simply the stroke of the pen" can and has done much to foster the growth of MSEs (Haggblade et al., 1987).

At the project assistance level, one of the most important implications from the survey findings is the recognition that the clients of this assistants, the MSEs, are *heterogeneous*. Among the MSEs there are different target groups, each with different opportunities and different needs. Those designing MSE assistance programs must recognize these differences and craft interventions that are appropriate to the needs of that particular group.

Enterprises that are starting up, for example, face different problems and constraints than those of existing firms seeking to expand. In view of the already large number of new starts in the region each year, along with the high attrition rates in early years of an enterprise's life and the multiple needs of new enterprises, one might seriously question whether many scarce resources should be allocated to facilitating new starts. If there are strong pressures to support this group, then it would be important to build on any existing experience of these new entrepreneurs.

Existing firms that have survived the first three years or that have grown even slightly would appear to be more likely candidates for assistance. Even in this instance, however, a distinction might usefully be made between three categories of existing MSEs: those that are not growing, those that seek to grow just a little, and those that seek greater grow or even to "graduate" to the upper end of the small enterprise scale.

These different types of existing MSEs have different contributions to make to the dual objectives of poverty alleviation and growth. Nongrowing MSEs, for example, are primarily survival activities and thus are a particularly appropriate target group for those concerned with poverty alleviation. Programs aimed at this group can increase the likelihood that such enterprises can survive or earn somewhat higher levels of income. Assistance focused on enterprises that seek to add to their labor force, by contrast, makes its major contribution in the area of growth.

For the first two categories of existing enterprises, small amounts of a single missing ingredient, working capital, are often all that is required to sustain the enterprise or to enable it to expand slightly. Until recently, there were few proven cost-effective mechanisms for making such funding available to MSEs. Fortunately, the innovative microenterprise credit schemes that originated in Asia have now been adapted and applied with some success in Latin America and Africa. The Get Ahead Foundation in South Africa, the Kenya Rural Enterprise Program, Banco Sol in Bolivia, and ADEMI in the Dominican Republic, for example, have demonstrated that it is possible to reach relatively large numbers of MSEs with credit schemes that are at least operationally self-sufficient and that can generate borrower repayment rates exceeding 95 percent (Otero and Rhyne, 1994).

What about those MSEs that seek greater growth or even to "graduate" to an enterprise with more than ten workers? Although only 1 percent of all MSEs succeed in managing this transition, this is an important group since it provides substantial numbers of jobs, is a major source of today's intermediate enterprises, and is often most closely attuned to market opportunities. Findings from the survey countries reveal that the "graduated" enterprises tend to exhibit a higher level of "human capital" (including both experience and education), to more likely be engaged in manufacturing than in trading, and to be involved with more complex marketing patterns (for both inputs and outputs) than their counterparts that have not graduated (Liedholm and Mead, 1999). Efforts to assist entrepreneurs seeking to "graduate" must thus address a more complex set of requirements than the simple provision of working capital. Business Development Support institutions typically have played a central role in providing much of this assistance, particularly by addressing the nonfinancial constraints to "graduation." One of the key and difficult challenges facing such institutions is finding ways to ensure that the needed services are provided to this extensive and widely dispersed client group in a reasonably cost effective manner. Recent experience has shown that a subsector approach, which focuses on the interrelationships between enterprises in a particular subsector (such as furniture), may be one way of meeting this challenge.[26]

In summary, MSEs are a major feature of the economic landscape of Latin America and Africa. There is much churning and diversity within this MSE universe. Policies and projects grounded on a solid understanding of this changing universe can help ensure that the important contributions of MSEs to the development process in these areas can be fully realized.

Notes

[1] This paper was commissioned for a project on The Role of Small & Medium Enterprises in Development organized by the World Bank Institute (WBI). The data and evidence surveyed in this paper are from studies undertaken in these regions by GEMINI project, which was supported by USAID and under the overall supervision of staff from Michigan State University.

[2] The sources for the country survey reports are listed in Liedholm and Mead (1999).

[3] For details, see Liedholm and Mead (1999). South Africa, for which countrywide data were not collected, is not included.

[4] A more recent survey of starts in Zimbabwe for the year 1997 reports a MSE birth rate of 20.3 percent (McPherson, 1998).

[5] New start (birth) rates are typically calculated by dividing all new firms appearing in a given time period (usually one year) by the number of firms already in existence at the beginning of the year. The number of firms at the end of the year served as the base. Given the net increase in the number of firms, this creates one source of downward bias. A second source of downward bias, present in all countries, is the omission of the short-lived firms that appear and the disappear within the year. A study of short-lived firms in the Dominican Republic indicates that if these are included in the analysis the birth rate in the Dominican Republic would have increased by 6.5 percentage points. For more details of these methodological issues, see Liedholm and Mead (1993).

[6] The birth rate is higher for smaller than for larger firms. For industrialized countries, the annual average birth rate for all firms is approximately 6.5 percent (Caves, 1998).

[7] Specifically, on the basis of area-based panel surveys, the annual closure rate was 29 percent in 1992 and 22 percent in 1993 (Cabal, 1995). In Zimbabwe, a closure rate of 11.5 percent per year (from 1991 to 1993) was reported from a similar area-based panel survey of MSEs (Daniels, 1995); 42 percent of the firms, however, could not be located in the resurvey, so this closure rate must be considered a lower-bound estimate. The area-based panel surveys, where all enterprises in the same areas are surveyed over time, generate much more accurate closure rates than those generated from either tracer or closed enterprise surveys, both of which are subject to severe selectivity biases that understate the closure rates. Annual closure rates derived from tracer surveys range from 1.3 in Nigeria (Kilby, 1995) to 4.1 percent in Jamaica (Fisseha, 1994), while those from closed enterprise surveys hover around 6 percent per year.

[8] In Kenya (Parker, 1994), those who closed for demand reasons were much more likely to start a new enterprise than those who closed because of a lack of working capital. Indeed, overall, of those who closed, 60 percent subsequently opened new business, 15 percent worked in agriculture, 8 percent accepted paid employment, and 17 percent were no longer economically active.

[9] More incomplete data from Malawi indicate that approximately one-third of the MSEs had closed three years after startup.

[10] The hazard analysis is more attractive than other statistical techniques for examining such patterns, because it not only permits time varying explanatory variables to be included in the analysis but also deals with the sample censoring problem that arises because not all the firms in the data set have closed. The observations about them are thus incomplete and these observations are called "censored." Standard econometric analyses, such as ordinary least squares, ignore this fact and count these firms as if they had closed and thus yield results that would be quite misleading. Hazard analysis, on the other hand, only included information on those firms that are at risk of failing. The "hazard rate" is defined as the probability that the firm will close during the period, usually one year, given that it has survived until the beginning of the period. It is computed by dividing the number of firms that closed in a period, by the number of those firms that have not yet closed at the beginning of the period. For more details see, Liedholm and Mead (1993).

[11] The complete sector ranking of MSEs by survival probabilities from highest to lowest in Swaziland and Zimbabwe combined was (McPherson, 1992) as follows: real estate, wood processing, wholesale trade, nonmetallic minerals, textiles, other services, food and beverage processing, construction, miscellaneous manufacturing, metal fabrication, hotels and restaurants, chemicals, retail trade, and transport. The rank differences, however, were not always statistically significant.

[12] The rural–urban distinction, however, was not statistically significant in the Dominican Republic analysis (Cabal, 1995).

[13] The compound growth measure provides a lower-bound estimate of the growth rate compared with the average growth rate measure, which uses initial employment in the base. An absolute measure, the annual change in jobs per firm, is also presented in Table III; it can be particularly useful in assessing the overall contribution of the smallest firms to job creation. The data for all the growth measures were generated by asking entrepreneurs retrospective information (event histories) about their firms.

[14] About 5 percent of the enterprises had declined in size since startup (see Liedholm and Mead, 1995).

[15] For an review of the relative theoretical literature as well as the available empirical evidence, see Liedholm and Mead (1999).

[16] Jovanovic's (1982) "learning model" of enterprise growth, which supersedes the "stochastic" models in which growth and size are independent, posits that the older firms grow more slowly than younger ones because managers learn more accurately over time about their efficient size of operation. It also predicts larger firms will grow more slowly than their smaller counterparts.

[17] See, for example, the work of Piore and Sable (1984) on the importance of these agglomeration externalities.

[18] Pakes and Ericson (1998) have extended Jovanovic's model to allow the manager's efficiency level to be changed through human capital formation.

[19] An updated version is reported in McPherson (1996).

[20] Parker (1994) also used ordinary least squares estimation techniques to examine the growth relationship in Kenya. In addition to the linear function employed by McPherson, she also used two additional functional forms, log-log and log-log with weights. Moreover, her dependent variable was the annual number of workers added by the enterprise since start rather than the percentage growth rate used by McPherson. Cabal (1995) used an ordered logit analysis in which the dependent variable was increased employment, decreased employment, or no change in employment since startup.

[21] In addition to the linear function reported in this paper, alternative functional forms were run, including a log-log formulation as well as one with a complete set of firm age-firm size quadratic and interaction terms included. These yielded similar findings, but the overall results were somewhat less robust than the ones reported in the paper.

[22] Specifically, the estimated equation was as follows:

$$\begin{aligned}\text{GROWTH} = \alpha + \beta\,(\text{INITIAL SIZE}) &+ \\ c\,(\text{ENTERPRISE AGE}) + d\,(\text{SECTOR}) &+ \\ e\,(\text{LOCATION}) + f\,(\text{GENDER}) &+ \\ e\,(\text{COUNTRY}) + \varepsilon &\end{aligned}$$

where

SECTOR = three dummy variables representing ISIC industries 3,6,9.
LOCATION = eight dummy variables representing various aspects of the MSE's location.
GENDER = two dummy variables representing male and female MSE entrepreneurs.
COUNTRY = six dummy variables representing Botswana, Kenya, Lesotho, Malawi, Swaziland, and Zimbabwe.

[23] The Heckit tests were run on the data from Zimbabwe and Swaziland. The estimates of lambda were 15.77 (25.70) for Zimbabwe and 22.34 (20.66) for Swaziland (the standard errors are in parentheses).

[24] There was no statistical evidence in Kenya, however, that entrepreneurs who had previously been civil servants or employed in either the formal or informal sector grew differently than those entrepreneurs who were previously unemployed.

[25] See Liedholm and Mead (1987), for the cross section evidence. See Parker (1994) and Parker et al. (1995) for time series evidence.

[26] Subsector analyses examine the vertical marketing and production channels within each sector, identify the links between large and small firms, analyze the competitive forces between and within channels, and identify those points that provide the greatest leverage for growth. Many times these leverage points act indirectly on the targeted MSEs. In Botswana, for example, the leverage point was the establishment of a commercial malting firm, which lowered the cost of malt to the small sorghum beer producers and enabled them to compete effectively with the large scale beer producers. See Boomgard and others (1992).

References

Boomgard, James, S. Davies, S. Haggblade and D. Mead, 1992, 'A Subsector Approach to Small Enterprise Promotion and Research', *World Development* **20**(2), 199–212.

Cabal, Miguel, 1995, 'Growth, Appearances and Disappearances of Micro and Small Enterprises in the Dominican Republic', PhD Dissertation. Michigan State University, East Lansing.

Caves, Richard, 1998, 'Industrial Organization and New Findings on the Turnover and Mobility of Firms', *Journal of Economic Literature* **36** (December), 1947–1982.

Daniels, Lisa, 1995, 'Entry, Exit and Growth Among Small-Scale Enterprises in Zimbabwe', PhD Dissertation. Michigan State University, East Lansing.

Daniels, Lisa and D. C. Mead, 1998, 'The Role of Small Enterprise to Household and National Income in Kenya', *Economic Development and Cultural Change* **47**(1), 45–71.

de Soto, Hernando, 1989, *The Other Path*, New York: Harper and Row.

Downing, Jeanne and L. Daniels, 1992, 'The Growth and Dynamics of Women Entrepreneurs in Southern Africa', Technical Report No. 47. GEMINI.

Fisseha, Yacob, 1994, 'A Dynamic Study of Jamaican Micro and Small Enterprises', Technical Report No. 70. GEMINI.

Grierson, John, D.C. Mead and S. Moyo, 1997, 'Business Linkages in Zimbabwe: Helping to Shape "Win-Win" Economic Structures', *Development Practice* **2**, 304–307.

Gustafson, Todd, and C. Liedholm, 1995, 'Patterns of Change Among Jamaican Microenterprises: Results from a Quarterly Panel Survey', Technical Report No. 81. GEMINI.

Haggblade, Steve, C. Liedholm and D. Mead. 1986, 'The Effects of Policy and Policy Reforms on Nonagricultural Enterprises and Employment in Developing Countries: A Review of Past Experiences', Employment and Enterprise Policy Analysis Project Discussion Paper 1. Harvard Institute for International Development, Cambridge, Mass.

Jovanovic, Boyan, 1982, 'Selection and Evolution in Industry', *Econometrica* **50**(3), 649–670.

Kilby, Peter, 1995, 'Nigeria, 1961–1991: Closure, Survival and Growth of Small Enterprises', Working Paper No. 54. GEMINI.

Liedholm, Carl and D. C. Mead, 1987, 'Small Scale Industries in Developing Countries: Empirical Evidence and Policy Implications', International Development Paper 9. Michigan State University Department of Agricultural Economics, East Lansing.

Liedholm, Carl and D. Mead, 1993, 'The Structure and Growth of Microenterprise in Southern and Eastern Africa: Evidence from Recent Surveys', Working Paper No. 36. GEMINI.

Liedholm, Carl and D. Mead, 1999, *Small Enterprises and Economic Development: The Dynamic Role of Micro and Small Enterprises*, London: Routledge.

McPherson, Michael A., 1992, 'Growth and Survival of Small Southern African Firms', PhD Dissertation. Michigan State University, East Lansing.

McPherson, Michael A., 1995, 'The Hazards of Small Firms in Southern Africa', *The Journal of Development Studies* **32**(1), 253–277.

McPherson, Michael A., 1996, 'Growth of Micro and Small Enterprises in Southern Africa', *Journal of Development Economics* **48**(21), 31–54.

McPherson, M. A., 1998, 'Zimbabwe: A Third Nationwide Survey of Micro and Small Enterprises: Final Report', Development Alternatives, Washington, D.C.

McPherson, Michael A. and C. Liedholm, 1996, 'Determinants of Small and Microenterprise Registration: Results from Surveys in Niger and Swaziland', *World Development* **24**(3), 481–487.

Mead, D. M. and C. Liedholm, 1998, 'The Dynamics of Micro and Small Enterprises in Developing Countries', *World Development* **26**(1), 61–74.

Otero, Maria and E. Rhyne, 1994, *The New World of Microenterprise Finance: Building Healthy Financial Institutions for the Poor*, West Hartford, Conn.: Kumarian Press.

Pakes, A. and R. Ericson, 1998, 'Empirical Implications of Alternative Models of Firm Dynamics', *Journal of Economic Theory* **79**(1), 1–45.

Parker, Joan. 1994, 'Patterns of Business Growth: Micro and Small Enterprises in Kenya', PhD Dissertation. Michigan State University, East Lansing.

Parker, R., L. Riopelle and W. Steel. 1995, 'Small Enterprises Adjusting to Liberalization in Five African Countries', Discussion Paper 271. African Technical Department, World Bank, Washington, D.C.

Piore, M. J. and C. Sabel, 1984, *The Second Industrial Divide*, New York: Basic Books.

Snodgrass, D. and T. Biggs, 1996, *Industrialization and the Small Firm: Patterns and Policies*, San Francisco: International Center for Economic Growth.

Van Dijk, M. P. and R. Rabellotti (eds.), 1997, *Enterprise Clusters and Networks in Developing Countries*, London: Frank Cass.